CW01236899

Warfare in History

GERMAN WAR PLANNING, 1891–1914

Warfare in History
ISSN 1358–779X

Editorial Board
Matthew Bennett, Royal Military Academy, Sandhurst
David Parrott, University of Oxford
Hew Strachan, University of Oxford

This series aims to provide a wide-ranging and scholarly approach to military history, offering both individual studies of topics or wars, and volumes giving a selection of contemporary and later accounts of particular battles; its scope ranges from the early medieval to the modern period.

New proposals for the series are welcomed; they should be sent to the publisher at the address below.

Boydell and Brewer Limited, PO Box 9, Woodbridge, Suffolk, IP12 3DF

*Previously published volumes in this series
are listed at the back of the volume*

Printed in Great Britain by
Cambridge University Press, England

GERMAN WAR PLANNING, 1891–1914

SOURCES AND INTERPRETATIONS

Terence Zuber

THE BOYDELL PRESS

© Terence Zuber 2004

All Rights Reserved. Except as permitted under current legislation no part of this work may be photocopied, stored in a retrieval system, published, performed in public, adapted, broadcast, transmitted, recorded or reproduced in any form or by any means, without the prior permission of the copyright owner

The right of Terence Zuber to be identified as the author of this work has been asserted in accordance with sections 77 and 78 of the Copyright, Designs and Patents Act 1988

First published 2004
The Boydell Press, Woodbridge

ISBN 1 84383 108 2

The Boydell Press is an imprint of Boydell & Brewer Ltd
PO Box 9, Woodbridge, Suffolk IP12 3DF, UK
and of Boydell & Brewer Inc.
668 Mount Hope Avenue, Rochester, NY 14620, USA
website: www.boydellandbrewer.com

A CIP catalogue record for this book is available from the British Library

Library of Congress Cataloging-in-Publication Data
Zuber, Terence.
German war planning, 1891-1914 : sources and interpretations / Terence Zuber.
  p. cm. — (Warfare in history, ISSN 1358-779X)
Documents in English translation.
Includes bibliographical references and index.
ISBN 1-84383-108-2 (hardback : alk. paper)
1. Germany—History, Military—20th century—Sources. 2. Military planning—Germany—History—20th century—Sources. 3. World War, 1914-1918—Germany—Sources. 4. World War, 1914-1918—Causes—Sources. I. Title. II. Series.

DD101.5.Z77 2004
355′.033543′09041—dc22
2004019694

This publication is printed on acid-free paper

Typeset by Keystroke, Jacaranda Lodge, Wolverhampton
Printed in Great Britain by
Cambridge University Press, England

Contents

List of maps	vii
Acknowledgements	viii
Introduction	1

Part I:
German War Planning to 1914 — 5

1	Greiner: The German Intelligence Estimate in the West	7
2	Dieckmann: *Der Schlieffenplan*	49
3	Dommes: Operations against Russia	122

Part II:
Schlieffen's *Generalstabsreisen* — 131

4	1894 *Ost*: Tannenberg	133
5	1901 *Ost*	140
6	2nd 1902 *Ost*	143
7	1903 *Ost*	151
8	1st 1904 *West*	155

Part III:
The Great 1905 War Game — 167

Part IV:
The 'Schlieffen Plan' — 187

Part V:
Moltke's War Planning — 205

9	Moltke's 1908 *Generalstabsreise West*	207

Part VI:
The German War Plan in August 1914 — 221

10	6th Army *Aufmarschanweisung*	223
11	5th Army *Aufmarschanweisung*	228
12	6th Army Evaluation of the Situation	231
13	Wenninger's Description of the German War Plan	240

Part VII:
The Birth of the Schlieffen Plan — 243
14 The Development of the German Operational Concept — 245

Part VIII:
The Schlieffen Plan Debate 1919–1930 — 259
15 1919: Hans Delbrück Criticizes the German War Plan — 261
16 1920: Kuhl Reveals the Schlieffen Plan — 265
17 1921: Delbrück Criticizes the Schlieffen Plan — 272
18 1921: Foerster Defends the Schlieffen Plan — 279
19 1920/1929: Groener Explains the Schlieffen Plan — 289
20 1929: Ludendorff Critiques the Schlieffen Plan — 297

The Schlieffen Plan Debate in *War in History* — 302

Further Reading in English — 303
Index — 305

Maps

1	German 1914 estimate of French deployment	46–7
2	Eastern Front	124
3	First 1904 *Generalstabsreise West*	158–9
4	November–December 1905 *Kriegspiel Ost*	169
5	November–December 1905 *Kriegspiel West*	176–7
6	Ritter's Schlieffen plan	190–1

Acknowledgements

In keeping with the highest traditions of German scholarship, the professors of history at the University of Würzburg, where I attended graduate school, concentrate on the impartial evaluation of source materials – *Quellenkritik* in German. Due to scholars such as my *Doktorvater*, Professor Wolfgang Altgeld, and Professor Rainer Schmidt, graduate school was always fascinating, rigorous and intellectually honest. In addition, in three years in the 12th Panzer Division serving under Colonel Klaus Kleffner and Lieutenant-colonel Heinz Eilers, I had become thoroughly familiar with the German army. When my time came to conduct archival research, the Germans had prepared me as thoroughly as I could possibly be.

To my joy, every day in the German archives was like Christmas. The archivists were continually bringing me dusty bundles of fascinating documents, secured with the curious German archive knot, and many of these were 'new' – they had never been mentioned in any historical publication. The Wall had just fallen, the German Militärarchiv in Freiburg had piles of new documents, the archive in Dresden was now open and it seemed worthwhile to really dig into the extensive holdings of the archive at Munich as well as those at Karlsruhe and Stuttgart. Archival research became an adventure.

When Professor Hew Strachan asked me if I wanted to publish a collection of documents on German war planning before the Great War, I therefore accepted immediately. This was a chance to follow in the tradition of German scholarship and at the same time share these documents with the Anglophone historical community.

I have attempted to translate these documents into readable English while retaining the content of the German original. Since the structure of the two languages is so dissimilar, this has been difficult at times. There is also the tendency in written German to construct complex, run-on sentences which can grow to a paragraph in length. In addition, these are generally military documents and not great literature. While Hans Delbrück was a very effective writer, he was an exception. In all cases, content took precedence. Nevertheless, the responsibility for the translation is mine.

I would also like to thank Boydell and Brewer for this opportunity, as well as my editor, Peter Sowden, for his patience and assistance. Sarah Pearsall, the project editor, was a real help. Graham Bradbury, my copy editor, found errors I would never have seen, and I am most grateful. The maps, as well as the photographs of the original documents, are once again the fine work of Herr Klaus Schinagl of Veitshöchheim, Germany. I would like to thank the staff of the Kriegsarchiv in Munich, the Bundesarchiv-Militärarchiv in Freiburg, the Hauptstaatsarchiv Stuttgart, the Generallandesarchiv Karlsruhe and the Hauptstaatsarchiv Dresden for their assistance. *Oberstleutnanant der Reserve* Bantle at Mittler was forthcoming and helpful. It is unfortunate (for historians) that Dr. Fuchs, the Director of the Kriegsarchiv in Munich, will retire in the summer of 2005 (though, for his part, Fuchs is happy to leave the big city for Amberg in the Bavarian Upper Palatinate). His encyclopedic knowledge of the archive will be sorely missed.

My wife, Tina, has tolerated a great deal as I spent our time and money, first in graduate school, then months in various archives and further months of translating and writing. She has seen more battlefields and bunkers than most military historians, which is asking much of a woman whose tastes are in art and literature. This book would not have been possible without her support.

For our grandchildren
Benjamin, Nadine and Lea
May they build a proud, prosperous and peaceful Germany
in the 21st century

Introduction

The First World War was one of the greatest catastrophes in European history, perhaps comparable in its effects only with the Black Death in the fourteenth century. The causes of the war have been hotly debated from the day it began to the present, and German war planning has been in the forefront of this debate.

In 1919 critics of the German General Staff contended that it had inadequately prepared for the war, that it had failed to anticipate the strength of British, Belgian and finally French resistance and therefore lost the battle of the Marne in the first and second weeks of September 1914. Worse, the General Staff's plan required that the German army immediately violate Belgian neutrality, which gave the Entente an immense propaganda advantage and placed Germany definitively in the wrong in the eyes of the world.

Hans Delbrück, the author of the groundbreaking military history *The History of the Art of War within the Framework of Political History*, the editor of the prestigious journal, the *Preussische Jahrbücher*, and a persistent critic of the General Staff, went one step further and argued in an article titled 'The German Declaration of War in 1914 and the March into Belgium' in 1919 that Germany had used the wrong war plan. If the Germans had attacked in the east and stayed on the defensive in the west, there would have been no need to violate Belgian neutrality. Germany could have quickly defeated the Russians and arrived at a negotiated peace with the western powers.

Former General Staff officers such as Generals Wilhelm Groener and Hermann von Kuhl and Lieutenant-colonel Wolfgang Foerster immediately replied that the Chief of the General Staff from 1891 to 1905, Count Alfred von Schlieffen, had bequeathed to his successor, Helmuth von Moltke (the younger) a virtually infallible plan, which was laid out in a *Denkschrift* (study) written in December 1905, immediately before Schlieffen retired. This was the culmination of fourteen years of Schlieffen's work in perfecting the German war plan. In this Schlieffen plan seven-eighths of the German army would advance to the north of Metz through Luxembourg and Belgium into northern France, continually turning the French left flank, if necessary moving to the west of Paris, and finally surrounding the French army or forcing it into Switzerland. Only one-eighth of the German army would deploy to protect Lorraine. If the French attacked into Lorraine they would be doing the Germans a favor, for they would accomplish nothing and the French forces in northern France would be that much the weaker. This enormous *Vernichtungsschlacht* (battle of annihilation) would be quickly concluded and the German army could redeploy to the east to meet the slow advance of the Russians. The General Staff officers contended that the only reason that this strategy was not successful was because the younger Moltke failed to understand Schlieffens concept and had 'watered it down', weakening the decisive right wing in order to strengthen the German forces in Lorraine. Therefore, at the critical time and place in the battle of the Marne the German right wing was too weak and the German armies were forced to retreat. The General Staff officers also argued that Germany was not strong enough for Delbrück's eastern offensive and that an attack into the vast Russian interior would have been pointless.

The point of the Schlieffen plan was to absolve from any blame for the failure on the Marne both the General Staff as an institution and its most important officers as individuals (except the scapegoats: Moltke, as well as Bülow, the 2nd Army commander, and Hentsch, Moltke's intelligence officer, who all conveniently were dead).

Hermann von Kuhl first revealed the Schlieffen plan to the public in 1920 in an article 'Why did the Marne Campaign Fail?', Kuhl had every reason to place the blame on Moltke, in order to deflect scrutiny from his own errors, for it was actually Kuhl's refusal, as the Chief of Staff of the right-wing 1st Army, to follow Moltke's orders to protect the right flank which caused the Germans to lose the battle of the Marne. The moving force behind the propagation of the Schlieffen plan idea, however, was Wilhelm Groener, the last *de facto* Chief of the General Staff and still an immensely ambitious man, who used his influence to insure that the Reichsarchiv official history followed the 'Schlieffen plan' line. The third principal architect of the Schlieffen plan project was Wolfgang Foerster, who actually wrote that official history.

The debate concerning German strategy continued between the 'Delbrück school' and the 'Schlieffen school' throughout the 1920s and into the early 1930s. Nevertheless, one fact was now considered certain: the German war plan in 1914 had been generally based on the concept of the 1905 Schlieffen plan *Denkschrift*.

In the early 1950s the German historian Gerhard Ritter was faced with explaining the German disaster in the twentieth century. His conclusion was that the fatal German flaw was militarism. By this he meant the preference for military patterns of thought and solutions over those of negotiation, law and diplomacy. To Ritter, the pre-eminent militarist was Alfred von Schlieffen and the apotheosis of militarism was the Schlieffen plan. The Schlieffen plan was one of the principal causes of the Great War, indeed it was the proximate cause. The requirement to violate Belgian neutrality in order to quickly defeat France not only forced Germany to turn a Balkan quarrel into a world war, it also cut short the time available for negotiation and blackened Germany's good name for ever. Ritter's influence was immense and his exegesis on the Schlieffen plan has become canonical.

I called this explanation into question in 'The Schlieffen Plan Reconsidered', which appeared in *War in History* in 1999 and in *Inventing the Schlieffen Plan*, which was published in 2002. These contend that there never was a Schlieffen plan, the most obvious proof being that the Schlieffen plan *Denkschrift* was written for a one-front war against France and required an army of 96 divisions, while Germany faced a war against both France and Russia and the German army never had more than 72 divisions available in the west. In fact, Germany was heavily outnumbered by the Franco-Russian alliance. Schlieffen wrote the *Denkschrift* in order to argue for a massive increase in the German army through the utilization of all of Germany's trained manpower as well as the implementation of universal conscription. The concept of Schlieffen's real war plans was to compensate for Germany's numerical inferiority by conducting a defense based on rail mobility in order to counterattack against the expected Franco-Russian offensives.

The fact that Moltke's plans in 1914 had only a superficial resemblance to the Schlieffen plan proves not that Moltke failed to understand the Schlieffen plan and 'watered it down', but rather that he had an entirely different concept, one which, not unreasonably, focused on winning the first battles.

The Documents[1]

The most serious deficiency in the discussion of German war planning prior to the Great War has been the dearth of reliable primary and secondary sources. After the war the Reichsarchiv, which was the custodian of the German army's archives, printed practically nothing and restricted access to the documents to reliable retired General Staff officers, who in turn distorted their description of the sources to preserve the reputation of the General Staff. The Reichsarchiv was then destroyed by British incendiary bombs on the night of 14 April 1945. Until the fall of the Wall, the only planning document which survived and was published (in 1956) was the text of the 1905 'Schlieffen plan' *Denkschrift*. Five of Schlieffen's General Staff rides in the east were made public only in 1938.

This problem is compounded for Anglophone historians by the fact that the most interesting parts of the secondary literature were printed in German periodicals in the early 1920s.

The fall of the Wall and German reunification brought about a significant change in the primary document situation. The Militärarchiv der DDR – the East German military archive – had in its possession a few documents that survived the destruction of the Reichsarchiv. The Communists saw no reason to make these documents available to historians, but the unified German Militärarchiv at Freiburg did so immediately. Nevertheless, the significance of these documents was not recognized at once, in large part because of the 'Schlieffen plan' dogma, but also due to the fact that many of them are written in nineteenth-century German Standard script, which most historians today cannot read.

This book makes available many of these documents in English translation, along with other documents from German archives as well as some of the 1920s literature.

---

[1] This book may be supplemented by Robert Foley's *Alfred von Schlieffen's Military Writings* (Frank Cass, London and Portland, OR, 2002). In addition to the 1894, 1901 and 1903 *Generalstabsreisen Ost*, the 1905 *Kriegsspiel* and the 'Schlieffen Plan' itself, which are also included here, Foley translated the 1897 and 1899 *Generalstabsreisen Ost*, Schlieffen's tactical-strategic test problems for 1892, 1896 and 1905, one of the German army's intelligence evaluations of the Russian army in 1905, and four essays that Schlieffen wrote after his retirement and which were included in a collection printed as *Cannae* by Mittler in 1925.

These newly discovered documents include two by Reichsarchiv historians: Hellmuth Greiner's history of the German west front intelligence estimate from 1885 to 1914 and Wilhelm Dieckmann's history of Schlieffen's war planning to 1904, as well as the notes for Wilhelm von Dommes' briefing on the German war plan in the east to 1905, and Schlieffen's 1902 *Generalstabsreise Ost* and 1st 1904 *Generalstabsreise West*. The last document is one of the only two of Schlieffen's General Staff rides in the west to be found. It is particularly significant because in this exercise the decisive battle took place in Lorraine, not northern France. A secret 1919 history of German war planning was also found in the papers of Wilhelm Groener at the Bundesarchiv.

This is supplemented by Schlieffen's 1894 and 1903 *Generalstabsreisen Ost*. In his November–December 1905 war game, which is also presented here, and was held only days before he retired, far from invading France Schlieffen conducted a strategic defensive on both the east and west fronts. Together, these exercises show the development of Schlieffen's doctrine of counterattacks based on rail mobility.

The younger Moltke's planning from 1906 to 1914 has been almost completely unknown. This book includes Moltke's 1908 *Generalstabsreise West*, which was acquired from the East Germans, and is one of the only two of Moltke's war games to survive. It gives the best insight available into Moltke's operational concept in 1914. Other documents from the Bavarian archives show Moltke's actual war plan in 1914: Moltke's instructions in August 1914 to the commander of the 6th Army, the 6th Army Chief of Staff's evaluation of the situation in August 1914 as well as a senior Bavarian officer's description in September 1914 of the German war plan. Moltke's instructions to the 5th Army were found in Freiburg.

The picture of German war planning which now emerges is both more complex and more believable than the previous single-minded emphasis on the 'Schlieffen plan'.

Last, there are several pieces, primarily journal articles, which show the crucial debate in the early 1920s over the German war plan. The description of the Schlieffen plan provided by the German officers can be compared with the actual 'Schlieffen plan' *Denkschrift* itself.

In order to include as many documents as possible, the commentary has been kept to the bare minimum. Numbers in square brackets are the page numbers of the original documents. The underlining replicates that in the original documents. For anyone seeking a larger context, reference has been made to the appropriate parts of my book, *Inventing the Schlieffen Plan*. Since 1999 there has also been a debate in the journal *War in History* concerning the significance of these new sources for the evaluation of the German war plan. A list of these articles is included, as well as a list of other books and articles in English on German war planning from 1891 to 1914.

Part I

GERMAN WAR PLANNING TO 1914

1

Greiner: The German Intelligence Estimate in the West[1]

The first element in considering a military situation is the enemy estimate. Sometime after the Great War, Archivrat Hellmuth Greiner[2] in the Reichsarchiv was given the mission to write a study on the following topic: 'What intelligence information did the German General Staff possess concerning the French mobilization and deployment in the period 1885–1914? What was the German enemy estimate? What were the actual French plans?' The result was a 157-page paper evaluating the German intelligence estimate in the west, perhaps the most remarkable intelligence document in the pre-war period. This document was held by the Militärarchiv der DDR and has only become available to us since the fall of the Wall.

Intelligence work is not primarily about grand strategy. It is a laborious process of assembling information in order that a picture of the enemy movements and deployment can be pieced together. Seemingly pedestrian questions such as order of battle, the composition of the covering force and routes of march had to be painstakingly resolved. From that, enemy capabilities can be estimated and finally a guess towards enemy intentions may be made. Greiner's Denkschrift *provides an excellent picture of the real-world problems that faced the German intelligence analysts.*

I. 1885/86 Mobilization Year

[2] In the spring of 1885 the 3rd Department[3] of the Great General Staff possessed voluminous material concerning the French mobilization and deployment for the

---

[1] Greiner, 'Welche Nachrichten besaß der deutsche Genetralstab über Mobilmachung und Aufmarsch des französischen Heeres in den Jahren 1885–1914? Wie würden sie ausgewertet, und wie lagen die tatsächlichen Verhältnisse?' BA-MA W10/50267. Greiner's *Denkschrift* is integrated throughout *Inventing the Schlieffen Plan*.
[2] Greiner was born on 20 April 1892, and served as a General Staff first lieutenant during the Great War. He studied at the University of Berlin after 1920, and from 1919 was at the Reichsarchiv, moving to the Reichswehr ministry in 1935. After 1939 he kept the war diary in the Führerhauptquartier.
[3] The 3rd Department was in charge of intelligence on the western countries, the 1st on the eastern countries.

1885/86 mobilization year from a French agent,[4] the authenticity of which, as was expressly stated, could not be doubted. It consisted of hand-written excerpts of the instructions for each rail serial[5] for the rail transport of the active army corps and the forces of the Paris military region for border security as well as the rail movement of the army corps, reserve divisions, reserve artillery, supply units, fortress troops and headquarters using the eastern rail system. The instructions for each rail serial included loading, transit and unloading rail stations on the eastern rail system, the date for loading, the arm of service, parent unit (active army corps, reserve division, etc.), so that from this material it was possible to obtain an exact picture of the planned French deployment in case of a war with Germany.[6] In August 1884 the 3rd Department also received from a French source a detailed hand-written order of battle for the French army as well as information concerning the troops designated as the covering force. Using changes which the 3rd Department knew had been made in position and organization, it was possible to update the order of battle for 1885/86, in the assumption that except for minor errors this accurately reflected the French intentions.

On the basis of this material, in June 1885 the chief of the 3rd Department of the Great General Staff at that time, Colonel Count von [3] Schlieffen wrote his estimate of the mobilization and deployment of the French army . . . [Pages 3 to 5 give a detailed breakdown of the French order of battle.] The French field army would contain 18 active army corps, 17 reserve divisions, 3 combined brigades, 6 cavalry divisions, several independent units in the strength of 14 light infantry battalions and 9 mountain battalions, a Marine infantry division and a reserve artillery of 32 depot battalions . . . Together: 486 infantry, 12 Marine, 168 territorial infantry, 24 light infantry battalions, 266 cavalry and 37 territorial cavalry squadrons, 352 field, 55 horse and 12 territorial artillery batteries: 690 battalions, 303 squadrons, 419 batteries, 1,033,086 men, 2,514 guns, 274,836 horses. In addition, territorial forces included 267 battalions and an unknown number of cavalry squadrons and artillery batteries, from which two reserve divisions [8] were to be formed to garrison Paris that were capable of field operations . . . while the rest were to form the garrisons of the fortresses as well as Algiers, Tunis and Corsica and coastal defense. There was no information concerning the formation of further reserve divisions.

Of the field army, the following forces would be deployed:
<u>against Germany:</u>
16 active corps and the entire artillery reserve, organized as 1st–4th Armies, each with 4 corps and an 8-battery artillery reserve.

12 reserve divisions (1–5, 8–13, 17) organized as the 5th–7th Armies, each with 4 divisions; the 14th Infantry Division and 7th Corps cavalry brigade [organized as an independent unit]

---

[4] Greiner footnote: "An official of the French Eastern Railway, who due to his position had access to all the papers concerning the mobilization and deployment."
[5] Complete train.
[6] Greiner footnote: "Only the information concerning movements for border security had gaps, so that it was necessary here to make conjectures."

5 cavalry divisions (1–5) . . . .
in total: 559 battalions, 258 squadrons, 358 batteries (including 96 territorial battalions and 24 territorial squadrons) with 849,698 men, 2,148 guns, 234,950 horses.

against Italy, as the 8th Army: [XIV and XV Corps, 2 reserve divisions]
in total: 95 battalions, 39 squadrons, 49 batteries (including 36 territorial battalions and 7 territorial squadrons) with 136,000 men, 294 guns, 31,823 horses.

against Spain, as the 9th Army: [3 reserve divisions]
in total: 36 battalions, 6 squadrons, 12 batteries (all territorial troops) with 46,588 men, 72 guns, 8063 horses.

The 3rd Department of the Great General Staff did not know where the 8th and 9th Armies were to deploy. It assumed that the 8th army would spread out in small detachments along the Italian border and that the 9th Army would assemble at Toulouse.

[In left margin] see map 1[missing].

The forces opposing Germany would . . . deploy
1st Army [in the south at Epinal, Charmes and Mirecourt]
2nd Army [in reserve, east of Neufchâteau]
3rd Army [in the center, at Toul–St. Dizier]
4th Army [in the north, south-east of Ste. Ménehould]
[all four armies contained four corps each and would deploy between the 4th and 15th days of mobilization]
5th Army [on far right at Belfort]
6th Army [behind 2nd Army]
7th Army [behind 4th Army]
[5th, 6th and 7th Armies consisted of 4 reserve divisions each and would deploy by the 18th day.]

[On pages 10–13 the French covering force operations are discussed. Schlieffen expected no offensive actions by the French covering force except possibly a raid by the 2nd Cavalry Division on Avricourt.]

[13] "The deployment of the French army", closed Schlieffen's *Denkschrift*, "is noteworthy in that the right wing has been made significantly stronger than the left. On or behind the short stretch of the Moselle between Epinal and Pont St. Vincent about 52.5 kilometers in length [the 'Trouée de Charmes'] the 1st, 2nd, 5th, 6th and part of the 3rd Armies are massed, while only the 4th Army is on the 90-kilometer stretch between Frouard and the Belgian border, and the rest of the 3rd Army as well as the 7th Army can be considered as a reserve for both wings. Obviously the principal emphasis has been laid on the defense of the gap in the fortress line between Epinal and Pont St. Vincent with the strongest possible forces. That the sector that has been chosen to defend is also the easiest one for a transition to the offensive has probably also been taken into consideration. The enemy appears to consider an offensive through the other gap in the defensive line to the north of Verdun [14] to be unlikely. On the other hand, the possibility of a march by the German army through Belgium has not been left out of consideration. This eventuality has probably been provided for, as is indicated by the deployment of

the entire left wing very far to the rear, by the deployment of elements directly on the Belgian border and by concentrating the mass of the French cavalry here."

[On pages 14 to 16 Greiner said that the German estimate generally matched the information provided on the French Plan VII in the official French history of the Great War, *Les armées françaises dans la grande guerre, tome première, première volume*, pp. 2 ff. and Marchand's *Plans de concentration*. Greiner said that the French active corps would complete their deployment by the 11th mobilization day – three to four days earlier than the Germans expected, but that the French reserve divisions would only complete theirs by the 19th day – one or two days longer than the Germans expected. The French also moved enough troops to France from Algeria to form a XIX Corps, replacing them with 36 territorial battalions, and provided a variant to deploy the XIV and XV Corps from the Italian border to Belfort. Greiner erroneously stated that Plan VII was effective in 1885, instead of 1886 as was actually the case.]

II. 1887/88 Mobilization Year

[17] .... In December of this year [1886] the French agent delivered a new, completely changed French deployment plan[7] for the 1887/88 mobilization year. [1st Army, 3 corps, in the north at Mézières–Dun; 2nd Army, 3 corps, to its right at Verdun–Ste. Ménehould; 3rd Army, 3 corps, in the center at Toul; 4th Army, 3 corps, on the right at between Toul and Epinal; 5th Army, 3 corps, behind the centre at Neufchâteau; 6th Army, 3 corps, assuming Italian neutrality, at Besançon–Vesoul; 7th and 8th Armies, 7 reserve divisions in total, at Langres and Châlons sur Marne.]

[18] The 3rd Department regarded this deployment plan as false, probably correctly. At least it has not been mentioned, so far as is known, in any of the French military literature. Nevertheless, it could be regarded as a study concerning German violation of Belgian–Luxembourg neutrality, which had also been considered in earlier deployment plans. That the 3rd Department received no new material from June 1885 to late fall 1886 was explained by the fact that the plan that had evidently been put in effect in 1885 was retained unchanged in the next mobilization year.

In the first quarter of 1887 the 3rd Department again received the hand-written march tables for all the elements of the active army corps and the military district of Paris involved in border security, as well as the deployment of the active army corps, reserve divisions, numbered army headquarters, ration dumps, and the army headquarters itself, so far as they used the eastern rail net. On the basis of this material, Captain von Rohr wrote a *Denkschrift* titled 'Deployment of the French Army against Germany in the 1887/88 Mobilization Year, Including Consideration

---

[7] Greiner footnote: "The material consisted of a detailed order of battle with the names of the senior officers down to regimental commanders, locations of the army and corps headquarters as well as the deployment areas of the corps and cavalry divisions."

of Changes since Previous Years', which was not to be found in the files of Great General Staff now held by the Reichsarchiv. As a consequence the German estimate of the French deployment can be discerned only from the march tables worked out by the 3rd Department.
[In left margin] see Map 2 [missing].

[On pages 19 and 20 Greiner gave the French march tables for the headquarters, numbered army headquarters, active army corps and reserve divisions. On pages 20 to 22 he gave the covering force deployment, generally down to cavalry brigade and light infantry battalion level.]

[22] It was not possible to make more precise statements concerning the German estimate of the order of battle and strength of the French army, as the relevant materials were not available.
[23] We learn from the French official General Staff history[8] only that the deployment plan for 1887/88, Plan VIII, which was written in January 1887, had a purely offensive character. In order to conduct the planned offensive, the main body was to assemble closer to the border than previously, the quantity of infantry employed in the covering force was increased and the advance of the first-echelon armies was planned for the 11th day of mobilization.
The German estimate of the French plan corresponded completely with that provided by Marchand,[9] with the exception of the 7th Army, which was to be unloaded further to the rear in the area of Blesmes–Vitry–Châlons–St. Hilaire.

[On pages 24 and 25 Greiner discussed details of the French covering force and German estimate of it, as well as French plans written towards the end of the year to pull back their deployment all the way back to Belfort–Langres–Châlons–Reims in case of a possible raid in the first days of mobilization by a German three-corps advance guard army. In December 1887 a second variant left the 1st Army on the right in place but pulled back the left somewhat. The German General Staff apparently learned of neither plan. The missing map 2 compared the German estimate of the French 1887/88 rail deployment with that provided by Marchand.]

[26] III. 1888/89 Mobilization Year

The 3rd Department received the march tables for the French deployment on the eastern rail line in the 1888/89 mobilization year from the same source as those of 1885 and 1887. This time the agent added small sections of maps, on which were printed the rail lines on the eastern rail net to be used by the individual corps, through the intermediate points to the unloading stations. The material describing the deployment of the covering force showed considerable gaps, so that the 3rd Department had to make conjectures.

---

[8] Greiner footnote: "See p. 11 . . ."
[9] Greiner footnote: "*op. cit.*, pp. 75 ff."

The *Denkschrift* titled 'The Deployment of the French Army Against Germany in the 1888/89 mobilization year, Including Changes since Previous Years', written in June 1888 on the basis of this material, was found in the archives of the 3rd Department only as a heavily corrected draft: the fair copy has not yet been found. This was true also for the attached annexes: it is uncertain if these are even all present. On the other hand, a detailed map presents a complete explanation of the German estimate of the French deployment.

[In left margin] see Map 3 [missing].

[On pages 26 to 28 Greiner gave a summary of the march tables for each numbered army headquarters, active army corps, and reserve divisions. He also noted that 4½ more reserve divisions were deployed in the east, two from the Spanish border, one from Paris, plus a new division and a new brigade, while there is no further mention of the third reserve division on the Spanish border or the second reserve division in Paris. On pages 28 to 30 Greiner described the deployment of the French covering force.]

[31] . . . . On the other hand, the Marine Infantry Division no longer appeared on the eastern border. According to the calculations of the 3rd Department there was an increase of the total French forces opposed to Germany of 48 battalions, 31 squadrons and 98 batteries with roughly 81,100 men and 588 guns. The total French forces now numbered 607 battalions, 289 squadrons and 465 batteries with approximately 930,800 men and 2,736 guns.

Concerning the reasons that may have motivated the French to make such a drastic change in their deployment from the previous year, the 3rd Department's *Denkschrift* said:

"The deployment planned in the previous year appeared too risky. First, it brought the left wing too far forward and relied on rail lines that were not adequately secured. Second, it placed too high demands on the capacity of the rail lines by requiring two lines to move three corps each[10] and required a daily capacity of from 54 to 58 trains.

[32] For this reason, this year the border security forces were reinforced, the Mézières rail line was only used for border security troops, not for first-line active army corps, the left flank of the deployment line was pulled back and each rail line was assigned only two corps.

The border security was given a reduced sector to the left and therefore gained strength and cohesiveness. The defense of the Vosges appeared to be adequately secured by the *Sperrforts* and the Vosges detachments. Therefore the reserve army here was dissolved.

The fear of a possible violation of Luxembourg and Belgian neutrality may have contributed to the decision to pull the left flank back. This same fear caused the placement of two cavalry divisions near Verdun, the extension of the left wing of the 4th Army to Challerange as well as the echelonning of a reserve army behind

---

[10] Greiner footnote: "The IV, XI and XVIII Corps on the line Revigny–Lérouville–Toul and the XII, IX and V Corps on the line Bricon–Chaumont. See Map 2 [missing]."

the left wing at Reims. Uncovering the Vosges and the establishment of a strong central reserve army permits the conclusion that the French thought they needed to hold this army ready for employment in the north, for they felt that the danger was stronger from this side than from the south-east.

Last year's two-day gain in the speed of mobilization has been reduced by a day. The desire to spread out [33] in order to allow the full exploitation of the available road net is even more evident this year, for all the active corps would march in one line with the exception of the IX.[11]

Once again the German estimate of the French deployment corresponded with the actual French Plan IX, which went into effect on April 1888, and which reflected the principles for the second variant in Plan VIII.

[On pages 33 to 35 Greiner compared the German estimate to Marchand's description of Plan IX. There were some minor errors, but the German evaluation was generally correct. In particular, the French had decided that the previous plan had taken too many risks with the capacity of the rail net. On the other hand, it was not possible to determine if the French had pulled back their left wing out of fear of a German attack through Belgium and Luxembourg.]

[36] IV. 1889/90 Mobilization Year

On 13 July 1889 the 3rd Department received the following material concerning the French plan for the 1889/90 mobilization year from the same agent as previously:

1.) Five printed books with march tables for the eastern rail line which gave the rail movement for the covering force from the 1st to 4th days of mobilization.

2.) A hand-written list of the rail stations used by the eastern railway for the rail deployment after the 4th day of mobilization, with the number of trains arriving each day at each station.

3.) A sketch of the rail line used by each corps.

4.) The report that each active army corps would be followed on the same rail line by a second corps with the same number but the additional designation *bis*.[12]

The material under 1.) gave the Germans a completely accurate view of the French border security [Greiner then described this information in detail, continuing onto page 37.]

[37] The actual deployment, however, could only be determined in its general outlines, for the material under 2.) to 4.) did not stipulate which units were to move with which trains, nor which elements were to compose the active army corps or the corps *bis*. Even in answering the question as to which off-loading rail stations belonged to which corps, it was necessary to resort to conjectures and for that reason errors were possible.

---

[11] Greiner footnote: "Probably also XVIII Corps. It was assumed that the V Corps would march in the gap between the XVII and XII Corps."

[12] Greiner footnote: "The agent received 6,000 francs for this material."

On the basis of this material, in addition to the peacetime stationing of the French forces, as well as what were apparently very loquacious statements in the French press, in October 1889 the 3rd Department *Denkschrift* determined that the following forces would deploy against Germany: [16 active army corps, 6 cavalry divisions and an independent cavalry regiment, 18 light infantry battalions and 4 mountain batteries, 3 Marine brigades, 12½ corps *bis*] = 720 battalions, 326 squadrons, 501 batteries.

[On pages 38 and 39 Greiner discussed the details of the German estimate. It was still believed that the XIV and XV Corps would initially be deployed against Italy. XIX Corps would be left in Algeria. It was thought that the French would not organize the three Marine brigades into the XX Corps. The 3rd Department noted that the corps *bis*, according to French press reports, were made up of the previous reserve divisions, with few corps troops and no corps artillery: it took only 80 trains to transport a corps *bis*, whereas 110 trains were needed for an active army corps. Each active corps, except for VI and VII, whose reserve troops garrisoned the border fortresses, would form a corps *bis*. Though Greiner did not mention it, the conclusion that the Germans would probably draw from this change was that the French intended to make more use of reserve units in maneuver operations – hence the corps organization. On pages 40 and 41 Greiner discussed the description of the Plan X (1889) order of battle in the French official history and Marchand and the errors in the 3rd Department's order of battle, which were minor. On page 41 Greiner mentioned Map 4, which gave the German estimate of the French deployment, but this map is missing. On pages 41 and 42 he discussed the errors in the German map and estimate, all of them being purely of tactical, not operational or strategic, interest. On pages 42 to 45 he described the deployment of the French covering force down to light infantry battalion level.]

[45] On the 5th mobilization day the deployment is in high gear. We can assume, analogous with the preceding years, that the combat troops of the active army corps will deploy by the 8th day of mobilization and their supply units by the 10th. The corps *bis* will begin to unload in the forward assembly areas on the 10th day and will be complete by the 15th.

[46] V. 1890/91 Mobilization Year

[The French official history (p. 5) noted that Plan X was provisional, which could be changed incrementally. A final change would be made in the following year.]

Some of these changes were visible to the 3rd Department in the material which it received on 19 May 1890 from the same source as previously. This consisted of hand-written, detailed information concerning extracts from the rail plan, an overview of the off-loading rail stations with the number of trains arriving daily and a rail map of the eastern rail net on which was sketched the routes of active corps and their terminal rail stations. During the exchange the agent also gave the following, completely accurate, information: the printed movement tables for Plan X turned over last year under 1.) remained in force and had only been modified;

German Planning: Greiner, Intelligence Estimate

they were now designated X M (*modifié*) and were effective on 15 April. The most significant changes [47] arose due to the fact that the rail line Bricon–Chaumont had been expanded to four lines. On the whole they were not so significant that it was worth the risks he would have had to take to steal the new books and movement plans. Recently all possible new security measures were being instituted, for example, numbering the copies, so that he had not dared to take one. Since 15 April work had already begun on Plan XI, which would probably be effective on 1 April 1891. He was asked if the reserve units would continue to be designated corps *bis*, and said that they would. He could not give any information concerning the employment of XIX Corps.

[In left margin] see Map 4 [missing].

[On pages 47 and 48 Greiner discussed the details of rail movement on the Bricon–Chaumont rail line changed by Plan X M. Though the agent did not give any indications for it, the 3rd Department decided that the French would form a XX Corps from Marine units, which was essentially true. On pages 48 and 49 Greiner explained that the 3rd Department assumed – erroneously, and in opposition to the information provided by the agent – that the French had dissolved the corps *bis* in order to establish 16 reserve divisions as well as add a reserve regiment to each active brigade. The basis for this error was not evident. On page 49 Greiner also discussed German errors in the order of battle for the covering force by St. Mihiel.]

[50] VI. 1891/92 Mobilization Year

The material that the 3rd Department of the Great General Staff received on 17 September 1891 for the French 1891/92 deployment plan against Germany was considerably less complete than that of previous years. It consisted of an overview, listing the troops arriving in the border areas to the 4th day of mobilization by arm [infantry, etc.], but not their points of embarkation on the rail line. Furthermore, there was an overview by day of the eastern rail operations from the 5th to 21st mobilization days, listing arrivals at the terminal rail station, but without noting the point of origin or arm. Finally, there was a sketch of the transportation routes of the active corps as well as XXV and XXXII Corps. [Greiner made reference to the applicable Map 5, which is missing.]

[On pages 50 and 51 Greiner gave the descriptions in the French official history and Marchand of Plan XI, which went into effect in August 1891. According to pages 5 and 6 of the official history, the French now committed against Germany 17 active army corps and 9 reserve corps – XXII, XXIII, XXV, XXVIII, XXIX, XXX, XXXII, XXIII, XXXVII – while attaching 6 reserve divisions to active corps.]

[52] The positions shown for the French deployment on Map 5 cannot have any pretentions of exactitude. In the French General Staff work there is no map for Plan XI and Marchand's work contains only a general sketch of the <u>assembly areas</u>

of the corps and armies. By using these sketches as well as the undoubtedly accurate off-loading rail stations provided by the French agent to the 3rd Department the off-loading areas are shown in Map 5. In this manner we can arrive at the most accurate picture of the French 1891 deployment.

On the basis of the agent material, on 4 October 1891 the 3rd Department produced a *Denkschrift* concerning the French deployment. This refers to a map showing the off-loading areas of the corps and armies that – according to a penciled note – was later burned. We must therefore rely on the summary description of the deployment in the *Denkschrift* itself. It says that "the 1st line armies were unloaded at:

1st Army [3 active corps, Epinal]
2nd Army [4 active corps] west of the Moselle line Charmes–Pont St. Vincent
3rd Army [4 active corps, Toul–Nancy] [53]
4th Army [4 active corps, a day's march west of the Meuse on the line St. Dizier–Ste. Ménehould]
14th Infantry Division [Belfort]
2nd Line. [Eight reserve divisions would follow their respective active army corps. The XX (Marine), XXV and XXXII Corps were probably regarded as 2nd line formations.]
3rd Line. [3 territorial divisions at Vesoul, 2 territorial divisions north of Chaumont, 4 reserve divisions and 3 territorial divisions at Reims.]

[On pages 53 and 54 Greiner said that the 3rd Department's estimate was fully correct in so far as it concerned the four armies of the 1st Line and the XX, XXV and XXXII Corps, as well as being largely correct concerning the number and employment of the reserve divisions. On pages 55 and 56 Greiner gave the estimate of the 1891/92 French deployment which the 3rd Department revised on 14 March 1892. Greiner's conclusion was that "These assumptions arrive at a better approximation of the actual intent of the organization of the reserve units, but on the other hand are farther from reality, because they contain a reserve corps and a reserve division too many." On pages 56 to 59 Greiner discussed border security, on pages 59 and 60 technical details of the use of French rail assets. On pages 60 and 61 he summarized Marchand's description (pp. 107–8) of three variants to the French deployment which were developed, two in case the Germans gained an advantage in the deployment race, one for a German violation of Belgian neutrality. The 3rd Department had no knowledge of these plans.]

[61] For the 1892/93 mobilization year the 3rd Department received no new material from its agent. It therefore assumed, correctly, that the deployment plan for the previous year was still in effect. Only the creation of new units resulted in changes in border security. [On page 62 Greiner described the changes that the 3rd Department estimated these new units caused in the French border security.]

[63] VII. 1893/94 Mobilization Year

The 3rd Department of the Great General Staff received the following hand-written material from its agent in the French eastern railway on 9 April 1893 concerning the French Plan XII,[13] which went into effect in February 1893:

1.) An overview of the "first priority transports for the covering force" including the rail station where the unit uploaded or the rail station where it entered the eastern railway net, if it uploaded outside of it, the departure time in hours and minutes after the mobilization order had been issued (the first train left seven hours after the issuance of the mobilization order, the last 32 hours 28 minutes after the issuance of the mobilization order), the arm of the unit being transported and the off-loading rail station for each train.

2.) An overview of the "second priority transports for the covering force", that is, from 1800 hours on the 2nd mobilization day to the 4th mobilization day. It included an indication of the departure and arrival day, the uploading or initial intermediate rail station on the eastern rail net, the off-loading rail station and the number for each train according to the rail movement table, as well as the description for each train which transported rations or reservists that would reinforce units already deployed forward. [64]

3.) An overview of the off-loading rail stations of the deployment transport, including the number of trains that would arrive per day at each off-loading rail station from the 5th to the 20th mobilization day, not only for the actual Plan XII but also for Variant I written in March 1893.

4.) A sketch of the transportation routes of the active corps as well as for the XXV and XXXII Corps.

[In left margin] Map 6 [missing].

[From pages 64 to 71 Greiner analyzed the information available to the 3rd Department concerning the French covering force, down to battalion, squadron and battery level. On pages 71 to 73 Greiner said that the 3rd Department thought six reserve divisions would be attached to active corps, instead of the previous seven, which was the number given by Marchand.[14] On page 74 Greiner said that the 3rd Department thought that the French would raise 13 reserve corps, when in fact they only intended to establish 9. The 3rd Department thought that these would be distributed behind the front, with three concentrated at Reims. The 3rd Department also did not know that the French were going to organize the XX (Marine) corps. On pages 74 and 75 Greiner said that the French really intended to form three reserve armies.]

---

[13] Greiner footnote: "Marchand, *Plans de concentration de 1871 à 1914*, pp. 115 ff. According to *Les armées françaises dans la grande guerre, tome première, première volume*, p. 6, Plan XII was to have already gone into effect in February 1892. This is obviously a typographical error."
[14] Greiner is in error. In the 1891/1892 estimate he said that the 3rd Department thought that six French corps would receive reserve divisions, p. 51; Marchand said seven, pp. 106, 115.

[75] Map 6 [missing] was accurate concerning the off-loading areas of the French active corps. In the 4th Army it inverted X and II Corps, and I and II Corps.

In Variant I to Plan XII the off-loading areas were moved back somewhat behind the line Epinal–Mirecourt–Baritey–Bar-le-Duc–Révigny. As has already been mentioned[15] the 3rd Department had already been informed by its agent of the location of a number of these off-loading rail stations for this plan and the number of trains to arrive there. In Variant II, which was not known to the 3rd Department, the 1st Army was to deploy forwards of Vesoul, the 2nd at Damblain [?], the 3rd at Bologne [Chaumont], the 4th in the area of Vitry le François–Reims, the 7th at Gray, the 5th at Brienne le Château and the 9th in the area of Sommesous–Epernay.

The transport lines designated by the agent for the active corps as well as the XXV and XXXII Corps in Plan XII were accurate.

[76] VIII. 1894/95 and 1895/96 Mobilization Years

The agent reported in again in March 1894, but brought no material with him. He could only say that Plan XII was still in effect for the next mobilization year and that work had begun on a new plan XIII. He appeared in the spring of 1895 for the last time, again with empty hands, because the access to the war march tables and all the supporting documents had been restricted to senior bureaucrats, and the security measures had been significantly increased. He gave the following information concerning the deployment plan for 1895/96 (Plan XIII) [changed routes for III, X, I, II and Marine Corps]. There was only one variant to Plan XIII, which moved the off-loading points further to the rear on the same march routes. The agent could give no further information.

In fact, Plan XII remained in force during the 1894/95 mobilization year. There were only a few changes made in March 1894 to the covering force.[16]

[On pages 76 and 77 Greiner described organizational changes to the French covering force. There were no changes to the covering force in the 1895/96 mobilization year. On pages 77 and 78 Greiner described the 3rd Department's December 1894 evaluation of the French covering force. On pages 78 and 79 Greiner summarized the description of the French Plan XIII, effective as of February 1895, as given on page 6 of the official history and page 123 in Marchand.]

[79] The 3rd Department of the Great General Staff had already reported to the 2nd [Operations] Department in January that it could be regarded as certain that in war the French would attach a reserve division to the I–V, VII–XIII and XVI–XVIII Corps, and that the remaining reserve corps would, with the addition of corps artillery and two territorial brigades, be organized into seven two-division reserve corps. [80] It is not clear where the 3rd Department received this completely

---

[15] Greiner footnote: "p. 64."
[16] Greiner footnote: "*Les armées françaises dans la grande guerre, tome première, première volume*, p. 7; Marchand, *op. cit.*, p. 124."

correct information from. In May 1895 the 3rd Department estimated that the French field army would include:

15 active army corps composed of two active army divisions and a reserve division (I–V, VII–XIII, XVI–XVIII)

4 active army corps composed of two infantry divisions (VI, a regional corps composed of the 39th and 40th Inf. Divs, XIX and Marine Corps)

2 independent infantry divisions (41st (the Vosges division) and 42nd)

7 reserve corps composed of two reserve divisions and two territorial brigades

. . . .

In total, 40 active and 29 reserve divisions as well as 14 territorial brigades, or 1½ divisions and 5 territorial brigades too many.

The 3rd Department said that these troops would off-load at:

1st Army [5 active corps, 2 reserve corps, Belfort–Epinal]

2nd Army [5 active corps, reserve corps, Vezelise–Mirecourt–Neufchâteau] [81]

3rd Army [4 active corps, 2 reserve corps, Toul–Nancy]

4th Army [4 active corps, 2 reserve corps, Ste. Ménehould–St. Dizier–Reims]

[There were numerous errors in the exact locations.]

The 3rd Department was unable to obtain further information concerning the variation to Plan XIII mentioned by the agent. It also appeared not to know that as of the winter (15 October to 15 April) of 1896 the French intended to bring three divisions from the Alpine front to the right flank of the main body. They would form the XXXIX Corps in the area Belfort–Lure–Besançon–Montbéliard (or in the variant, deploy to Dole). There is no evidence to support German suspicion that the corps was to be dispersed on the rail line.

[82] IX. 1896/97 to 1898/99 Mobilization Years

Plan XIII remained in force for the 1896/97 and 1897/98 mobilization years and was replaced in April 1898 by Plan XIV,[17] which was based on entirely different principles. The active corps would henceforth consist only of active army units. [Greiner then described changes in the structure of an active army French corps.] It was no longer intended to create reserve corps and territorial troops were no longer to be part of the field army. Instead, there were to be 17 reserve divisions . . . . of which 12 would deploy against Germany, with the remaining 5 being employed either on the Italian border or as fortress garrisons.

[In left margin] Map 8 [missing; Greiner said it contained Marchand's description of the Plan XIV rail march routes.]

[On pages 82 and 83 Greiner described the composition of the new 1st (advance guard) Army at Nancy (VI, XX and I Corps). On pages 83 and 84 he described the covering force, the largest elements of which were VI and XX Corps, 13th, 14th and 41st Infantry Divisions and all seven cavalry divisions. The main body deployed behind the advance guard and covering force] [84]

---

[17] Greiner footnote: "*Les armées françaises*, p. 7–8; Marchand, *op. cit.*, p. 130–40."

2nd Army [4 corps, Epinal]
3rd Army [4 corps, Mirecourt–Neufchâteau]
4th Army [4 corps, Gondrecourt–St. Dizier]
5th Army [3 corps, Chaumont–Joinville]
behind these 1st line troops three groups of four reserve divisions each would deploy at Vesoul, Troyes and Reims.

In total 40 infantry, 12 reserve and 7 cavalry divisions would be deployed against Germany.

[In left margin] Map 7 [missing]

The Germans thought that the French deployment plan for 1896/97 would be the same as in the preceding year.[18] It was now assumed that the reserve corps would consist of two reserve divisions and one territorial brigade, instead of two, which was in fact true for only one of the five reserve corps.[19]

[On pages 84 and 85 Greiner listed a number of other errors of tactical interest only. In a 1 October 1896 estimate the Germans correctly identified the XX Corps near Verdun–Stenay. This information may have come from newspaper reports.]

In general the guesses the Germans made above were probably based on information gained by the German military attaché in Paris. There is no evidence of other sources, such as agent reports.

In 1897/98 the 3rd Department retained in large part the estimate of the French deployment it had used in the previous two years.

In the fall of 1897 the German military attaché in Paris submitted a detailed report to the Great General Staff [86] concerning the French mobilization plan XIV, not the deployment plan, which had gone into effect on 1 April 1898. The manner in which this information was evaluated by the 3rd Department can be seen in the following document, "Remarks on the French Deployment for 1898", written by the section chief on 10 October 1897:

1.) The reserve divisions have been withdrawn from their previous attachment to the active corps. The active army corps I–V, VIII–XIII, XVI–XVIII (= 14 corps) consist of two divisions, each division of 16 battalions. The XIX, XX and Marine Corps consist, as before, of two divisions, each division of 12 battalions. The VI and VII active army corps, to which the 41st and 42nd Infantry Divisions will be attached, consist of three divisions, each division of 12 battalions. The reserve light infantry battalions are also no longer considered to be first-line troops. The corps artillery of all the active army corps has been increased by a section with three batteries. Each army has only 12 batteries of heavy field artillery attached, 6 batteries of short 120mm and 6 of short 155mm canons.

To this, the following should be said. According to Marchand,[20] in wartime all active infantry regiments would consist of four battalions, including the VI, VII

---

[18] Greiner footnote: "pp. 80–1."
[19] Greiner footnote: "p. 79."
[20] Greiner footnote: "*op. cit.*, p. 130; there is no reference to this in the French General Staff work."

and XX Corps, which was in conformity with the Law of 4 March 1897.[21] The four regiments of Zouaves and four of Algerian Tirailleurs [87] that composed the XIX Corps had always consisted of four battalions. It was possible that the 4th battalions of the three border corps VI, VII and XX in wartime could be used to form the mobile reserve of the eastern fortresses and that the 4th battalions of the XIX Corps could remain in Africa, but this could not be proven. It was also not possible to confirm if the eight battalions of Marines that comprised the Marine Division would deploy to the field with three battalions or four. The estimate concerning the field and heavy artillery can be considered correct.

[On page 87 Greiner pointed out errors in the German estimate for the order of battle for the VI, VII, XX and Marine Corps. These errors were apparently corrected on 1 May 1898. On pages 87 and 88 he said that the reserve corps had been broken up and replaced by 14 reserve divisions. The estimate of the deployment areas for the reserve divisions was wrong, but since he referred to Map 8, which is missing, it is not possible to know exactly why. He said the 3rd Department maintained this incorrect estimate through 1898. On pages 88 and 89 he noted that the active corps debarkation rail stations designated in the May 1895 estimate were in large part retained through 1898.]

[89] The corps of the new (1st) advance guard army, the existence of which was completely unknown to the Germans, were still counted as part of the 3rd Army (VI Corps) and 4th Army (I Corps) as was the newly formed XX Corps. In 1898 the VI Corps was switched with XX.

The result was that the 3rd Department of the Great General Staff, thanks to the information provided by the German military attaché concerning the new French mobilization Plan XIII [sic: XIV], was able to almost correctly estimate the strength and organization for combat of the forces to be deployed against Germany. But it had no knowledge of the completely changed deployment plan and therefore retained the 1895 estimate, which even at that time contained many errors.

[90] X. Plans for the Mobilization Years from 1899/1900 to 1905/1906

The political tension between England and France that resulted from the incident at Fashoda was the cause for a change in Plan XIV in the 1899/1900 Mobilization Year. The XIX Corps was to remain in Algiers, to be replaced on mobilization by the 43rd Infantry Division, which was to be formed from excess active army units. Otherwise, Plan XIV was in force until it was replaced by Plan XV in March 1903.[22] In this plan, 39 infantry, 12 reserve and 8 cavalry divisions were deployed against Germany. [On page 90 Greiner gave the composition of the French corps and reserve divisions.]

---

[21] Greiner footnote: "p. 82."
[22] Greiner footnote: "*Les armées françaises*, pp. 8–10; Marchand, *op. cit.*, p. 144–56."

[91] The planned French deployment is shown on Map 9 [missing]. [On page 91 and 92 Greiner described the French covering force.]

The Germans, in the absence of any newer information, retained in the 1899/1900 mobilization year the estimate from the previous year which, as has already been related, was incorrect.

[On pages 92 and 93 Greiner gave the German estimate of the French covering force. He cites the missing Map 8.] [93]

1st Army [4 corps, Epinal–Belfort]
2nd Army [5 corps, Vézelise–Mirecourt–Neufchâteau]
3rd Army [3 corps, Toul]
4th Army [4 corps, St. Dizier–Ste. Ménehould]
finally the four groups of reserve divisions, as on page 88.

The 3rd Department retained this estimate of the French deployment until 1904. Changes were made only on the basis of relatively certain information concerning inspections or war games held by French generals who were assumed to be the designate army commanders in wartime, from the construction of rail lines, or due to changes in peacetime stationing of units.

[On page 94 and 95 Greiner listed changes in the French order of battle, the most noteworthy being the replacement of the Marine Corps with the Colonial Corps in January 1901, which the Germans initially, and erroneously, credited with three divisions, as well as a new (8th) cavalry division. The Germans made some changes in the fall of 1903 in the debarkation points for some corps and switched a few from one army to another in their estimate of the French order of battle.]

[95] In midsummer 1904 the 3rd Department came to the conclusion that the French had extended their deployment to the north, for the following reasons:

A French offensive, which until 1904 was a possibility, appeared unlikely in light of the Russo-Japanese War. It was far more probable that at the beginning of a war the French would not attack immediately, but rather await the German offensive in an assembly area behind their fortifications. They would most likely expect that their left flank would be turned to the north of their fortress front. A deployment quickly conducted to the north seemed more favorable for such an assembly area than the previous one which was assumed to be opposite German Lorraine.

[In left margin] Map 9 [missing].

The 3rd Department was reinforced in this conviction by the news that the XX Corps, whose appearance at Nancy was considered certain, belonged to the 2nd Army. It was therefore concluded that this army must have been pushed to the north, and that the 3rd and 4th Armies must also therefore be further to the north. The 2nd Army was therefore moved from the area of Mirecourt to one nearer to Toul, the 3rd from Toul to the area of Bar le Duc and the 4th Army [96] whose left wing had been assumed to be on the Aisne, was pushed up to the area of Rethel. The 4th group of reserve divisions was also expected to be farther to the north, at Laon–La Fère instead of Reims. The August 1904 estimate was therefore:

1st Army [VII Corps – 3 divisions – on Vosges from Belfort to St. Die, with 4 corps behind it at Belfort–Epinal][23]
2nd Army [5 corps, Vézelise–Toul]
3rd Army [5 corps, Commercy–St. Dizier]
4th Army [5 corps, Challerange–Toul]
1st Group of Reserve Divisions [4 reserve divisions, behind right wing] [97]
2nd Group [3 reserve divisions, Neufchâteau]
3rd Group [3 reserve divisions, Châlons sur Marne]
4th Group [4 reserve divisions, Laon]
The covering force troops not indicated were assumed to be at the same locations as previously.

The 3rd Department's estimate of <u>lines of deployment transportation</u> are indicated (in green) on Map 9 [missing].

This estimate of the French deployment was retained during the following years. If it is compared with the actual French deployment in Plan XV, it is clear that the estimate of the German General Staff was in large part wrong both overall and in the details. Above all what is most striking is that the Germans assumed that four French first-line armies were widely extended from Belfort to the north of Rethel while the actual plan massed these forces in the Belfort–Verdun area. Depending on the direction of the German attack, the French intended to insert the 3rd Army between the 2nd and the 1st or between the 1st and the 4th. The Germans also did not calculate that the French would deploy the middle of the first-echelon armies as an advance guard army so close to the border (at and south of Nancy). It was assumed to be further to the west, with the centre of mass at and south-west of Toul.

[98] XI. 1906/07 and 1908/09 Mobilization Years

In <u>March 1906</u> Plan XV was changed, because the French General Staff believed they had received information that made German violation of Belgian neutrality a likelihood.[24] Therefore a 5th Army was assembled out of the IV, X and Colonial Corps in the area of Revigny–Bar le Duc–St. Dizier and the 4th Army, consisting of the VI, I, III and IX Corps, was moved forward to the line Commercy–Verdun–Challerange. The remaining three armies generally maintained the positions they had been assigned in Plan XV. [Greiner then described changes in the composition of the 2nd and 3rd French armies.]

Due to the continually growing possibility of a German advance through Belgium, Plan XV was again significantly changed in the following spring, which

---

[23] Greiner footnote: "On the basis of evidence that is no longer available, it was assumed that there was a I and II Colonial Corps."
[24] Greiner footnote: "*Les armées françaises*, p. 10 ; Marchand, *op. cit.*, p. 149 and map for Plan XV." Marchand does not support Greiner's assertion. He says the change in question was due to the fact that the French could count firmly on being able to commit the XIV and XV Corps against the Germans, not against the Italians, and the French intent was to attack with their *right*: Marchand, *op. cit.*, p. 155.

gave it an entirely new face and which was formalized in Plan XV*bis*, which went into effect on 22 May 1907.

[99] [In left margin] Map 10 [missing].

A mass of three armies (1st, 3rd and 4th) with 14 corps between them were now to deploy on the border with German Lorraine.[25] A cavalry division was attached to each army. It did not, as previously, deploy to the covering force area but rather assembled to the rear of the corps, because it was felt that the army-level cavalry did not have room to maneuver between the two deploying armies, and should therefore be saved for the decisive battle.[26] The main body was covered to the north by the 5th Army, consisting of two corps and two cavalry divisions, while only one army (2nd), consisting of four corps, was now deployed in the south on the Vosges front. The southern group of reserve divisions was moved back into the area of Gray–Langres–Is sur Tille. The northern group was widely dispersed from the Camp de Châlons to La Fère. The middle two groups were deployed on both sides of Troyes. The covering force consisted only of the VII Corps (13th and 41st Infantry Divisions), XX Corps with the 2nd Cavalry Division and 5 light infantry battalions, as well as the VI Corps with the 4th Cavalry Division and 8 light infantry battalions. The Burgundian Gate [Belfort] was still blocked by the 14th Infantry Division, 8th Cavalry Division and the 21st Light Infantry Battalion. The XIX and XXI Corps would be employed as the situation required.[27] The deployment transportation lines according to Marchand are shown in Map 10.[28] Plan XV*bis* was in effect until the spring of 1909.

[100] In the summer of 1906 Agent 35 delivered the complete deployment of the active French corps including their transportation routes to the 3rd Department of the German Great General Staff. He named as his sources three officials in the French General Staff and War Ministry whom he had befriended for a considerable period. He explained that the march plans were compiled only by officers, but over the years the necessary changes were made by officials working under the supervision of officers. In this way his friends had become aware of the actual deployment plan and had conveyed this information in conversation to Agent 35, who they held to be a good patriot. According to Agent 35, the corps deployed as follows:

XIX Corps at Besançon
XIV, XVI Corps, 30th Inf. Div. (XV Corps) at Belfort
XIII Corps, Epinal
XVII Corps, Toul
VIII, XII Corps, Sorcy [north of Toul?]
V, IX Corps, both sides of Lérouville [north of Toul?]
IV Corps, Verdun
I, II, III Corps, both sides of Montmédy on the Belgian border

---

[25] This looks very much like this deployment is designed for a battle in Lorraine, and it is hard to see how it was to stop a German advance through Belgium. Nor does Greiner try to justify his assertion, which serves only to reinforce the idea of the inevitability of the Schlieffen plan.
[26] Greiner footnote: "Marchand, *op. cit.*, p. 157."
[27] Greiner footnote: "p. 98."
[28] Greiner footnote: "Marchand, *op. cit.*, Map for Plan XV*bis*."

X, XI, XVIII Corps at Châlons sur Marne
VI, VII, XX Corps were not mentioned [covering force].

In a *Denkschrift* of January 1907 the 3rd Department thoroughly evaluated the probability of this information from the agent and compared it with its August 1904 estimate of the French deployment.[29] According to [101] its estimate, the French army currently had 14 independent double-tracked rail lines available for its deployment to the German border. The VI, VII and XX Corps were employed in border security. The Colonial Corps[30] was dispersed throughout France and would deploy by piggy-backing on the other corps. Important documents from the 30th Infantry Division had come into the hands of the 3rd Department which allowed significant conclusions to be made concerning the employment of the French Alpine Army: since 1905 the XIV and XV Corps were added to the forces deployed against Germany. Therefore, including the XIX Corps, the French had 17 corps to transport on 14 rail lines. Since the XIX Corps linked up with its supply units in France, it was assumed that it would deploy with the corps moving on each side of the Rhone. It was not possible to move two corps in addition to the third. "And these would be" said the *Denkschrift* "presumably the XIV and XV Corps. On the one hand, they would be available if the benevolent neutrality of Italy would ever come into question, on the other hand they could be employed according to the circumstances [against Germany.] They will initially remain stationary as a deceptive measure. In addition, they will wait until the reserve and territorial units are ready on the alpine border. It was therefore not absolutely certain that they [XIV and XV Corps] would, as the agent reported[31] appear [102] at Belfort. It could only be assumed that they would possibly reinforce the 1st Army[32] in order to strengthen it for a powerful offensive into Alsace. However, some other use of the former Alpine Army is not out of the question."

The 3rd Department thought that a strong offensive into Alsace was possible because the French Headquarters, given the peculiarities of the French character and out of consideration for domestic politics, would attempt to gain a quick first

---

[29] Greiner footnote: "pp. 96–7."
In both Plan XV (1903) and Variant I to the Plan (1906) the deployment for the first three armies was:
   1st Army, 4 corps, Nancy (advance guard)
   2nd Army, 5 corps, Epinal (right wing)
   3rd Army, 4 corps, Neufchâteau (reserve)
   In Plan XV the left-wing 4th Army with 4 corps, was at St. Dizier–Bar le Duc
   In Variant I it was moved forward to Challerange–Verdun–Commercy.
Agent 35's information most closely corresponded to Variant I. Nevertheless, it placed the left-wing army (I, II, III Corps) too far forward and the reserve army (X, XI, XVIII) too far to the north.

[30] Greiner footnote: "The assumption that two Colonial Corps would be created at mobilization (see p. 96) was soon dropped."

[31] Greiner footnote: "In opposition to the agent's report that the 29th Division of XV Corps would remain at Nizza, the 3rd Department thought that the entire corps would be deployed against Germany".

[32] Greiner footnote: "This was the designation given to the army that assembled in the Belfort–Epinal area".

success. The occupation of Mühlhausen and perhaps the investment of Strasbourg beckoned. Another possible employment for the XIV and XV Corps was apparent in an agent's report of a *Generalstabsreise* held at the end of May 1906 by the Chief of the French General Staff. It started near Gondrecourt[33] and concerned the movement of five active army divisions from the rail debarkation points on the left bank of the Meuse at and north of Neufchâteau in the middle of the French deployment to the left flank of the army. The movement was conducted with the rail line Bar le Duc–Ste. Menehould–Apremont as well as the rail net of the Departement of the Western Meuse. The 3rd Department thought that these five active divisions could represent either the XIX and Colonial Corps or the former Alpine Army. Since it was more likely to assume that XIX Corps would appear at Belfort (and not, as the agent said, at Besançon, where it was, for no reason, too far removed from the 1st Army), it became more likely that this exercise concerned the XIV [103] and XV Corps as well as the 2nd Colonial Division garrisoned in Toulon, which was held behind the middle of the deployment as a reserve army in order to be employed as the circumstances dictated.

For these reasons the 3rd Department did not include the XIV and XV Corps in the deployment and retained the August 1904 model for the organization of the 1st Army.[34] However, it moved XVI Corps from Epinal–Dounoux to Aillevillers and XIII Corps was off-loaded at Epinal instead of Chatel s. M.–Thaon.

In the view of the 3rd Department, the 2nd Army was deployed to defend against the German attack that they almost surely expected against the gap in the fortress line between Toul and Epinal. The 3rd Department considered the close concentration of forces reported by the agent to be unlikely, as well as the deployment of the corps to the north and north-west of Toul, because this would leave an uncovered section of front 600 [sic – 60?] kilometers long. The 3rd Department therefore saw no reason to significantly change its estimate of the deployment of this army. Instead it switched the location of VIII Corps with that of XVII Corps and moved V Corps from Toul to Sorcy.

Concerning the 3rd Army, the *Denkschrift* says: "The establishment of a group of corps behind the middle of the deployment, such as Agent 35 reports for the X, XI and XVIII Corps, has many advantages and has been reported in a similar manner by other sources. According to an agent report of a new plan in 1904,[35] [104] an army, indeed the 2nd, was stationed to the rear at Châlons. This army consisted of the V, IX, XII, and XVII Corps. In an article in the *France Militaire* of 14 February 1906 the author, M . . . . , says that individual corps will be off-loaded behind the front in order to be committed only later at the decisive point. Also, in Hargon's[36] *Generalstabsreise* in May of this year (1906) it appears not unlikely that an army was deployed farther to the rear – somewhere in the area of Châlons. The exercise, according to press and agent reports, began near Châlons and ended at Sedan. The objective of the exercise may have been to test the

---

[33] Gondrecourt le Château is 22 kilometers by road to the north-west of Neufchâteau.
[34] Greiner footnote: "p. 96."
[35] Greiner footnote: "Mentioned for the first time here; not in the file of deployment plans."
[36] Greiner footnote: "In 1906 commander designate of the 3rd Army, in 1907 *Generalissimo*."

commitment of the 3rd Army next to the 4th in case of a German attack through Belgium. Deployment in depth, in conjunction with the use of the double-tracked rail line through Reims to Laon or Rethel, facilitates shifting forces to the north to a greater degree than the previous linear formation. It cannot be assumed that the organization of the armies was violated in order to create this reserve army at Châlons. There is also no reason for the isolated appearance of IV Corps near Verdun. If forces are held in reserve, it is a only question of using the entire 3rd Army. For technical reasons, this cannot be tightly assembled around Châlons, and therefore may perhaps be assumed to be in the area of Châlons s. M.–Vitry le François–Revigny–Ste. Menehould. This would certainly create another 50-kilometer-long gap on the Meuse north of Toul to Verdun, which would however be covered by the Meuse forts and the border security of the 40th and 42nd Infantry Divisions. In addition, the forward corps of the 3rd Army could reach the Meuse from the line Revigny–Ste. Menehould in two short day's marches."

The 3rd Department therefore assumed the deployment for the 3rd Army shown in Map 11 [missing]. Contrary to the information provided by Agent 35 it retained the composition of the army from the 1904 estimate, for which it believed it found confirmation [105] in the previously mentioned *Generalstabsreise* of General Hargon, in which the IV, IX, XI, and XVIII Corps[37] as well as the 5th Cavalry Division had participated.

According to the agent's information, the 4th Army was to be transported over Mézières to the area of Montmedy. The 3rd Department thought this to be completely unlikely for technical reasons: the three corps would have to be moved over one double-tracked rail line, which in addition was not provided with off-loading ramps. These corps would also be deployed far forward and east of the Meuse, for which there was no logical basis, considering the initially wait-and-see attitude the French were expected to adopt. The 3rd Department considered a concentration behind the Meuse at and south of Mézières more likely. This was supported by a *Generalstabsreise* conducted by the probable commander designate of the 4th Army, General Metzinger, which began at Ste. Menehould and took place in the Department of the Ardennes. This also could have indicated an advance by the 4th Army from the Aisne prior to an attack. General Hagron was supposed to have moved the 3rd Army from Châlons s. M. to Sedan, which argued for the employment of the reserve 3rd Army to the left of the 4th Army. Finally, according to an agent report, during the negotiations for a British-French military convention General Brun, the Chief of the General Staff, was supposed to have developed a plan for the movement of the French army to the Meuse, once the British had arrived. Nevertheless, the [106] 3rd Department thought that there were strong reservations concerning the deployment of the 4th Army on the Meuse. The French concept, which can be characterized best as strategically defensive and tactically offensive, required above all things freedom of movement, which was all the more available the further 4th Army deployed to the rear. In addition, the employment

---

[37] Greiner footnote: "The actual composition of the 3rd Army in Plan XV (1903). According to Variant I to Plan XV (1905) the Army included the XI, XII, XVII, XVIII Corps. In Plan XV*bis* (1907) it included V, IX, XII, and XVIII Corps as well as the 7th Cavalry Division."

of the 3rd Army next to the 4th would be more difficult if the 4th deployed forward on the Meuse.

Based on these considerations, and in the absence of sufficient information, the 3rd Department decided that it was not advisable to assume that the 4th Army was on the Meuse. It assumed, as in 1904, that it was on the Aisne, but due to the reorganization of the rail system pushed it somewhat to the north, so that the left wing (I Corps) was now at Liart instead of Novion Porcien.

The off-loading point for the 1st Group of reserve divisions in the 1904 estimate was, in general, retained. Given the new organization of the rail system, the three divisions exchanged positions and the 66th Division was at Lure instead of Aillevillers. From the 2nd Group the 62nd Reserve Division was put at Neufchâteau, the 55th at Gondrecourt, the 59th at Joinville and a reserve Zouave Brigade from XIX Corps at Bologne. The 3rd Group could no longer be placed at Châlons sur Marne, Vitry la Ville and Vitry le François, because the Germans thought that the 3rd Army would deploy here. Given the new organization of the rail net, it was assumed that they would deploy to Epernay, Fère [107] Champenoise and Sommesous. The 4th Group was put at St. Quentin, Laon and Soissons.

The covering force was divided into three sectors. The right sector included the VII Corps (14th, 41st, 13th Infantry Divisions, 7th Cavalry Brigade), the 8th Cavalry Division and the 21st Light Infantry Brigade; a middle group with the XX Corps (11th, 39th Infantry Divisions, 20th Cavalry Brigade), 1st, 2nd, 6th, 7th Cavalry Divisions, 1st, 2nd, 4th, 17th, 20th and 26th Light Infantry Battalions; the left group with the VI Corps (40th, 42nd, 12th Infantry Divisions, 6th and 6bis Cavalry Brigades[38]), 3rd, 4th, 5th, Cavalry Divisions and the 25th, 29th, 19th, 8th, 18th, 16th, and 9th Light Infantry Battalions.

If the January 1907 3rd Department estimate of the French deployment is compared to the French Plan XVbis of May 1907, the result is that 3rd Department in general correctly evaluated the operational idea on which the plan was based, but had an often incorrect picture of the details, as the following comparison shows [108]

The deployment according to
Plan XVbis (Map 10)[missing]

the German estimate (Map 11) [missing]

2nd Army (XV, XIV, XIII, VII Cav. 8 Cav. Div.) Belfort–Lure–Aillevillers–Epinal–St. Dié

1st Army: (XIX, XVI, XIII, VII, 8 Cav. Div.) Belfort–Aillevillers–Epinal–St. Dié

1st Army (VIII, XVII, XVI, XX, 6th Cav. Div.) Charmes–Neufchâteau–Toul–Nancy

2nd Army (XVII, VIII, XII, V, XX Vézelise–Sorcy–Toul–Nancy

3rd Army (V, XVIII, XII, IX, 7th Cav. Div.) Vaucouleurs–Gondrecourt–Joinville–St. Dizier–Commercy

---

[38] Greiner footnote gives the organization of the French cavalry.

4th Army (IV, XI, Colonial, X, III, 3rd Cav. Div) Bar le Duc–Revigny–Ste. Menehould–Consenvoye–Verdun

3rd Army (IX, XVIII, XI, Colonial, IV) Revigny–Vitry le François–Camp de Châlons–Ste. Menehould

5th Army (II, I, 1st and 5th Cav. Div.) Challerange–Rethel–Chaumont Porcien

4th Army (X, III, II, I) Challerange–Rethel–Liart

VI Corps (3rd Army) on a line Gironville–Azannes

VI Corps (3rd Army) on a line Gironville–Sedan

Southern Group of Reserve Divisions (58th, 63rd, 67th, 66th) Gray–Is sur Tille–Langres

1st Group of Reserve Divisions (66th, 67th, 58th, 63rd) Lure–Vitrey–Passavant

Middle Group of Reserve Divisions (55th, 59th, 61st, 54th) south of Troyes–Arcis sur Aube

2nd Group of Reserve Divisions (62nd, Zouave Brigade, 59th, 55th) Neufchâteau–Bologne–Joinville–Gondrecourt [109]

3rd Group of Reserve Divisions (68th, 61st, 54th) Sommesous – Fère Champenoise–Epernay

North Group of Reserve Divisions (53rd, 60th, 52nd, 51st) St. Hilaire–Reims–Laon–La Fère

4th Group of Reserve Divisions (52nd, 53rd, 60th, 51st) Laon–Soissons–St. Quentin

The inaccuracies in the 3rd Department estimate were probably in large part due to the fact that it thought the French had 14 deployment rail lines available, when in fact they only planned to use 9 (see Map 10) [Missing].[39]

Reports that reached the 3rd Department in the course of 1907 caused a change in their estimate of the French 1908/09 army order of battle from that of January 1907. There was considerable discussion in the French press and parliament that in the case of war five armies would be deployed to the north-east border, including a "covering force army". Further, according to a private report that was considered very reliable, General Lacroix had inspected the three border corps (VI, VII and XX) as "inspector of the army" and repeatedly toured the eastern border. Before being named the Generalissimo in 1907 he was supposed to have been selected to be the commander of an army composed of these three corps. On the basis of these reports the 3rd Department now thought there would be five French armies, the 5th Army [110] being a covering force army composed of the VI, VII and XX Corps. They considered the role of this commander at the beginning of the campaign to consist of bringing the movements of the widely dispersed covering force troops in harmony with each other as well as with the intentions of the army command. It was left undecided how long after the commencement of operations this army would continue to exist. This assumption was confirmed in 1907 by an agent report.

---

[39] The 3rd Department has made the French much stronger on the left, 10 corps as opposed to the actual 7, while the French have an entire 4-corps army in the centre and the 3rd Department has none.

Another deployment plan delivered by Agent 35[40] also provided for five armies, including a 3rd Army under General Lacroix around Nancy composed of the IV, VI, VII and XX Corps.[41] The 3rd Department thought that the agent had misunderstood what he had learned concerning the covering force army. Perhaps he had heard that the army headquarters initially would be at Nancy and had therefore thought that the border corps would be concentrated there, with the addition of the IV Corps, which he put to the south of Toul. A concentration of the border corps at Nancy could be considered completely out of the question and there was no support for the idea that IV Corps belonged to the covering force army. The 3rd Department therefore maintained its previous estimate. In addition, the new deployment plan delivered by this agent was very similar to the one he had delivered in 1906.[42] On the right flank there was supposed to be an army (4th) with about six corps (XIV, XVI, Colonial, elements of XV and XIX Corps would deploy around Belfort, XIII at Epinal) [111]. The centre (2nd) Army (V, VIII, XII, XVII Corps) was no longer tightly concentrated in the Toul–Lérouville area, but now was between Toul and Verdun. The left flank army (1st) with I, II, III, and X Corps was to stand on the east side of the Meuse, between Verdun and Montmédy. The reserve army (5th) now composed of IX, XI, and XVIII Corps, was again at Châlons sur Marne. The 3rd Department took the same position concerning this deployment plan that it had towards the one delivered in 1906 and maintained its January 1907 estimate for the 1908/09 mobilization year,[43] with one exception. It now thought that the three border corps had been consolidated into a 5th Army. The army order of battle given by the agent generally agreed with that of the 3rd Department, as the following comparison demonstrates:

Right-wing army:
Agent 35: 4th with XIII, XVI, XIX, XIV, XV, Colonial Corps
3rd Department: 1st with XIII, XVI, XIX, perhaps XIV, XV Corps
Middle Army:
Agent 35: 2nd with V, VIII, XII, XVII Corps
3rd Department: 2nd with V, VIII, XII, XVII Corps
Reserve Army:
Agent 35: 5th with IX, XI, XVIII Corps
3rd Department: 3rd with IV, IX, XI, XVIII, Colonial Corps [112]
Left-wing army:
Agent 35: 1st with I, II, III, X Corps
3rd Department: 4th with I, II, III, X Corps
Covering Force army:
Agent 35: 3rd with IV, VI, VII, XX Corps
3rd Department: 5th with VI, VII, XX Corps.

---

[40] Greiner footnote: "p. 100."
[41] This was entirely wrong. According to Plan XV*bis* (1907) IV Corps was part of 4th Army at Bar le Duc, VI Corps was north of Toul and part of 3rd Army, XX Corps at Nancy and part of 1st Army, and VII Corps at St. Dié and part of 2nd Army.
[42] Greiner footnote: "p. 100."
[43] Greiner footnote: "3rd Department *Denkschrift* of 31 March 1908 concerning the French deployment 1908/09."

The 3rd Department had not come any closer in its new estimate to the actual French deployment in Plan XV*bis*.

XII. 1909/10 and 1910/11 Mobilization Years

The application of the law of 25 March 1905, which instituted two-year conscription in France, and the improvement of relations with England made a new plan appear necessary. This was implemented on 1 March 1909 as <u>Plan XVI</u>. The concept of the new plan was presented to the Supreme War Council by the Generalissimo designate, General Lacroix, on 15 February 1908.[44]

[On pages 112 and 113 Greiner discussed organizational changes in the French army. Sixteen of the nineteen corps areas were to raise one reserve division each; VII, XIV and XV Corps areas raise two each. XIX Corps was to definitely return to France in case of war. XXI Corps was raised from units excess to XIV and XV Corps.]

[114] Therefore, in case of war the French army included:
22 corps (I–XXI, and Colonial Corps) of which 2 (VI and VII) had 3 divisions, therefore a total of 46 infantry divisions,
22 reserve divisions,
8 cavalry divisions; in addition
9 territorial divisions.
All the corps and cavalry divisions were to deploy against Germany. Of the 22 reserve divisions, the four to be raised by the XIV and XV Corps districts were to remain on the Italian border. The two from VII Corps district became the mobile reserves of Belfort and Epinal, the reserve division from the XX Corps district the mobile reserve of Toul, that of the VI Corps the Verdun reserve, two further reserve divisions would comprise the garrison of Paris. That left 12 reserve divisions available for the field army opposing Germany.
In the course of the year in 1909 (the exact date cannot be determined) the <u>3rd Department of the Great General Staff</u> received, either from the German military attaché in Paris or from agent "Peter", copies of parts of the <u>mobilization section of Plan XIV</u> [this leads to a discussion on pages 114 and 115 of the German impression of the organizational changes in the French army described on pages 112 and 113.]
[116] The Germans calculated that the French had in total
21 active corps (I–XX and Colonial Corps, of which two – VI and VII – each had three divisions = 44 divisions)
1 independent colonial division (2nd)
20 reserve divisions
8 cavalry divisions

---

[44] Greiner footnote: "*Les armées françaises*, pp. 10 ff."

14 territorial divisions, and two territorial brigades as well as the regional brigade from Lyon of nine battalions[45] and

13 Alpine groups, each of a battalion[46] and a battery, in addition

12 reserve Alpine battalions

Therefore one corps (XXI) and two reserve divisions too few, but six territorial divisions too many, if the Lyon regional brigade and the Alpine groups are not considered. It was assumed that, of the active and reserve forces only two reserve divisions (64th and 65th) as well as the 13 Alpine groups in addition to the 12 reserve Alpine battalions would remain on the Italian border: everything else would be employed against Germany.

[117] The deployment of the French army against Germany in Plan XVI is shown on Map 12 [missing]. It shows a mass of three armies on the border with German Lorraine with a total of 10 active corps and three cavalry divisions. On each wing is an army of two corps and a cavalry division. At Rethel there is in addition a group of three cavalry divisions. As reserves there are the 6th Army with four corps, the XIX Corps at Orléans, the XXI Corps south-east of Paris, four groups of three reserve divisions each, one behind the right wing, one behind the centre and two behind the left wing. Finally there are the XIV and XV Corps, which if possible would be moved to Dôle, in order to be sent forward, either through Besançon to Lure or through Chatillon sur Seine to Chaumont–Langres. Two territorial divisions were also to be employed with the field army, the 121st, which was to assemble at the camp D'Auvours, and the 136th, which was to assemble at the camp de la Braconne. The deployment was to be covered by the three border corps (VII, XX, VI), three cavalry divisions (8th, 2nd, 4th) and 14 independent light infantry battalions. Their missions were to prevent an encirclement of Belfort, to secure the rail lines to the west of the fortress as well as the crest of the Vosges, the Forest of Haye[47] and the ridge line between Toul and Verdun, prevent an enemy crossing over the Moselle, Madoce and Meuse before the 11th day of mobilization, and finally to cover the assembly of the 5th Army. As [118] support for the covering force the 6th, 7th, 5th, 3rd and 1st Cavalry Divisions were to be given accelerated mobilization and deployment, as was the 15th Infantry Division (VIII Corps) to Charmes, the 9th Infantry Division (V Corps) to St. Mihiel and the 1st Division (I Corps) to Dun–Doulcon (opposite Dun sur Meuse). Now ten rail lines were available for deployment instead of the previous nine; they are marked on Map 12 with the letters A – K. [Greiner then discussed peculiarities in the rail transport for VII Corps.] Plan XVI remained in effect until the fall of 1911.

The *Denkschrift* of July 1910 by the Vice-President of the Supreme War Council, appointed in February 1911, General Michel,[48] need not be considered here,

---

[45] Greiner footnote: "The two infantry regiments that belonged to the brigade and the third regiment from the XIV Corps district (see p. XII, 2, footnote 1), each with three infantry battalions."

[46] Greiner footnote: "6th, 7th, 11th, 12th, 13th, 14th, 22nd, 23rd, 24th 27th, 28th 30th Alpine Battalions as well as the provisional 31st Alpine Battalion established in the middle of 1909 from companies of other Alpine battalions in XV Corps area."

[47] Greiner footnote: "Between Toul and Nancy."

[48] Greiner footnote: "*Les armées françaises*, pp. 13–15."

because the Supreme War Council rejected its suggestions in July 1911. General Joffre, appointed Chief of the General Staff at the end of June, retained the fundamental principles of Plan XVI, but in a variant in September 1911[49] made the following changes:

[119][In left margin] Map 13[missing].

The XIV and XV Corps definitely became part of the 4th Army. It was possible the XIX Corps, which was to move to Lyon, might also be added. The deployment assembly area of the army was moved north to the area of Mouzon–Amagne–Liart–Mézières. The 6th Army was also moved northward to the area of Ste. Menehould (X Corps)–Suippes (IV)–Camp de Châlons (XI)–Reims (III).[50] The XXI Corps, which was transported to Meaux, might also be added later to this army. Finally, the four groups of reserve divisions received assembly areas either on or directly behind the front line. The 1st on the line Vesoul – Jussey, the 2nd between Toul and Commercy, the 3rd south of Ste. Menehould, at Apremont and Dun sur Meuse, the 4th at Riems, Liart and Charleville. Finally, the 1st, 3rd and 5th Cavalry Divisions were grouped around Mézières, while the 4th Cavalry Division was transferred from the 5th to the 3rd Army.

Variant 2[51] to Plan XVI went into effect in April 1913. The 6th Army was moved forward to the area of Ste. Menehould–Grandpré–Reims–Camp de Châlons "in order to facilitate and increase the speed of its movement over the Meuse to the north of Verdun, either to the east, crossing the river between Dun and Stenay, or northwards towards the Meuse between Sedan and Dun." In addition, the 3rd Group of reserve divisions would now deploy with the 54th Reserve Division south of [120] Verdun, the 53rd around Montfaucon and the 52nd on both sides of the Meuse between Dun and Stenay, in order to occupy the Meuse heights on both sides of Verdun.[52]

The entire rail deployment was divided into three phases.[53] During the first four days after the announcement of mobilization the covering forces, the 1st, 9th and 15th Infantry Divisions, the 1st, 3rd, 5th, 6th, and 7th Cavalry Divisions, the first echelon of both General Headquarters and the Army headquarters, the corps cavalry brigades, as well as one infantry brigade each with an artillery battery from the II–IV, IX–XVIII Corps, would be moved to the deployment assembly areas. From the 5th mobilization day they would be followed by the second echelon of the General Headquarters and the Army headquarters. By noon of the 11th mobilization day the rail movement of the combat troops and combat trains[54] of

---

[49] Greiner footnote: "*Les armées françaises*, p. 16; Marchand, *op. cit.*, pp. 181–4."
[50] The deployment in Variant I to Plan XVI was now practically identical to that reported by Agent 35 and the 3rd Department's January 1907 estimate.
[51] Greiner footnote: "*Les armées françaises*, pp. 16–17; Marchand, *op. cit.*, p. 184."
[52] Greiner footnote: "According to the French General Staff history, Vol. 1, p. 16 and Map 6, in the 1st and 2nd Variants the assembly area for the 4th Group of Reserve Divisions was around Mézières. According to Marchand, p. 183 and Map to Plan XVI, for Variant 1 the assembly area was at Riems–Liart–Charleville. I have followed Marchand and entered the Group on Map 13 according to his information."
[53] Greiner footnote: "Marchand, *op. cit.*, pp. 176–80."
[54] Combat and field trains are supply units. Combat trains include medical and ammunition units, field trains rations and other supply units.

the active army units, the balloon and telegraph troops, the mobile heavy artillery of the field army, the reserve units of the Paris garrison as well as the garrisons of the fortresses will have been completed. At 2359 hours on the 11th mobilization day the remaining troops and trains would follow, beginning with the reserve brigades of the active corps and the reserve divisions. The entire rail deployment was to be concluded at noon on the 17th mobilization day.

[121] Due to a lack of new information, the 3rd Department of the German Great General Staff retained its March 1908 estimate of the French deployment[55] until 1911. However, it expressly noted in a *Denkschrift* of March 1909 "that the assumed deployment, due to a lack of official materials, rests in large part on deductions from a variety of indicators and reports. There is no complete assurance that this estimate is correct, and it is not out of the question that the actual deployment deviates from it more or less." In particular, the reports concerning the French *Generalstabsreisen* for 1908, 1909 and 1910 were so uncertain that no secure conclusions about the order of battle for the armies could be drawn from them. In the opinion of the principal agent of the 3rd Department, and according to press reports, the composition of the armies was purely arbitrary and had nothing to do with the war plan. Strict measures were taken to keep unauthorized personnel away from the exercise critiques in the field. Reports that in the French deployment, in addition to a "covering force army, which would probably exist only until the beginning of operations" five first-line armies were to be established, were so uncertain that the 3rd Department did not feel it immediately necessary to change its estimate of the army order of battle.

[122] In 1911 several events caused a review of the estimate of the French deployment. First, a plausible source (Agent 17) reported that on 1 April 1912 a new deployment plan would go into effect. In addition, there were signs that the active army troops of the XIV and XV Corps (Corps districts of Lyon and Marseilles) would in large part be employed immediately against Germany. The French also seemed to be certain that the British army would land on French territory and provide them effective support. Finally, it was apparent from the most recent French military literature that the French had changed their evaluation of the probable German operation. "Until about 1909 they certainly expected to be attacked frontally from Lorraine and the Vosges and thought that an advance by the German right wing through south Belgium and Luxembourg was very likely, although not certain." Since that time they seem to believe that the decisive German attack would be made through Belgium and Luxembourg. An old school expected in addition an attack by strong forces against Toul–Epinal. The new school did not expect a serious attack from Lorraine, but supposed that the mass of the German forces would advance through Belgium and Luxembourg against Maubeuge–Verdun, with the far right flank even advancing north of the Meuse and through Holland. Only weak forces would deploy in Lorraine, which would feint an attack or stay on the defensive.

[123] These changed military-political conditions were the reason, as has been said, that made it appear necessary to re-evaluate, based on consideration of French

---

[55] Greiner footnote: "p. 111 and Map 11."

German Planning: Greiner, Intelligence Estimate

operational and tactical thought, how the French would conduct their deployment. This resulted in a *Denkschrift* in May 1912 concerning 'French Deployment and Operational Intentions in a Future Franco-German War.'[56]

The *Denkschrift* had the following to say concerning the basic considerations of the French deployment:

"So long as the French were certain that they could count on a German attack in Lorraine, the French main body deployed on and west of the line Epinal–Toul, with weak forces on the wings . . . It may be assumed that . . . due to a change in French assumptions concerning the German operation that the location of French *Schwerpunkt* has been shifted." This was because a deployment of the French main body on and west of the line Epinal–Toul "would only be reasonable in case the Germans actually attacked from Lorraine. It was not suitable for a situation, which now is considered probable, in which the Germans advance with all their forces through Belgium and Holland. Shifting the deployment from the area around Neufchâteau to the Belgian border either during or after the completion of the rail deployment is in reality not [124] possible."

"It is therefore obvious that the deployment cannot be moved further to the south, if the French assume that the offensive by the German main body will be made through Belgium. A counterattack with the French main body into upper Alsace is unanimously rejected in the French military literature."

"In the same manner the French will not deploy on the Belgian border. Their right flank would be too threatened from Lorriane. An attack from this direction would severely threaten their lines of communication, which run to that part of France to the south of Paris. The French would run the danger of being driven to the north, a course of events that they definitely want to avoid. As long as the French right flank is not completely secure, it is hardly credible that they will deploy their *Schwerpunkt* on the Belgian border. If the German main attack is made through Belgium and not from Lorraine, the French forces deployed on the Belgian border will merely oppose the Germans frontally. It is out of the question that the French will extend the left flank farther to the north, close to the sea, in order to envelop the German right. They would then expose themselves to the danger of being pushed into the sea.[57] It is completely contrary to their operational concept to meet an envelopment with a further envelopment of their own."

[125] "The French have probably moved the *Schwerpunkt* of their deployment from the area west of Epinal–Toul somewhat to the north, approximately in the area west of the middle Meuse (west of Toul–Verdun). The form of the deployment is essentially the same as it has been proven to be in the past. The main body is concentrated in a central mass, in depth, so that it can immediately be employed to the east, north or south. There are smaller armies on the wings to protect the flanks."

Map 14 [missing], which was attached to the *Denkschrift*, shows the German estimate of the French deployment for the 1912/13 mobilization year.

---

[56] Preserved in the Bundesarchiv-Militärarchiv Freiburg im Breisgau, (BA-MA) PH 3/256 Großer Generalstab, 3. Abteilung, Geheim! (A.O.K. 4 – 2a) *Aufmarsch und operative Absichten der Franzosen in einem zukünftigen deutsch-französischen Kriege.*
[57] A fair description of the strategic situation in May 1940.

Concerning the Alpine Army, the *Denkschrift* said: "Official documents from June 1905 showed without a doubt that the XIV and XV Corps, 2nd Colonial Division and the reserve troops of the 14th and 15th Corps districts would initially defend the Alpine border. According to reliable sources there was a contingency plan to transport the Alpine army to the principal battlefield. Since, as a consequence of the Italo-Turkish War, Italian intervention at the beginning of a Franco-German war has become very unlikely, the French military literature and the press has drawn the conclusion that a "system of surveillance" (using mountain infantry, reserve and territorial units) would be adequate on the Alpine border, [126] and that the XIV and XV Corps (and perhaps also the 2nd Colonial Division and the Alpine light infantry) would immediately be employed against Germany." The 3rd Department saw confirmation for this opinion of the French military literature and the press in the fact that in the course of the artillery reorganization conducted in 1910[58] the XIV and XV Corps received the normal 30-battery artillery component. Previously both corps had lacked the two horse batteries which at the time were a part of the normal corps complement, and XV Corps had only 17 instead of 21 field artillery batteries.[59] Above all, it was known from a reliable source that the French General Staff had decided to move the XIV and XV Corps to the main body immediately upon mobilization. Both corps would now, according to their peacetime garrisons, move with the right flank units first. Similarly, it was thought that the entire XIX Corps would immediately be moved from Africa to France to be employed against Germany.

The French military literature and press also showed, as the *Denkschrift* demonstrated in great detail, that the French hoped for the immediate military support of the British Expeditionary Force and did everything they could to smooth the way for their landing and engagement in combat. It was generally assumed in France [127] that the British landing would take place at Dunkirk, Calais and Boulogne, because the sea movement to these ports could be made the most quickly and was the easiest to secure and the three fortresses offered the British good operational bases. In addition, it was clear from statements in the French press that the costly expansion of the Dunkirk harbor and the recent build-up of the fortifications were made to facilitate a British landing. Further, in the debate concerning the demilitarization of the Lille fortifications a weighty argument for their retention was that Lille would form an important base for the expected British intervention. To make it easier for the British to take the decision to land, the French intended to leave I Corps and perhaps several reserve divisions on the Belgian border, perhaps at Maubeuge, as support. This intent was proven without a doubt by the statements concerning Lille and Dunkirk and confirmed by a letter from General Townsend to General Haldane of 23 October 1911, which was obtained by the German military attaché in London.

Concerning the timetable for the completion of the deployment, the 3rd Department thought that the border security forces (VI, VII, XX Corps, 2nd, 4th,

---

[58] Greiner footnote: "pp. 112–3."
[59] Greiner footnote: "The corps artillery brigade prior to the reorganization included 21 field and 2 horse batteries in two regiments."

8th Cavalry Divisions as well as the . . . [11] independent light infantry battalions
. . .) [128] would arrive in their deployment assembly areas on the 1st day of
mobilization. The 6th, 7th, 3rd, 5th and 1st Cavalry Divisions as well as the corps
cavalry brigades would arrive on the 4th, the active army corps, including their
supply trains, by the 10th, the XIX and Colonial Corps by the 11th, the reserve
brigades on the 10th and 11th, the reserve divisions by the 13th day of mobilization.
That is, the corps, reserve brigades and reserve divisions were expected to deploy
much earlier than was actually the case.[60]

In accordance with the change in the deployment, the 3rd Department changed
the last evaluation of composition of 14 rail deployment lines, which had been
made in January 1907. Of 21 French corps, in addition to the border corps (VI, VII,
XX) two more corps, I and II, no longer needed to be deployed by rail: I Corps,
because its assembly area was presumed to be at Maubeuge, II Corps because a
deployment on its own rail line was unnecessary as it was in part garrisoned on the
border. Of the remaining 16 corps, XIX did not need to be considered because its
rail movement would be conducted at a later point in time, after its sea movement
to France. There remained 15 corps, which the 3rd Department distributed on the
12 available rail lines in such a way [129] that the line Paris–Château Thierry–
Châlons and the line Paris–Soissons–Reims–Cuperly each transported 1½ corps
(IX, ½ XVIII and XI, ½ XVIII), the line Lyon–Bourg–Besançon– Belfort–Lure
and Paris–Coulommiers–Vitry le François two corps each (XIV, XV and XVII,
Colonial Corps).

Given a lack of new information, in the 1913/14 mobilization year the 3rd
Department maintained the previous year's estimate of the French deployment. In
the meantime, the estimate presented in the *Denkschrift* of May 1912 seemed to
be confirmed in many respects by numerous articles written by competent French
military writers and in statements in the daily press, as was demonstrated in detail
by a new 3rd Department *Denkschrift* in February 1913.[61] Two French mobilization calendars that were obtained in the summer of 1912 provided a wealth of
information concerning the French mobilization in general and that of the covering
force in particular. In addition to a large number of other individual reports of
various provenance, they proved that the French mobilization plan XVI was still
in effect. On the other hand, they also considerably expanded the 3rd Department's
understanding of the French covering force. These were described in a December
1912 *Denkschrift*, Expected Initial French Actions 1913/14. It stated that: [On
pages 130 to 133 Greiner discussed the 3rd Department's estimate of the deployment of the French covering force and the security of vital French installations in
great detail. The expected French actions on the flanks are interesting:]

[130] I. Section: Belgian–French Border and Verdun
It is possible that the I Corps (without its reserve brigade) will assemble near
Maubeuge, and, perhaps reinforced by the II Corps (without its reserve brigade)

---

[60] Greiner footnote: "p. 120."
[61] Also preserved in the Bundesarchiv-Militärarchiv, (BA-MA) PH 3/628 Großer Generalstab, 3. Abteilung, Geheim! *Aufmarsch und operative Absichten der Franzosen in einem zukünftigen deutsch-französischen Kriege, berechtigt für Mob. Jahr 1913/14.*

and cavalry, move into Belgium early to seize the Meuse line between Namur–Givet. According to various reports, the French may under certain circumstances intend to launch a surprise attack into Belgium with strong cavalry forces. For this purpose the following units will assemble at the times stated above: 4th Cavalry Division between Sedan and Stenay, north of it perhaps 5th and 1st Cavalry Divisions, east and north-east of Verdun perhaps 3rd and 7th Cavalry Divisions. In addition perhaps a newly formed [131] cavalry division . . . .

[132] IV Section: Vosges–Belfort
[133]. . . . It is possible that French forces will attack early with VII Corps and the 8th Cavalry Division from Belfort and the southern Vosges into the upper Alsace against Mühlhausen (Mulhouse) . . . .

[134] The degree to which the German estimate of the French covering force corresponded to the actual French plan is shown by a comparison with the covering force positions shown on Map 13 [missing]. We know nothing concerning the initial measures planned by the French for 1913/14. Otherwise a comparison of the German estimate in the time period under consideration from 1909/10 to 1913/14 with the deployments for Plan XVI and both subsequent variants shows that in general on the one hand the 3rd Department expected the French left flank to extend too far to the north, with the left wing of the active corps at Liart. In 1912/13 there was in addition an army group at Maubeuge. In fact, in 1910/11 the French left was at Rethel. As of 1911 the left wing was assumed to be at Liart, with the left-wing reserve divisions at St. Quentin, when it was in fact at La Fère, and as of 1911 at Liart–Charleville. On the other hand, the 3rd Department did not recognize that as of 1911 the French forces were concentrated closer to the border. The French had given up their principle, to which they had previously been strongly attached, of maneuvering in depth, in favor of an immediate offensive. According to the 3rd Department's estimate during this entire time the line Vesoul–Chaumont–Soissons–St. Quentin formed the western boundary of the deployment. In fact, this line had been moved forward in 1911 from the line Dôle–Dijon–Troyes–Soissons–La Fère to the line Montbéliard–Vesoul–St. Dizier–Reims–Liart. Concerning the details, [135] such as the number of armies, the corps in each army, their deployment assembly areas, the rail deployment routes and the use of the reserve divisions, now as previously, the 3rd Department was groping in the dark.

[136] XIII. 1914/15 Mobilization Year

1913 was a year of great importance for the development of the French army. First, due to the new law on infantry cadres of 23 December 1912, ten new infantry regiments were created in the spring of 1913, for the most part from already existing 4th battalions,[62] along with the 31st Light Infantry Battalion in St. Dié[63] and five

---

[62] Greiner footnote: "p. 113, footnote 3."
[63] Greiner footnote: "The provisional 31st Light Infantry Battalion, created in the middle of 1909 in the XIV Corps area received the number 32 (See p. 116, footnote 3)."

new native Tirailleur regiments in North Africa. [On pages 136 and 137 Greiner recapitulated the French peacetime order of battle]
[137] On the other hand the regional infantry brigade from Lyon was expanded into the 43rd Infantry Division in St. Dié and a new 87th Infantry Brigade was formed in Stenay, so that the following units now stood on the Franco–German border:
4th Infantry Division (II Corps) (Mézières) with the 7th, 8th and 87th Infantry Brigades
VI Corps (Châlons) with the 12th (Reims), 40th (St. Mihiel) and 42nd (Verdun) Infantry Divisions
VII Corps (Besançon) with the 14th (Belfort) and 41st (Remiremont) Infantry Divisions
XX Corps (Nancy) with the 11th (Nancy) and 39th (Toul) Infantry Divisions
the new XXI Corps (Epinal) with the 13th (Chaumont) and 43rd (St. Dié) Infantry Divisions.
[Greiner then discussed the organization of the cavalry.]
[138] The peacetime French army therefore consisted of:
20 Corps (I–XVIII, XX, XXI) with 41 Infantry Divisions
10 Cavalry Divisions (1st–10th)
12 Fortress Infantry Regiments (six with four battalions, six with three) in Maubeuge, Verdun, Toul, Epinal, Belfort, Briançon as well as a regiment with four battalions on Corsica
Colonial Corps with three divisions
in North Africa there were
XIX Corps with divisions in Algiers, Oran and Constantine,
the Tunis garrison division
the Moroccan garrison, which was composed of colonial troops, elements of the XIX Corps as well as the Tunis Division.[64]
The third law in 1913 was the Three Year Law, which was promulgated on 7 August, and as a result of which two recruit classes were conscripted in November, which increased the peacetime strength of the French army by 200,000 men. This resulted in a significant increase in the authorized strength of the troop units[65] as well as an increase in the ease and speed of mobilization.
[139] This expansion of the French army had as a consequence a new mobilization and deployment plan, which came into effect on 15 April 1914 as Plan XVII.

---

[64] Greiner footnote: "In July 1914, 64 battalions, 24 squadrons and 22 batteries strong (*Les armées françaises* I, p. 139).''
[65] Greiner footnote: "Normal authorized strength of a company rose from 115 to 140 men, reinforced strength was increased from 160 men to 200. [This was effectively wartime strength – Z] All light infantry battalions, cavalry regiments and horse batteries were brought to reinforced strength (cavalry regiments 780 instead of 680 or 720 troopers, horse batteries 175 instead of 120 or 160 men. The border corps (VI, VII, XX, XXI), 4th Infantry Division and II Corps were all brought up to reinforced strength.''

The order of battle for this plan included:

1.) 21 active army corps with 43 divisions [Greiner then discussed the order of battle for the individual corps.]

2.) 3 independent divisions [140] [37th and 38th Infantry Divisions to be established in XIX Corps area in North Africa – the rest of the garrison would initially have to stay in North Africa – and the 44th Infantry Division to be created from the fortress garrisons of Nizza and Briançon.]

3.) 25 reserve divisions [Greiner discussed the composition of the reserve divisions.] [141]

4.) 12 territorial divisions and 1 territorial brigade [Greiner discussed the organization of the territorial units.]

5.) 10 independent Alpine light infantry battalions . . . .

6.) 10 fortress infantry regiments and 9 reserve regiments [Greiner gave the garrisons of the 10 French fortresses in battalions.]

7.) 10 cavalry divisions [142] [Greiner then gave the organization of the cavalry divisions.]

8.) Mobile Heavy Artillery of the Field Army:
26 batteries 155mm howitzers[66]
15 batteries 120mm canons and
6 batteries 220mm mortars.

The total strength of the French field army, including territorial divisions, mobile fortress reserves as well as active and reserve fortress garrison regiments was therefore: 46 Infantry, 25 reserve and 12 territorial and 10 cavalry divisions, 1 territorial brigade with a strength of 1175 battalions, 444 squadrons, 1020 batteries.[67]

[143][Greiner gave a breakdown of battalions, squadrons and batteries by category: active army, reserve, territorial, colonial, etc.]

This total strength was to be employed as follows:

1.) The field army against Germany, including territorial divisions, excluding fortress garrisons on the eastern border: 21 army corps with 43 infantry divisions and 2 independent divisions = 45 infantry, 17 reserve, 11½ territorial and 10 cavalry divisions and the mobile heavy artillery of the field army with a total of 971 [144] battalions, 422 squadrons, 935 batteries.[68]

2.) the fortress garrisons on the eastern border (excluding territorial troops): 4 reserve divisions (57th, 71st, 72nd, 73rd) as well as 10 active and 4 reserve fortress regiments with a total of 90 battalions, 8 squadrons and 36 batteries.

---

[66] Greiner footnote: "Five of these batteries were established in the spring and summer of 1914."
[67] Greiner footnote: "On mobilization in August 1914 these numbers were increased by 32 battalions, 2 squadrons and 44 batteries, because a total of 53 battalions and 18 batteries were brought over from North Africa, so that not only were the 37th and 38th Infantry Divisions significantly reinforced – the first to 15, the second to 14 battalions, 4 squadrons and 9 batteries – but with the addition of 2 reserve squadrons and 18 reserve batteries two more divisions were established: the 45th, with 12 battalions, 0 squadrons and 9 batteries, and the Moroccan Division with 12 battalions, 2 squadrons and 6 batteries. The mobile heavy artillery of the field army also reached a strength of 67 batteries instead of the planned 47."
[68] Greiner footnote: "These numbers were increased at mobilization in August 1914 by 32 battalions, 2 squadrons, 44 batteries (see p. 142, footnote 3 [64])."

German Planning: Greiner, Intelligence Estimate   41

3.) the Alpine Army on the Franco-Italian border : 1 Infantry (44th), 4 reserve (64th, 65th, 74th, 75th) and 1 territorial division (91st) as well as 10 Alpine light infantry battalions with a total of 104 battalions, 14 squadrons, 49 batteries.

4.) the fortress garrisons on the Franco-Italian border (excluding territorial troops): 8 battalions; the garrison of Corsica: 2 battalions, for a total of 10 battalions.

In contrast, the 3rd Department of the German Great General Staff estimated that in the 1914/15 mobilization year

1.) the field army against Germany, including territorial divisions, but excluding the fortress garrisons on the eastern border would consist of 22 active army corps with 45 infantry divisions and 20 reserve infantry brigades [Greiner discussed the German estimate of the composition of each French corps.] [145] with a total of 689 battalions, 144 squadrons, 789 batteries.

18 reserve divisions [Greiner discussed the German estimate of the composition of the reserve divisions.] [146]

1 reserve Zouave Brigade . . .
12 mobile territorial divisions . . .
20 mobile territorial brigades . . .
10 cavalry divisions . . .
21 batteries of mobile heavy artillery of the field army
in total, 1297 battalions, 502 squadrons, 1044 batteries.

2.) the fortress garrisons on the eastern border [Maubeuge, Verdun, Toul, Epinal, Belfort] . . .

in total, 71 battalions, 10 squadrons, 41 batteries [147]

3.) the Alpine army [13 Alpine light infantry groups of one Alpine light infantry battalion and a mountain battery, 12 reserve light infantry battalions, 2nd Colonial Division, 64th and 65th Reserve Infantry Divisions, 2 mobile territorial brigades]

in total, 85 battalions, 14 squadrons, 40 batteries.

4.) the fortress garrisons on the Franco-Italian border [14 battalions]
   the garrison of Corsica [7 battalions, 2 batteries]
in total, 21 battalions, 0 squadrons, 2 batteries.

Therefore, according to the German estimate, the total strength of the French field army, including territorial divisions and brigades, the mobile reserves of the fortresses as well as the active and reserve fortress regiments was: 46 infantry, 25 reserve,[69] 12 territorial and 10 cavalry divisions and 22 territorial brigades with 1474 battalions, 526 squadrons, 1127 batteries

which was 21 territorial brigades or 299 battalions, 82 squadrons and 107 batteries more than the actual French strength.

[Greiner broke down the German estimate of the French army by battalions squadrons and batteries by category – active, reserve, territorial, colonial, etc.- as he did for the actual French army on page 143 of his text.]

[148] The 3rd Department arrived at this significantly higher strength primarily because it assumed that the reserve regiments had three battalions instead of the

---

[69] Greiner footnote: "Including 4 1/2 fortress divisions and the reserve Zouave Brigade."

actual two, that 20 of the [149] 22 corps had 36 batteries instead of the actual 30, and that there were 21 more territorial brigades available than was actually the case. Because of this, and because the Germans assigned only two reserve divisions to the Alpine Army instead of the actual four, the Germans thought that the French field army consisted of 1297 battalions, 502 squadrons, 1044 batteries, when it really included only 971 battalions, 422 squadrons, 935 batteries.

[Greiner's Description of the Actual Plan XVII]

According to Plan XVII the French forces employed against Germany were divided into five armies, a cavalry corps and forces at the disposition of the Generalissimo. These deployed:
[In left margin] Map 15 [missing].

1st Army (HQ Epinal; VII, VIII, XIII, XIV, XVI Corps, 6th and 8th Cavalry Division), centre of mass Epinal;

2nd Army (HQ Neufchâteau; IX, XV, XVI, XVIII, XX Corps, 2nd and 10th Cavalry Divisions, 2nd Group of Reserve Divisions with the 59th, 68th and 70th Divisions) centre of mass between the Meuse and the Moselle in the area of Mirecourt–Toul;

3rd Army (HQ Verdun; IV, V, VI, Corps, 7th Cavalry Division, 3rd Group of Reserve Divisions with the 54th, 55th and 56th Divisions) centre of mass in the area of St. Mihiel–Verdun;

4th Army (HQ St. Dizier; XII, XVII, Colonial Corps, 9th Cavalry Division) in the area of Gondrecourt–Commercy–Revigny,

5th Army (HQ Rethel; I, II, III, X, XI Corps, 4th Cavalry Division, 52nd and 60th Reserve Divisions) in the area of Ste. Menehould–Stenay–Hirson; [150]

Cavalry Corps (1st, 3rd, 5th Cavalry Divisions) between Mézières and Sedan.

The following units were at the disposal of the Generalissimo:

the 37th and 38th Divisions from North Africa, eventually the 44th Division which was originally attached to the Alpine Army; these three divisions were to be moved either to Epinal or Mézières;

the 1st Group of Reserve Divisions (58th, 63rd, 66th Divisions) at Vesoul;

the 4th Group of Reserve Divisions (51st, 53rd, 69th Divisions) at Vervins, Sissone and Cormicy. The fortresses of Belfort, Epinal, Toul and Verdun with their mobile reserves of the 57th, 71st, 73rd and 72nd Reserve Divisions were also directly subordinate to the Generalissimo.

The 67th Reserve Division at the Mailly maneuver area and the 61st and 62nd Reserve Divisions in the fortified camp of Paris remained at the disposal of the Minister of War. These three divisions were to be returned eventually to the control of the Generalissimo. Finally, there remained 11½ territorial divisions, of which 4½ (83rd, 85th, 86th, 89th Divisions and the 185th Territorial Brigade) formed the garrison of Paris, while three (81st, 82nd, 84th) were responsible for the security of the [northern] Franco-Belgian border and four (87th, 88th, 90th, 92nd) guarded the coasts at Cherbourg, Nantes, Bordeaux–Bayonne and in the XVI region (Montpellier).

German Planning: Greiner, Intelligence Estimate

The covering force was provided by:

VII Corps and 8th Cavalry Division in the High Vosges Sector from the Swiss border to the Schlucht pass. At the beginning of hostilities they were to occupy the Vosges passes and cover the arming of Belfort as well as [151] secure the Montbéliard–Belfort–Lure rail line;

the XXI Corps and 6th Cavalry Division in the Upper Meurthe Sector from north of the Schlucht pass to Avricourt; they were to hold the line of the Meurthe, secure the crossings and occupy the Vosges passes from Col du Bonhomme to Saales;

the XX Corps and 2nd Cavalry Division in the Lower Meurthe Sector from north of Avricourt to Dieulouard; they were to cover Toul and the off-loading of troops on the Moselle and Madon, and for this reason take up positions on the right bank of the Meurthe and prevent the enemy from crossing the river;

the VI Corps with three divisions and the 7th Cavalry Division in the Southern Woevre Plain Sector; they were to cover the off-loading in the Meuse valley between Commercy and Verdun and oppose an enemy offensive between Toul and Verdun;

initially the 4th Infantry Division with three brigades and the 4th Cavalry Division, eventually the entire II Corps in the Northern Woevre Plain Sector; they were to cover the off-loading in the Meuse valley north of Verdun and secure the fortress against an envelopment from the north. The 8th Infantry Brigade was to secure the Meuse crossings between Sedan and Givet.

In case the Germans violated Belgian neutrality the Cavalry Corps, which was to assemble between Mézières and Sedan, would oppose their advance; it could receive the attachment of the 8th Infantry Brigade.

Ten rail lines were used for deployment: Line A (XIV Corps), B (VIII and XIII), C (XV and XVI), D (IX and XVIII), E (XII and XVII), F (V and Colonial Corps), G (IV and XI), H (III and X), J (II), and K (I). The British Expeditionary Force [152] was to disembark at Calais, Boulogne and Le Havre and move by two rail lines (W) to the area of Maubeuge–Le Cateau–La Nouvion. The rail deployment was to be conducted in two phases. From the 4th to the 11th mobilization days the combat troops of the corps and part of the reserve divisions as well as the combat trains, from the 12th to the 17th mobilization days the remainder of the reserve divisions as well as the field trains and higher echelon supply units.

[In the left margin] Overlay for Map 15 [missing].

A variant was prepared in case the Germans violated the neutrality of Belgian and Luxembourg. The deployment of the rear corps of the 5th Army was pushed somewhat closer together towards the north and the deployment of the 4th Army moved north into the area of Bar le Duc–Ste Menehould–Suippes. In this case it was to be prepared by the 12th day of mobilization to move forward into the first line between the 3rd and 5th Armies. In the variant the corps deployment assembly areas were changed: III Corps from Attigny–Poix to Signy l'Abbye, X Corps from Grandprè–Vouziers to Attigny, XI from Ste. Menehould–Ville sur Tourbe to Grandpré–Vouziers. The XII Corps of the 4th Army would move through St. Dizier–Revigny to Ste. Menehould instead of through Commercy–Void and the XVII Corps through Vitry le François–Châlons to Suippes instead of through

Gondrecourt. The Colonial Corps would continue to off-load at Bar le Duc. This variant was implemented on 2 August 1914.[70]

[153] The <u>German estimate of the deployment</u> of the French army in the 1914/15 mobilization year was given in a *Denkschrift* written by the 3rd Department in April 1914.[71]

"We have no concrete information concerning the French deployment. The following estimate concerning the army orders of battle, off-loading areas and grouping of the corps, reserve divisions and cavalry divisions is based on uncertain sources and assumptions.

The assumed deployment is based on the presumption that the French will conduct a strategic defensive in order to counterattack with the support of their fortifications.

The actual deployment can differ considerably from our assumption. The French have planned for the possibility of shifting units during the rail movement.

The French will presumably conduct their deployment in the following fashion:

the cavalry divisions and any units in the interior with accelerated mobilization	1st to 4th mobilization days
corps' combat troops (without reserve brigades)	4th to 7th
combat and field trains and corps supply units	7th to 10th
corps' reserve brigades	9th to 10th
combat troops of reserve divisions	10th to 12th
reserve divisions supply units	12th to 13th
mobile territorial divisions and brigades	14th to 18th
Operational readiness can be assumed to be:	
Covering force	immediately
cavalry divisions from the interior, at the latest	4th mobilization day
corps, including reserve brigades, trains and supply units	10th
reserve divisions, including trains and supply units	13th
territorial divisions and brigades	18th

The covering force presumably includes the troops in II, VI, VII, XX, XXI Corps areas and the 2nd, 4th, 5th, and 8th Cavalry Divisions. It is probable that until the end of the rail deployment the covering force [154] is under one commander. The Army headquarters is possibly in Nancy. In the first days of mobilization border security will probably be reinforced by cavalry divisions from the interior and perhaps by troops of other corps given accelerated mobilization. It is possible that the I Corps, perhaps followed also by II Corps, will assume the border security mission on the [northern] Franco-Belgian border.

---

[70] Greiner omitted to mention the most important part of the French plan, which was Joffre's intent to "assume the offensive as soon as the armies are assembled".

[71] Also preserved in the Bundesarchiv-Militärarchiv, (BA-MA) PH 3/628 Großer Generalstab, 3. Abteilung, Geheim! *Aufmarsch und operative Absichten der Franzosen in einem zukünftigen deutsch-französischen Kriege, berechtigt April 1914.* The 3rd Department qualified everything with words like "probably", "may" or "possibly". Within the brackets these have been eliminated.

German Planning: Greiner, Intelligence Estimate

The covering force is deployed:

1.) In the sector on the Franco-Belgian border to Longuyon [II Corps on the Meuse, 1st, 3rd and 7th Cavalry Divisions. Possible locations are given down to brigade and light infantry battalion level.]

2.) In the Verdun–Toul Sector [VI Corps (12th, 40th, 42nd Divisions), 4th and 5th Cavalry Divisions, later also 9th Cavalry Division]

3.) In the Nancy–Blâmont Sector [XX Corps, 2nd, 10th and 6th Cavalry Divisions]

4.) In the Cirey–Col du Bonhomme Sector [XXI Corps. Possible positions given to infantry regiment and light infantry battalion level. All roads crossing the Vosges will be immediately occupied.] [155]

5.) In the Schlucht pass–Belfort Sector [VII Corps and 8th Cavalry Division. The Ballon d'Alsace and Bärenkopf and the roads will be immediately occupied.]

The field army will deploy against Germany roughly on and west of the line Belfort–Mézières, in addition to weak forces (I Corps, possibly reinforced by several reserve divisions and perhaps by a cavalry division) which will probably be in the area of Maubeuge. The covering force army (see above) will be dissolved at the beginning of operations; the covering force units will come under the command of the armies behind them. A portion of the cavalry divisions will presumably be united into a cavalry corps immediately subordinate to the *Oberste Heeresleitung*. [OHL: in French *Grande Quartier Général* – GQG, the senior headquarters].

The French may deploy:

1.) an army at Epinal, about five corps, one cavalry division, perhaps the corps from south France: VII, XIV, XV, XVI, XXI Corps and the 8th Cavalry Division;

2.) an army at Toul, about four corps, four cavalry divisions, perhaps the corps from central France: V, VIII, XIII, XX Corps and the 2nd, 6th, 9th, 10th Cavalry Divisions;

3.) an army around Vouziers–Rethel, about four corps, three cavalry divisions, perhaps the corps from northern France: II, III, IV, X Corps and the 1st, 3rd and 7th Cavalry Divisions;

4.) on the middle Meuse at St. Mihiel–Verdun perhaps VI Corps (with three divisions) perhaps reinforced by several reserve divisions;

5.) a strong army group, probably organized into two armies, west of the middle Meuse somewhere inside the area of Ste. Menehould–Neufchâteau–Chaumont–Châlons sur Marne, with at least seven corps, perhaps the corps from western and south-west France: IX, XI, XII, XVII, [156] XVIII, Colonial, XIX, Reserve Zouave brigade and possibly several reserve divisions. Part of this force will perhaps initially be retained at suitable rail junctions further to the rear;

6.) a group of reserve divisions on the right wing at Lure–Vesoul, about four divisions, perhaps 57th, 63rd, 66th, 71st Reserve Divisions;

7.) a group of reserve divisions on the left wing at Laon–La Fère, about six divisions, perhaps 51st, 52nd, 53rd, 54th, 60th, 61st Reserve Divisions;

The remaining reserve divisions, perhaps 55th, 56th, 58th, 59th, 62nd, 67th, 68th, 70th Reserve Divisions will presumably be added to the *armées de manoeuvere* (see 5.) or perhaps will be used to occupy the fortified Meuse line.

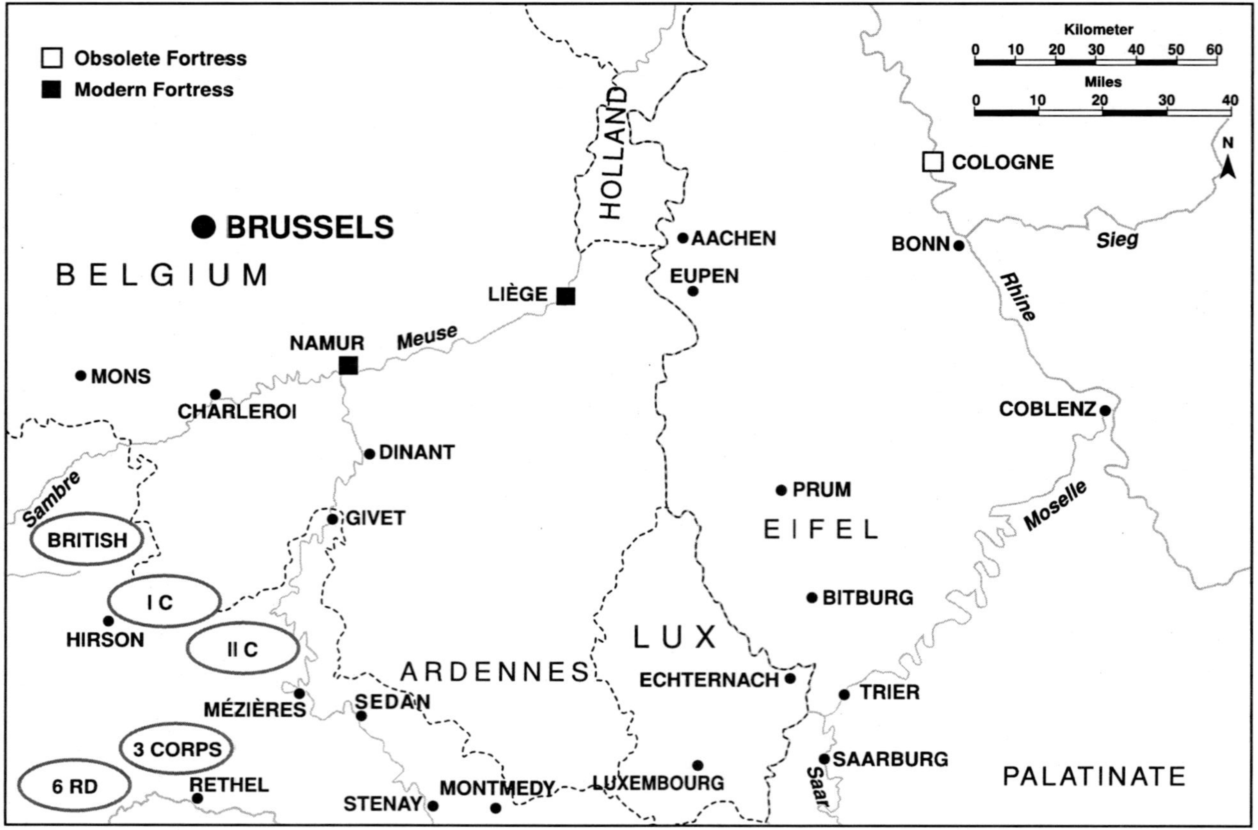
Obsolete Fortress
Modern Fortress
Kilometer
0 10 20 30 40 50 60
Miles
0 10 20 30 40
N
BRUSSELS
BELGIUM
HOLLAND
LIÈGE
NAMUR
Meuse
MONS
CHARLEROI
Sambre
DINANT
GIVET
BRITISH
I C
HIRSON
II C
MÉZIÈRES
SEDAN
3 CORPS
6 RD
RETHEL
STENAY
MONTMEDY
ARDENNES
LUX
LUXEMBOURG
ECHTERNACH
AACHEN
EUPEN
PRUM
EIFEL
BITBURG
TRIER
SAARBURG
Saar
COLOGNE
BONN
Sieg
Rhine
COBLENZ
Moselle
PALATINATE

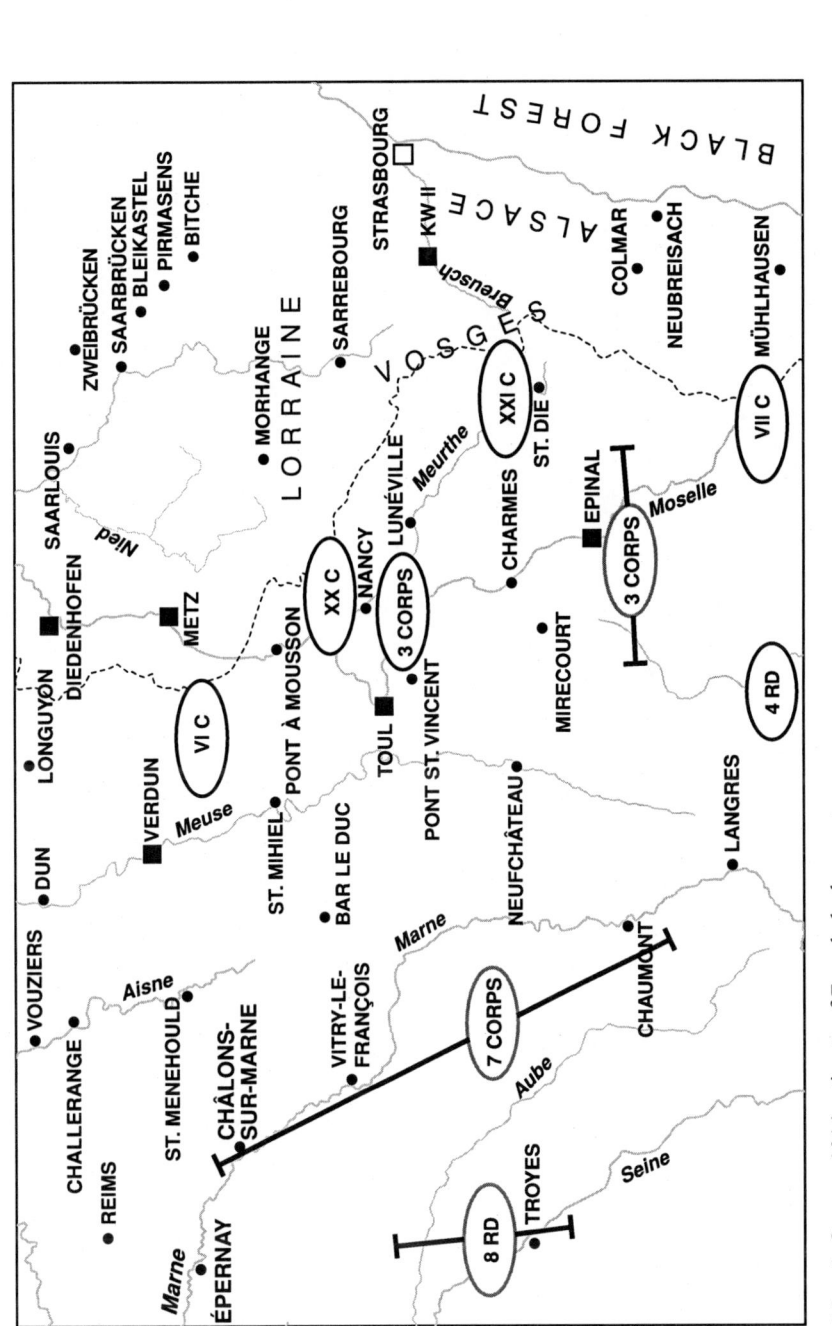

Map 1 German 1914 estimate of French deployment

A comparison of the French deployment projected by Plan XVII for the 1914/15 mobilization year with the German enemy estimate for that year shows that the 3rd Department almost exactly established the furthest extent of the French army to the north. Their estimate was that the French left wing would be at Charleville–Liart, when it was actually at Hirson. Allowance needs to be made in this regard for the incorrect placement of the I Corps at Maubeuge, where the English were to be moved. On the other hand, as in previous years it was thought that the French would deploy in far greater depth than was actually the case. In the German estimate the western border of the deployment was at Vesoul–Chaumont–Soissons–St. Quentin, when it actually was at Vesoul–Neufchâteau–Bar le Duc–Reims–Vervins. The Germans had not recognized the full extent of the recent inherent tendency of the French General Staff to concentrate the strongest possible forces along the border in order to conduct an immediate offensive. They still [157] expected the French to conduct a strategic defensive and were therefore led to the completely incorrect assumption that initially a strong army group would be held far behind the centre, when in fact only three corps would deploy in the second line, in addition to the fact that in the variant these forces could be very quickly inserted into the front line. Under these circumstances the Germans' conclusions concerning the organization of the field army into maneuver armies, the assignment of the corps to the maneuver armies and the employment of the reserve divisions must for the large part be wide of the mark. That the estimate of the French covering force was on the other hand generally correct was due to the fact that its deployment was in large part predetermined by the location of the peacetime garrisons and the geographic conditions.

2

Dieckmann: *Der Schlieffenplan*[1]

The most important of the newly found documents is Major Dr. Wilhelm Dieckmann's Der Schlieffenplan. Dieckmann was born on 17 July 1893. He volunteered for military service in August 1914 and served as a lieutenant in 161st Infantry Regiment, winning the Iron Cross I Class. After the war he completed his studies as an economic historian and was brought into the Reichsarchiv in 1920 to help write the Kriegsrüstung und Kriegswirtschaft *(armaments and war economy) volume of the official history, which was published in 1930. He also worked on several other papers, including one on an aspect of the Schlieffen plan which is in Foerster's* Nachlass.[2] *During the Second World War he was recalled to active duty as a replacement battalion commander. Major Dieckmann was arrested after 20 July 1944 as one of the Stauffenberg conspirators and executed by machine-gun fire in the courtyard of the Lehrterstrasse prison in Berlin on 15 September 1944.*[3]

Dieckmann left us a working manuscript some two-hundred-seventy typewritten pages long. The text includes numerous hand-written corrections. It is undated, but appears to have been written in the late 1930s, probably in conjunction with the other works on Schlieffen published in 1937 and 1938. Most of what Dieckmann presents becomes known to us for the first time. The manuscript gives summaries of Schlieffen's Aufmarschpläne, *selected* Denkschriften *concerning force structure and operational planning and* Generalstabsreisen *as well as the texts for twenty other* Denkschriften, *which are included as annexes. He stated where he obtained information from published documents and where information was not available, and he made it clear when he was drawing inferences. It is therefore important in utilizing Dieckmann to be aware of whether he is citing Reichsarchiv documents, published documents, or is merely giving his own opinion. While his summaries of the lost Reichsarchiv documents are unique and invaluable, Dieckmann's own opinions are generally uninteresting. It is unfortunate that the maps which*

---

[1] W. Dieckmann, *Der Schlieffenplan*, BA-MA, W10/50220.
[2] W. Dieckmann, *Hat Graf Schlieffen während der ersten Marokkokriese 1905 den Präventivkrieg gegen Franhreich gefördert?* BA-MA N121/30 *Nachlass* Foerster. Some of Dieckmann's other work is listed in Herrmann, *Das Reichsarchiv*, 533–42, 601–2.
[3] Personalakten Wilhelm Dieckmann, BA-MA 8/618; Karl Demeter, *Das Reichsarchiv* (Frankfurt, 1969), 48. Demeter discusses Dieckmann's work on the *Kriegsrüstung und Kriegswirtschaft* book on page 30. Also Sigrid Wegner-Korfes, '*Realpolitische Haltung bei Offizieren der Familien Mertz von Quirnheim, Korfes und Dieckmann', Militärgeschichte* (25) 1986 *Heft* 3, 226–33.

Dieckmann prepared were separated from the manuscript and apparently lost (as were several annexes).

Dieckmann's manuscript is not a great piece of historical writing. Nevertheless, due to the destruction of the Reichsarchiv, this manuscript is likely to remain the only source of information for most of Schlieffen's war planning, which makes Dieckmann's manuscript absolutely irreplaceable.

Dieckmann's manuscript was apparently evaluated by Wolfgang Foerster.[4] Foerster wrote numerous question marks and critical comments in the margins of the first 43 pages (up to the Aufmarschplan of 1894/1895). Foerster was obviously intimately familiar with Schlieffen's planning, had some very firm ideas concerning Schlieffen's strategy and criticized Dieckmann when Dieckmann's interpretations did not agree with his own. Foerster's penultimate marginal comment was the most important: he took Dieckmann to task for suggesting that Schlieffen's war planning in the east in 1894 ran counter to German foreign policy. Foerster wrote, "?? Particularly nowadays one must avoid making such judgements."[5] It was already clear to Foerster that Dieckmann had produced a view of Schlieffen's strategy which differed in many ways from his own ideas. Foerster did not have the work revised or the mission assigned to another historian, but apparently let the matter drop.[6] It is significant that Foerster did not criticize Dieckmann's summaries of Schlieffen's war plans and Denkschriften: *we can therefore take them to be accurate.*

It is interesting to speculate why, at this late date, Wolfgang Foerster directed that an analysis of Schlieffen's 1891–1905 war planning be written. The W10 file (Reichsarchiv working papers) in Freiburg shows that, as an internal procedure, the Reichsarchiv produced exhaustive studies which were never published as well as detailed first drafts that were drastically cut back before publication. Dieckmann's manuscript may therefore have been an internal working document. On the other hand, the style and tone of the writing are not at all that of a professional General Staff document, but are similar to the official history of the Great War. Dieckmann's study may have been ultimately intended for publication. Had it been published, it would have been one of the most controversial military histories ever written. A strong possibility therefore exists that Dieckmann's manuscript was an experiment to determine what sort of problems such a book would raise.

---

[4] "Apparently" because the reviewer is identified only as "F". The tenor of the comments makes it clear that the writer is superior in rank to Dieckmann, an important factor in a Reichsarchiv made up of former officers and organized along military lines, and which would limit the possible reviewers to two or three individuals. This was also Foerster's particular area of expertise in a highly compartmentalized archive where documents were made accessible purely on a 'need to know' basis. These factors together seem to point pretty clearly to Foerster.

[5] *"Vor solchem generellen Urteil muss man sich zumal heute hüten.* F." Dieckmann, *Der Schlieffenplan*, p. 42.

[6] Stig Foerster says the war caused the termination of this project. Stig Foerster, 'Der deutsche Generalstab', *Militärgeschichtliche Mitteilungen* pp. 54, 87. Nevertheless, the Forschungsanstalt finished the *Weltkriegswerk* during the war. Reymann, *Reichsarchiv*, Blatt 373. The war was therefore probably not the determining factor.

The irony of this manuscript is that there is no evidence that Dieckmann ever saw the original 'Schlieffen plan' Denkschrift, which was not in the Reichsarchiv but in the possession of Schlieffen's daughters until 1931, and was surely thereafter a closely held secret.[7] Dieckmann's comments concerning the Schlieffen plan are no better informed that those of the general population. The army had allowed a military historian access to the Denkschrift *in 1919, and he had come to a raft of dangerously unorthodox conclusions.[8] Wolfgang Foerster had every reason to deny Dieckmann access to the Schlieffen plan until Dieckmann could prove that his ideas were acceptable, a test Dieckmann never passed.*

I. The Operations Plans of the Great General Staff in the First Half of the Decade of the 1890s

1. The political-military situation at the beginning of the 1890s
[In the first eight pages Dieckmann gave his interpretation of the significance of the fall of Bismarck – which he accounted to have been an inexplicable disaster – and the balance of forces between the Triple Alliance and the Franco-Russian alliance in the early 1890s. Foerster's marginal notes complained that his view is simplistic and told him to move on to Schlieffen's documents. The tendency to insert his own opinions about political and military affairs – which were generally no better informed than those of the well-read public at large – was characteristic of this paper. They will therefore not be included in the translated text, which will focus on Dieckmann's summaries of Schlieffen's planning.]

2. The first changes to the previous operations plans

a.) Causes

[On pages 8 and 9 Dieckmann described the German war plan under Moltke and Waldersee, which he said consisted in the west of a defensive–offensive operation with two-thirds of the German army on the Saar. In the east Moltke intended with one-third of the army to conduct a double envelopment of the Russian armies in Poland, with the German and Austrian pincer movement linking up behind Warsaw. The patriotic interpretation of Moltke's planning was that his *Ostaufmarsch* would have led to a decisive victory in the east. In fact, an envelopment of the Russian armies in Poland was not a realistic possibility and Moltke's eastern offensives were conducted as frontal attacks north of the Vistula.[9] Dieckmann cited both Schmerfeld's 1929 book and Foerster's 1931 books as his sources, and not a study of the Reichsarchiv documents. A reasonably conscientious reading of both Schmerfeld and Foerster would have shown Dieckmann that in the east Moltke

---

[7] Zuber, *Inventing the Schlieffen Plan*, pp. 44–5.
[8] See the chapter on '1919 Entwicklung des operativen Gedankens'.
[9] Zuber, *Inventing the Schlieffen Plan*, pp. 127–34.

was not nearly so optimistic, and that in 1888 he intended nothing more than a spoiling attack on the Russian armies as they assembled, and then to defend east Prussia.[10] To this point Dieckmann was only repeating the popular nationalistic interpretation of the geo-political situation in the early 1880s. His description of Moltke's planning is therefore generally erroneous.[11] Dieckmann would also do his best to explain the Schlieffen documents on the basis of the development of the "Schlieffen plan", which everyone believed to have been the template for the German war plan in 1914.

On page 9 Dieckmann started to consider Schlieffen's planning documents:]

[9] Soon after becoming Chief of Staff, Schlieffen began to consider undertaking a fundamental change in this operations plan. First of all it seemed questionable to him if the offensive in the east was still practical, since the Russians, who were obviously aware of the German plans, had continually reinforced their defense through troop concentrations in the northern and western military districts as well as strengthened their fortifications on the Narew and Niemen. "Russia has", said Schlieffen in a *Denkschrift* [10] in December 1892, "in years of work both organized its mobilization and the peacetime stationing of its units to meet its wartime needs, and expanded and improved its rail system to such a degree that, in spite of the immense size of the country and the low density of the population, its readiness for war is little, or not at all, inferior to that of its more favorably situated western neighbor. In addition, since it is careful enough to execute its deployment behind a fortified river line, it has less to fear from a surprise attack or having its armies overrun in their assembly areas than any other Power." In addition, according to reliable information the Russian General Staff had recently changed its deployment plan and, obviously out of concern for a German offensive, no longer intended to deploy the principal mass of its forces in Volnya and Podolia against Austria-Hungary, but on the Narew and the Niemen against Germany, indeed "precisely behind Lomza, exactly the point where we wanted to conduct our attack". Therefore "the intended breakthrough of the Narew Line has been made almost impossible". "Even if it should succeed", Schlieffen continued, "the enemy would not withdraw to the south, in order to run straight into the Austrians, but rather to the east, where he will find the railheads that he used to conduct his deployment. We will therefore not succeed in fighting a decisive battle and destroying the Russian army [11] but rather engage in frontal battles against an enemy who could withdraw into the interior of an immense Empire, while our lines of communication would be the least favorable that we could imagine and endangered to the highest degree."

---

[10] F. von Schmerfeld, *Die deutschen Aufmarschpläne 1871–1914* (Berlin, 1929); W. Foerster, *Aus der Gedankenwerkstatt des Deutschen Generalstabes* (Berlin, 1931), pp. 20ff, pp. 42ff. Dieckmann said on page 8 of his text that Moltke intended to rest his right flank on Metz, to which Foerster quite correctly added a question mark. In pp. 42–4 of his book Foerster described the offensive portion of Moltke's 1888 plan in the east as a spoiling attack and expressly said that Moltke did not anticipate what would happen thereafter: he did not plan for a great double-envelopment of the Russian armies in Poland.
[11] See Zuber, *Inventing the Schlieffen Plan*, pp. 107–34.

A change in the plan appeared necessary not only due to the disappearance of the preconditions for the eastern offensive itself, but principally because the offensive committed too many forces in the east and therefore weakened the west front. To Schlieffen this appeared even more dangerous "because of the constant increase in the French forces and the complete standstill in our current military development, which will continue into the future, and which means that the balance of forces will become even less favorable for us".[12] The Verdy-Program to build up the army had not been approved and the subsequent increases had been postponed.

Therefore the Chief of the General Staff gave more consideration to the momentous decision to commit *the Schwerpunkt of the German army definitively in the west.*[13] The first indications of this change are to be found in a note written by Schlieffen in August 1892. Based on the concept that in a two-front war one must "turn first against the stronger and more dangerous enemy", he considered it necessary to take the initiative [12] and instead of waiting for the French offensive in a defensive position, to anticipate it through his own offensive. Schlieffen thought that it could come to a battle against France before both the Russian and the Austro-Hungarian armies had completed their deployments. In addition he harbored doubts about the assumption held to that point by the General Staff concerning French offensive intentions;[14] in fact the *Aufmarschplan* of the French General staff since the beginning of the 1890s did *not* foresee an immediate offensive, but rather, because the assembly areas of the French main body were located in and behind the French border fortifications, demonstrated "principally a tendency towards the strategic defensive".[15]

Schlieffen first extensively addressed the grounds for his decision to take the offensive against France in a *Denkschrift* in 1894. As tactically advantageous as it might appear to wait for the enemy attack in a favorable defensive position, as previously planned,[16] it was nevertheless "doubtful if the enemy would direct his attack against our strong front and allow his flanks to be enveloped by our attacks. Even if he had the intention of accommodating our desires in this manner, the size of his army would make it exceptionally difficult for him to do so. In order to bring 32 corps[17] on [13] unfavorable roads and paths in a front of 40–50 kilometers, one would have to assume endlessly long march columns and the concentration

---

[12] Dieckmann footnote: from a Schlieffen *Denkschrift* of April 1891. Foerster added a marginal note: "I think this *Denkschrift* must be discussed before the planned changes."

[13] In fact, the German *Schwerpunkt* had been in the west since 1888.

[14] Greiner did not mention any such tendency at the time, and Schlieffen's own analyses as the head of the 3rd Department pointed to a French defensive–offensive operation.

[15] It is important to note that here Dieckmann is not quoting one of Schlieffen's documents but rather, as he expressly states in a footnote at this point, Foerster's 1931 book *Aus der Gedankenwerkstadt des deutschen Generalstabes*, p. 109. Foerster himself didn't agree with Dieckmann's interpretation of his work. In a marginal note he said that "This applies only for 1891. In 1894 Schlieffen actually expected a French offensive. See the next page. F."

[16] This is the real difference between Schlieffen's planning and that of his predecessors.

[17] Dieckmann's footnote: "This means reserve corps as well as active corps; the former really possessed the strength of divisions. In fact the French at this time had available only 17 active corps and nine 'reserve corps' available to deploy against Germany."

of masses that would be impossible to move or supply." Due to these constraints Schlieffen concluded that the French would be required "to outflank our position with at least a portion of their massive army". This supposition served as an additional argument for his latest decision [to concentrate in the west]; for in order to defend against the enemy outflanking maneuver, the Germans needed to "hold ready . . . considerable forces not only near Diedenhofen but also in the Rhine valley south of Strasbourg". But even this appeared inadequate, for in his opinion an enemy envelopment was quite possible on the right bank of the Saar to the west of the Vosges. To defend against this the previous *Aufmarschplan* had, to be sure, provided a strong defensive flank pushed forward to Saarburg. The troops deployed here found themselves, in spite of terrain that supported the defense "in a quite exposed position". "You can consider the French advance any way that you like – the first battle will take place at the far forward position at Saarburg. Regardless of the degree of determination that the defenders display, the relatively weak German forces will be defeated by the superior attacking forces. If the German forces in the Rhine valley are fixed in place by the French attack, the loss of Saarburg will open a path into the left flank of the German [14] position in Lorraine (at Saarunion, D.), which will then be almost impossible to hold. In order to avoid such a situation, the German army will have no other choice, once the enemy attacks the detachment at Saarburg, than to attack all along the entire line. We will probably be forced to take the course of action that we wanted to avoid, that is, an attack against superior enemy forces."[18] Even the choice of another defensive position, Schlieffen said later, would not alleviate this situation, for one could not force the enemy "to attack such long positions uniformly along their entire length. Intentionally or accidentally the enemy will only attack part of this carefully chosen and prepared position. Where he does attack, however, he can or will do so with considerable superiority."[19]

Due to all these considerations it was not at all practical for the Germans to conduct a defensive operation against the French. In the last analysis, it was a question of winning, and to win one had to attempt to be "the stronger at the point of collision. We only have the prospect of being so when *we* determine the course of the operation, [15] not when we await the enemy's decision passively in a defensive position." It was therefore imperative to anticipate any French attack.

---

[18] Dieckmann's footnote: "To this argument it could be objected that this enemy attack fit precisely the intention of the Moltke-Waldersee operations plan, because it created the possibility that the enemy offensive group attacking Saarburg could itself be attacked by strong forces from the north advancing out of the German defensive position between Bolchen and Saarunion and forced to fight a battle with a reversed front. In this way the decisive battle could very likely be fought on this side of the French fortress line." Foerster's comment was that "We would be forced to attack other enemy forces frontally before we could conduct the flank attack! F." This sort of amateur generalship is a favourite sport of some military historians, but Foerster obviously did not consider it part of Dieckmann's mission.

[19] Schlieffen was adding his comments to a debate concerning the proper defensive position and German offensive options in Lorraine that had been conducted by Moltke and Waldersee between 1882 and 1888. In spite of the fact that Dieckmann refers to a Moltke-Waldersee defensive position, at no time did they agree on the conduct of operations in Lorraine: Zuber, *Inventing the Schlieffen Plan*, pp. 94–134.

It was clear that offensive operations in the west required considerably stronger forces than were previously provided. The Chief of the General Staff therefore wanted to deploy ¾ of the field army in the west. This resulted in such a *weakening of the forces in the east* that the planned offensive on the Niemen and Narew[20] was completely impracticable. Under these circumstances it was reasonable to restrict oneself to a pure defensive in the east. Considering that the Austro-Hungarians were dependent on German support, Schlieffen considered a complete renunciation of offensive operations in the east to be inadvisable. In spite of the changed Russian deployment plan[21] it appeared to Schlieffen that, if the Germans did not attack in the north, then without a doubt the Russians would commit their entire strength against their principal, Austro-Hungarian, opponent. "Our ally will scarcely take any risks. If we are in the defensive, they will revert to the defensive too. And they will conduct theirs more effectively behind the Carpathians [16] than we will with our 900 kilometers of open unprotected border. When the Austrians no longer threaten the Russian left flank from Galicia, but withdraw to wait passively behind their border mountains, our eastern enemy is no longer prevented from crossing over to the left [south] bank of the Vistula, marching into Posen and West Prussia and advancing on Berlin, while forcing us to evacuate East Prussia. It is therefore in our interest to preserve the Austrian offensive and we are therefore forced, in one fashion or another, to do the same."[22] Schlieffen decided for the most obvious solution, which was an immediate reinforcement of the Austrian army. The mass of the German army in the east would deploy in Silesia and in the southern portion of the province of Posen and from there link up with the planned Austro-Hungarian offensive from Galicia against the Russian southern group of forces. This offensive offered Schlieffen favorable chances of success, not only because the Russian forces deployed in Volnya and Podolia had recently been weakened in favor of the northern group on the Niemen and Narew,[23] but also because the Russian deployment area extended over a line more than 370 kilometers long.[24]

When this change in Schlieffen's operational concept was first incorporated in an *Aufmarschplan* of the General Staff can no longer [17] be determined with certainty. It was clearly implemented by the beginning of the 1893/94 mobilization year, that is, on 1 April 1893. In any case the remaining documents show that the new *Aufmarsch* was in force during that year.[25]

---

[20] Dieckmann's footnote: "In a November 1893 *Denkschrift* Schlieffen reiterated once again his initial reservations against this offensive (see p. 9). See Foerster, op. cit., p. 50."
[21] Dieckmann's footnote: "p. 10."
[22] Dieckmann's footnote: "From a *Denkschrift* by Schlieffen dated December 1892."
[23] Dieckmann's footnote: "p. 10."
[24] Dieckmann's footnote: "From a *Denkschrift* by Schlieffen dated August 1892."
[25] Foerster's marginal comment: "I doubt that the German west offensive had already been planned by this time. It is not discussed in the 1892 *Denkschriften*."

b.) The new Westaufmarsch *and the plan for the conduct of the offensive against France*

The new deployment plan required few changes in the measures that had been taken on the German frontier with France to secure the deployment of the army. A considerable force was already deployed in peacetime along the relatively short and militarily not unfavorable Franco-German border. In Alsace-Lorraine alone there were 2½ corps (XV, XVI and elements of XIV Corps) whose units were maintained for the most part at a higher level of peacetime strength and therefore could be mobilized relatively quickly. All measures for protecting and blocking the border were prepared well in advance, in addition the border security was backed up by the great fortresses of Diedenhofen, Metz and Strasbourg, whose own security however required not a few troops.[26]

In keeping with Schlieffen's new operational concept in the *Aufmarschplan* for 1893/94 the *Westheer* [18] included more than ¾ of the entire German field army:[27]

16 active corps
15 reserve divisions
6 cavalry divisions   together, 48 divisions
12½ mixed Landwehr brigades

The principal mass, organized in four armies, would deploy along the general line Diedenhofen–the Moselle between Diedenhofen and Metz–Contchen–the course of the German Nied–Falkenburg [Faulquemont, SW of St. Avold]–Gross Tännchen–Lörchingen [Lorquin, SW of Sarrebourg]–Wasselnheim [Wasselonne, W of Strasbourg]–Rosheim [near Obernai, SW of Strasbourg], while only a weak detachment was provided for the defense of the upper Alsace.

Schlieffen had already given a more detailed description of his concept for the planned offensive in the notes of July 1894 mentioned previously. First he addressed the question of the point where the French fortress line should be attacked. Strategically[28] this can be divided into five sections:[29]

1. Belfort–Moselle forts–Epinal
2. Moselle between Epinal and [Fort] Pont St. Vincent
3. Nancy including [Forts] Frouard and Pont St. Vincent
4. Toul–Meuse forts–Verdun
5. Meuse below [north of] Verdun

The first section was immediately rejected as unsuitable for an attack, because according to Schlieffen's conviction [19] it was "difficult for the artillery to deal with", as was the fifth section. It was true that the fifth section appeared to him to

---

[26] Foerster underlined "Diedenhofen" and "not a few troops" and wrote a large "? F." in the margin.
[27] Dieckmann's footnote: "See Table I" [Missing].
[28] Foerster underlined "strategically" and put "?" in the margin.
[29] Dieckmann's footnote: "See the attached annex . . . giving an overview of the development of the French fortress system" [Missing]. For a discussion of the French fortress system between 1874 and 1914 see Zuber, *Inventing the Schlieffen Plan*, pp. 107–13.

be the most suitable for a German attack. A crossing of the Meuse below Verdun, that is, an attack to the north of the fortress around the left flank of the French fortress line offered the greatest chances for success, because here "we would expect to encounter the fewest fortresses and [enemy] troops". Schlieffen thought nevertheless that it was not possible to conduct such an attack; when a German army had crossed the Meuse below Verdun, it must, "swing south in order to reach the enemy main body. Thereby it distances itself from its contact with neutral Belgium to its rear and must protect both its left flank against Verdun as well as its right against French forces that might be remaining there." An envelopment to the north of Verdun is only possible "when another army attempts to break through between Toul and Verdun at the same time". That is, this force conducts a frontal attack. This attack must be covered in turn by an operation against Nancy, which is a bastion projecting forward from the French fortress line. Therefore, three attacks would be necessary and in addition "the rest of the line had to be secured". In Schlieffen's opinion, in a two-front war the German *Westheer* was not strong enough for such an operation. "We must therefore do without an envelopment to the north of Verdun."

[20] Only one offensive was possible, and that would be directed either against the Meuse between Toul and Verdun or against the Moselle above [sic: below][30] Epinal. For both offensives "an attack against Nancy is a precondition. It is obvious that any offensive against France includes an attack on Nancy and therefore our offensive movement must be directed against this forward point."[31]

Schlieffen thought that the attack on Nancy could be conducted without great difficulty. The city itself was unfortified.[32] Nevertheless, not only was Fort Frouard located to the north, but to the south of the city it was thought that "many battery positions had been prepared in conjunction with Fort Pont St. Vincent". In addition "it is to be expected that the initial resistance would be encountered on the heights on the right bank of the Meurthe, more of less reinforced with field fortifications" and which could not be taken without the employment of a considerable quantity of heavy field artillery. Once these heights had been taken, the attack could be continued against the left bank of the Meurthe and Fort Frouard. "Once we are in possession of the plateau west of Nancy, it will only be necessary to silence Fort Pont St. Vincent in order to make the section of the French line above Nancy untenable and thereby break the entire French defensive line."[33]

[21] Schlieffen wanted the centre German army, which was deployed behind the German Nied, to conduct the attack on Nancy. The armies to the left and right would support it with offensive operations if necessary.

---

[30] Foerster underlined "above" and put "? F." in the margin.
[31] Moltke also thought that the first German offensive operation had to be directed against Nancy, but he did so because he felt that an attack here would bring on a decisive battle with the French army: Zuber, *Inventing the Schlieffen Plan*, pp. 60, 91–6, 116.
[32] Dieckmann footnote: "See the overview of the development of the French fortress system Annex . . ." [Missing].
[33] Dieckmann footnote: "Schlieffen's note does not contain any indication of the manner in which the attack would be continued after the fall of Nancy. From the last sentence one may conclude that he intended an advance against the broad gap in the French defensive position, towards the stretch of the Moselle between Nancy/Toul and Epinal."

Schlieffen said that the "most essential precondition" for the success of the attack on Nancy was "the formation of a powerful heavy field artillery".[34]

What was the condition of the heavy field artillery? What was available?

In order to anticipate any French attack, the attack [on Nancy] had to be conducted immediately on the completion of the deployment of the *Westheer*. Therefore, artillery support could only be provided by the "mobile foot artillery" (*Fussartillerie mit Bespannung*), whose principal mission, according to the doctrine of the time, was to support the field army in attacks on *Sperrforts* and fortified positions. The formation, rail deployment and forward movement of the large and awkward artillery siege trains, in which the mass of material (guns, equipment, vehicles, munitions, etc.) necessary to attack larger fortresses was concentrated, required so much time that their employment at the beginning of operations could not be counted on. They were therefore not available for this sort of surprise attack on Nancy.

[22] From the beginning of his tenure as Chief of the General Staff, Schlieffen laid particular emphasis on building up the mobile foot artillery created by his predecessor to give it the equipment and organization suitable for maneuver warfare. In large part due to his intervention, the cumbersome guns (heavy 12cm cannons, short 15cm cannons and light 15cm mortars) of the horse-drawn foot artillery, which were unsuitable for field operations, were replaced in 1893 by the very effective 15cm howitzer, which later became the heavy field howitzer. The armament, which consisted thereafter of only two calibers, the 21cm mortar in addition to the 15cm howitzer, was thereby considerably simplified.

[From the last half of page 22 to the end of page 27 Dieckmann discussed in great detail the attempts by Schlieffen and the Chief of Artillery, Generalleutnant Sallbach, to increase the number of heavy field artillery batteries. The general staff calculated that 72 heavy howitzer and 24 heavy mortar batteries were needed for the attack on Nancy alone, while the other armies on the western front would require a further 16 heavy howitzer batteries. In 1893, without counting the requirements for the east (which probably wouldn't get any heavy artillery), the German army needed another 38 heavy howitzer and two heavy mortar batteries. Schlieffen convinced the War Minister to transform siege artillery units into heavy field artillery, and largely due to this measure, by the 1896/97 mobilization year there were 82 howitzer and 18 mortar batteries, which Dieckmann said was almost enough for the offensive against Nancy. As of 1896 the "mobile foot artillery" was renamed the "heavy artillery of the field army" (*Schwere Artillerie des Feldheeres*)].[35]

c.) The new Ostaufmarsch *and the defense of eastern Germany*

[28] After the reinforcement of the *Westheer* undertaken for the first time in the 1893/94 mobilization year, there remained for the *Ostheer* in total only:[36]

---

[34] Dieckmann footnote: "Underlined by Schlieffen."
[35] Foerster wrote a marginal note asking: "This raises the question: how did Schlieffen intend to conduct the offensive until the 1896 mobilisation year with insufficient artillery? F."
[36] Dieckmann footnote: "See Table I" [Missing].

4 active corps
6 reserve divisions
4 cavalry divisions   together, 15 divisions
14 mixed Landwehr brigades

Of which the following forces were to participate in the joint offensive with the Austro-Hungarian army:

3 active corps
4 reserve divisions
3 cavalry divisions   together, 11 divisions
7 mixed Landwehr brigades

These were to be organized into one army and, as explained previously, were to deploy in Silesia and the southern part of the province of Posen. The army should move as soon as possible in the direction of Iwangorod, cross the Vistula above [south of] the fortress and then link up with the left flank of the Austro-Hungarian forces advancing from Galicia.

For East and West Prussia there remained therefore only:

1 active corps
2 reserve divisions   together, 4 divisions
1 cavalry division
7 Landwehr brigades

[29] a very limited number of field units, which would be opposed by a Russian force several times greater.

Therefore the question of protection of the area east of the Vistula, which due to its geography was very exposed to enemy attack, assumed a more serious character than previously. This was even more so the case, because the Germans had since the middle of the 1880s begun to perceive the unusually systematic concentration of war-ready Russian troops, especially cavalry, in the immediate proximity of the border. The Germans had long been concerned that the Russians intended to flood the Prussian border lands with groups of cavalry immediately on the outbreak of hostilities, and possibly even beforehand, in order to delay, and perhaps even prevent altogether, the German mobilization and deployment there. The political leadership shared this concern.[37] It was confirmed by the nature of Russian training, in particular the emphasis on long-range operations and forced marches, and even more so by several Russian secret orders that came into the possession of the German General Staff [30] from which the Russian intention to immediately conduct a ruthless attack across the German border with strong cavalry forces was unambiguous.

---

[37] Dieckmann footnote: "In September 1891, during the first flowering of the Franco–Russian friendship, Chancellor Caprivi told the War Minister that according to reliable information, the concern could not be rejected out of hand 'that the Russians could begin the war with an attempt to disrupt our mobilisation'." Foerster wrote a marginal comment: "Waldersee had already said this at some time. F."

In order to defeat such attacks, the Germans had always endeavored to go above and beyond the normal measures to prepare and reinforce the border security in the exposed eastern provinces. Even though the war could be decided by the results of the opening battles, nevertheless important moral and political considerations made it impossible under all circumstances to abandon, to "sacrifice", the border districts to enemy incursions. A possible interruption of the delivery of products from the agriculturally rich areas of the German east could in addition endanger the supply of horse fodder to the army and indeed significantly reduce the national food supply.

In addition to the reinforcement of the active army units,[38] the intent of the carefully prepared border security measures strove principally, in case of mobilization, through the earliest possible assembly of the troops and the deployment of security detachments to block the most important border crossing points. For this reason special measures were taken for the accelerated recall of reservists [31] who would be formed into units to reinforce the border security as quickly as possible. Nevertheless, the implementation of such measures, in spite of all preparations, would require a considerable period of time due to the exceptionally poor state of the road and rail net in the east. The local commanders frequently made reference to this problem. If too many reservists and active army units were committed to border security, a risk arose that that they would be broken up throughout the countryside, and thereby the formation and concentration of maneuver units to operationally ready formations would be impaired and an already extremely complicated mobilization would become even more difficult.

Under these circumstances the employment of the Landsturm became even more important. Its use for border security was regulated by the Military Service Law of 11 February 1888 which established the legal basis that had been to that time lacking. For this purpose of course only the trained Landsturm (II mobilization group) came into consideration, whose members would in any case form the Landsturm units provided in the mobilization plan. In order to employ the Landsturm if necessary as soon as possible in border security, since the 1890s it was intended that, simultaneously with the mobilization order, the Kaiser would issue an Imperial order to commanders of the eastern border corps, giving them the authority to immediately call up the Landsturm of their districts. [32] In order to employ the Landsturm in these districts as soon as possible, weapons, ammunition, uniforms and equipment were stored at the mobilization stations. However, all preparations for the call-up, formation and employment of the Landsturm lacked a sound basis because the law of 11 February 1888 stipulated that in peacetime the Landsturm men could not be "subject to military control or training of any kind". The military authorities were therefore unable to establish an accurate overview of the number and fitness of the available Landsturm men. The immediate employment of the Landsturm in case of mobilization as border security and their

---

[38] Dieckmann footnote: "As a consequence of the Army Bill of 1890 a new XVII Corps was created between I and II Corps and thereby the number of units stationed in East and West Prussia increased by 10 infantry battalions to 74, by 10 [cavalry] squadrons to 70 and by 24 field artillery batteries to 64."

cooperation in the defense against enemy surprise attacks and raids was therefore naturally rendered unusually difficult, if not entirely called into question.

For all that, the defense of the eastern provinces could to this point in general have been considered adequate, because in case of war a considerable force would deploy to East and West Prussia and immediately begin offensive operations against the Russian forces. In opposition to the many concerns voiced by the local commanders, <u>Schlieffen was of the opinion</u>[39] that "it was not necessary to give the possibility of attacks by Russian cavalry the degree of importance that would require the deployment of forces for border security to a greater degree than is currently [32] planned". To do so would "not only retard the mobilization of the active army units to an even greater degree, but would also cause a detrimental delay in the concentration of the active corps and the prompt commencement of operations". Admittedly, the Chief of the General Staff did not fail to recognize "that a truly successful penetration by enemy cavalry" which the border security was not completely able to prevent, "could be quite uncomfortable for our mobilization and deployment". It was only necessary to consider the dependence of the mobilization of many other corps on the supply of horses from the eastern provinces as well as the importance for the mobilization of the vital West and East Prussian rail lines. Schlieffen therefore proposed that stronger consideration of the "more extensive employment of the local Landsturm in the border districts" was called for. If the Russian cavalry found "that all of the vital points that they had identified in peacetime were occupied – and indeed with stronger forces than was possible with mere detachments" then "attempts to penetrate into the interior had little prospect of success from the very beginning".[40]

Due to the change in the *Ostaufmarsch*, which left only a very weak force in the eastern provinces, the question of the eastern border security assumed a more serious character. The previous [34] measures were no longer at all sufficient to provide relatively adequate protection against the overwhelmingly superior Russian forces. It was absolutely necessary to find other ways and means for this purpose.

[In pages 34 to 36 Dieckmann discussed the proposals of the commanders of I Corps, stationed on the eastern tip of East Prussia, in the late 1880s and again in 1893, for more active army units and the arming of the entire population (*Volksbewaffnung*). Neither request was implemented.]

[36] Schlieffen was less enthusiastic about the proposal of General von Werder [Commander, I Corps] to institute a mass militia [*Volksaufgebot*] in the eastern provinces. On the other hand, Schlieffen considered "better preparation in the assembly of small detachments of reservists and Landsturm capable of defensive missions" in the east to be an urgent requirement for the national defense. In order to create the necessary preconditions for this the Chief of the General Staff

---

[39] Underlining by Foerster, with marginal comment "When? 1891? F."
[40] Dieckmann footnote: "Letter from the General Staff to the War Minister of 11 November 1891."

approached the War Minister[41] with the request that at the minimum the Landsturm in the border districts be subject to the same degree of military control as the Landwehr. "Regularly conducted recall of Landsturm men with appropriate instruction concerning the sector that they will defend, conducted by the officers who will lead them, [37] will pave the way for the instruction of the population for the tasks expected of them in an emergency and will counteract the indifference of the population which has been, correctly, emphasized by I Corps." At the same time, "we should strive for a more expedient arrangement of the individual Landsturm detachments". The important thing was not to assemble stronger units at a few places, "but to hold very many points – preferably defiles near the local villages – with small, militarily organized detachments by the evening of the 1st mobilization day at the latest. In my opinion only in this manner, and not through a mass militia as proposed by the commander of the I Corps, should we attempt to utilize the assistance of the local population in a war against Russia." Considering the importance of this measure, the problems associated with such a course of action concerning the peacetime storage of weapons and ammunition in numerous depots scattered along the border had to be overcome.[42] In addition, the Chief of the General Staff considered it desirable to place obstacles, such as abatis, to reinforce the local defense as well as the preparation of field fortifications to protect militarily valuable objects.

Schlieffen was not successful in convincing War Minister von Kaltenborn of the necessity of these proposals. Kaltenborn successfully opposed peacetime preparation of Landsturm for domestic political reasons. In truth, he had not been informed by the General Staff [38] of the change in the *Ostaufmarsch*. Therefore his opposition proceeded from the incorrect assumption that the mass of the German *Ostheer* would deploy on the Vistula.

After Kaltenborn stepped down in the fall of 1893, Schlieffen attempted to win his successor, General Walter Bronsart von Schellendorff, over to his proposals. Bronsart, in contrast to his predecessor, fully recognized the inadequacy of the military protection for the eastern German border. While he opposed for the same reasons as his predecessor the introduction of peacetime military preparation of the Landwehr so strongly favored by Schlieffen, he added that the capabilities of the Landsturm would be little improved and it appeared to him dangerous "in peacetime to inform a large number of persons that we intended to keep the maneuver units in the rear and entrust the border security to the oldest year groups". On the other hand the new War Minister wanted to increase the active forces in the eastern border corps, which he considered inadequate, far beyond the level proposed by the General Staff. If there was a danger, he wrote to Schlieffen at the end of December 1893, "that [Russian] cavalry deployed along our East and West Prussian borders can attack us by surprise before our mobilization is far advanced and the deployment has not yet begun", it appeared imperative [39] – as Bronsart, also completely unaware of the operational intentions of the General Staff,

---

[41] Foerster marginal note: "When? F."
[42] Dieckmann footnote: "Letter from the Chief of the General Staff to the War Minister of 15 June 1893."

explained – "that we *anticipate* the Russian offensive and for this purpose deploy the cavalry regiments which we intend to commit to the east on or near the border in peacetime. The assembly of additional infantry along the sectors which should be protected would also be required." Accordingly Bronsart declared himself prepared to reinforce the cavalry of the three eastern army corps in the east (I, II and XVII) from other parts of Germany, so that each of these corps – in addition to the cavalry of the infantry divisions – disposed in peacetime of a complete cavalry division. In addition he wanted to move six light infantry battalions "to East and West Prussia in order to block sectors and support offensive operations of the cavalry".

These considerable concessions by the War Minister with the intention, so to say, of providing an offensive reinforcement of the north-eastern corps to be sure fit in poorly with Schlieffen's new operations plan. Schlieffen once again examined the advisability of this plan.[43] Without informing the War Minister of his real motives, [40] he characterized "in the most praiseworthy terms" the planned increase in the strength of the eastern corps as "very valuable", but futile, because the proposed increase in the strength of the German cavalry was insufficient in view of the masses of Russian cavalry. The peacetime preparation of the Landsturm would be much more important; even a larger reinforcement of the border corps would never make "the support of a well-organized Landsturm unnecessary". Schlieffen repeatedly petitioned the War Minister to work with all his power for the peacetime preparation of the Landsturm, reiterating his previous arguments as well as pointing out that most of the other Powers had similar organizations.

His efforts were fruitless, for in the meantime Bronsart's own proposals had been completely rejected by the Kaiser and the Chancellor. Thereupon the Landsturm proposal of the General Staff, with which the War Minister now as before was still not happy, met a similar fate. Chancellor Prince Hohenloehe flatly rejected it on the grounds that he did not consider "the extension of peacetime service to the Landsturm at this time to be either necessary or advisable".[44]

The question of the reinforcement of the border security in the east, with which the new *Ostaufmarsch* rose and fell, had not advanced one step forward. [41] It did little good for Schlieffen when the War Minister told him to wait for the future and promised him to keep the improvement of the Landsturm in mind! In addition, the reorganization of the Reserve and Landwehr in the east proposed by the War Minister, which, should the occasion arise, would make them available for border security somewhat earlier, brought about no appreciable improvement in the existing untenable situation. When Bronsart, as he explained to Schlieffen, wanted to see to it that the cavalry divisions earmarked for service in the east would be brought to operationally ready status by an acceleration of their mobilization, he

---

[43] Dieckmann footnote: "In an exhaustive *Denkschrift* of 26 November 1893 Schlieffen once again examined the strategic situation on the eastern front in case of a two-front war and decided once again to conduct a joint offensive from Silesia and Galicia, which, given the widely dispersed Russian deployment in several armies of about equal strength, he still thought to be very promising." Foerster's marginal note: "This cannot be discussed in a footnote. F."

[44] Dieckmann footnote: "Letter from the War Minister to the General Staff at the end of April 1894."

had no idea that the new deployment plan of the General Staff provided only one cavalry division for the northeastern theatre of war.[45] In any case, while the General Staff retained the planned common operation with the Austro-Hungarian ally, the border security in the provinces of East and West Prussia was completely inadequate.

It was doubtless <u>very important political motives</u>, of which neither the Chief of the General Staff nor the War Minister were informed, that caused the Kaiser and the Chancellor to deny all military measures for the reinforcement of the German east. One cannot go wrong when this military policy is brought in relation with Wilhelm II's [42] energetically pursued efforts at that time <u>to reconnect the line to Russia</u>. For this purpose it is well known that Wilhelm personally encouraged the trade treaty with Russia that was signed in the spring of 1894, and which the German Reichstag approved only after a fierce battle because its advantageous conditions to the Russians came at the expense of German agricultural interests. To take or propose military measures that were unmistakably directed against Russia was <u>incompatible</u>[46] with such a policy.

d.) Another change in the Ostaufmarsch

The final disapproval of his [Landwehr] proposals presented the Chief of the General Staff with the serious <u>question</u> as to whether he could <u>maintain the new Ostaufmarsch</u> without running the risk in time of war of abandoning the eastern German lands as far at least as the Vistula to the superior Russian forces. In the meantime he had thoroughly discussed his new operations plan in the east with his colleague in Vienna, Generalfeldzeugmeister Freiherr von Beck, who was not pleased with the modification of the plan that he had arranged earlier with Moltke and Waldersee, but to which he had reconciled himself.[47] To accommodate his wishes, [43] the Chief of the German General Staff had recently even changed the original direction of attack of the German army, whose northern wing he had originally intended to direct towards Kalisch–Lodz–Radom in order to leave open the option of swinging in the direction of Warsaw. When Beck objected that the threat against the eastern flank of the Austro-Hungarian army from Podolia might require a weakening of the forces employed in the offensive from Galicia to the north, Schlieffen said that he was prepared to give the German offensive a principal direction of attack over Kielzy–Radom towards the Vistula between the mouth of the San and Iwangorod, in order that the cooperation of two armies would be assured under all circumstances.[48] Finally, Schlieffen reinforced the offensive of

---

[45] Dieckmann footnote: "p. 28."
[46] Underlining by Foerster. Foerster's marginal comment: "?? Especially nowadays one must avoid making such judgements! F." A second comment is not entirely legible, but Foerster seems to be saying that he does not agree that defence policies and foreign policy in this case were linked.
[47] Dieckmann footnote: "Glaise-Horstenau, *Franz Josephs Weggefährte. Das Leben des Generalstabschefs Grafen Beck*, Zürich, Leipzig, Vienna, pp. 346 ff." It is important to note that Dieckmann is *not* citing German planning documents.
[48] Dieckmann footnote: "Glaise-Horstenau, *op. cit.*, p. 353."

the German army in the east for the 1894/95 mobilization year by three divisions (one corps and two reserve divisions).⁴⁹

In the meantime the Chief of the German General Staff adhered to his plan for a joint offensive with his ally, in spite of the endangered position of the eastern provinces. But soon he appeared to waver. This can be concluded from the fact that in the 1895/96 mobilization year he drew up two *Ostaufmärsche* – A and B.

[44] *Aufmarsch A*, which was therefore obviously the primary plan [?], assembled one main army in East and West Prussia, as previously. This was to deploy:

a northern group, composed of one active corps, one reserve division (together three divisions) and one cavalry division on the Angerapp between Insterburg and Darkehmen

a main group, made up of four active corps, two reserve divisions (together 10 divisions) and two cavalry divisions, on the southern border of West and East Prussia behind the general line Strasburg–Soldau–Neidenburg–Willenberg–Ortelsburg

as protection for the right flank a group consisting of four reserve divisions and one cavalry division in the area Thorn–Bromberg–Graudenz–Strasburg.

In Silesia only one reserve division and ⅓ of a cavalry division were available for border security.

In contrast, according to *Aufmarsch B* the main body of the German *Ostheer* would assemble in Silesia and south Posen and attack in the direction of the mouth of the San–Iwangorod to conduct the previously planned joint offensive with their ally.

It is no longer possible to determine with certainty what Schlieffen's operational intent for *Aufmarsch* A was. Obviously, he planned to conduct an operation on a broad front, with the right flank attacking down the Vistula in the direction of Warsaw.⁵⁰

[45] As soon as the following year, doubtless in the main due to the completely inadequate protection provided the German eastern provinces, Schlieffen definitively abandoned *Aufmarsch* B and thereby with it the planned joint offensive with the Austro-Hungarian army. He obviously already reported his intention to his colleague in Vienna in the spring of 1895.⁵¹ Therefore in the 1896/97 mobilization year only one single *Ostaufmarsch* was prepared, for the concentration of the main body of the German *Ostheer*, which was at the same time reduced to 15 divisions (three active corps, nine reserve divisions), in East and West Prussia. This would be conducted in a manner similar to that of *Aufmarsch* A in the previous

---

⁴⁹ Dieckmann footnote: "XII Corps, which had three divisions, was replaced by VI Corps with two." Foerster marginal comment: "Which reserve divisions were these? Were they new formations? F."
⁵⁰ Dieckmann footnote: "Glaise-Horstenau, *op. cit.*, p. 377." This is not at all "obvious". In his 1894 *Generalstabsreise Ost* Schlieffen played the battle of Tannenberg.
⁵¹ Dieckmann footnote: "Glaise-Horstenau, *op. cit.*, pp. 377 ff."

year, with the important difference that the main body on the south border of West and East Prussia was to deploy on a considerably smaller front, with the left flank at Neidenburg instead of Ortelsburg. This change was obviously made at the request of the Chief of the Austro-Hungarian General Staff, who in general agreement with the old Moltke-Waldersee plan intended a flank attack against the lower Narew over Rozan-Ostrolenka onto the rear of Warsaw.[52] As before, the Chief of the German General Staff found it necessary to preserve the intention to conduct offensive warfare against Russia out of consideration for his ally.[53]

II. The Envelopment Plan

1. The origin of the plan

When one considers the operations plan of the German General Staff at this time, which provided for offensive operations on both fronts and therefore required in all cases an unwelcome operational dispersion of forces which were in any case inferior to those of the enemy, it appears to be a compromise solution, which was hardly in harmony with the strategic principles of Frederick the Great, Napoleon and Moltke. In fact the plan was just such a compromise, which came into being under the influence of political considerations. We know that Schlieffen thought prior to the planned offensive in the east, that an offensive was necessary there principally for political reasons, to keep the weak Austro-Hungarian ally engaged in the fight.[54] Political considerations also appear to have played at least a part in the development of the offensive war plan against France.

This is because Waldersee, in his memoirs, maintained that the decision to shift the *Schwerpunkt* in a two-front war to the west, beginning with a frontal attack on the French fortress line, originated less from Schlieffen's initiative, who, due to his [47] many years of service in the General Staff understood the reasons that spoke against such a course of action, but was rather much more influenced by Kaiser Wilhelm II.[55] He disapproved in the sharpest terms with the changes to the well-

---

[52] Dieckmann footnote: "Glaise-Horstenau, *op. cit.*, p. 378."
[53] It is hard to follow Dieckmann's logic, except as another expression of his conviction that both Moltke and Waldersee always intended to conduct a massive envelopment of the Russian forces in Poland by linking up with the Austrians east of Warsaw. By moving his left wing from Ortelsburg to Neidenburg Schlieffen was shifting it 25 to 30 kilometers to the *west*. This would make an envelopment of Warsaw harder, not easier. Schlieffen's intent was not offensive, but to draw his left flank back and protect it against a Russian attack.
[54] It is not clear what "political" reasons Dieckmann is referring to. Schlieffen clearly said that if the Germans did not attack, then neither would the Austrians, and the Russians could drive directly on the German core provinces. This is purely a military calculation.
[55] Dieckmann footnote: "Waldersee, *Denkwürdigkeiten* II, p. 318. The accuracy of Waldersee's assertion has been challenged by Foerster in his *Gedankenwerkstatt*, p. 28. Foerster refers to a *Denkschrift* written personally by Schlieffen in July 1894 (see pp. 18 ff.). This proof is not necessarily convincing, since although Schlieffen wrote it, this does not necessarily mean that he was the sole originator of the ideas it contained. Foerster is also in error when he contends that Schlieffen thought it "most likely" that the French would assume the offensive, and that it

considered plan developed by Moltke and himself and spoke in this context of Schlieffen's responsibility to talk the young Kaiser out of these "unripe ideas". If Waldersee's assertions are accurate, and as has been said, there is no reason to doubt this, the ideas which helped bring into being the shift in the *Schwerpunkt* from the east to the west front were not "unripe", but very serious political considerations. One would not go wrong by attributing this decision to the Kaiser's lively interest, which we have already mentioned, in [48] improving Germany's relationship with its eastern neighbor.[56] The monarch obviously considered the reduction in the German pressure against Russia caused by this shift in forces from east to west as an additional means in furthering his rapprochement with Russia.[57]

Be this as it may, there can be little doubt that Schlieffen was <u>operationally little satisfied by the frontal attack against the strong French fortress line</u>. His *Denkschrift* of July 1894 proceeds from the basis that in no way did he consider this a favorable solution, but rather one which had been adopted because the much more promising operation, namely an attack north of Verdun around the left flank of the French fortress line, was impossible due to political and military considerations.[58]

There was a second factor: the precondition for an offensive to penetrate the French line was that the French maintain a defensive posture or, if that was not the case, that it was at least possible to precede the French offensive. Schlieffen assumed, as he stated in his July 1894 *Denkschrift*, that it was "certain" "that the French had for many years [49] intended in a possible war against Germany to maintain a strictly defensive posture". He maintained that it was at that time also entirely possible "that at the current time they had not altered their previous plans, because it appears that they do not believe the time has yet come for them to realize their ideas of revenge". On the other hand, he also believed the French "when they had decided for war and push for war . . . . they will very likely at the same time make the decision to take the offensive". He had expressed himself in a similar sense at the beginning of 1894 to the War Minister and called attention to the fact that, in view of the increasing concentration of considerable elements of the French peacetime army on the border, and considering, in addition their relatively simple and therefore very rapid mobilization capability and the high capacity of the French rail net, the danger of a surprise attack of enemy forces into Alsace-Lorraine

---

was "less likely" that the French would stay on the defensive, which was the prerequisite for a German offensive. To be sure, Schlieffen did think that the French would assume the offensive, and we will later discuss this (p. 48 ff.). However, as he makes thoroughly clear in precisely the same July 1894 *Denkschrift*, he wanted to <u>anticipate</u> the French attack. In my opinion there is no reason to doubt the correctness of Waldersee's assertion, still less so because it is based on statements by General von Verdy, the one-time War Minister, who at the time was the presumptive Chief of the General Staff of the German *Ostheer* and therefore frequently consulted with Schlieffen."

[56] Dieckmann footnote: "pp. 41 f."

[57] Dieckmann footnote: "Of course one does not need to assume that the Russians were officially informed of such operational intentions, but there were sufficient indicators that were easily obtainable by the usual means and that could not be kept secret, from which the Russians could draw the appropriate conclusions." This is merely the last in a long chain of unsupported assertions that renders Dieckmann's political speculations both unproven and unlikely.

[58] Dieckmann footnote: "p. 19."

could not be ruled out. "For long years after 1870 the French have sought their salvation solely in the defensive. The more that their self-confidence has risen through the growing size and improvements in their army, and the surer they have become of Russian support, the more the idea of the offensive has made itself felt. It is demonstrable that their military press today makes the unchallenged assertion that the offensive is necessary in a war against Germany. There is every reason to believe that this point of view is shared by the leading circles." Doubtless the idea of a surprise [50] attack was quite common in the French General Staff. For twenty years the French had "lived in constant fear of being overrun by the Germans. They know very well the bad situation in which the surprised army finds itself. It would not be miraculous if now, when they would like to move from the period of sufferance to one of action, they would come upon the idea of inflicting on us that which they so long felt they had been threatened by." As in the case of the Russians, the French could easily be thought capable of attacking into German territory without a declaration of war. As early as 1870 the question of declaring a state of war or not had been considered in France. "Twenty-three years later the opinions will certainly have clarified themselves to allow the French to go beyond this formality if the enemy can be damaged thereby."[59]

In these circumstances it appeared doubtful to Schlieffen that the Germans would still succeed in preceding the French. "The French mobilization is compressed to the highest degree. It will be difficult to surpass our opponent. The French deployment has also become just as fast as ours." Everything depended on whether it was possible to further increase the speed of the German [51] mobilization and deployment. But even if the Germans gained an advantage here over the French, they must still "be prepared to meet a French attack either during the deployment or during the German advance".[60]

The preconditions for the planned offensive in the west were therefore uncertain at the very least.

But apart from this, Schlieffen would also have been even less optimistic concerning the difficulties of a frontal attack against the French fortress line because he knew that his great teacher Moltke as well as his immediate predecessor Waldersee wanted to allow the French to attack first precisely because of these difficulties, in order to draw them out of their fortress line and then strike them with a counterattack. These difficulties had not become any less due to the fact that he had reinforced the *Westheer* to the highest degree possible, given the forces available,[61] nor because since 1896 an immediately operational assault artillery, in

---

[59] Dieckmann footnote: "In fact the deployment plan of the French General Staff which went into effect in 1893, as can be seen in Marchand, *Plans de Concentration de 1871 à 1914* (Nancy–Paris–Strasbourg, 1926), pp. 118 ff., in contrast to the official French history (see also Foerster, *Gedankenwerkstatt*, p. 110) was based on the same defensive intentions as previously."

[60] Dieckmann footnote: From the July 1894 *Denkschrift*. Schlieffen had expressed a similar opinion to War Minister von Bronsart at the beginning of 1895, saying that in the west the Germans must "always be prepared . . . to fight on the defensive", "as long as we are not sure that our deployment will be completed before that of the French".

[61] Dieckmann footnote: The temporary weakening of the *Westheer* for the benefit of the *Ostheer* (p. 43) was rescinded after the second change in the *Ostaufmarsch* (p. 45). In addition, at

the form of the of the heavy artillery of the field army, was available in the necessary quantity as calculated by the General Staff for the surprise attack on Nancy [52].[62] For in the interim the French had begun a drastic alteration and redesign of their fortresses system. The previous system of groups of fortifications centered on one location were fully independent of one another and had the operational purpose of immediately supporting the field army and serving, if necessary, as the backbone of offensive operations. The French now sought to establish a closer defense both within the fortress belts and between the individual fortresses by establishing intermediate forts both in the main fortresses and between them. This redesign naturally considerably reinforced the defensive power of the French fortifications by creating a sort of extended defensive zone or areas along the border. However, the resulting expansion of the fortifications required in addition a considerable increase in the garrisons at the expense of the field army, which could only lead to the conclusion that the French finally intended to limit themselves to defensive operations.[63] Such a French plan was one of the [53] prerequisites for Schlieffen's planned offensive; its execution was however made significantly more difficult by the reinforcement of their fortifications undertaken by the French.

In August 1895 the *Oberquartiermeister* in the Great General Staff, General-major Köpke, wrote a thorough *Denkschrift* giving his appreciation of "The Conditions, Directions and Prospects for a German Offensive Against France". He

mobilisation it was planned to create two new corps (XVIII and III Bavarian) for the *Westheer* out of the third divisions excess to normal corps tables of organization. Therefore the strength of the *Westheer* in the 1896/97 mobilisation year was (see Table . . .) [Missing].
   19 active corps
   12 reserve divisions
   6 cavalry divisions (together 50 divisions)
   13½ mixed Landwehr brigades
[62] Dieckmann footnote: "p. 27."
[63] Dieckmann footnote: "The new French plan written by the Chief of the French General Staff of the time, General Miribel, which became effective in 1895, was obviously already written to reflect the recent changes in the French fortress system. It provided for a strategic defensive [53] operation. See Marchand, *op. cit.*, p. 112 ff.; Foerster, *op. cit.*, p. 110 ff. Foerster properly calls attention to the fact 'that Miribel's suspicions concerning the probable German operation were by and large correct'." It is difficult to understand where Dieckmann got his ideas concerning the French fortifications. Significantly, he does not cite Reichsarchiv documents, so this is probably another case where Dieckmann is giving his own ideas. His description of the state of fixed fortifications at this time is completely wrong. The introduction of high-explosive shells in the late 1880s had rendered the massive French and German masonry fortress systems built in the 1870s and 1880s obsolete practically overnight: Zuber, *Inventing the Schlieffen Plan*, pp. 107–13. Neither Greiner nor Marchand say anything about fortresses in the 1890s. Marchand does say that "There is little to comment on concerning the deployment of forces [in the 1891 Plan XI]. The ideas concerning the general employment of forces are little changed", the concept of the operation still being purely defensive. Plan XII (1893) was no different. Plan XIII in 1895 changed "many details" and the French "returned to a tighter concentration" but the concept was not altered. The Plan XII and Plan XIII maps are practically identical. Greiner shows that in the early 1890s Schlieffen was thoroughly informed about the French deployment and hardly needed to draw inferences from changes in the French fortress system. This is another demonstration of the unfortunate fact that the further Dieckmann strays from the original Reichsarchiv documents, the less valuable his paper becomes.

came to the conclusion that an offensive both to the north as well as to the south of Verdun, whether it was directed against the Meuse between Verdun and Toul or against the Moselle below [north of] Epinal required numerous supporting attacks against other points on the strong French fortress front, which went beyond the strength of the German forces, and that it was "a great gamble" which "if it failed had incalculable consequences". Because in a two-front war the Germans were already numerically considerably inferior to the French, a German offensive in the west could only have "limited objectives". Therefore the only offensive that could be considered was the one already planned by the German General Staff against Nancy, the projecting cornerstone of the French fortress line. Even this offensive was not easy, but it could be conducted given the available means and forces and in case of success [54] would create favorable conditions for further offensive operations. Nevertheless, the capture of Nancy "was worthwhile more for intangible than material reasons", first as a tactical success. One could not deny that the real difficulties would begin at this point, and would be that much greater if "the enemy would commit everything . . . to take the valuable hostage, Nancy, away from us again". If the Germans had to renounce a continuation of the offensive because of a lack of forces, this would be "felt by both the army and the people to be an admission of weakness and therefore has a hazardous side". On the other hand one could not under any circumstances be drawn into operations "that were not only hopeless, but as far as can be anticipated would take an ominous course for us". After taking Nancy we would probably find ourselves in a position in which "nothing further could be attained . . . with the offensive spirit" and "than through a step-by-step, laborious and bloody creeping advance – in some places by way of formal siege warfare – to gradually make gains". Because a hasty attack[64] made with insufficient preparation, equipment and forces on strong enemy positions was "discouraged in the strongest terms", one must for better or worse be satisfied with the goal of achieving "the sum of a series of small partial successes". "Only through the tough, patient and courageous perseverance of each individual [55] in a fight for a small piece of the larger and wider battlefield will we perhaps be able to attain a final success in the whole. Perhaps the enemy will, in his thirst for action, here and there allow himself to be drawn into poorly considered enterprises, which if successfully turned back and then exploited could in the course of events bring us lasting and decisive advantages. There is no reason to count on such a turn of events."

Köpke's *Denkschrift* closed with an almost prophetic view of the future: "In any case there are indications that the war of the future will have a different appearance than that of 1870/71. We have no reason to expect quick, decisive victories. The army and the people must accustom themselves to this unpleasant prospect well in advance, if an ominous pessimism is not to spread at the very beginning of the war and become a serious danger for its favorable conclusion. We must be able to successfully conduct large-scale trench warfare, the battle over long fronts reinforced with field fortifications, and the siege of great fortresses. Otherwise we

---

[64] *Gewaltsame Angriff*: attack on a fortress using field artillery in a hurricane bombardment to support an infantry assault which attempts to bypass the main centers of resistance.

will not be able to attain success against the French. Hopefully we will not lack the necessary intellectual and material preparation for this and at the decisive moment we will be thoroughly practiced and well equipped for this form of warfare."

[56] Schlieffen shared completely the views that Köpke expressed in his *Denkschrift*. He too thought that the prospects for a purely frontal attack against the French fortress line, which was continually being reinforced, were at the minimum questionable. It is certain that he neither overestimated the power of the French defense, nor did he underestimate either the German offensive power or equipment. But he justifiably feared that a purely frontal assault against the wall of fortresses, even if all available forces were employed, would only lead finally nevertheless to a laborious and costly struggle, trench warfare of indeterminate length and yet to an uncertain conclusion.[65] In light of these difficulties, if one were determined to conduct an offensive against France [57] – and in addition to the military, as has been said, weighty political grounds as well argued for it – time and again the question arose concerning the possibility of mastering this problem. Time and again the answer was that there was only one solution, which Schlieffen had already characterized in his 1894 *Denkschrift* as being the most promising: an outflanking offensive swinging around the left flank of the French fortress front to the north of Verdun, supported by a frontal attack against the fortress line.[66]

To this time two problems made this solution appear unacceptable and unworkable: first the insufficient strength of the *Westheer* in a two-front war; then the operational requirement, to which we shall return, that the outflanking offensive, if it were to be effective and successful, must necessarily transit Belgian territory.

Of itself the idea of the outflanking maneuver was neither new nor original, so that it is not permissible, as often occurs, to characterize it as "Schlieffen's brilliant idea". Bismarck had already asked Waldersee at the end of the 1880s – at the time of the aftermath of the Boulanger crisis – if it was not "expedient in a war against

---

[65] Dieckmann footnote: "The accusation made by technical specialists such as Justrow in his highly regarded book, *Feldherr und Kriegstechnik (Command and Military Technology)* that due to his lack of understanding of modern technology Schlieffen had a false conception of the strength of the means of attack and defence, is completely incorrect inasmuch as it misses the essential point. This is not the place to refute in detail the charge that Schlieffen was technically ignorant. To name only a few points, it is only necessary to recall Schlieffen's unquestionable service in the creation of the heavy artillery of the field army, the adoption of the light field howitzer, the development of military communications technology, etc. Concerning Schlieffen's aversion when faced with the impregnability of the French fortress front, which Schlieffen's critics in their arrogance falsely attribute to his technical ignorance, such aversion was never evident in the real Schlieffen. However, he understood even better than his critics, who had the advantage of hindsight, that a purely frontal attack against the French fortress front conducted with the number and capacity of the offensive equipment available at the time did not necessarily need to be hopeless, but had no prospects of leading to a quick, decisive, end to the war. This quick decision, however, was exactly the goal that he was pursuing with all means available, in order to spare the people and the army under all circumstances long, ruinous, arduous trench warfare of uncertain [57] duration. This strategic-operational goal was also unobjectionable from the technical point of view, for proof of which one needs finally only to call to mind the experience of the World War."

[66] Schlieffen saw *two* solutions, the more promising being a counterattack against the French left, as Dieckmann's own description of Schlieffen's planning demonstrates.

France to accept the violation of neutrality and march through Belgium".[67] [58] Immediately after becoming Chief of Staff, Schlieffen had himself stated in a note written in April 1891 concerning possible cooperation of the Austro-Hungarian and German armies against France, which he admitted was a very unlikely situation, that in such a joint offensive the French fortresses "did not need to be a disqualifying obstacle to any offensive" "because they could be avoided by going through Belgium". The German and foreign press repeatedly and openly discussed the question of the violation of Belgian neutrality, either by France or by Germany. Many in Germany were of the opinion that the French were capable of taking such a step to outflank the Germans to the north. It is true that Moltke in 1887 incidentally took a position once on this question, but thought that such an operation was highly unlikely not only for military but principally for political reasons. If anything could move Britain to actively participate against France, he thought it was "the occupation of Belgium by a French army; for all these reasons the entire operation is in the highest degree unlikely".[68] We know that Schlieffen had also already concerned himself repeatedly with the question of the violation of Belgian neutrality [59] and in contrast to Moltke did not reject without hesitation the possibility of a French envelopment through Belgium out of hand. When the National Defense Commission (*Landesverteidigungskommission*) considered the question of erecting a chain of forts (*Sperrforts*) in Lorraine,[69] Schlieffen opposed such a measure above all on the grounds that in this manner the French would be forced to avoid the German front by moving through Belgium. The military press, as Schlieffen said at the time, "had concerned itself a good deal with the march through Belgium; the possibility that the German army would choose this route has led the French to reinforce their border fortifications opposite Belgium. Belgium has gone to the trouble through new fortifications to make a march through her territory impossible, without success. For Namur and Liège together block a single road; the trafficability of the terrain that comes in question for transiting Belgium is so great that even large forces will find an adequate number of useable roads." The Belgians would in addition hardly delay the transiting forces; their troops "will pull back to the fortresses". When reference was made to international law guaranteeing Belgian neutrality and in particular to Britain's interest in the maintenance of this neutrality, Schlieffen did not doubt that Britain, like most of the other Powers guaranteeing [60] Belgian neutrality, would be involved in a general European war and also expressly in that case would take an active part if vital British national interests were at stake. But even if England considered only the violation of Belgian neutrality by a foreign Power as grounds for war and therefore took up arms, it could "not thereby stop enemy forces from marching through Belgium. This will have long since taken place before British troops had landed in Antwerp", because "the organization of the British army" was "not suitable for immediate deployment".

---

[67] Dieckmann footnote: "Waldersee, *Denkwürdigkeiten* I, p. 412."
[68] Dieckmann footnote: "Schmerfeld, *op. cit.*, p. 125."
[69] Dieckmann footnote: "For details see pp. 89 ff."

The idea of a march through Belgium was therefore to a certain degree in the air, just as an enveloping attack north of Verdun automatically presented itself as the most promising route for a German offensive against France. But as obvious and attractive as this idea was, the German General Staff could not to this time explore it further, principally out of consideration for Britain, for Britain as the founder and protector of the Belgian state saw the maintenance of its neutrality, which was intended to prevent a European Great Power from establishing itself on the North Sea coast opposite the island nation, purely and simply as a question of national life or death. As long as the traditional friendship between the two kindred nations on both sides of the English Channel was preserved, it was impossible for the German General Staff to develop a plan which was expressly hostile to Great Britain, [61] and should the occasion arise, by violating Belgian neutrality threaten a vital British interest and thereby quite possibly drive Britain into the arms of France, with whom it had for a considerable time by no means been on good relations.

In the meantime the German–British friendship had been very seriously clouded. On the other side of the Channel the quick and powerful rise of the German economy was followed with growing mistrust. The British saw with unconcealed envy the manner in which German trade connections spread over the entire world, and how German trade pushed back British influence on the world markets, which they practically viewed as their monopoly. They suspected that Germany intended to follow the same imperialist road that Britain had herself so boldly, consistently and unscrupulously followed, to aspire to become a world power and thereby to threaten the power position and continued existence of the British world empire. All kinds of colonial quarrels increased the existing tension. They arose because Britain, swimming in the excess of the greatest colonial empire of all times, was petty and unyielding with Germany, which had come too late in the division of the world. The clumsiness of the German government added to the tension, as at the beginning of 1896 with the ill-considered and unnecessary folly of the Krüger telegram, which inflamed nothing short of a war fever in Britain. It was not difficult to foresee that the build-up of the German High Seas Fleet, pursued with passionate enthusiasm by Kaiser Wilhelm II, [62] and as little a threat to British sea power as it was, would deepen the opposition between the two countries. It was no wonder that, in view of British conduct, the opinion grew in ever larger groups of the German population that the rise of Germany from continental to world power had its strongest opponent in Britain.

There were recently grounds enough available that justified the assumption that in any war with France, Germany would also have Britain as an enemy. If this were so, then consideration for Britain's interests in Belgian neutrality were no longer operative, the more so because if Britain participated in a war against Germany it was hardly possible in any case to avoid the spread of military operations to Belgian territory.[70] It became for Germany even more than before a question of life or death that the war not be allowed to become a lengthy trench war, but rather a decision needed to be reached quickly in the operationally most favorable fashion, before

---

[70] Dieckmann footnote: "See pp. 59 f."

the British world empire was in the position to summon up and employ its entire power.[71]

It is no longer possible to state for certain when Schlieffen seriously began to approach his enveloping operation through Belgium. There are numerous [62] indications, which we will discuss later[72] which show that he first began to consider these ideas in the fall of 1896. There is, however, no written proof of this, or at least none has survived. The first written expression of his new operational intention is found in a *Denkschrift* which Schlieffen personally wrote on 2 August 1897.

From the very first this fundamental *Denkschrift* established the requirement that a German offensive against France must "find a way" "which is blocked by as few fortifications as possible". Only two avenues of approach came into consideration: either the gap in the French border fortifications between Toul and Epinal or the outflanking maneuver north of Verdun. The first route was not very promising, because "the main body of the French army would be assembled at Epinal and behind the Moselle below [north of] Epinal.[73] The Germans would find the French in a strong position here, with the flanks secured by two strong fortresses."

"The circumstances are more favorable to the north of Verdun. The line of the Meuse will be occupied to be sure, but not in significant strength. Here at least the right flank is free and it will probably be possible to force a crossing of the river through an envelopment. Once this has succeeded, the attack can be directed against the enemy's lines of communication [64] and if this is successful the French army can be forced away from Paris."

The goal of the operation, the destruction of the enemy, was expressed in a few short sentences.[74]

Schlieffen explained that the space between Verdun and the Belgian border was inadequate for the envelopment. "Only five discrete march routes can be found here for a maneuver around Longwy and Montmedy. If the two or three routes are subtracted for those units which are necessary for blockading Verdun, there are not enough lines of communication available for a sufficiently powerful offensive. The small force which can continue the advance over the Meuse will disappear trying to fulfill all the necessary missions it will have to perform."

Therefore "an offensive which must swing to the north of Verdun must not be shy of violating the neutrality of Belgium in addition to that of Luxembourg".

---

[71] Dieckmann intended this passage from pages 60 to 62 to provide the geo-political explanation for the German decision to attack through Belgium. It is not based on Reichsarchiv documents and adds nothing to what Hans Delbrück said in his articles on the *Preussische Jahrbücher* in 1914. (See Zuber, *Inventing the Schlieffen Plan*, pp. 9–11.) For an analysis of the German decision to invade Belgium based on Reichsarchiv intelligence documents to which Dieckmann did not have access, see Zuber, *op. cit.* pp. 239–52.

[72] Dieckmann footnote: "pp. 73 ff."

[73] Dieckmann footnote: "According to the French Plan XIII, which was in effect at that time, this was perfectly accurate, see Marchand, *op. cit.*, pp. 126 ff."

[74] Simply untrue. Schlieffen expressly stated that the French would be driven away from Paris, which was a colossal fortress. There is no mention of destroying the French army. Nevertheless, Dieckmann is trying to lay the foundation for the Schlieffen plan and its *Vernichtungsgedanke* (annihilation of the enemy).

Schlieffen then presented his concept for an offensive against France.[75] The strength of the enveloping wing was dependent on the capacity of the rail lines. He set this at eight active corps, in two armies (1st and 2nd) deploying between St. Vith and Diedenhofen, which was the southern pivot. Six reserve divisions, assembled in the area of Aachen, were adequate to cover the right flank against [65] the weak Belgian army. On the other hand the two armies moving on the Meuse required a powerful covering force against Verdun. For this purpose it was necessary to form a further eight reserve divisions into the 3rd Army, "which must be deployed by rail in a manner which allows them to cross the Moselle between Diedenhofen and Metz. Part will advance against the east front of Verdun, part will swing gradually against the north and north-west fronts of the fortress on both banks of the Meuse."

As soon as the two maneuvering armies had reached the level of Verdun, they would then "lose contact with the remainder of the German army" and "would be alone confronting the French masses". It was therefore absolutely necessary that they not only receive immediate support, but also that "the largest possible number of enemy forces be fixed in place". In order to give the maneuvering armies the necessary reinforcement, a 4th Army, consisting of four corps and liberally provided with artillery, would attack from the area south of Metz over Fresnes-Thiaucourt against the Meuse between Verdun and Toul and force its way over the river by capturing one or two forts. "Their mission is a very difficult one. They not only have the ridge in front of them which is on the east side of the Meuse, but also the forested plateau and the forts and batteries on the bank of the river, and they will be threatened on their left flank from Toul and Nancy." In order to negate this flank threat a 5th Army would conduct a double envelopment [66] of the Nancy position. For this purpose two corps would attack across the Moselle at Pont à Mousson and then swing south, while two more corps would attack from Nomeny and Delme on the right [east] bank of the Moselle against the heights north-west of Nancy. To support this attack a 6th Army, four corps strong, would attack from the woods north of Parroy against the Meurthe between Nancy and Lunéville.

"The left flank, which will initially be refused, will be formed by the 7th Army" composed of five active corps and three reserve divisions. It would only move towards the Moselle in conjunction with the 6th Army when the Nancy position had been taken. One corps and the three reserve divisions of this army had the mission of protecting the upper Alsace; the active corps would later participate in the 7th Army advance.

If all these corps are added up it is evident that in order to conduct this operation not only was it necessary, as Schlieffen expressly said, to "employ <u>the entire German army</u>".[76] In addition, he assumed that the number of active corps – created during the mobilization from new units as well as from existing units excess to normal tables of organization[77] – be increased by three to 25. In addition to the reserve divisions actually available he required a number of additional reserve

---

[75] Dieckmann footnote: "See Map 1" [Missing].
[76] Dieckmann footnote: "Underlined by myself."
[77] Dieckmann footnote: "for details, see p. 77."

divisions for the creation of one or two reserve armies. For the security of the rear area communications all [67] available Landwehr units had to be employed, most of which were to be assembled behind the right (maneuvering) wing so as to allow them to "march immediately behind the active corps". Finally, it would be necessary to reinforce the reserve division artillery in order to give them roughly the same amount as the French reserve divisions.[78]

One would ask with astonishment, what was left over for the east, if according to Schlieffen's own statement it was necessary to employ the entire German field army in the west? Did Schlieffen, who only recently had unceasingly pointed out the Russian threat, now in a two-front war want to leave the German eastern border fully defenseless and unprotected? How can this be reconciled with his previous views on the necessity of supporting the Austro-Hungarian ally and the understandings concluded with them? Or had the German Chief of Staff suddenly come to surprising conclusion, given all that had gone on before, to consider an operation, the obvious precondition for which was complete freedom in the east in a two-front war? Was this precondition only a highly questionable assumption by a politically clueless general who glided beyond reality in order to make the wish the father of the deed? In view of the long-standing Franco-Russian alliance, what was Schlieffen's justification [68] which allowed him to make such an assumption which stood in complete contradiction with his previous views?

Since Schlieffen himself does not give us an answer to these questions, we must attempt to find an answer by considering the political situation at the time.

[From pages 68 to 73 Dieckmann tried, in what is actually a political essay, to show that Schlieffen's 2 August 1897 *Denkschrift* was based on his intent to support German foreign policy, which was to draw closer to Russia. Dieckmann's thesis was that the Russians were turning their interest to the Far East. Russia was opposed both there and in Turkey by Great Britain. This offered Germany an opening to re-establish close ties with Russia, a course of action which Kaiser Wilhelm favored. The plan for an attack on Belgium "created another opportunity to direct Russia and Germany onto a common front". Whether and how the Russians got wind of Schlieffen's top-secret war plans was left unexplained. Flipping the argument around, Dieckmann then contended that the new plan was an "exhortation" to the German political leadership to make just such an alliance with Russia, which in turn would leave Germany's rear free for the one-front war that the new plan required. At the same time Schlieffen dropped plans both to reinforce East Prussia and to conduct an offensive in the east, while assuring the Austrians that nothing had changed. He then stopped talking to the Austrians altogether. Schlieffen's intent was to reduce German dependency on Austria and encourage the German government to restore the old Bismarckian system of playing off Russia against Austria. This was too clever by half. Dieckmann himself noted that between 1893 and 1897 even the War Minister wasn't informed of his operations plans,[79] in spite

---

[78] Dieckmann footnote: "A German reserve division was provided with, on average, six reserve field artillery batteries as opposed to the eight to twelve of a French reserve division."

[79] pp. 39–40, 79.

of the fact that this secrecy made planning the force structure for the entire army and covering force mission in the east nearly impossible. Now Dieckmann contended that the war plan was in effect a foreign policy position paper. He offered absolutely no documentary proof of his assertions. Nor did Dieckmann explain where, even in a one-front war, Schlieffen was going to get the three additional active corps, extra reserve divisions or additional artillery for the reserve divisions to fill up Schlieffen's order of battle for the attack on France. Dieckmann was trying desperately to hammer the evidence to fit his preconceived idea that Schlieffen's planning must be leading to the 1906 Schlieffen plan.

The simplest solution is frequently the most likely. Schlieffen should be taken at his word. As Dieckmann himself noted,[80] there was considerable speculation prior to 1897 concerning a German attack through Belgium. Nevertheless, Schlieffen did not consider the operation until he had been Chief of the General Staff for over six years. When he did consider the right flank maneuver, his conclusion was that to be feasible it would require a one-front war, the violation of Belgian neutrality, three more active corps, an unstated number of additional reserve divisions and an increase of somewhere between 66% and 100% in the reserve artillery – some 80 to 120 batteries. Any objective observer would have to conclude that Schlieffen thought an attack through Belgium was impossible unless there were massive increases in the size of the German army.]

2. Preparations for the implementation of the envelopment plan

Schlieffen's *Denkschrift* of 2 August 1897 was by no means based on an already completed and fully operational war plan. It was concerned first of all merely with reflections on operational possibilities conducted by Schlieffen. Before such intentions could be implemented in an official *Aufmarschplan* of the General Staff numerous practical preparations were necessary, which were dependent on the feasibility of the envelopment plan. We can conclude from the fact that the envelopment idea had assumed such a firm form that Schlieffen had begun such preparations in the late summer of 1896.

[74] a.) Changes in the order of battle

As we have shown, the Chief of the German General Staff thought the entire strength of the German army was not sufficient to implement his new operational concept. For this he required a number of additional active and reserve units. In addition he considered it advantageous, considering the manifold missions involved in the planned operation, and also in order to promote ease of command, to organize and equip the units as symmetrically and uniformly as possible.

In the 1896/97 mobilization year the German field army consisted of:[81]

22 active corps (Guard, I–XVIII, I–III Bavarian)[82] each with two infantry divisions (in total, 44 divisions)

---

[80] pp. 57–8.
[81] Dieckmann footnote: "See Table . . ." [Missing].
[82] Dieckmann footnote: "The XVIII and III Bavarian Corps were to be formed on mobilisation from units excess to the normal tables of organization as well as from reserve units (see p. 51, footnote 2 [57])."

20 reserve divisions (1st and 2nd Guard, 1, 3, 5–7, 9, 11, 13, 15, 17, 19, 21, 23, 25, 26, 28, 35, 1st Bavarian)
10 cavalry divisions
31½ mixed Landwehr brigades.

The organization of active corps sometimes varied quite considerably, particularly in the number of infantry units.

The so-called "small infantry brigades" gave Schlieffen a lever with which to realize his goals of both <u>increasing the number of active corps</u> while <u>giving all corps a uniform organization</u>. [75] These brigades were being established from the 4th (half) battalions that had been created during the expansion of the army in 1893.[83]

During the planning discussions concerning Kaltenborn's ill-starred creations, which had already proved to be completely unsuccessful,[84] the General Staff initially suggested that the half-battalions be reorganized into normal (three-battalion) regiments at regular strength. In the interests of providing necessary reinforcement for the border corps most of them would be transferred to the I, XIV, XVI and XVII Corps sectors and there, with the addition of other elements, be formed into six new divisions.[85] War Minister Bronsart von Schellendorf, Kaltenborn's successor, who wanted to transform his unwelcome legacy as soon, and naturally as inexpensively, as possible into a militarily effective organization, rejected Schlieffen's suggestion due to the expected difficulties from the Treasury and the Reichstag. As a consequence there remained only the plan that had been proposed by the War Ministry from the start, which permitted the conversion of the half-battalions without the expense of creating new units. Therefore,[86] with individual exceptions as in Bavaria, as a rule the half-battalions of each army corps were formed into two regiments consisting of two full battalions, and these were formed into a so-called "small" brigade [76] and remained in their parent corps as the fifth brigade. Without making further objections to this measure, which deviated considerably from its own, the General Staff proposed only that this opportunity be used at least to provide vitally necessary reinforcement to the VIII Corps in the west and especially the I Corps in the east through the transfer of units from other corps areas.

---

[83] As part of the introduction of two-year service in 1893 each infantry regiment received a half-strength (two-company) 4th battalion, which was to be the home of personnel tasked out for special duties. This was supposed to relieve the other battalions of the responsibility for the special duty personnel and allow them to train at full strength. The 4th battalions were never given enough personnel to fulfil this function and the other battalions continued to receive personnel taskings. Nor could the 4th battalions conduct effective training. On 1 April 1897 there were consolidated into two-battalion regiments: Jany, *Geschichte der Preußischen Armee vom 15. Jahrhundert bis 1914*, vierter Band (Osnabrück, 1967), pp. 300–1.

[84] Dieckmann footnote: "*Kriegsrüstung und Kriegswirtschaft*, Text volume, p. 46; Annexes, p. 370."

[85] I Corps was headquartered at Königsberg, XVII Corps in Danzig. Schlieffen was proposing to increase the strength of two corps in the east, which contradicts Dieckmann's assertions on p. 72 that he had dropped such plans in favour of his policy of rapprochement with Russia.

[86] Dieckmann footnote: "See *Kriegsrüstung und Kriegswirtschaft*, Annex, p. 370."

[The rest of the page is filled with footnote 1 (see below). Dieckmann was clearly concerned that Schlieffen's advocacy of reinforcing the east in 1896 undermined his thesis that Schlieffen was pursuing a policy of rapprochement with Russia. More to the point, Dieckmann is forced to acknowledge that in 1896 there was no sign that the Russians had turned militarily to the east. Rather, Schlieffen saw a continual build-up on the East Prussian border.]

1) From the correspondence between the General Staff and the War Ministry which continued to the spring of 1896, we can conclude that Schlieffen to this point had no knowledge of the policy of rapprochement with Russia initiated by the German government. In keeping with his previous proposals to reinforce the border security against Russia (p. 36 ff.), Schlieffen urgently enjoined the War Minister that the I Corps was seriously in need of reinforcement, as the Corps Commander was of the opinion that he was not in a position with the available troops to defend the border against the superior Russian forces. This request was turned down by Bronsart, who in the meantime had obviously gotten wind of the new policy towards Russia, on the significant grounds that "the Chancellor has characterized the transfer of reinforcements to East Prussia and other measures aimed against Russia in this province as politically inappropriate and has advised against such plans. Since in the case at hand the proposed measures are directed against Russia, we must give even more weight to the approval of the Chancellor, due to the fact that we know here of no political factors or significant facts which would call for a conspicuous reinforcement of the eastern border areas" (Letter to the General Staff of 30 April 1896). Schlieffen did not back down and continued to insist on the reinforcement of I Corps, because Russia "was continually reinforcing its troops near the East Prussian border". [!] All available reports agreed "that a war would begin with a purposefully planned attack into Prussian territory, carefully prepared to the last detail . . . . The intent of this attack will be the large-scale and thorough disruption of our mobilization and deployment, which can – as I have repeatedly emphasized and which is also recognized by the War Ministry – only be met when adequate forces are immediately available." The War Ministry finally yielded to the repeated pressure of the General Staff to the degree that it declared itself prepared to transfer the fifth brigade which was to be established at the III Corps to the I Corps area, [77] after the necessary construction of buildings had been completed.

[Return to text] After the [77] approval of the law by the Bundesrat and the Reichstag, in the spring of 1897 the reorganization of the half-battalions was conducted according to the plans of the War Ministry.

Initially the Chief of the General Staff intended to dissolve the fifth brigades upon mobilization and distribute most of their regiments, so that as a rule each army corps would receive two brigades of three regiments each.

Schlieffen soon gave up this intention, a decision which was undoubtedly made in connection with his new operational plans, which were taking firmer form. The "small" brigades offered him the opportunity to increase the number of maneuver units, which appeared to him to be urgently necessary for the realization of those plans. Consequently he recommended to the War Minister that a number of the "small" brigades be employed during mobilization in the same manner as that which was already planned and prepared to create the XVIII and III Bavarian Corps,[87] to create more maneuver units, in this case two corps (XIX and XX) and an infantry division (3rd Guard). In spite of serious reservations concerning the numerous improvisations that were necessary, the War Ministry finally acceded to this proposal.

[78] At the same time the General Staff recommended that the command and control arrangements for the reserve divisions be changed. It had been planned that they be organized into three special army detachments. The General Staff wanted to subordinate two reserve divisions "which often . . . were ordered to move along one and the same road" "to be subordinate to the same commander for purposes of marching and combat" in a manner analogous to active corps. The General Staff thought that it could dispense with a corps headquarters for reserve corps structured in this fashion and be content with the senior division commander and an appropriately reinforced division staff exercising the corps command. This recommendation was also approved by the War Ministry, which proposed to establish six of this sort of reserve corps with reinforced division staffs. In the order of battle these reserve corps were numbered XXI–XXV Corps and the Guard Reserve Corps.[88]

Finally, also at the request of the General Staff, at mobilization a further cavalry division was to be established[89] as well as planning and preparation for the expansion of the three army detachments into complete army headquarters, so that the number of army headquarters of the field army rose from five to eight.

[Jany's *Preußische Armee*, which is authoritative, did not mention these new corps. The *Kriegsrüstung und Kriegswirtschaft* (Armaments and War Economy) volume of the official history, which Dieckmann helped write, said in 1898 that XX and XXI Corps consisted of an active and a reserve division, with no corps artillery and few corps troops, that is, they were active army corps in name only. There were five reinforced reserve division staffs, but these are *not* identified with active army corps designations. Only two had any reserve corps artillery and none had any corps troops. Both works say the XX–XXIII Corps and the Guard Reserve Corps were *Kriegskorps* which Schlieffen only succeeded in convincing the War Minister to organize *in 1902*. Schlieffen may well have recommended that these corps be created in 1897, but this did not occur until five years later. In any case, the War Minister succeeded in getting XXII and XXIII Corps disbanded in 1904.[90] From the next paragraph it is clear that Schlieffen was going to try to reorganize the army after mobilization. Neither the War Minister nor the Kaiser were pleased.]

---

[87] Dieckmann footnote: "p. 51, footnote 2 [57]."
[88] Dieckmann footnote: "Letter from the General Staff to the War Ministry of October 1896."
[89] Dieckmann footnote: "Table" [Missing].
[90] C. Jany, *Preußische Armee* IV, pp. 296–7; Reichsarchiv, *Kriegsrüstung und Kriegswirtschaft 1. Die militärische, wirtschaftliche und finanzielle Rüstung Deutschlands von der Reichsgründung bis zum Ausbruch des Weltkrieges* (Berlin, 1930), pp. 66, 74–5, Tables 1898, 1902.

[79] This constituted in fact a far-reaching <u>reorganization of the field army</u>, which corresponded to Schlieffen's new operational ideas and became effective at the beginning of the 1897/98 mobilization year.[91] Schlieffen did not communicate these intentions to the War Minister – Generalleutnant von Goßler having replaced Bronsart – in any way or form. He was therefore unaware of the purpose of this new organization, with which he could not be particularly satisfied due to the many improvisations it required. Goßler told the Kaiser in the spring of 1897 that he could not bring the peacetime organization of the army into harmony with the order of battle for the field army developed by the General Staff. The Kaiser responded that he "felt it was henceforth expedient" that the War Minister, in his presence, be informed by the Chief of the General Staff "concerning the relevant aspects of the order of battle, in order to be able to have a firm foundation for the future peacetime formation of the army".[92] In spite of that the Chief of the General Staff still did not brief the War Minister of his intentions, obviously because for the present they were still a matter of developing ideas. He merely told Goßler that primarily it was a question "of disposing of a greater number of active corps in the order of battle [80] than previously", which "must be of approximately the same strength and consist of two uniformly organized infantry divisions".[93] Schlieffen's intent, which the chief of the deployment section (*Aufmarschabteilung*) Colonel von Wittken in a subsequent conference told the representative of the War Ministry, was to utilize the "small" brigades and other units excess to normal tables of organization to increase the <u>number of the active army corps</u> in the *peacetime* organization of the army <u>by seven to a total of twenty-seven</u>. Such an increase could obviously be implemented at the earliest with the next scheduled adjustment of the peacetime strength of the army in 1899.

b.) Reorganization of the border security in the east

Even though the *Denkschrift* of 2 August 1897 was based on the assumption that Russia would not participate in a Franco-German war, Schlieffen was of course not so naive that he would rely on this assumption and neglect to provide for the protection of the German eastern border. As long as the Franco–Russian alliance was in effect, so long as it was not guaranteed – perhaps by the conclusion of an alliance – that the still very loose bonds of the new friendship [81] between the two empires possessed lasting durability, in short, so long as the possibility of a war with Russia was not completely out of the question, the General Staff had, it goes without saying, the duty to continue to take measures to provide for adequate protection for the German eastern border. On the other hand Schlieffen's new operational intent required considerable alteration to the previous preparations, if only because under the changed circumstances it was no longer a question of conducting offensive operations against Russia.

---

[91] Dieckmann footnote: "Table" [Missing].
[92] Dieckmann footnote: "Letter from Goßler to Schlieffen of 19 March 1897."
[93] Dieckmann footnote: "Letter from the General Staff to the War Ministry of 10 April 1897."

[From pages 81 to 88 Dieckmann discussed in great detail Schlieffen's changes, beginning in the spring of 1897, in border security in the east. On the strategic level Schlieffen concentrated border security on East Prussia east of the Vistula, while in Posen and Silesia Russian operations were considered unlikely and only local security was adequate. Tactically, Schlieffen changed the cordon system of defense to a deep and flexible system that intended to block the most likely enemy avenues of approach. The mission was now simplified to one of protecting the rail communications to Königsberg, Allenstein and Insterburg. The mobilization was accelerated to the highest degree possible. In border districts the call-up was to be complete in less than 24 hours. The two East Prussian Corps, I and XVII, were given the authority to integrate all year groups, including Landwehr, immediately into active army units and employ them in all operations, including offensive operations. Nevertheless, the two East Prussian corps still complained that they were not strong enough and required additional units in peacetime. Field fortifications were built, particularly at communications nodes and, beginning in 1899 very large bunkers (*I-Werke*), reinforced barrack buildings, artillery positions and machine-gun emplacements in the defiles of the Masurian Lakes. These, Dieckmann admitted, were intended to prevent the Russian Niemen and Narew armies from uniting in eastern East Prussia. More permanent and larger fortifications were also built on the Vistula bridgeheads. Dieckmann contended that these permanent fortifications proved to the Russians that the Germans had no intention of attacking in the east. If this were so, it would be hard to reconcile the construction of large modern fortifications at Königsberg, Posen and Thorn in the 1880s (which were far more obvious than bunkers built in the East Prussian forest in the late 1890s) with Moltke's war plan, which Dieckmann said was aimed at a massive double envelopment of the Russian armies in Poland. In the next chapter he would make precisely the opposite argument: that the truly gigantic build-up of the super-fortress of Metz allowed Schlieffen to attack in the west. In fact, on both fronts Schlieffen's intent was to use fortifications to aid the maneuver of the field army.]

[88] c.) The expansion of Fortress Metz–Diedenhofen

Next to the reorganization of the field army and the redesign of the border security in the east, finally the expansion of Metz–Diedenhofen was a further prerequisite for the feasibility of the new operational intent of the Chief of the General Staff. Although <u>Metz</u>, as the strategically most important fortress on the German west front, had been built in the course of the last twenty years into a strong bulwark,[94]

---

[94] This is simply inaccurate. After the Franco-Prussian war the Germans had modernised Metz by building a belt of masonry forts around the city. In 1886 and 1887 the new high-explosive artillery rounds made these fortifications obsolete and rendered them as much a liability as an advantage: the masonry fortifications were so vulnerable to high-explosive fire that they were practically abandoned (Zuber, *Inventing the Schlieffen Plan*, pp. 111–13).The debate concerning the refortification of Metz with "armoured" works out of concrete and steel was motivated by the need to make Metz defensible again and not, as Dieckmann would have it, to fit Metz into the Schlieffen plan.

it remained, however, like all the other German fortresses [89] to this time, an isolated entrenched camp. [The next two sentences contradict each other].[95] No less than the other German fortifications, and in contrast to those of the French, Metz was also intended to this time to perform an operational function, that is, to operate in close conjunction with the field army. On the contrary it should, as necessary, take pressure off the field army, and otherwise perform an exclusively defensive function, securing the border and the deployment of the army. The belt of [masonry] fortifications surrounding the fortress was located only a few kilometers from the city wall, which was far too close, and it possessed no immediate connection to the other two great entrenched camps in Alsace-Lorraine, Diedenhofen in the north and Strasbourg in the south. When in 1892 the War Ministry recommended establishing such a connection by means of a chain of *Sperrforts* [intermediate forts], the National Defense Committee unanimously turned the project down, on the basis of a joint recommendation[96] submitted by Count Schlieffen and the Inspector-General of Engineers and Fortifications at that time, Generalleutnant Goltz. According to their statement as well as the opinion of the Commission, blocking off [90] Lorraine in this way would accomplish nothing more than to delay and make more difficult fighting a decisive battle in the open field. It was unanimously decided to reaffirm the old proven rule that it was more important to reinforce the army than to build a dead mass of fortifications, and that fortresses have value only so far as they are able to supplement "the necessary preparation of all available living forces of the Empire".[97] Similarly Schlieffen, in agreement

---

Dieckmann footnote: "In addition to the [medieval and early modern] city wall, Metz possessed ten forts in close proximity to the city, which had already been begun by the French. In the 1870s the Germans completed and expanded the city fortifications and the fortress belt. Further reinforcement, modifications and new construction, principally in the forts on the most likely enemy attack sector, were started during the growing tension [89] between Germany and France during the Boulanger crisis and continued in the following years (completion and partial reconstruction of secondary "annex" batteries, establishment of numerous bombproof barracks and magazines, increase in the *Sturmfreiheit* [invulnerability to infantry assault] in the area before the ditch and glacis, [all this was construction outside of the existing masonry forts, remedial measures which were necessitated by the effect of high explosive on the masonry forts] construction of armoured observation posts and the erection of barbed-wire obstacles. The construction to reinforce and improve the defensive installations was in the main completed by 1895."

[95] The phrase, "was intended . . . with the field army" was originally written "was not intended . . .", which would have made sense in conjunction with the second sentence, "On the contrary . . .", but would have been factually incorrect. Dieckmann struck out the "not" but didn't correspondingly change the second sentence, which should also have been deleted. (In the original German my English second sentence is another clause in a run-on sentence which I broke in half for reasons of clarity.) Metz was most definitely intended to assist the maneuver of the field army, as both Schlieffen's and the younger Moltke's exercises demonstrate (see Zuber, *Inventing the Schlieffen Plan*).

[96] Dieckmann footnote: "As has been said (p. 59), the recommendation stated that blocking Lorraine by means of Sperrforts would cause the French to outflank the German front to the north through Belgium, which would force the Germans to fight the decisive battle under significantly less favourable conditions."

[97] Dieckmann footnote: "In the question of fortifying Alsace Schlieffen stood in some degree in opposition to this principle. Soon after becoming Chief of the General staff, Schlieffen pushed

with the responsible military authorities, recommended against a project to expand Metz through construction of a second fortress belt far beyond the existing one. In the mid-1890s this project was considered more closely in connection with the question of the use of modern "armored" fortifications.[98] [91] A commission was established for this purpose in the spring of 1895, composed of representatives from the War Ministry, the General Staff and the General Inspection [of Engineers and Fortifications], which unanimously rejected the necessity of constructing such a fortress belt, stating that "the resources that are available for Metz . . . should be employed within the existing fortress line".

This was the situation in the fortress question in the fall of 1896 when it was reopened again by the Kaiser personally, that is, at the time that Schlieffen's envelopment plan began to take firm form. First he ordered that the project for reinforcing or expanding Metz, possibly with the use of armor, be re-examined. It can well be assumed with certainty that this initiative was taken at Schlieffen's instigation and stood in immediate connection with his new operational intentions.[99] Schlieffen's concept gave Metz a completely different strategic

---

through the controversial plan for a fortress on the Molsheimer Höhe in front of Strasbourg, which had been considered since 1884." Dieckmann exaggerated both the importance of the fortress and Schlieffen's role in bringing it about. It was originally planned to build five separate major fortresses at Molsheim, but due to the expense only two were ever constructed. The fortress remained a torso. Naturally, the construction of a major fortress such as Kaiser Wilhelm II at Molsheim was a complicated process extending over decades, and Schlieffen's role was as far from decisive as Dieckmann would make it appear. Kriegsarchiv Munich, Kriegsministerium, 4605/2 Ingenieur-Komitee Abteilung 4, *Die Entwicklung des deutschen Festungssystems seit 1870*, esp. pp. 23–6. "This fortress, which was begun in 1893, and was named 'Fortress Kaiser Wilhelm II' formed the support for the right wing of the German forces deploying in Alsace, which with Fortress Strasbourg would hold the Breusch line and therefore block the Rhine valley against a French force approaching from the south. Schlieffen had also requested in addition that the weak, indeed militarily worthless, fortress of Neu-Breisach be built into a strong bridgehead which would assure German forces a secure crossing point on both sides of the Rhine. For the protection of the Rhine bridges above this point he proposed that several smaller fortifications be erected at Müllheim, Bellingen, Istein and Oettingen. To this time these projects were not approved because of financial difficulties."

[98] Dieckmann footnote: "To this time German fortresses had made little use of 'armoured' works. At the beginning of the 1890s the larger fortresses had a total of two hundred 5cm canons under armour [these were close-range anti-personnel weapons, generally mounted in casemates]. In addition, several heavy armoured turret guns were mounted in the outer forts of Metz and Thorn. [91] After considerable back and forth, the budget of 1895/96 finally appropriated a larger sum of money for armoured fortifications. Since there was still a difference of opinion concerning which fortresses should be armoured, no work had begun."

[99] It is certain that the refortification of Metz had nothing to do with operational plans in 1896 or any time during Schlieffen's tenure as Chief of Staff. First, the fortress question was reopened in 1897 because of purely technical considerations, not due to Schlieffen's war planning. It was felt that the development of armoured fortifications had proceeded to the point where confidence could be placed in them and it was worthwhile to build armoured fortresses. Second, the refortification of Metz was a colossal undertaking that would not be completed in Schlieffen's lifetime. Only three of the five major forts on the west side of Metz were completed by 1904, just before Schlieffen retired in 1905, and none of the three major forts on the east side had even seriously been started. In addition, it was necessary after 1905 to build a further mass of infantry bunkers and secondary batteries on both sides of the Moselle. Metz was in no fit state to support

importance than previously, for the envelopment plan transformed the fortress not only into the pivot and support of the enveloping wing, it also allowed the fortress to immediately support the field army. At the same time, as the central joint of the German army front, the stronger and more extensively Metz was reinforced, the more maneuver forces it would free up for offensive operations. [93] An expanded Metz was in a position to provide immediate reinforcement to the field army, which Schlieffen, as we know, required for the conduct of his planned offensive. But the expansion of Metz for Schlieffen did not rest there; his proposals for the fortress went even further, proposals which stood in opposition to his previous views in the same manner as his changed opinion concerning the expansion of Metz. These proposals included the extension of the fortifications of Diedenhofen to the left [west] bank of the Moselle in addition to securing the most important Moselle crossings between Diedenhofen and Metz through smaller fortifications. Therefore Schlieffen wanted to establish a connection between the two fortresses, which would provide a sort of hinge, with security on both sides, for the enveloping wing.[100] After all, in his *Denkschrift* of 2 August 1897 Schlieffen advocated the realization of the long-considered plan to build a fortress in the area of Saarburg [92] in order to secure the south flank of the front in Lorraine against any possible French outflanking maneuver.

The preparatory work for the expansion of Metz was begun in the winter of 1896/97. [On pages 93 and 94 Dieckmann discussed technical details for planning the use of armored fortifications at Metz and recommendations submitted by Vogel von Falkenstein, the Inspector of the Engineers and Fortresses.[101]]

[94] Schlieffen stated that he was in general in agreement with these [Falkenstein's] recommendations. In his written opinion he emphasized in particular that through the planned expansion of Metz "a very worthwhile increase in the

---

any of Schlieffen's war plans. R. Rolf, *Die deutsche Panzerfortifikation. Die Panzerfesten von Metz und ihre Vorgeschichte* (Osnabrück, 1991, esp. pp. 83, 111, 189).

[100] Dieckmann footnote: "In his book, 'The Fortress Problem in Germany and its Effect on the Strategic Situation 1870–1914 (Volume 1 of the New German Research, Military Science Section) Berlin, 1935, Major (Retired) Dr. Grabau completely misunderstands Schlieffen's intent in the expansion of Metz–Diedenhofen. This poor piece of work contains numerous inexcusable errors concerning the development of German fortifications that are incompatible even with a complete ignorance of the material. It would both exceed the scope of this work and hardly reward the effort to refute them in detail."

[101] Dieckmann footnote page 93: "The stated justification for the dissolution [in 1897 of the National Defense Committee, which had not met since 1892] was the progress in the development of weapons, the introduction of new technical devices for the defense in addition to similar measures on the enemy side, etc., which made it necessary to implement 'numerous changes or new installations in fortresses, etc., expeditiously, and excluding agencies other than those that are immediately involved'. The main purpose of the dissolution doubtless was that it was held to be dangerous to give a commission consisting of several members, a sort of 'council of war', insight into the operational plans of the General Staff, which was correlated in many ways with the fortress system, and to make these plans to some degree dependent on the conclusions of this 'council of war'." Dieckmann offers no proof for this assertion. The elder Moltke had to fight to assert his authority against other members of the King's entourage who wanted to determine military strategy, which he labelled 'councils of war', making this a powerful pejorative term in the German army. Dieckmann's intent was clearly to reinforce the

[95] value of the fortress for the operations of the field army" would ensue. "The expansion of the zone of influence of the fortifications would allow troops to be saved for employment in other areas. In conjunction with the expansion of Diedenhofen they together reinforce the defense of the intervening section of the Moselle and contribute to covering the deployment of the field army. The enlargement of the protected interior area will also provide larger maneuver elements an adequate and secure space for crossing over the Moselle as well as for transiting the fortress. The secure possession of the dominating high ground on the western approaches to the fortress will significantly improve the ability of our forces to deploy on the left [west] bank of the Moselle and permit forces that are withdrawing to break contact with the enemy at the proper time."[102] Schlieffen disagreed with Falkenstein's recommendations on two important points. First, he felt it was necessary that all new gun positions be fully armored, rather than some being emplaced in naval-style gun turrets (*Panzerschirme*). Above all he objected to the proposed construction of fortifications on the right [east] bank of the Moselle, that is, on the south and east fronts of Metz, which increased the defensive power of Metz, to be sure, but were not able "to increase the significance of Metz for the conduct of field operations". For the operational mission that Schlieffen intended to assign to Metz, the expansion of the southern and eastern fronts could be dispensed with, or was at least less pressing. This mission required above all the reinforcement of the west front, that is, [96] the construction of advanced works on the left bank of the Moselle. The Kaiser agreed with Schlieffen and in an order of 25 November 1897 directed that priority be given to the fortifications on the north-west and south-west sides of Metz, while the south and east fronts would receive only a few weak positions, for the most part just prepared infantry and artillery positions.[103]

---

idea that Schlieffen was working on a brilliant secret plan. He wants to leave the impression that for this reason Schlieffen was now the one who decided on questions of fortifications. In fact, according to the official secret history of German fortifications, the subsequent procedure for deciding on matters of fortification, which was regularized in 8 April 1899, was that the Chief of the General Staff, the Inspectors-General of Fortresses, of the Foot Artillery and of Transport troops and the local corps commanders were to come up with proposals and the War Minister would comment on the availability of funding. The Kaiser would then give his decision. (Kriegsarchiv Munich, Kriegsministerium, 4605/2, *Die Entwicklung des deutschen Festungssystems*, 32–3) By Dieckmann's definition this would have to be considered a 'council of war'. This was, in fact, normal staff work on a complicated proposed course of action, which could not be decided by the Chief of the General Staff in isolation.

[102] This is a statement of the manner in which Schlieffen would use Metz in all of his subsequent exercises: principally as a springboard for a counterattack by the right wing into Lorraine, and not as a dead anchor for the left flank of a right-wing attack through Belgium. See Zuber, *Inventing the Schlieffen Plan*, pp. 191–211.

[103] Dieckmann footnote: "Although a closer examination of the Metz construction project is not the subject of our investigation, the opinion of the General Inspector of the Foot [Heavy] Artillery, General of the Artillery von der Planitz, who completely rejected it, is particularly interesting and should be mentioned. In his written opinion of 2 October 1897 he said, among other things, that the performance and power of resistance of the proposed armoured works was being seriously overrated. Above all, the 'expense . . . of such a gigantic project and the requirement for such a large garrison to perform such a short-term and limited mission is so significant, that the consideration cannot be rejected out of hand, that these sums of money and

[97] It seemed that everything had been clarified to the degree that the technical work would commence and soon the construction of the forts could begin.

The execution of construction plans however suddenly experienced a longer interruption. The cause for this was without doubt once again political events, which were so grave as to threaten to put even Schlieffen's new operational intentions in question.

[From pages 97 to 101 Dieckmann included his second political essay. He said that Schlieffen's strategy was strongly influenced by two political factors. First, the German-Russian friendship was cooled in November 1897 by the German seizure of the port of Tsingtao: "Russia's conduct demonstrated on what an insecure basis the friendship between the two Empires stood, and how illusory was the German hope for a reduction in the threat of two-front war. But the realization of this hope was precisely the essential precondition on which the practicability of the new operational concept of the Chief of the German General Staff depended. There is no doubt that Schlieffen was as little pleased by the hasty and ill-considered initiatives of the Imperial government, or rather of the Naval Ministry, which did not adequately consider the disruption to Russo-German understanding that it would cause, as was Baron Holstein, the actual director of German foreign policy, with whom Schlieffen frequently discussed political matters, and who Schlieffen, we have every reason to assume, probably informed of the train of his operational thoughts."[104]

Dieckmann contended that the advocacy by Joseph Chamberlain, the British Colonial Secretary, of an alliance with Germany (which was opposed by the Prime Minister, Lord Salisbury), while not an official offer of alliance from the British, constituted "an approach from London which presented the Imperial German government with the extremely difficult question, simply stated, whether it should decide for Britain or Russia". In fact, Germany had no such choice, for neither country was willing to ally itself with Germany. It should also be noted that British adoption of such a policy would have required a change in the British government, with Chamberlain replacing Salisbury, a very unlikely turn of events. Dieckmann's sole support for this remarkable assertion was a long, rambling note from May 1898 in which Kaiser Wilhelm II mulls over what he thinks are his diplomatic possibilities,[105] and which Dieckmann took quite seriously. The Kaiser's note spoke of the possibility of an Anglo-German alliance against Russia and France, or a

---

troops might not be better used for a larger purpose elsewhere'. Planitz was thinking in the first case that the resources were 'to be employed' in the expansion of the heavy artillery of the field army, a project which he had been energetically advocating, 'and the necessary reinforcement of the Fortress of Metz should be restricted to a more limited space, that of the current fort line'. The planned fortress groups were too weak by themselves and in addition were so widely spaced from one another that they were exposed to being enveloped and destroyed individually, one after the other, which would significantly increase the difficulties in defending the fort. It was therefore 'his strongest' recommendation that 'the proposed expansion of the fortress be rejected'. At least one German senior officer saw the situation clearly.

[104] pp. 97–8. Dieckmann may assume anything he likes but, as so often, his theories lack any proof.
[105] Grosse Politik, XIV (1) No. 3799.

Russo-German alliance against France and perhaps England. In the latter case, England could destroy German trade but the Kaiser said "on land we could attack France with our entire army, perhaps even reinforced by the Russians, crush them and save our Empire".]

[101] It is obvious[106] that a possible consideration of the British overtures must not only change the course of German foreign policy but also the basis on which the German military-political situation rested. Above all it would invalidate the new operational intent of the Chief of the German General Staff, for if Britain were allied with Germany then the planned enveloping operation through Belgium was self-evidently out of the question. This would be prohibited not only out of consideration for British vital interests in Belgian neutrality, but also because such an alliance would unquestionably cause the Franco-Russian Entente to bring increasing pressure against Germany on both fronts. Due to the significance of the deliberations concerning such a possible change in the foreign and military-political course it is only too understandable that precisely those measures would be postponed which were closely connected with the now-questionable new operational intent of the Chief of the General Staff, to which belonged, in addition to the construction of fortifications on the German eastern border,[107] above all the expansion of Metz.[108]

[From pages 102 to 105 Dieckmann tried to connect the debates concerning the fortification of Lorraine with German foreign policy. On 26 May 1898 Kaiser Wilhelm decreed that Metz be provided with an enormous fortress belt, which he designed himself, some 60 to 70 kilometers in diameter, which Dieckmann said "admits of no other conclusion, than that the Kaiser, as can be seen from other indications," (Dieckmann again cited in a footnote the Kaiser's memo of May 1898) "was completely determined to accept the English overtures and reorient German policy from Russia to England. Schlieffen wanted to make Metz into an offensive weapon for his encirclement plan; the Kaiser's plan would transform Metz into a great defensive bulwark. This [the Kaiser's plan] only made sense if it were put in immediate connection with the intention to ally with Britain, for then the important thing in fact was to reinforce the defensibility of the German borders against the anticipated increase in Franco-Russian pressure, for which purpose the expansion of Metz into a huge fortified camp was doubtless well-suited." Colmar Freiherr von der Goltz, the General-Inspector of Engineers and Fortresses, replied with a project to build a chain of *Sperrforts* at Sierck, Han an der Nied, Mörchingen, Bensdorf, Saarburg and Wasselnheim north of Molsheim to seal off the border completely.[109] Graf Heaseler, commander of XIV Corps at Metz and the Fortress Governor then both submitted their own recommendations.]

[106] Again Dieckmann attempts to assume something that requires considerable proof.
[107] Dieckmann footnote: "pp. 85 ff.".
[108] The official secret history of German fortifications does not mention any such considerations. Kriegsarchiv Munich, Kriegsministerium, 4605/2, *Die Entwicklung des deutschen Festungsystems seit 1870.*
[109] Dieckmann footnote: "Goltz briefing to Wilhelm, 30 June 1898."

[105] It is not possible to determine from the records how in the end Schlieffen succeeded in bringing the [Metz] question back to the line that he consistently pursued [refortify only the west front] and to win the Kaiser over to his ideas. Doubtless the fact that the German-British rapprochement quickly came to nothing played a role. The Kaiser was never able to deny the objections put forward, particularly by the Foreign Minister, von Bülow, that a hasty acceptance of the very vague English offers of friendship, given the weakness of the German fleet and the grave repercussions from Russia, was a great risk and a dangerous experiment. Enough, Schlieffen succeeded in winning over the Kaiser, so that the construction of the Metz forts proceeded according to his intentions.[110] This was obviously not easy and required a considerable period of time. Only after the British-German negotiations had completely faded away in the winter of 1898/99 and relations between the two had soured so much due to colonial differences (the Samoa dispute) that Berlin considered breaking off diplomatic relations with Great Britain[111] did the Kaiser finally approve Schlieffen's suggestions. In orders on [106] 18 March and 4 April 1899 he directed that armored forts were to be built in an accelerated manner at . . . [Festen Lothringen, Kaiserin, Kronprinz and Graf Heaseler].

Initial construction finally commenced at the beginning of April 1899. At the same time construction was begun at Obergentringen [near Diedenhofen].

3. Provisional continuation of previous deployment plan

When Count Schlieffen first began to consider the idea of an envelopment operation in the fall of 1896, he surely would have expected to implement these intentions without delay in the official deployment plan of the General Staff. It can be assumed that this oft-mentioned *Denkschrift* of 2 August 1897 was supposed to serve as the basis of such a new formulation of the *Aufmarschplan*. But the great insecurity in the position of German foreign policy, which was caused by the events that have been related, had repercussions which interfered with establishing the preconditions necessary for its implementation. As we have seen, these circumstances first called the plan into question, and now they put an end to the planning. [107] In any case, Schlieffen's intended envelopment plan was the basis of neither the *Aufmarschplan* for 1897/98 nor for the following year.[112]

In the 1898/99 mobilization year the *Westheer* consisted of (the figures for 1897/98 are in brackets) six (six) armies with

17 (18) active corps with 35 (37) divisions

---

[110] Aside from Dieckmann, there is no reference to Schlieffen playing an important role in the design of Metz. *Entwicklung des deutschen Festungssystems*, Rolf's *Panzerfortifikation* and Stéphane Gaber's *La Lorraine Fortifiée* (Metz, 1994) all demonstrate that the principal question involved at Metz was technical, not strategic, and that the great breakthrough was in the development of a new fortress type, the *Feste*, which was an engineering feat far beyond the competence of Schlieffen or the General Staff.

[111] Dieckmann footnote: "*Grosse Politik* XIV (2) No. 4053 and 4055."

[112] Dieckmann footnote: "It states on page 54 of volume one of the official history of the World War that the draft for the *Aufmarschplan* of 1898/99 was based on the new operations plan. This is not accurate and requires correction."

    4 (4) reserve corps with 8 (8) divisions
    3 (3) reserve divisions   (in total, 46 (48) divisions)
    6 (6) cavalry divisions
    13½ mixed Landwehr brigades

In both years the deployment area on the Franco-German border was the same as it had been previously, with the right flank accordingly on the south border of Luxembourg. This leads unmistakably to the conclusion that the operation was to be conducted in the same manner as the plan in force since 1893.[113]

The *Ostheer* in these years was composed of two (two) armies with

    7 (6) active corps with 14 (12) divisions
    1 (2) reserve corps with 2 (4) divisions
    6 (4) reserve divisions   (in total, 22 (20) divisions)
    5 (5) cavalry divisions
    15 (14) mixed Landwehr brigades

not inconsiderably increased from 1896/97. [108] The deployment area for the *Ostheer* was essentially the same as that in the 1896/97 mobilization year.[114]

4. Redesign of the German operations plan in 1899

a.) The army bill of 1899, building the High Seas Fleet and the "politics of the Free Hand"

In 1899, after the expiration of the five-year army bill of 1894, which saw the last, and it should be noted, significant, increase in the German army, according to the provisions of the statute a further adjustment in the strength of the peacetime army was due. This, as had been customary, should have resulted in an increase in the peacetime strength of the army[115] which was made necessary by the rapid growth in the German population alone.

Count Schlieffen's expectations for the further growth of the army have already been explained. His priority, in particular in light of his new operational intentions, lay in an increase in the number of uniformly organized divisions and corps. As we know, to this point his wish had been to use the "small" brigades to increase the number of active corps by seven from 20 to 27.[116]

[109] The new army bill did not come close to these expectations. Concerned with holding the costs of an increase in the army to the very minimum, the War Minister asked only for the creation of three new active corps (XVIII, XIX and III Bavarian),[117] which in any case were already included in the mobilization plan, plus

---

[113] Dieckmann footnote: "pp. 17 ff."
[114] Dieckmann footnote: "p. 45."
[115] Dieckmann footnote: "For details see *Kriegsrüstung und Kriegswirtschaft*, Text volume, pp. 52 ff."
[116] Dieckmann footnote "p. 80."
[117] Dieckmann footnote: "See p. 51, footnote 2 [57]."

a reorganization of the field artillery[118] and the creation of some technical units.[119] Far from making a serious attempt to fully implement universal conscription, the army bill proposed only a modest increase in peacetime strength, which was reduced by one-third by the Reichstag.

The reason for this far-reaching restraint, which fatally restricted the further development of military preparation of the Empire, was primarily consideration for the expansion of German sea power. This had begun recently on a large scale, and the consequent pressure on German finances, according to the completely incorrect opinion of the bureaucrats and parliamentarian guardians, ostensibly prohibited a rigorous expansion of the army.

It has been asked why Count Schlieffen remained silent, why he did not employ his entire influence to obtain a larger increase in the army which would have been appropriate to the actual military needs, the necessity for which he, as no other, was convinced. This question seems all the more justified, when one considers that [110] the Chief of the General Staff regarded a considerable increase in the peacetime army as simply one of the essential preconditions for execution of his envelopment plan. In fact, Schlieffen made no objections and pronounced himself satisfied with the limited increases, and even reconciled himself with the fact that these increases would not be introduced at once, as had formerly been the case, but in increments, this "being more appropriate to the financial capacity of the Empire".[120]

[From pages 110 to 117 Dieckmann included his third political essay, which concerned the construction of the German High Seas Fleet, the necessity to avoid a two-front war, and Bülow's politics of the "Free Hand", while presenting his own views justifying German *Weltpolitik*. Dieckmann admitted that "There are no statements or papers by Schlieffen from this period that would give any indication as to his attitude towards the creation of a High Seas Fleet." Nevertheless, he built an enormous case concerning what Schlieffen must have believed. He said that Schlieffen did not argue for a larger army bill in 1899 because he thought the expense of the fleet made it futile. Though Schlieffen was not in favor of building up the navy at the expense of the army, he supported both *Flottenpolitik* (the High Seas Fleet) and *Weltpolitik*. Schlieffen understood that this would lead to war between Great Britain and Germany, proof of which he found in *Der Krieg in der Gegenwart* (War in Modern Times, written after Schlieffen retired, in 1909). War with Great Britain – and of course, France – was possible according to Schlieffen only if there was no threat from the east of a two-front war. *Weltpolitik* to Schlieffen meant reconciliation with Russia. Instead, Bülow and Holstein pursued the "notorious politics of the Free Hand. This", and here Dieckmann dropped the pretense that he was interpreting Schlieffen, "was nothing other than a cowardly and weak policy of vacillation" which avoided clear decisions and sought to win small advantages, leaving Germany standing between two stools, with no freedom to maneuver.

---

[118] Dieckmann footnote: "*Kriegsrüstung und Kriegswirtschaft*, Annex volume, pp. 376 ff."
[119] Dieckmann footnote: "ibid., p. 384."
[120] Dieckmann footnote: "In a letter from the War Ministry to the General Staff of July 1898."

In addition, they underestimated the ability of Britain to reconcile itself with France and Russia and the sacrifices that France was willing to make to gain British support for a war of revenge against Germany.]

[117] b.) German deployment plans for the 1899/1900 mobilization year

Therefore two important preconditions for the feasibility of Schlieffen's new operational concept remained unfulfilled: first the creation of the number of new army corps that he felt were necessary and second and most important, relief from the threat of a two-front war. It was thus obvious that the insecurity in Germany's foreign relations was not without repercussions on the operational plans and intentions of the Chief of the General Staff. [118] It required him above all to base his operational planning on the possibilities of both a one-front and a two-front war.

That being the case, for the 1899/1900 mobilization year initially two different deployment plans were prepared, specifically

Aufmarsch I for a war in the west only (one-front war)
Aufmarsch II for a war in the west and the east (two-front war)

In *Aufmarsch* I the entire German field army[121] was assembled on the west front in eight armies in a strength of

> 23 active corps with 49 divisions
> 7 reserve corps with 14 divisions
> 5 reserve divisions   (in total 68 divisions)
> 11 cavalry divisions
> 13½ Landwehr brigades

with the exception of 5 Landwehr brigades for coastal security and 13 Landwehr brigades left at the disposition of OHL [*Oberste Heeresleitung*, the German Headquarters in the First World War] initially in their mobilization stations. Since, aside from the order of battle, no other documents from this *Aufmarsch* I have survived, it is no longer possible to determine where and how it was intended to deploy the army. On the other hand there is in the archives a document written personally by Schlieffen, dated October 1898, which [119] obviously served as the basis for this *Aufmarsch* and provided the guidance for its preparation.[122]

In this document the Chief of the General Staff first considered the possibility of a French offensive, which he thought must always be the case, because the mobilization and deployment of the French army took place faster than that of the Germans.[123] Consequently the German deployment could "not be moved so close

---

[121] Dieckmann footnote: "Table" [Missing].
[122] The October 1898 *Denkschrift* was obviously written for a two-front war, that is, *Aufmarsch* II, and not the one-front war of *Aufmarsch* I. According to Dieckmann's description, in the October 1898 *Denkschrift* 62 divisions were to be deployed in the west, leaving 6 for the east, and Schlieffen specifically makes mention of the necessity over time to transfer more troops to the east to meet the growing Russian threat.
[123] Dieckmann footnote: "At this time the mobilisation and deployment of the German army to include the complete assembly of all elements required about four weeks; the French army on the other hand could be operationally ready in two to three weeks."

to the enemy lines that the French offensive could find us unready". It was indeed "inadvisable" for the Germans "to go any considerable distance over the line of the Saar". This insecurity in the situation already presents a deviation from Schlieffen's original intentions, which he stated in his *Denkschrift* of 2 August 1897. Probably in expectation of a prompt understanding between the two Empires, at that time Schlieffen was not anticipating Russian interference and obviously for that reason also did not expect a French offensive. He therefore had no qualms about deploying the German army immediately on the German-French border. This now did not appear "advisable" to him.[124]

The October 1898 document said that a French attack against the German deployment front on the Saar was most promising [120] "if it were made in conjunction with an envelopment of our left flank". This was admittedly "made considerably more difficult by the upper Rhine, Strasbourg, Fortress Kaiser Wilhelm II, the Vosges and also through a small army which would assemble at Strasbourg and attack the French envelopment in turn". Even if the French, "for the sake of the overall plan", were not deterred by these difficulties from conducting an envelopment of the German south flank, it could hardly be assumed that they would remain totally inactive in the north, "completely refusing . . . their left flank". It was much more likely that they would attack with their left through Belgium and Luxembourg, so that the Germans had to expect a French attack "north of Diedenhofen, south of Diedenhofen or also south of Metz." Such an attack could only be welcome for the Germans, for it offered them the opportunity for a very promising counterattack in the enemy flank. If this was successful, they would be in position to "push the entire French army away from their fortresses and onto the upper Rhine". "We must therefore make our right flank strong and extend it if at all possible to the west. This will not be possible without violating the neutrality of Luxembourg, and perhaps that of Belgium".

Nevertheless, Schlieffen continued, it was "not absolutely" certain, "that the French would make use of their faster mobilization and quicker deployment to conduct an immediate offensive". Perhaps they would satisfy themselves with assembling their troops in good time in their defensive [121] positions. If this was the case, the Germans could hardly make the inexcusable error, and in spite of their "slowness", not take the initiative which had been put in their hands, but "inactively wait to see if our opponent did decide to attack after all". Not only the threatening dangers from the east speak against such passivity, but also the fact that after the Germans had completed their deployment, they could not expect a further improvement in their position, "unless we wanted to surrender ourselves to the illusion that the Italians will do something useful for us".

If the French did not advance, then under all circumstances <u>the Germans were well advised to themselves take the offensive as soon as possible</u>. Schlieffen repeated once more his reservations against an attack which was limited to a frontal assault against "the fortified Verdun–Belfort front". Such an attack required

---

[124] Stating Dieckmann's argument more clearly, it would be unlikely that the French would attack unless they expected Russian support. Therefore the October 1898 *Denkschrift* was written for a two-front war, that is, *Aufmarsch* II.

numerous sieges and, even if it succeeded, promised "no particular success" because the defeated enemy could withdraw directly to the rear. As a consequence it was "imperative" that the Germans go around the "great wall erected along the Moselle and Meuse", "but not through Switzerland, where a war-ready army had to be defeated and fortified Jura passes must be taken, only in order to begin a battle with the French under unfavorable circumstances". On the contrary, the French fortress line could be enveloped only to the north, "through Luxembourg, which possessed no army, and through Belgium, which [122] would withdraw its relatively weak army back into fortresses", particularly since it was "easier and more effective" here, "because it immediately threatens the enemy line of retreat". Schlieffen expressly added, however, that "this envelopment could not be too extensive" for operationally it was presented with "a double mission": "counterattack, if the enemy advances as soon as he has completed his deployment, and offensive, in case the enemy remains behind his fortifications".

In an annex appended to this document Schlieffen presented a recommendation for a deployment which met this dual mission, whose details are visible in the attached Map 2.[125]

Concerning the <u>conduct of the German operation</u>, Schlieffen said that in case of a <u>French</u> offensive, the Germans should conduct a pincers attack, with both right-wing armies (1st and 2nd Armies together with eight active corps) counterattacking against the French left, the 6th Army (three active corps, two reserve divisions) counterattacking against the French right, while the centre armies (3rd, 4th, 5th with 12 active corps) would allow the French to attack their strongly held front.

If the French decided not to assume the offensive and surrendered the initiative to the Germans, both right-wing armies (1st and 2nd) would [123] march to the right and "cross the Meuse between Donchery and Stenay", that is, push into the rear of the French fortress front from the north. Their right would be covered by the 7th Army composed of six reserve divisions, their left by the 3rd Army (four active corps, two reserve divisions), the latter "following later over the Meuse", that is, after the envelopment had been effective. The two armies deploying between Saarbrücken and Saarburg (4th and 5th Armies, together eight active corps) were to advance on Nancy and attempt, in a similar manner as previously, "to take the position east of this city as well as Forts Frouard and Pont St. Vincent". Then the mass of both armies were, while covering themselves against Toul, to advance "to the south across the Moselle in the direction of Neufchâteau", that is, through the gap in the French fortress front between Nancy/Toul and Epinal. The left-wing (6th) Army, including the forces deployed in the upper Alsace, (in total 4 corps, 6 reserve divisions) had the mission of covering the left flank of the German attack.

The conduct of the attack also differed in one important way from Schlieffen's original intentions. In the 2 August 1897 *Denkschrift* Schlieffen had planned to

---

[125] The map has been lost. Dieckmann footnote: "The order of battle, which is all that survived from *Aufmarsch* I, contains some insignificant differences concerning grouping and organization of units from this recommendation. See Table. . . ." [Missing].

German Planning: Dieckmann, Der Schlieffenplan

support the envelopment of the right wing through an attack by the 3rd Army against the French fortress line between Verdun and Toul. He had, however, characterized this attack as being very difficult.[126] [124] The Chief of the General Staff now decided he would do without this attack. In the October 1898 document he said that it was not possible "to obtain at the outset a breakthrough of the Meuse forts between Toul and Verdun. It is too difficult a mission to attack in the bend between Frouard and Verdun, and inside this enemy envelopment, and lay siege to one or two enemy forts, and requires too many forces. We should conduct it only if we are absolutely forced to." Schlieffen was obviously compelled to call off this attack because the Army Bill of 1899 did not provide him with the required number of new active army corps.

In case the French remained on the defensive, as has been noted, Schlieffen justified the necessity of an immediate German offensive above all with reference to the imminent threat in the east. In the October 1898 document he said "Each day and week that follows after the 1st day of mobilization, the Russians can come closer to our borders, perhaps even approaching the Vistula. With each day the situation in the east becomes more dangerous and the necessity to deploy stronger forces there more pressing, and therefore we weaken our forces in the west." To the related question of the division of German forces between the east and west fronts, Schlieffen said nevertheless that "all possible forces were initially" to be employed "in the west". "An exception can be made at most for those forces [125] that are already stationed and will be mobilized right [east] of the Vistula, if only because these troops will not be able to leave. If we divide our forces with about ⅓ in the east and ⅔ in the west, we will (remain) seriously outnumbered on both fronts and will not be able to assume the offensive in either direction. If we reinforce the west with two or three corps, we will nevertheless remain weaker here and will be so weak in the east, that we will not be able to execute the very difficult defensive mission on this front at all. We will have to withdraw behind the Vistula. For such a retreat, it is better to be weak than to be strong. It is necessary to gain a decisive victory in the west. If we have accomplished this, then we can see how we can regain what we have lost in the east."

The opinions here are obviously based on the idea that, in case of a Franco-German war, at least at first it could be expected that the Russians would not intervene. For this reason *Aufmarsch* I deployed the entire German field army in the west.[127]

On the other hand, in case the Russians perhaps did take up arms <u>at the same time</u> as the French, <u>*Aufmarsch* II</u> was fashioned for a <u>true two-front war</u>. The deployment in this case was: [126]

<u>in the west</u>:
six armies with
16 active corps with 34 divisions

---

[126] Dieckmann footnote "p. 65."
[127] In the October 1898 *Denkschrift* Schlieffen expressly said that the forces in eastern Germany, which in the October 1899 *Aufmarsch* I Dieckmann said included 10 divisions, would stay in the east.

    4 reserve corps with 8 divisions
    3 reserve divisions
    5 cavalry divisions   (in total, 45 divisions)
    13½ mixed Landwehr brigades

in the east
two armies with
    7 active corps with 15 divisions
    2 reserve corps with 4 divisions[128]
    4 reserve divisions   (in total, 23 divisions)
    5 cavalry divisions
    15 mixed Landwehr brigades

Aufmarsch II divided the German forces between the east and the west fronts in a manner that went beyond the proportion of ⅔ in the west and ⅓ in the east that Schlieffen had said was unwise.[129] The limited strength of the *Westheer* permits the conclusion, even if there are no documents in the archives to prove this directly, that in the case of a two-front war the General Staff would forego the envelopment to the north of the French fortress line and limit itself to conducting the old operations plan for the attack on Nancy. The correctness of this line of reasoning is confirmed by the fact that the units that compose the *Ostheer* in *Aufmarsch* II were in large part drawn from the armies that would conduct the envelopment in *Aufmarsch* I.

[127] From the surviving initial instructions for the eastern armies (*Aufmarschanweisungen*) in *Aufmarsch* II, the German *Ostheer* would deploy with elements as before on the Angerapp, and with the main body on the general line Thorn–Lautenburg–Neidenburg–Masurian Lakes. It is uncertain whether the intent was defensive or, as earlier, offensive.[130]

These initial *Aufmärsche* prepared for the 1899/1900 mobilization year were subjected to a fundamental revision in the same year. In order to forestall the serious disruption to the mobilization and deployment mechanism that could easily arise, significant changes to the plans during that mobilization year were avoided as a matter of principle. The grounds for this change must therefore have been extremely important. What they were cannot be determined due to a lack of documentation. One would probably not go wrong by again seeking them in international politics. Russo-German relations had indeed once more recently deteriorated due to many differences, principally in the near east (Baghdad rail line). These arose from the inevitable collision between Germany's [128] interest in expanding its economic

---

[128] Dieckmann footnote "In *Aufmarsch* II one fewer reserve corps was created. Therefore, the number of independent reserve divisions was increased by two. See Table" [Missing].
[129] Dieckmann footnote "p. 125."
[130] Dieckmann footnote: "The presumption is for defensive employment. A *Denkschrift* prepared by *Oberquartiermeister* von Lessel of 15 April 1899 states that in view of the Russian superiority only the strategic defensive came into question, which to be sure must exploit 'every available opportunity' 'to gain partial successes against the Russian armies, which were advancing separately, and to make their operations more difficult'."

German Planning: Dieckmann, Der Schlieffenplan

influence with the traditional, purely power-political ambitions of Russia. The increase in the two-front threat that this occasioned had obviously caused Schlieffen to give up hope of having his back free in the east. He was constrained to modify the 1899/1900 *Aufmarschplan* during the mobilization year in order to meet the changed circumstances.[131]

This *Aufmarsch*, which went into effect on 1 October 1899, was of fundamental importance for the future. It was based on the expectation that in any Franco-German war,[132] Russia would take such a hostile stance that defensive measures beyond those of normal border security would be imperative. The concentration of the entire German field army on the west front was thereafter completely out of the question. In fact, two armies would deploy and remain in the east with

    2 active corps
    1 reserve corps
    3 reserve divisions   (in total, 10 divisions)
    3 cavalry divisions
   14 mixed Landwehr brigades

all of which were units which had their peacetime garrisons in the east or were created during mobilization in the east. The mission of the *Ostheer* was the strategic defense of the territory east of the Vistula according to the plans mentioned earlier.[133]

[129] Therefore, the strength of the *Westheer* was

    6 six armies with
  21 active corps with 45 divisions
    5 reserve corps with 10 divisions
    3 reserve divisions   (in total, 58 divisions)
    8 cavalry divisions
  13½ mixed Landwehr brigades

The assembly areas planned for these forces are shown in Map 3 [Missing]. It is evident that, even without the "complete security in the east" and in spite of the weakening of the *Westheer*, it was intended to proceed with the enveloping

---

[131] Dieckmann's attempts to link radical alterations in the war plan to minuscule changes in relations between Germany and Russia are simply not credible. He fails completely to prove that between April and October 1899 Russia had drawn so close to Germany that it would fail to uphold its alliance with France and allow the Germans to crush the French in a one-front war – thereby establishing German hegemony on the continent.

[132] Dieckmann uses a semantic trick to reinforce his thesis that Schlieffen was striving to fight a one-front war with France. On the basis of no discernible evidence, he assumes that a one-front war against France was the German base plan. However, since 1894 at the latest France and Russia had a firm military alliance and the Germans knew it. Thereafter, a one-front war was extremely unlikely. It would be more logical to assume that the two-front war was the most likely case, and that this war could be started by Russia, not France. This was, after all, the actual situation in August 1914.

[133] Dieckmann footnote: "pp. 80 ff."

operation planned according to Schlieffen's document of October 1898.[134] Aside from the fact that the *Westheer* in the new *Westaufmarsch* was weaker than in the October 1898 document and *Aufmarsch* I in 1899/1900, it deviated little in principle from its predecessors, mainly having less depth. The two maneuver armies, (1st and 2nd) had the same strength, eight corps. Only the number of reserve divisions in support was reduced to five, there being one fewer on the north and three fewer in direct support of the maneuver armies. The 3rd Army, which had the mission of protecting the left flank of the maneuver armies, was considerably reduced, retaining only two active corps and one reserve corps. [In the October 1898 document it included four active corps and two reserve divisions: p. 123.] This leads to the conclusion that the attack on the Verdun–Toul front was completely out of the question. On the other hand, the two armies (4th and 5th) which were to attack Nancy and subsequently [130] penetrate through the gap in the French fortress line [between Toul and Epinal] were reinforced by a further active corps and now contained a total of eight active corps and a reserve corps. The left wing of the German deployment was weakened by an active corps and a reserve corps, giving it a strength of three active corps, one reserve corps and three reserve divisions.[135]

The supporting documents finally provide the details concerning the assembly areas for the army of five corps and two cavalry divisions[136] that in the latest

[134] Dieckmann footnote: "pp. 118 ff."
[135] This is the first mention of reserve divisions following the two maneuver armies. This may have been explained in a table which Dieckmann mentions, but it has been lost. Dieckmann's comparison of his own figures for the various plans does not add up, and either the table provided more information or he was confusing the 2 August 1897 *Denkschrift* with that of October 1898.

To recapitulate:

	Denkschrift 2 Aug 1897	*Denkschrift* Oct 1898	*Aufmarsch* I 1 Oct 1899
right flank	6 RD	7 RD	5 RD
1st, 2nd Armies	16 ID	16 ID	16 ID
3rd Army	8 RD	8 ID	4 ID
		2 RD	2 RD
4th, 5th Armies	16 ID	16 ID	16 ID
			2 RD
6th Army	8 ID	8 ID	6 ID
		6 RD	5 RD
left flank	10 ID		
	3 RD		
Total divisions	67 +	62	56

[136] Dieckmann footnote: "See Map 3" [Missing].

German Planning: Dieckmann, Der Schlieffenplan

bilateral agreement the Italian General Staff[137] had consented to send to Germany's assistance. The cavalry was to assemble between the 7th and 12th mobilization day on the right [east] bank of the Rhine, one between Ottenheim and Kappel [east of Lahr] and one in the area of Altbreisach. Later, the first division would move forward to the area of Saarburg, the second to Colmar–Münster. The first two army corps were to arrive between the 14th and 20th mobilization day, one in the area of Offenburg and one at Kenzingen–Altbreisach and then move forward, the first through Schlettstadt to Markirch and the second through Colmar to Münster. The three remaining Italian corps would arrive later, between the 16th and 18th day of mobilization in assembly areas at Offenburg, Emendingen and between Freiburg and Breisach. Their further employment was open.

That the Germans counted on the arrival of the Italian reinforcements is at least doubtful, in spite of the Italians' demonstrative show of solidarity to the Triple Alliance, [131] which concealed certain political objectives,[138] in spite of the agreement recently concluded between the two General Staffs. Schlieffen at least did not. We should not "allow ourselves any illusions", he said in his document of October 1898, "that Italy will do anything of tangible value for us. If France leaves two active corps with their reserve troops on the Alpine border, that is all the advantage that we can expect the alliance with Italy will provide."

What was the French deployment at the time that this fundamental change was being made in the German operations plan? In fact, the French plan had also been changed, which came into effect as Plan XIV on 1 April 1898.[139] According to this plan, in case of war the French would dispense with an immediate offensive and on the contrary initially await the enemy's actions. Therefore, the French General Staff history called this plan "*un dispositif d'attente*". Territorial units garrisoned fortresses and coastal fortifications in order that the field army would remain undiminished for utilization in field operations. The field army,[140] minus covering force units on the border (principally cavalry and light infantry), would deploy with [132]

the 1st Army with three active corps as "advance guard" army at Nancy
the 2nd Army with five active corps in the area of Epinal
the 3rd Army with four active corps behind the gap between these fortresses.

They were to oppose any enemy force attacking through this gap, in fact the attack planned by the German 4th and 5th Armies, which also would have been threatened in the left flank by the French 2nd Army from Epinal. The French 4th Army, four active corps strong, would assemble west of Toul between the Meuse

---

[137] Dieckmann footnote: "Foerster, *op. cit.*, pp. 78 f."
[138] Dieckmann footnote: "See J. L. Glanville, *Italy's Relations with England 1896–1905* (Baltimore, 1938)." Italian 'betrayal' of the Triple Alliance in 1914 and 1915 was a sore point in the German officer corps. This entry was made by hand and the 1938 date it bears is the best indication of the period in which Dieckmann conducted his work.
[139] Dieckmann footnote: "Foerster, *op. cit.*, pp. 112 ff.; Marchand, *op. cit.*, pp. 130 ff."
[140] Dieckmann footnote: "See Map 2" [Missing].

and the Marne, in order to be able to gain the right[141] flank of an enemy attacking Nancy, or to oppose a flank attack from the north into the rear of the French fortress line, in other words the enveloping operation of the German 1st and 2nd Armies. The French 5th Army, three active corps strong and assembled north of Langres in the area of Joinville–Chaumont, was the "maneuver army". It would be employed where the *Schwerpunkt* of the German offensive lay. The two groups of reserve divisions, consisting of four divisions each, one in the north in the area of Reims, one further to the south near Troyes, apparently had the same mission, while a third group, also of four reserve divisions, deployed in the area of Vesoul to cover the French right flank.

It cannot be denied that Plan XIV was remarkably well-fashioned and undoubtedly very well adapted to [133] the German operations plan of the time.[142]

As has been said, the plan of the German General Staff which went into force on 1 October 1899 included both a *West* and an *Ostaufmarsch*. The *Westaufmarsch* was intended for a Franco–German war in which Russia would certainly commence hostilities, but was not expected to immediately commit strong forces against Germany. The *Ostaufmarsch* assumed the Russians would commit strong forces immediately. In this case, as the *Aufmarsch* working papers show, a considerable reinforcement of the *Ostheer* was planned: altogether five active corps, one reserve corps and two cavalry divisions for a total of

7 active corps with 14 divisions
2 reserve corps with 4 divisions   (in total, 22 divisions)
4 reserve divisions
5 cavalry divisions

These units were once again, if necessary, drawn for the most part from the armies comprising the enveloping wing of the *Westheer*. Obviously, in case of immediate Russian participation in a Franco-German war the envelopment plan [134] in the west would be dropped. Therefore, before the turn of the century Schlieffen did not yet plan under all circumstances to conduct the enveloping operation.

---

[141] The text says "reste", which makes no sense.
[142] Dieckmann footnote: "Foerster (*op. cit.*, p. 114) leaves the question open as to whether the French General Staff already reckoned with the German enveloping operation, 'as indications for this are not available in the French military literature'. Perhaps the character of the changes that were made – *dispositif d'attente* – permit the assumption that the French suspected or had ascertained that a revision of the German operations plan was considered or had been conducted, without being aware of the specifics."

5. The development of the envelopment plan in the first years of the new century

a.) The 'Free Hand' foreign policy at the turn of the century

[From pages 135 to 142 Dieckmann attacked Bülow's 'Free Hand' foreign policy, which he characterized as attempting to gain advantages by maintaining a neutral position between Russia and England, while pursuing Germany's colonial and commercial interests, especially in the Near East. He was of the opinion that by cooperating with Russia on colonial matters against England, Russia could have been moved to break her alliance with France, clearing the way for a German one-front war against the French, which he said was Schlieffen's goal. On the other hand, Dieckmann contended that Chamberlain could have convinced Salisbury of the advantages of an Anglo-German alliance, had the Germans really wanted one. Such topics are each worthy of a book by themselves. Dieckmann presented little more evidence than his own opinion and three footnotes, one from the *Grosse Politik* and two from the *Berliner Monatshefte*, a journal dedicated to fighting the charge of German "war guilt". This is far too weak a foundation to support such an enormous superstructure. Usually Schlieffen is criticized for failing to inform the political leadership of the intent of his war planning. Dieckmann turned this spear around nicely, and criticized the politicians for their failure to consult Schlieffen concerning the military implications of their foreign policy. Dieckmann, speaking through Schlieffen, concluded: "There is no reason to doubt that an agreement with England would not have been any less welcome for Schlieffen, even though it would not have decreased the pressure on both fronts, but increased it, not to mention the fact that an alliance with England would have made the execution of the envelopment plan impossible. Schlieffen thought that it was unsupportable for Germany to pursue *Weltpolitik*, and with it English enmity, while under pressure on two fronts. He watched with growing mistrust the renewed and considerable reinforcement of German sea power which was initiated by the Fleet Bill of 14 June 1900."]

b.) The Aufmarschpläne *in the first years of the new century*

The great uncertainty in the political situation, which was both the consequence and the reverse side of the policy of the Free Hand, required the Chief of the German General Staff, now as before, to alter his operational concept, and therefore his deployment and operations plans, to meet the various constellations of German foreign policy. The French-German tension formed, so to say, the solid core of these possible constellations. That this tension could discharge itself at any time into war was therefore the basis and the precondition of all his calculations. From this proceeded the most likely case, that France's Russian ally would if necessary [143] support her. Nevertheless, it was still an open question whether Russia would at first passively[143] adopt a waiting attitude or commit itself at once

---

[143] Dieckmann used the military command "Gewehr bei Fuß", which can be translated as "At ease" or "Rest". The sense is that the troops are under arms, but there is no forward movement. Bethmann-Holweg used the same term during the July 1914 crisis.

actively in a war against Germany. The slow and unwieldy Russian mobilization and deployment would presumably exclude decisive action at the beginning in any case.[144] In *Fall* I,[145] where the larger part of the German army deployed in the west while only a few units remained in the east, it had to be calculated that in addition to Belgium, England would also take sides against Germany.[146]

Fall II was also based on a two-front war, but now the larger portion of the German field army was employed against *Russia* [emphasis mine – Z].[147] This situation could become particularly probable if there were an alliance between Britain and Germany.

The deployment plans of the German General Staff in the first years of the 20th century were based on these two situations. They will therefore be considered below in more detail.

1900/01 mobilization year

Fall I
   Westaufmarsch[148]
     6   armies with
    23   active corps[149]
    12   reserve divisions   (in total, 58 divisions)
     7   cavalry divisions
   13½ mixed Landwehr brigades

[144] The assembly of the *Westheer*[150] displayed several <u>considerable changes</u> from that of the plan put into effect in 1 October 1899 for the 1899/1900 mobilization year.[151] Due to a lack of documentary evidence only suppositions can

---

[144] Dieckmann is again trying to show that a one-front war with France was both a practical possibility and Schlieffen's goal. It would be more reasonable to assume that the Russians would recognize that German victory over France meant German hegemony in Europe and that Russia would do everything in its power to prevent this. The variable was the length of time the Germans estimated that the Russians would need to deploy their forces. Hence the two *Aufmarschpläne*. In fact, Schlieffen tested various scenarios to defend East Prussia with small armies – *Aufmarsch* I – until reinforcements arrived from the west. See Zuber, *Inventing the Schlieffen Plan*, pp. 146–9 (1894 *Generalstabsreise Ost* – 'Tannenberg'), pp. 153–6 (1897 *Generalstabsreise Ost*), pp. 164–7 (1899 *Generalstabsreise Ost*), pp. 171–4 (1901 *Generalstabsreise Ost*).

[145] Dieckmann switches terminology. *Aufmarsch* I becomes *Fall* (case) I, *Aufmarsch* II is now *Fall* II. Each *Fall* is now divided into a *Westaufmarsch* and an *Ostaufmarsch*. This probably reflects the terms used by the General Staff at the time.

[146] Schlieffen's west front war games make no such assumption until November–December 1905. The question is, who speaks here, Dieckmann or Schlieffen?

[147] In 1902 and 1903 Schlieffen's *Generalstabsreisen Ost* played an outright *Ostaufmarsch* with the mass of the German army in the east. Nevertheless, the strategy in both was defensive–offensive. Zuber, *Inventing the Schlieffen Plan*, pp. 181–9.

[148] Dieckmann footnote: "See Map 4 and Table . . ."[Both missing].

[149] Dieckmann footnote: "Including the XX Corps, which was to be formed on mobilisation from the excess division of two corps with three divisions, as well a the Guard Reserve Corps, which was to be formed from the 3rd Guard Infantry Division and the 1st Guard Reserve Division."

[150] Dieckmann footnote: "Map 4" [Missing].

[151] Dieckmann footnote: "p. 128 and Map 3" [Map missing].

German Planning: Dieckmann, Der Schlieffenplan

be made concerning possible changes in the operational intentions of the Chief of the German General Staff. It has already been mentioned[152] that Schlieffen had discarded the attack he originally planned to make with the 3rd Army against the Meuse front between Verdun and Toul.[153] He seems to have drawn conclusions from this, for he extended the enveloping wing further to the south to the level of Diedenhofen and considerably reinforced it. Instead of two armies, three (1st, 2nd, 3rd) were provided for the envelopment operation. Because the force protecting the right flank was also strengthened, the strength of the enveloping wing was increased from 8 active corps and 5 reserve divisions to 12 active corps and 6 reserve divisions, more than half of the *Westheer*. The left flank of the enveloping force, in addition to being covered by elements of the 3rd Army, was also protected by the expanded, or expanding, fortresses of Metz and Diedenhofen.[154] The mission of the enveloping wing was, as before, to advance through south Belgium and Luxembourg on the Meuse below Verdun, cross the river and drive onto the rear of the French fortress front.[155]

[145] The centre group of armies of the *Westheer* (4th and 5th), which was to attack Nancy and then drive through the gap in the French front between Toul and Epinal, was weakened (by one active corps and one reserve division) while the left-wing (6th) army was correspondingly strengthened.[156] These changes in the order of battle permit the further assumption that Schlieffen had also decided not to conduct the attack on Nancy. Perhaps he calculated that the increased pressure of the enveloping wing would cause the French to attack the comparatively weak German centre, either by means of a frontal attack or an envelopment. It is probable, however, that the centre armies were to fix the enemy by demonstrations, not by attacking Nancy.[157] Such intentions are thoroughly understandable, for the more enemy forces that were fixed in this manner, the better the situation would be for the enveloping wing.[158]

---

[152] Dieckmann footnote: "p. 123."
[153] Dieckmann footnote: "p. 65."
[154] Dieckmann may have enlarged the size of the enveloping wing by the simple expedient of adding to it the strength of the 3rd Army, which still clearly has the principal mission of providing protection against Verdun. He does so in order to show the further development of Schlieffen's envelopment plan. An indication of his methods can be gained from the fact that he is already attributing defensive capabilities to the fortresses at Metz that they won't possess for at least four years: at this point the construction at Metz and Diedenhofen consisted of little more than raw holes in the ground.
[155] According to Schlieffen's October 1898 document, the principal mission of the right wing was to counterattack against a French advance into south Belgium: pp. 119–21 in Dieckmann's manuscript.
[156] Dieckmann footnote: "The deployment of the Italian army to Alsace was planned and prepared in the same manner as in the previous year."
[157] Schlieffen always said that demonstrations alone would never succeed in fixing the enemy: only an outright attack could accomplish this. See p. 110 below and Zuber, *Inventing the Schlieffen Plan*, p. 211. It would be curious if Schlieffen had made such radical changes as Dieckmann described to his plan without *ever* leaving a written record of any kind. What Dieckmann has again done is construct a case purely out of unsupported assumptions.
[158] And if the relatively passive demonstrations did not fix the French in Lorraine, the enveloping wing was in big trouble.

The preceding assumptions are to a certain degree confirmed by an *Operationsstudie* written on 18 January 1900 by the *Oberquartiermeister* III at that time, Generalmajor Beseler. Beseler began by stating once again the reasons that required the Germans to make an advance to the north of the French fortress line, with the consequent violation of Belgian neutrality. He continued by saying that the enveloping wing [146] must be made "as strong as possible from the very beginning", in order to "permit it to conduct the decisive operations, in which the German armies at and south-east of Metz at first can only play a supporting part". While in the south the enveloping operation "was to be conducted... past Diedenhofen and Verdun", the northern extension of the enveloping wing was limited "by the necessity" "to keep it a certain distance from the Belgian Meuse fortresses of Liège and Namur". This resulted in an operational deployment area of about 80 to 90 kilometers, which provided maneuver space for 10–11 corps. Consequently the enveloping wing would advance from a line Malmedy–Sierck through the southern end of Belgium and through Luxembourg to the Meuse below Verdun, "cross the river, and the German offensive... will continue to the south towards Reims and Verdun". It was particularly important that between the enveloping wing and the forces deployed in Lorraine "a reciprocal action take place... so that" the forces in Lorraine "must draw as many French units to themselves or prevent them as much as possible from withdrawing and changing front to the north through energetic attack demonstrations". The "German units remaining on the Moselle" will first be able "to break through the French border fortifications and open the German lines of communication to the east at the point" when the enveloping wing has succeeded in "defeating the opposing French forces" [147] and penetrating into the rear of the French fortress front.

Beseler saw the principal difficulty in the entire operation in the fact that it would be hardly likely that the assembly of the main body of the German *Westheer* on the Belgian-Luxembourg border could be kept a secret and the French high command would at once arrange for countermeasures to insure the security of their northern flank. The most important precondition for the success of the German operation was therefore "to conduct the planned offensive quickly and with full force, in order, if at all possible, to arrive at a complete decision through the first blows".

Ostaufmarsch
Two armies would remain in the east with
  2 active corps
  5 reserve divisions   (in total, 10 divisions)
  3 cavalry divisions
  14 Landwehr brigades

The assembly of the *Ostheer* would be conducted in the same manner and with the same mission as it had been since the 1 October 1899 plan for the 1899/1900 mobilization year.[159]

---

[159] Dieckmann footnote: "p. 128."

Fall II
Ostaufmarsch
Four armies with
14 active corps
15 reserve divisions			(in total, 44 divisions)
 6 cavalry divisions
14 mixed Landwehr brigades

[148] Two of the *Ostheer* armies would deploy with a total of five active corps, ten reserve divisions and three cavalry divisions on the southern border of the provinces of West and East Prussia behind the general line Thorn–Strasbourg–Lautenburg–Rudzanny. The other two armies with nine active corps, five reserve divisions and three cavalry divisions on the eastern border of East Prussia behind the general line Arys–Orlowen–Darkehmen–Stallupönen–Pillkallen–Schmolleningken.

Although there is no documentary proof, the intent was obviously to conduct an offensive against the Narew and the Niemen.

Westaufmarsch
Four armies with
10 active corps
 3 reserve divisions			(in total, 24 divisions)
 5 cavalry divisions
14½ mixed Landwehr brigades

A document written by Schlieffen in November 1899, which gives an indication of his operational intent, obviously served as the basis for the *Westaufmarsch* in *Fall* II. The document states that when the greater part of the German army was employed against Russia and the smaller part against France, "the French will not be able to avoid assuming the offensive". If they do not do so, "in spite of their responsibilities towards their ally" "the campaign in the west" will be limited to "each side observing the other". "In such a situation the Germans cannot take the offensive".

[149] Thereupon, presuming that the French took the offensive, Schlieffen examined the probable French courses of action. Their advance would "hardly be restricted to the area Metz–Saarburg. There is not enough room here for their 19 corps. If they extend themselves to the east, their right flank will come up against Molsheim [Fortress Kaiser Wilhelm II] the Breusch position and Strasbourg. If they avoid these obstacles and send an army over the Rhine, it will be lost for the battle against the enemy main body." The question therefore arises for the French "as to whether they want to send their left wing to the north around Diedenhofen or just around Metz.[160] They can do one or the other, or they can send the left wing south

---

[160] Dieckmann's text said "... to the north around Metz or also just around Diedenhofen". Aside from the fact that the sentence is poorly worded in general, this makes no sense, because Diedenhofen is north of Metz. Dieckmann seems to have switched Metz with Diedenhofen.

of Metz, the moment will always come when this wing will lose its firm support [with the main body]. This offers the Germans the opportunity to attack the much stronger French army at a point where the Germans enjoy numerical superiority." The most promising operation was an attack on the French left wing; it was therefore imperative to mass the largest part of the German *Westheer* against it. If this attack were conducted "from the very beginning, as soon as the mobilization [sic – deployment] of the units has been completed, the French will take countermeasures and the intended flank attack will fail. We will only reach our goal if we attain surprise."

As preparation for the planned counterattack, Schlieffen considered the following:

[150] 1.) The border security measures would be conducted as in *Fall* I. Therefore, VIII Corps would assemble in the area of Trier, XIV Corps in and around Metz.

2.) The cavalry divisions would deploy in Lorraine in such a manner "that they can quickly be concentrated in one direction or the other".

3.) The majority of the active corps would remain "initially in their garrisons and would only be deployed on order". The deployment assembly areas would be prepared on both sides of the lower Moselle, approximately in the vicinity between Prüm and Saarbrücken.

4.) The reserve divisions would cover the left flank or be used to garrison Strasbourg and Metz.

Some indications concerning the planned operation are evident in the first *Grosse Generalstabsreise* in 1900, which was based on a situation in the west similar to that in *Fall* II. In his exercise critique, the Chief of the General Staff said, among other things, that in this situation it was not advisable for the Germans to stay purely on the defensive, principally because of the danger that the much stronger French could go around a defensive position, no matter how strong it was locally. In addition, the French had the ability, in case their attack against the German defensive front failed, to withdraw to their fortress line, which would naturally increase the difficulties for the Germans considerably.

[151] On the other hand, given their great numerical inferiority, it was obvious that the Germans could not take the offensive from the very beginning. They must rather allow the enemy to attack first. It would be just as great a mistake to conduct a frontal counterattack against the attacking enemy. It "was necessary to limit oneself to attacking an enemy wing with numerical superiority. In order to be successful, the strongest possible forces must be concentrated against the enemy flank. If this is conducted according to a fixed plan, on about the 5th day of mobilization, we must worry that the enemy will become aware of the danger that threatens him.[161] He will then not advance as he previously intended, but rather, using the protection of his fortified line, swing to present his front to our flank attack. It seems more promising to begin the rail movement of the forces with

---

[161] Dieckmann's text left out the "not", resulting in "it is necessary to insure that the enemy learns of the danger that threatens him", which is nonsense and contradicts the rest of the passage he is citing.

which we intend to conduct the flank attack only when the enemy has already begun his advance and has proceeded beyond his fortified line. If the enemy then hears that we have begun to move troops by rail, the conclusions he draws from this will hardly be sure enough to cause a fundamental change in the operation he has already begun. If he learns from his cavalry in the course of time of the danger that threatens his flank, it might well be too late for him to throw equal forces against it."

[152] A counterattack against the French left flank, which would probably seek to outflank to the north the German forces deployed on the defensive front between Metz and Saarburg, offered the best chance of success. If this counterattack were successful, it might be possible not only to push back the enemy left flank, "but to force . . . the entire French army away from its fortifications and onto the upper Rhine".

1901/02 mobilization year

Initial Situation: Two-front war. *Fall* I / *Fall* II: as in the previous year.

Fall I
Westaufmarsch:[162]
Six armies with
22   active corps
11   reserve divisions[163]   (in total, 56 divisions)
 8   cavalry divisions
13½ mixed Landwehr brigades

The assembly of the *Westheer*[164] was conducted in essentially the same manner as in the previous year.[165]

[153] *Ostaufmarsch*
Two armies with
3 active corps
4 reserve divisions   (in total, 10 divisions)
3 cavalry divisions
14 mixed Landwehr brigades

The assembly and mission of the *Ostheer* also remained the same, that being:
One active corps, a reserve division, a cavalry division and four mixed Landwehr brigades were to deploy in the Insterburg–Gumbinnen–Darkehmen area

---

[162] Dieckmann footnote: "Table . . ." [Missing].
[163] Dieckmann footnote: "In addition, one reserve division in Metz and one in Strasbourg."
[164] Dieckmann footnote: "Map 5" [Missing].
[165] Dieckmann footnote: "p. 144 and Map 4 [Map missing]. No documentation was available concerning the deployment of the Italian army. It is possible that it was no longer planned at all because the dispatch of Italian forces to the German west front appeared less and less likely (see Foerster, *op. cit.*, pp. 79 ff.)."

one active corps at Allenstein
one active corps between Deutsch-Eylau and Bischofswerder
one cavalry division at Strasburg and one cavalry division forward of Mogilno
one reserve division at Bromberg and one at Posen
six mixed Landwehr brigades between Allenstein and Posen
one reserve division and four mixed Landwehr brigades in Silesia

These weak forces had the mission of delaying an attack by the superior enemy forces against the Vistula for as long as possible, but in any case long enough to allow reinforcements to be sent to them from the west. Their arrival created a new military situation, which one could call *Fall* Ia. This situation was played in the 2nd 1901 *Große Generalstabsreise*. It was a continuation of the situation played in the 1st 1901 *Große Generalstabsreise*, in which the German *Westheer* was able in the fourth week of the war to win a decisive victory over the French on the left bank of the Rhine near the Belgian border. In the meantime the weak German forces in the east had withdrawn, [154] partly to Königsberg, partly behind the line Allenstein–Osterode–Rosenberg. At the same time the Austrians were advancing from Galicia, partly against the Russian South-West Army, partly against the Bug Army. As soon as the victory had been gained in the west, nine active corps and three cavalry divisions were sent by rail to the east. The exercise ended in a draw.

Fall II
Ostaufmarsch[166]
Four armies with
 15 active corps
 9 reserve divisions[167]   (in total, 39 divisions)
 4 cavalry divisions
 14 mixed Landwehr brigades

The assembly of the 5th and 6th Armies (six active corps, five reserve divisions, two cavalry divisions) was similar to that of the previous year[168] behind the line Thorn–Strasburg–Lautenburg. On the other hand the other two armies (7th and 8th with nine active corps, four reserve divisions and two cavalry divisions) in contrast to the previous year[169] deployed immediately to the East Prussian border on the line Johannisburg–Lyck–Maggrabowa–Filipow–Szittkehmen–Wyschtynez–Kibarty–Schirwindt.

Due to the lack of documentation it is not possible to state the concept for the operation in *Fall* II. Obviously it was intended that a decisive blow was to be delivered against the Russian Niemen Army, while [155] a simultaneous attack by the 5th and 6th Armies would fix the enemy Narew Army in place.[170]

[166] Dieckmann footnote: "Table . . ." [Missing].
[167] Dieckmann footnote: "In addition, one reserve division in Graudenz and one in Thorn."
[168] Dieckmann footnote: "p. 148."
[169] Dieckmann footnote: "p. 148."
[170] Dieckmann footnote: "See Boetticher, *op. cit.*, pp. 275 f."

Westaufmarsch[171]
Four armies with
- 10 active corps
- 6 reserve divisions[172]   (in total, 27 divisions)
- 5 cavalry divisions
- 14½ mixed Landwehr brigades

Concerning the mission of the *Westheer* the general instructions to the army commanders (*Aufmarschanweisungen*) for the previous year gave the following instructions:[173] "For the numerically inferior German *Westheer* it is important to assemble in the most favorable possible posture, that is to say, so that it can launch a surprise attack on the wing or flank of the enemy army. For this purpose it appears expedient to initially leave the active corps in their garrisons and to begin the rail movement as soon as the direction of the enemy offensive is determined." However, the probable assembly areas were determined: they are shown on Map 6 [Missing].

1902/03 mobilization year

Initial situation: Two-front war. *Fall* I: as in the previous year. *Fall* II: ⅔ of the field army in the west, ⅓ in the east.

[156] *Fall* I
Westaufmarsch[174]
Seven armies with
- 25 active corps[175]
- 10 reserve divisions[176]   (in total, 60 divisions)
- 8 cavalry divisions
- 14½ mixed Landwehr brigades

As Map 7 [missing] shows, the deployment of the German *Westheer* differed considerably from its predecessors. The principal mass (2nd–6th armies with 18 active corps, followed by four reserve divisions) should assemble closely massed together immediately on the border with France and Luxembourg, in the area between Echternach and Champeny, while the 1st Army (four active corps, four reserve divisions) was separated from the main body as the right wing and assembled widely dispersed behind the general line Eupen–Neuerburg. The left flank was formed by the 7th Army with three corps and two reserve divisions in Alsace.[177]

---

[171] Dieckmann footnote: "Table . . ." [Missing].
[172] Dieckmann footnote: "In addition, one reserve division in Metz and one in Strasbourg."
[173] Dieckmann footnote: "pp. 148 ff."
[174] Dieckmann footnote: "Table . . ." [Missing].
[175] Dieckmann footnote: "The increase in the number of mobilized army corps is discussed on pp. 166 ff."
[176] Dieckmann footnote: "In addition, one reserve division at Metz."
[177] Dieckmann footnote: "There is again no information at all concerning the deployment of the Italian army to Alsace in the 1902/03 mobilization year."

This deployment was obviously based on a <u>considerably different operational intent</u>, concerning which we can make no secure statement. Nevertheless there are a few indications available which permit certain suppositions and conclusions. What emerges from these indications first of all is that Schlieffen had assumed that the German envelopment plan was known to the French and that to meet this threat to their north flank they had taken defensive measures by assembling a strong force on their left [157] flank. Further, Schlieffen seems to have decided that German troops would be permitted to enter Belgian and Luxembourg territory only after their neutrality had been first violated by the French.[178] Proceeding from these assumptions, and on the basis of the deployment of the army and the available indications, Schlieffen's operational intent can be reconstructed as follows:

Of the three armies (4th–6th) deploying on the French border south of Diedenhofen, the 4th with four active corps and two reserve divisions was to immediately attack the Meuse front between Verdun and Toul, while the other two armies with seven corps and two reserve divisions advanced on Nancy and the gap in the French fortress front. It was expected that the French forces assembled on their left flank would at the same time attempt to envelop the north flank of the German attack front. To accomplish this they would, in order to avoid the area of the German fortress front of Metz and Diedenhofen, have to cross Belgian and Luxembourg territory. Thereby it would be possible for first the German 2nd and 3rd Armies (seven active corps) and then also the 1st Army (four corps, four reserve divisions), which was also responsible for flank security, to advance into Belgium and Luxembourg and fall on the enemy enveloping wing, and having defeated it, for their own part go over to the attack against the Meuse below Verdun.

[158] In fact, in the spring of 1902 Schlieffen gave several senior General Staff officers the requirement of studying a simultaneous attack against the Meuse front between Verdun and Toul as well as against Nancy. In his "comments" (of 16 May 1902) Schlieffen said: "An attack on the well-defended line of the Meuse forts between Toul and Epinal presents not inconsiderable difficulties and will probably only succeed if it is supported by an envelopment to the north of Verdun (! Dieckmann). Such an envelopment will not surprise the French. They evidently intend to defend their front with limited forces and hold five corps ready some distance behind their left wing. This force needs only to swing left and deploy in order to present a new front to the German envelopment. Four reserve divisions at Reims complete the defensive measures and threaten the right flank of the attacker.[179] The enveloping army must therefore be brought to a strength which would be capable of defeating the expected fourteen French divisions. Having said that, it cannot be expected that this alone will bring success. The hope . . . that the army, which advances against the Meuse forts, can rather quietly await the effect of the envelopment, will be sorely deceived.[159] The enveloping army, which will be completely separated from the rest of the German forces by the Meuse

---

[178] Dieckmann footnote: "Boetticher, *op. cit.*, p. 264."

[179] Dieckmann footnote: "These assumptions correspond, although not in every detail, still by and large to the actual intentions of the French General Staff, as contained in the French deployment plan XIV of 1898 which was in force at this time."

forts, if left without support, will finally have to deal with the entire French army. Here, as always, neither the frontal attack alone, nor the flank attack or envelopment alone, will lead to success, but only the two in conjunction. In order to assist the envelopment in achieving success, as many enemy forces as possible must be fixed by a [frontal] attack, not merely by waiting patiently before the enemy front." It was to be hoped that through such an attack the French forces in the fortress line would be held in place and "that they will not be able to turn towards the north".

What were the grounds that led the Chief of the General Staff to come to these truly most surprising changes in his operational intentions, which stand in stark contrast to his previous ideas? First, he may have done so due to the assumption mentioned above that the French had taken countermeasures against the expected German envelopment. But this does not explain why Schlieffen did not believe that he could march into Belgium and Luxembourg until the neutrality of these countries was first violated by France. It may be suspected that there is here a connection with the British–German alliance negotiations, which as we know, were in 1901 once again being very vigorously conducted.[180] After the collapse of the previous negotiations, no effort was spared to postpone reopening the issue. Then in the fall of 1901, that is, at the time that the General Staff commenced preparatory work for the next year's deployment plan, in Germany the option for Britain finally gained the ascendancy and the Germans began to press the British for a decision. If these led to a positive conclusion, then, as we know, for the Germans it would only be possible to conduct the march through Belgium after the French had violated Belgian neutrality. The negotiations continued through to winter. However, it now became clear that the procrastinating policy of Bülow and Holstein bore bitter fruit. They were too late! The British became less and less interested and finally turned down the German alliance flat. That was the beginning of the end for the policy of the Free Hand.

Ostaufmarsch: as in 1901/02[181]

Fall II
Westaufmarsch
Five armies with
19   active corps
 6   reserve divisions   (in total, 44 divisions)
 6   cavalry divisions
14½ mixed Landwehr brigades

In *Fall* II the deployment differed considerably from those previously. The strength of the *Westheer* had been increased considerably and now constituted about ⅔ of the entire German field army. Previously the assembly of the *Westheer* had been dependent on the general direction of the expected French offensive. Now it deployed immediately to the western border. The supporting documents are

---

[180] Dieckmann footnote: "pp. 139 ff."
[181] Dieckmann footnote: "pp. 153 f."

lacking, so that again only suppositions can be drawn concerning the intended [161] operation. Obviously the 1st Army (four active corps, four reserve divisions) assembled as a maneuver army in the Rhineland, was to attack in the flank any French attempt to outflank the north wing of the German main body assembled in Lorraine (2nd–4th Armies with 11 active corps). If the French stayed on the defensive or did nothing, the German deployment permitted the possibility of an outflanking attack against the Meuse below Verdun. In any case, even in *Fall* II the strength and deployment of the *Westheer* acquired a clearly recognizable offensive tendency.

Ostaufmarsch:
Three armies with
  9 active corps
  6 reserve divisions[182]   (in total, 24 divisions)
  5 cavalry divisions
  14 mixed Landwehr brigades

The *Ostheer* was to deploy with:
the 6th Army, with two active corps and four reserve divisions, behind the line Gollub–Ortelsburg–Puppen
the 7th Army, with five active corps, behind the line Bialla–Lyck–Maggrabowa–Goldap
the 8th Army, with two active corps and one reserve division, at and south of Stallupönen.

As far as it is possible to determine from the scant supporting documents, the 7th Army was to make the main attack against [162] the Niemen, covered on its left flank and supported by the 8th Army, while the 6th Army demonstrated against the Narew to fix in place, as far as possible, the Russian forces deployed there.

It can therefore be seen that the considerably changed *Fall* II also allowed the possibility of conducting an offensive in the west as well as in the east, a possibility that was suitable to the military-political situation that would have arisen after a possible German-British alliance.

1903/04 mobilization year

Initial situation: Two-front war. *Fall* I: Assembly of the largest part of the field army in the west. *Fall* II: Assembly of a larger part of the field army in the east.

---

[182] Dieckmann footnote: "Including a reserve division designated for Silesia. In *Fall* II there were two fewer reserve divisions, so that the field army included 14 reserve divisions in *Fall* I and 12 in *Fall* II."

Fall I
Westaufmarsch:[183]
Seven armies with
  25 active corps
  15 reserve divisions   (in total, 65 divisions)
   7 cavalry divisions
  17½ mixed Landwehr brigades

As Map 9 [missing] shows, the deployment of the previous year has again been changed. If the reasons we have given which motivated Schlieffen to adopt this unusual deployment are accurate, one must assume that in the meantime the final collapse of the British-German [162] alliance negotiations[184] were the grounds to return to the old deployment plans. In large part the assembly of the *Westheer* remained that as planned in the previous years, so that it can be assumed that the operational intentions of the Chief of the General staff remained the same as previously. The two armies (6th and 7th) with the mission to guard the left flank of the *Westheer* have been conspicuously reinforced. Together they now included six active corps and four reserve divisions, of which an active corps and two reserve divisions were indeed to deploy on the right bank of the Rhine. This reinforcement of the left wing of the army was obviously [164] due to the fact that in the future the Germans could not count at all on the appearance of the Italian forces in Alsace. The renewal of the Triple Alliance on 28 June 1902 contained a clause which so much as completely released Italy from the requirement to send forces to the German western front.[185]

Ostaufmarsch:
One army with
   3 active corps   (in total, 10 divisions)
   4 reserve divisions
  14 mixed Landwehr brigades

---

[183] Dieckmann footnote: "Table . . ." [Missing].

[184] Dieckmann footnote: "At the end of September 1902 the Chief of the General staff was sent, on the Kaiser's orders, a longish letter from the head of the German *chargé d'affairs*, Freiherr von Eckardstein, of 14 September 1902, in which he reported a discussion he had had with Chamberlain (*Große Politik* XVII No. 5094). While expressing vehement criticism of the previous conduct of the German government in the question of an alliance, which he had so strongly supported, the British minister told the German diplomat point-blank that an alliance between the two countries was no longer possible. Indeed, Chamberlain frankly stated that Germany must now reckon in the future with British hostility. This report is, in addition, the single document that can be shown from the records of the Foreign Office and the General Staff, that the Chief of the General Staff received concerning the British-German alliance negotiations." If this was the only document that it can be shown that Schlieffen had seen concerning British-German alliance negotiations, then Dieckmann's contention that Schlieffen altered his war plan to conform to every change in these negotiations collapses. Nor is there any indication that after September 1902 Schlieffen considered British hostility to be certain. The first time British units appear against Germany in one of Schlieffen's exercises in the November-December 1905 *Kriegsspiel*.

[185] Dieckmann footnote: "Foerster, *op. cit.*, pp. 84 f."

The deployment and mission of the *Ostheer* remained the same as previously.

Fall II

There is no information whatsoever concerning the planned _Westaufmarsch_. Certain indications can be gained however from the 1st *Große Generalstabsreise* in 1903, in which the *Westheer* contained only about half of the German field army. "Given an almost 2–1 enemy superiority" said the 'Situation for Blue' [German situation] "it appears advisable to concentrate the main body against one of the enemy wings, in hopes of attaining numerical superiority here, with the justifiable expectation of winning a decisive partial victory. For various reasons it was decided to attack the enemy left wing and consequently to deploy eight active corps, two cavalry divisions and four reserve divisions in the [165] Prussian Rhineland on the left [north] bank of the Moselle. In case the French attempt, as is not unlikely, to envelop the German right flank through Belgium or Luxembourg, or at least through Luxembourg, these eight active corps, etc., will be able to attack the enemy enveloping army concentrically in conjunction with two corps deployed on the lower Saar and the troops assembled in the area of Metz–Diedenhofen (three active corps, six reserve divisions). If we gain a decisive victory here, the Germans would then turn against that portion of the French forces which may have penetrated between Metz and the Vosges. In order to initially block these, seven reserve divisions were deployed between Saarlouis and Saarbrücken and two active corps behind their left flank. The mobile reserve of Strasbourg consisted of four reserve divisions and that of the upper Rhine fortifications two reserve divisions, while Neubreisach received one reserve brigade. In addition, the ersatz (replacement) battalions of the XIV, XV and XVI, as well as elements of those of the VIII and XIII Corps were concentrated in the fortresses of the theatre of war."

Concerning the intended _Ostaufmarsch_ in *Fall* II, for which supporting material is also lacking, an indication is provided by a document written by Schlieffen on 5 December 1902, which was obviously written to give directions for its preparation. In this document the Chief of the General Staff deployed 13 active corps, 10 reserve divisions and 5 cavalry divisions in the east. The main body (9 active corps, 4 reserve divisions) were to deploy on the general line Thorn–Ortelsburg–[166] Rudzany, from there advance on the Narew between Pultusk and Lomza and throw back the weak Russian army there. Thereupon it was to advance on a broad front against the Bug and link up with Austrian forces advancing from the south and fight the decisive battle. The German forces deploying in front of and north of the Masurian Lakes (4 active corps, 6 reserve divisions) had the mission of covering the left flank of the main army and to envelop the Russian forces assembled on the Niemen from the north.[186]

[The operational portion of Dieckmann's manuscript ends here.]

---

[186] This document contradicts practically everything Schlieffen had said over the last 13 years both concerning an offensive in the east as well as the need to be able to transfer forces from the east to the west. In addition, Dommes says in 'Operationen gegen Rußland' that the 1903/04 *Ostaufmarsch* in *Aufmarsch* II was reduced to 'a small force', p. 12.

c.) The "Schlieffen Corps"

[From pages 166 to 175 Dieckmann discussed Schlieffen's attempts to increase the number of maneuver units in the field army. This consists almost entirely of a repetition of what he had said earlier concerning the army bill of 1899 (p. 109) or what had been said in the *Kriegswirtschaft und Kriegsrüstung* volume of the official history (Text volume, pp. 65 ff., Annex volume pp. 52ff., 60 ff., 76, 78, Table 11), which primarily concerns the creation of the *Kriegskorps*. In 1899 Schlieffen maintained that Germany was not strong enough to fight a one-front war with France alone, not to speak of a two-front war against France and Russia. He demanded that all trained infantrymen, active or reserve, be formed into maneuver divisions and corps. Dieckmann acknowledged that there was no artillery, technical troops or supply units for new formations. Dieckmann said that the War Minister, Goßler, was blinded by the supposed successes of the 'Free Hand' policy and opposed any increase in the army as being unnecessary, indeed injurious: the army was already too large and Goßler wanted to concentrate on quality, not quantity. The War Minister said the money for new units was simply not forthcoming from a Reichstag that was focused on building a battle fleet. He also objected that Schlieffen's improvisations to avoid these problems did as much harm as good. Dieckmann's discourse on increasing the army closed in 1902. Schlieffen had succeeded in obtaining the creation of five *Kriegskorps*, a mix of odd excess active army and reserve units (XX, XXI, XXII, XXIII, XXIV, Guard Reserve Corps: however, it had already been intended since 1897 to organize XX and the Guard Reserve Corps on mobilization, and XXIII and XXIV would be disbanded in 1904). Dieckmann acknowledged that Schlieffen's intent was to transform the *Kriegskorps* into active army corps. On the other hand, the formation of the *Kriegskorps* had the result that the number of available reserve units was reduced. Schlieffen then argued for increasing the number of reserve units and upgrading them to give them the combat capabilities of active army units, although he acknowledged that there were no officers or non-commissioned officers for such units. The War Minister said that this was impossible. There already weren't enough supply units and artillery for the existing units: creating new ones would only make matters worse, and neither the government nor the Reichstag was going to approve funds to even repair the current deficiencies.]

[Dieckmann's text ends completely here]

[Dieckmann's intent for the rest of his study can perhaps be seen in the chapters of his work he listed in the 'Table of Contents' (see below) which were apparently never completed – unlike the completed chapters, these have no page numbers. These chapters surely leave the impression that Dieckmann thought that the Schlieffen plan was intended for a one-front preventive war with France in 1906. This was, however, a commonly held notion, which Dieckmann shared with none other than Wilhelm Groener. There is no evidence that Dieckmann ever had access to any of Schlieffen's planning documents in 1904, 1905, or the January–February 1906 Schlieffen plan *Denkschrift* itself.]

Table of Contents

II. The Envelopment Plan . . . .
   d. The Fortress Problem and the Operations Plans of the Chief of the General Staff

III. The Encirclement Plan
   1. The Franco-British Entente and the Russo-Japanese War
   2. The Great Chance
   3. Bülow's Victory over Schlieffen

Annexes

[In addition to the text and the missing maps and tables, Dieckmann's study also included at least twenty annexes, of which Annexes 1, and perhaps 3 or 4a (there is an unnumbered annex) are missing. The absence of annexes concerning operational planning is striking.]

Annex 2 is a typescript eight pages long of a *Denkschrift* written in Schlieffen's own hand on 25 August 1889, when he was an *Oberquartiermeister* in the General Staff. Schlieffen says that if war were to break out between Germany and France in that year, the balance of mobilized forces would be:

| Germany | 1482 battalions | 603 squadrons | 595 batteries |
| France | 1595 | 487 | 664 |

The French army grew more than the German from year to year because all conscripts in each year group were called to the colors. According to the most recent law this would be 224,595 men for the army, while in 1887 the Germans had only conscripted 174,194 for the army: the French conscripted 73.5% of each year group, the Germans 44% of theirs. By employing French standards, the Germans should conscript another 112,000 men annually. Nor should the Germans conscript a higher percentage of men, and in return reduce the period of service from three to two years.

"Although France has a population of only 37,103,689, with a yearly conscript group of 316,090 men, and Germany a population of 46,855,704 and a conscript year group of 404,599, they already have a larger army than we do in peacetime, and in the same manner they can in war put an enormous army in the field, and in the future this disparity in both areas will increase.

In spite of having the larger army, in war France, in comparison to Germany, has the easier mission. It will be opposed by two enemies, but it can deal with one of them without great difficulty. Two active corps and the fleet will, from their point of view, be sufficient to keep Italy on the defensive or inactive. The vast majority of their forces can be employed against Germany. Germany must, however, fight against the two most numerous armies in the world. With Austria's assistance we can admittedly gain numerical superiority on one front. On the other hand, as was said at the beginning, it will be only ⅔ as strong as the French army in infantry and only ⅗ as strong in artillery."

[Schlieffen's conclusion was that Germany needed a military reform along the lines of that instituted by King Wilhelm in the 1860s. This led to a constitutional crisis that only subsided after 1866 – reason enough for the German government to be unenthusiastic about Schlieffen's ideas.]

Annex ? – unnumbered – From War Minister Generalleutnant von Kaltenborn-Stachau to Chief of General Staff, 11 August 1893 (six pages): Increasing the authorized strength of corps in border districts; reinforcing East Prussia with four battalions; military control, arming and equipping of Landsturm.

Annex 4b Schlieffen to Kaltenborn-Stachau, hand-written draft, 30 August 1893 (four pages): Border security in East Prussia.

Annex 5 Schlieffen to War Minister Bronsart von Schellendorff, hand-written draft by the Chief of the *Aufmarschabteilung*, Lieutenant-colonel von Heeringen, 11 December 1893 (12 pages): Landsturm in the border security of East Prussia.

Annex 6 Schlieffen to Bronsart von Schellendorff, hand-written draft, 6 January 1894 (three pages): Defense against Russian cavalry raids in East Prussia on mobilization. Schlieffen says that

" . . . the discussions which the Imperial Chancellor had with the previous War Minister and myself concerning the contents of our alliances leave no doubt that the initiative will lie in the hands of our eastern opponent. Initially we are therefore required to await events."

" . . . the war that awaits us will not be conducted as in earlier times. The Russians have completely broken with the principle that an army does not fight the unarmed inhabitants of the enemy state. The Russian cavalry will not attack into our territory in order to seek out our cavalry and fight cavalry battles, but will intentionally set out to pillage and destroy in order to spread fear and panic. In a war which the enemy will conduct not against soldiers, but against all, then all must be armed."

Annex 7a Bronsart von Schellendorff to Schlieffen 30 January 1894 (two pages): Reply to above. Schlieffen's plans rejected.

Annex 7b Schlieffen to Bronsart von Schellendorff, hand-written draft, 1 February 1894 (two pages): Reply to above.

Annex 8 Schlieffen to Bronsart von Schellendorff, draft by Major Sixt von Armin, 17 February 1894 (five pages): Reply to letter of 30 January 1894 (Annex 7a). Employment of Landsturm in border security in neighboring countries.

Annex 9 Schlieffen to Kaltenborn-Stachau, draft, 18 January 1892 (2 pages): Argues for the use of heavy foot artillery, and not merely flat-trajectory field guns, against fortified positions in maneuver warfare.

Annex 10 General-Inspector of Foot Artillery Generalleutnant Sallbach to Schlieffen, hand-written, 12 June 1893 (three pages): Need for six more mobile heavy field artillery battalions, draught horses and drivers.

Annex 11 Schlieffen to Bronsart von Schellendorff, draft by Lieutenant-colonel Heeringen with corrections by Schlieffen, 24 December 1894 (six pages):

"I have already addressed to the Royal War Ministry the inadequacy of the mobile heavy artillery for the initial requirements of a future war. The preparatory work for the coming mobilization year has once again confirmed these concerns.

On the western theatre of war there are only two gaps in the entire French fortress line extending on our border along the Meuse and Moselle, one north of Verdun and the other north of Epinal. They lie so far separated from each other that it is not possible for our field army to use both.

If we attempt to advance north of Verdun, our corps advancing further to the south come up against the fortifications on the middle Meuse. In this case we would also have to attack Nancy, which projects forwards like a bastion. On both sides of Fort Frouard we can surely expect numerous batteries with heavy artillery from Toul in addition to extensive field fortifications, which we must also attack.

In an advance between Fort Pont St. Vincent and Epinal a similar attack on Nancy would be unavoidable for the same reasons. In addition, according to whether we employ our army further to the north or to the south, either our left wing will come up against the French forts on the upper Moselle or our right wing against the fortifications on the middle Meuse.

However we arrange our offensive against France, we will always be required to attack Nancy and at the same time either some forts on the middle Meuse or some on the upper Moselle.

If we do not take the offensive and allow the enemy to bring forward his reserve formations and attack us, this will not reduce our need for more mobile heavy artillery. If we defeat the enemy attack, we must still deal with those fortifications in the same manner as previously.

Therefore, we can only hope to attain success in a war against France if we have enough heavy artillery to overwhelm the enemy fortifications" [15 howitzer battalions and 9 heavy mortar battalions for the actual attacks, plus 4 battalions for the other armies. With one regiment in the east, the German army was short 9½ howitzer battalions, or 38 howitzer batteries. The heavy artillery also needed to conduct more realistic training.]

Annex 12 Schlieffen to War Ministry, draft by Colonel Rothe, 3 June 1891 (one page): Each corps should be able to form two maneuver brigades out of ersatz (replacement) battalions.

Annex 13 Schlieffen to War Ministry, 18 June 1892 (7 pages):

"The continual growth of the military power of Russia and France and especially the efforts of the latter power to make larger forces available for field operations through organizational measures, requires that we in turn strive to reinforce the field army by all possible means.

Aside from an increase in the army in peacetime, we can, with our current organization, take effective measures towards this goal.

1. Through increased use of the Landwehr in the field army and [their replacement] as fortress garrisons by the Landsturm [which Schlieffen says will free up 70 Landwehr battalions for the field army].

2. Through transfer to 4th battalions [which were to become field battalions on mobilization] or Reserve battalions of trained personnel that are currently assigned to replacement battalions of the field army [which Schlieffen says will allow the creation of 60 to 80 battalions, for a total of 130–150 battalions.]

3 . . . . I recommend further in this matter

a) That a 4th battalion be established in every infantry regiment

b) Each army corps creates as many reserve and Landwehr battalions as there are Landwehr districts, and in addition as many battalions as there are personnel available to fill them . . . .

c) Each three battalions are immediately to be organized into a reserve or Landwehr regiment, for each of which a replacement battalion is in general at first to provide the cadre . . . . For several corps this will result in nothing less than the establishment of a reserve corps of three to four brigades in place of a reserve division, by many others the formation of a Landwehr division will be possible in place of a Landwehr brigade. In order to save personnel for higher echelon staffs, the division headquarters can be eliminated and the brigades directly subordinated to the corps headquarters.

The current number of reserve cavalry regiments must be adequate for the future. An increase in the quantity of reserve artillery is imperative, so that each division receives its division artillery and for each corps a corps artillery of about six batteries can be created.

An increase in the number of reserve ammunition companies would be desirable. An increase in the number of reserve supply companies on the other hand can be dispensed with, at least for the corps to be deployed in the west.

The Landwehr divisions can draw on a number of Landwehr squadrons and Landwehr batteries now assigned as fortress garrisons and thereby obtain a makeshift provision of these types of units . . . . Given the missions that will be assigned to the Landwehr divisions, it will not be necessary to establish Landwehr munitions or supply companies.

These will in addition in general have to make do with requisitioned [horse-drawn] vehicles in place of military vehicles. To reduce the shortage of horses on the other hand, a number of corps-level supply companies could be eliminated in the corps earmarked to be sent to the west. According to calculations that I have had made, the ration supply in the west in the initial period of the campaign could be conducted with two supply companies fewer [per corps] than is currently planned . . . .

It is clear to me that my requests will cause further difficulties for the mobilization, including the provision of officers, but I am of the opinion that we must overcome these difficulties in order not to remain behind our neighbors in the utilization of our entire manpower . . . .

Finally, I would like to express my conviction that we must . . . prepare to utilize our entire manpower without delay and therefore cannot wait for a possible army bill in peacetime, nor need we wait for one."

Annex 14 Schlieffen to the War Ministry, draft by Major von Einem, 19 November 1892 (three pages): Use of oldest Landwehr men (Landwehr II) as fortress garrisons, thereby releasing Landwehr brigades to reinforce the field army "because I regard it as an unavoidable necessity in a two-front war to make all militarily useful forces immediately available".

Annex 15 Schlieffen to War Ministry, draft, with corrections by Schlieffen, 6 August 1895 (two pages): Reserve corps should be reinforced with Landwehr artillery batteries.

Annex 16 Schlieffen to Kaltenborn-Stachau, personally hand-written draft, 19 October 1893, (two pages): Reserve divisions are not equal in combat ability to active army divisions, but given Germany's position, must be used in combat to the limit of their capacity, as must the Landwehr. Reserve divisions must also be organized in reserve corps.

Annex 17 Letter from Bronsart von Schellendorf to Commanding General I Corps, draft, no date, the letter was never sent (four pages): Border security. Dieckmann probably included this document because Bronsart says that an additional cavalry division and an infantry brigade were not sent to East Prussia "for political reasons" [emphasis in document]. Bronsart also says that a Russian "bolt from the blue" is now no longer expected and that training need not be cancelled out of fear of such an attack – which had apparently been the case.

Annex 18a Commander I Corps to General Staff, 26 January 1899 (eight pages): Border and rail line security.

Annex 18b XVIII Corps security order, 12 December 1898, effective 1 April 1899 (three pages): In case of war the corps expected raids by Russian cavalry in up to four division strength, followed by light infantry battalions, the objective being to destroy the German rail net in the corps area.

Annex 19 Joint written opinion by Schlieffen and the General-Inspector of the Engineer Corps and Fortresses, Generalleutnant Goltz, for the National Defense Committee, hand-written draft by Schlieffen, June, 1892 (four pages):

"In a two-front war, for reasons that are explained elsewhere, in the west we must initially expect an enemy offensive. With the forces that we can assemble in a timely fashion in Lorraine, we have a well-founded expectation of being able to defeat an attack on our Metz–Saarburg front.

Our right flank is secured by Metz-Diedenhofen. If the enemy attacks further to the north to envelop us, he enters into the unfavorable terrain between the Mosel and the lower Saar and would be met by the attack of our reserves held back here. If we are forced by such an envelopment to retreat, we could nevertheless conduct it in the least unfavorable direction for us, towards central Germany.

On the other hand, the French would threaten our left flank as soon as they pass over the Vosges or enter the upper Alsace from Belfort, and they will attack us in the rear if they cross the Rhine and march on the right [east] bank to the north. The most suitable means to protect us against one as well as the other is to place forces at Strasbourg." [Schlieffen said that a more economical means would be to fortify Molsheim as well as so many of the Rhine crossings in the upper Alsace as possible.]

"Less pressing is a reinforcement of the Moselle below [east of] Metz in order to increase the security of our right wing. The least necessary would be a reinforcement of our Metz–Saarburg front.

A row of forts between Metz and Saarburg would admittedly provide our deployment with a considerably increased degree of security, even if it did not reach the capacity for resistance of the French *Sperrforts* in the strong Moselle and Meuse sectors. The fate of this fortified position would be the same as that of most fortified positions: it won't ever be attacked. The French will avoid it by going through Luxembourg and Belgium. The French will not lack the necessary spirit of enterprise. For if they now cannot decide whether to take the offensive or not, all their doubts will fall away when we give an open admission of weakness by adopting the same French fortification system that we have disparaged for the last twenty years.

German Planning: Dieckmann, Der Schlieffenplan

In order to oppose the march of our enemies through Belgium, we would have to move our forces out of Lorraine. It is very doubtful that we would come into better conditions to fight the French than those that we have in Lorraine. We would have only delayed the decision. That can hardly be an advantage, for in a war on two fronts our most pressing priority is to reach a decision on one side in order to gain a free hand for the other."

[Schlieffen said that security of the deployment can be better assured by a covering force than fortifications. A great fortified double bridgehead at Mainz would be useful in case of defeat, but reinforcing the border fortifications has a higher priority.]

Annex 20 Written opinion by the Engineer Committee concerning the reinforcement of fortresses, especially Metz, with detached fortress groups, 9 February 1895 (seven pages):

[On 16 June 1894 the Engineer Committee had recommended against the construction of individual detached works to reinforce Metz because individual detached works were too vulnerable. They were exposed to envelopment and defeat in detail and their loss would compromise the defense of the entire fortress. New forward works would only be effective if Metz were surrounded by a completely new belt of mutually supporting detached works. There was no money for a new continuous fortress belt. The garrison for a new belt would have to be dramatically increased, and there were doubts concerning the possibility of being able to exercise command and control of the defense of such widely-dispersed fortifications. In the current opinion, the Engineer Committee reaffirmed its previous findings. It recommended that any funds be used to increase the defensibility of the current belt of masonry fortifications.

This written opinion demonstrates that the question of refortifying Metz was far more complicated than Dieckmann's discussion, which presented it as a simple matter of expanding the fort to facilitate Schlieffen's envelopment plan.]

3

Dommes: Operations against Russia[1]

Wilhelm von Dommes was born on 15 September 1867. He joined the 5th Dragoon Regiment in 1885 and entered the Kriegsakademie in 1894. In May 1905 he was appointed the adjutant to the Chief of the General Staff. In 1930 he was the General Adjutant to the Kaiser, and in 1933 the administrator of the Imperial Household. He died in 1959.[2]

This appears to have been a briefing given by von Dommes to the incoming Chief of the General Staff, Moltke.

This document was also obtained by the Bundesarchiv-Militärarchiv from the East Germans.

Transcript [Hand-written]: (from Great General Staff Z No. 2345 concerning operations with Austria against Russia 1905.)
 [Typed]: Briefing notes May 05
 [Hand-written]: vD (probably von Dommes)

Operations against Russia

[Hand-written in the left margin]: 1. *Denkschrift* by Count Schlieffen December 92, (Number 17 of the series). The strength of the *Aufmarsch* 88/89 shows a different *Aufmarsch* in West Prussia. Older deployment strengths not available.

Operations plan in the 1880s
 German deployment
a) one army (7 infantry, 2 reserve divisions) Johannisburg–Lyck
b) one army (6 infantry, 2 reserve divisions) Goldap–Stallupönen
c) an army detachment (2 infantry, 2 reserve divisions) Soldau.[3]

The group under a) was supposed to force a crossing over the Narew at Lomza. The group under c) was to support this operation by an advance on Ostrelenka. The group under b) was to cover the advance by an attack against the Russian Niemen Army. General advance to begin on the 16th mobilization day.

The Austrians were to advance from their assembly areas in Galicia in the direction of Warsaw, leaving weaker forces on the defensive against the Russian South-West Army.

---
[1] (BA-MA) W10/50221.
[2] From the so-called 'Sammlung Krug' BA-MA MSg 109. My thanks to Herr Montfort of the Bundesarchiv-Militärchiv for this information.
[3] In total, 21 infantry divisions.

It was expected that the Russians would have to oppose the German and Austrian advance and defeat them before the completion of their [2] deployment.[4]

[Hand-written in the left margin: Waldersee wrote in a report to Moltke concerning the German strength in the east "not under 400,000". (Document #2 in military-political correspondence concerning Austria 1882–1902). The number 400,000 was also considered in the following drafts for operations plans. In a draft for a plan by Waldersee from 25 October 1882 the number 350,000 is used. (Illegible initials in bottom right corner)]

In August 1882 at Ischl Count Waldersee had a conference with Freiherr Beck. The result was that Austria obligated itself to attack from Galicia with all available forces, while Germany was to begin the war with Russia with a minimum of 350,000 men (= 18 divisions).

[Hand-written in the left margin: (Number 7 in the file)
And *Denkschrift* Count Schlieffen Dec. 92
(Number 17 in the file)]

Denkschrift Count Schlieffen of April 1891 (Chief of Staff since 7 February 91)
The preconditions under which the Field Marshal's plan was written no longer apply.
The Russians have increased their readiness for war to an extraordinary degree. In addition, there are the fortifications of the Narew line. The French deployment is faster than our own. If they deploy behind their fortress line, they can begin the war whenever they like. We must divide our forces. Distribution of forces in active corps:

Germany	20	Russia	21
Austria	15	France	20
Italy	12		
	47		41

[3] The additional strength that Italy provides cannot be used. The fortifications on the Italo-French border make an attack into France impossible. The employment of a significant part of their forces [in Alsace] in connection with the Germans is impossible due to the fear of enemy landings and out of consideration for public opinion. We must restrict ourselves to having inferior forces than the French.

In the east we run the danger that the Russians will stop us with inferior forces on the fortified Niemen–Narew line and throw the mass of their troops against the Austrians. The result of this operation could decide the entire campaign for us. If Austria is defeated it might make peace and then we would be alone against Russia and France.

---

[4] There is clearly no mention of a German-Austrian double envelopment of the Russian forces in Poland.

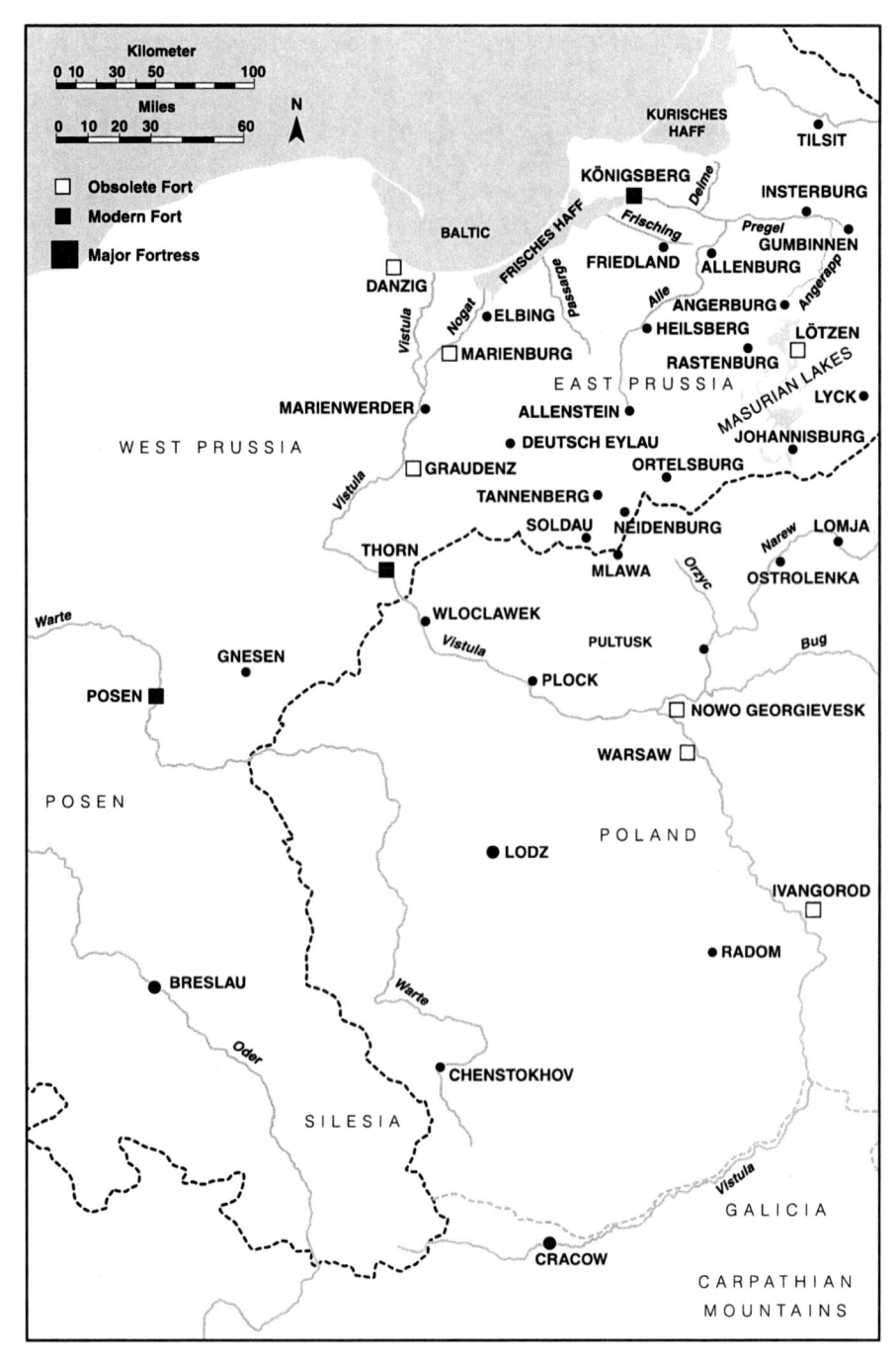

Map 2 Eastern Front

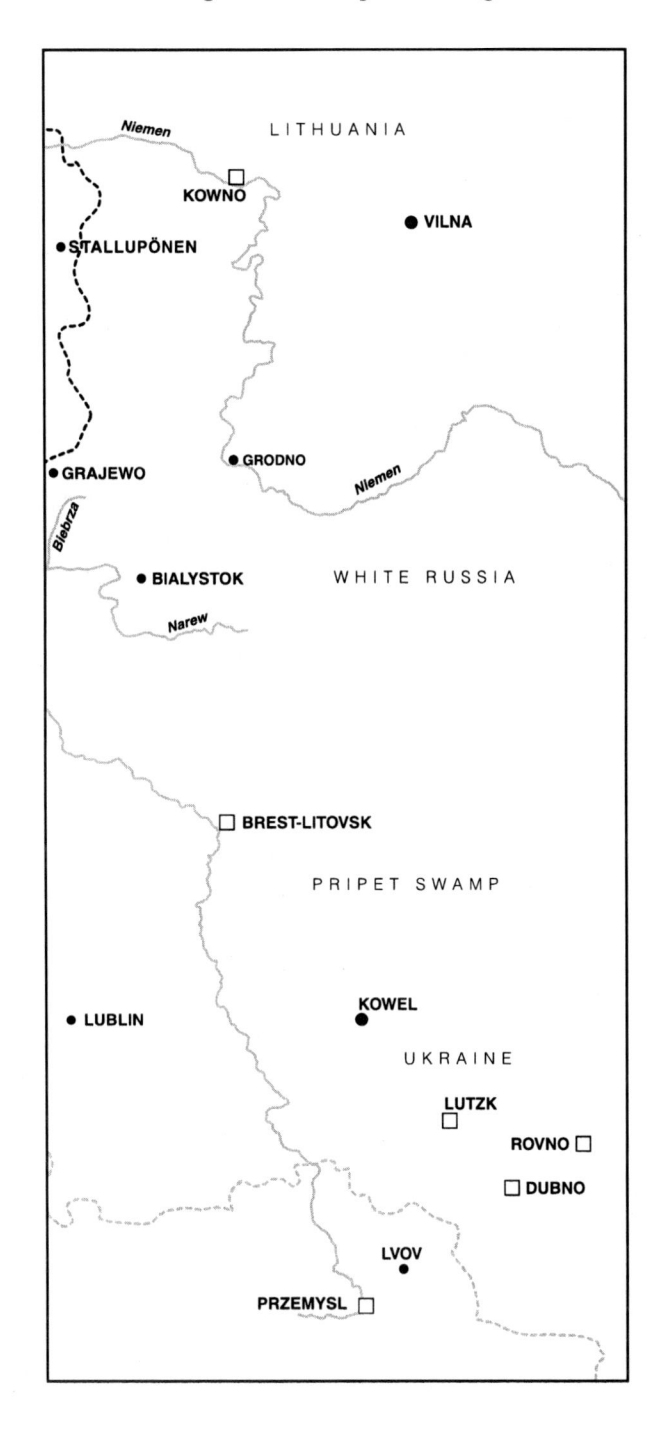

German Planning: Dommes, Operations against Russia

The German and Austrian armies cannot be employed as one army, which might operate effectively on interior lines. The Austrians are [4] tied to Galicia. Therefore, we must go to them. We must deploy in Galicia and seek to link up with them.

[Hand-written in left margin: 2]

In December 92 the military attaché, Colonel von Deines, presented this concept to the Feldzeugmeister, [Beck] at first unofficially as an academic study. The Feldzeugmeister and especially Archduke Albrecht, whose opinion was also solicited, were at first unwilling to depart from the idea that the Prussian operation against the Narew was the more suitable. Finally they probably convinced themselves that the deployment in upper Silesia was the more favorable for Austria.

The German *Aufmarsch* for 93/94 planned for:

7 active army and 2 reserve divisions on the line Beuthen–Jarotschin, [in upper Silesia] a reserve division at Soldau.

2 active army and a reserve division at Gumbinnen–Insterburg

It was initially planned to cross the Vistula between Warsaw and Ivangorod and link up with the Austrians to the east of that river. [5] This plan had to be rejected, because the Austrians could not advance so quickly and it was impossible that the Germans could cross between Warsaw and Ivangorod on their own. In addition, there was no suitable crossing point above [north of] Ivangorod. It was necessary to cross above [south of] Zawichost. The lead elements of the German army should reach the Vistula on the 22nd day [of mobilization].

The Austrian main force (1st and 2nd Armies) should advance with their left wing on the lower San towards Krasnick–Lublin and their right wing from the area of Sokal.

The Austrian 3rd Army would attack towards Dubno–Rowno.

The Austrians claimed the overall command in the theater (Archduke Albrecht or the Emperor; the leader of the German army would be the King of Saxony).

A letter from Feldzeugmeister Beck to Colonel von Steininger (13 April 1894) said "he had recognized the magnitude of the German sacrifice, which involved the [6] possible abandonment of East Prussia, from the very beginning, and he valued it even more, because the German military leadership had decided to conduct the *Aufmarsch* while ruthlessly disregarding all secondary considerations – and thereby create an operational situation which made it possible to conduct the first decisive battle after the armies of both allies had been united . . . ." Concerning the Italians, he wrote that "he had never believed that the Italians would provide the German army with substantial support. He always considered the plan for [sending] the [Italian] 3rd Army [to Alsace] a surety for Italian loyalty. In this sense he laid an exceptional value on the measures to secure Austria's back [against Italy] and he requested that everything be done to insure this."

[Typed in left margin: As Bismarck said: "so that the Italians don't bite the Austrians in the heels".]

Count Schlieffen abandoned the plan to move the German deployment to upper Silesia (95). He no longer believed that the Russians had the intention of attacking the Austrians. Their deployment rather [7] led far more to the conclusion that they would turn against the Germans. In this case our entire deployment and movement would have been unnatural. It was also extraordinarily threatened from the direction of Warsaw and in the last analysis only three corps would remain available to link up with the Austrians. The remainder would be required to provide the necessary protection for Germany's eastern border.

Count Schlieffen was in the retinue of Prince Albrecht on the occasion of the presentation of the Field Marshal's staff to the Emperor Franz Joseph. At this time Feldzeugmeister Beck was away conducting the *Generalstabsreise*. Count Schlieffen discussed with his deputy [hand-written in the left margin: Feldmarschall Leutnant Guttenberg] the factors which led him to believe that the deployment in upper Silesia appeared dubious. He advocated that the Germans deploy along the line Thorn–Ortelsburg while the Austrians shifted their deployment to the left with their left wing on Lublinitz.

[Hand-written in the left margin: German army Thorn–Ortelsburg
                  Austrian 1st Army Prussian Silesia
                  2nd   Forward
                  3rd   Eastern Galicia.]

[8] Feldzeugmeister Beck answered on 30 May 1895, saying that he had not even considered fundamental changes in the agreed-upon deployment. Austria could not think of deploying an army at Cracow–Lublinitz. In addition to other considerations, the Austrians in this case would be forced to leave so many forces to cover the south-east that the main operation would be too weak. He recommended the retention of the current deployment plan. He expressly emphasized, however, that in planning for joint operations of the allied armies the views of both sides had to be considered. He therefore refrained from any influence on the German plan.

After a short written exchange the Feldzeugmeister wrote that he interpreted a letter from Count Schlieffen of 21 December 1895 (the draft was not found) to mean that the joint operation, which had been agreed upon based on the German proposal of December 1892, was now terminated. He mentioned once again the advantages of this operation and said, somewhat resigned, [9] that he would become reconciled to a return to the agreement of the 1880s. (However, on 22 November 1900 he told the military attaché, Rittmeister von Bülow, that the return to the original operation had "satisfied him very much".)

[Hand-written in left margin: 3]

The German *Aufmarsch* 96/97 was made on the line Thorn–Ortelsburg, as *Ostaufmarsch* B in 95/96 had been planned.

[Hand-written in left margin: No. 637a Secret]

The military attaché Colonel Count Hülsen, wrote on 17 March 1896 that Feldzeugmeister Beck had complained about the lack of information concerning the German deployment plan. He said that there was a danger that in case of a war he would take this as an excuse for inactivity. Count Schlieffen supplied the Feldzeugmeister with the requested information – the general line of the deployment and composition of the army. He wrote to Count Hülsen that "We cannot allow ourselves to be beaten by the French on the 15th to the 17th day of mobilization, at a time when the Austrians calmly [10] complete their deployment in Galicia. The outcome of this first battle will determine whether even <u>one</u> Austrian crosses the San."

The fundamental difference in views was that Count Schlieffen said "We must first defeat the French", while Feldzeugmeister Beck said "Russia is the main thing". For this reason, the Feldzeugmeister suspected that Germany would draw even more troops to the west. We must for the meantime maintain the minimum of 18 divisions promised by Field Marshal Count Moltke.

In a letter of 8 January 1896 the Feldzeugmeister asked concerning the provision of Oder barges (for bridge laying, rations and supply). Our "special instructions" and transport orders provided that three trains daily from the 15th to the 22nd mobilization days and one train as of the 23rd day, each with four barges, would arrive in Myslowitz and be placed there at the disposition of the Austro-Hungarian General Staff. [Hand-written in left margin: now 13th–20th day, three trains a day, as of 21st day, one train] V Corps would prepare 32 barges at Glogau, 36 would be prepared at Breslau and VI Corps would prepare 32 at Brieg. [Hand-written in left margin: 26.11.01, Nr. 91 Secret] According to the statement of the Feldzeugmeister the barges would be used when the siege of Ivangorod [11] was begun.

A letter of the Feldzeugmeister to the military attaché Prince Schönburg of 20 January 1897 referred to the necessity to clarify the *casus foederis* (according to the reports of the military attaché the Feldzeugmeister broached this question at every opportunity). He requested adequate border security in Prussian upper Silesia to cover the deployment of the Austrian left wing, namely a cavalry regiment for eight days in the area of Myslowitz–Beuthen–Tarnowitz. [Hand-written in the left margin: 22nd Infantry Regiment with two batteries of 2nd Regiment.]

In discussions between the military attaché Rittmeister von Bülow and the Feldzeugmeister in 1900/1901 the question recurred, whether the Austrians wanted to first conduct their offensive to the east, against the Russian South-West Army, or towards the north. The Feldzeugmeister, who was always concerned for his right flank, obviously found this question unpleasant. [Hand-written in the left margin: 181a Secret, 190a Secret, 91a Secret.]

[Hand-written in the left margin: 9a Secret.]

In January 1902 Major von Bülow told the Feldzeugmeister that the German army intended to conduct an offensive into Poland at the same time as the Austrian army. [12] The advance against the Narew army would begin on the 12th day of mobilization. The Feldzeugmeister replied that the Austrian deployment would be concluded on the 16th day of mobilization. If the Germans attacked, then the Austrians would attack on the 18th day of mobilization with eight corps in the direction of Lublin against the Russian Bug army. What the South Army would do was dependent on the circumstances. The Austrians were more than sure that a joint offensive was the greatest guarantee for the success of both allies. The Austrians had to be concerned for their right flank, particularly because they were not completely certain of the Rumanians.

[Hand-written in the left margin: 4.]
   The drafts of the deployment plans read:[5]
   1897/98: 3 active corps, Bromberg–Thorn–Neidenburg
   　　　　　5 active corps, 3 reserve divisions, Lötzen–Gumbinnen[6]
   1898/99: 3 active corps, Bromberg–Thorn–Neidenburg
   　　　　　5 active corps, 6 reserve divisions, Lötzen–Gumbinnen[7]
   1899/00: 9 active corps, 4 reserve divisions, Thorn–Bischofsburg[8]
   1900/01: 16 active corps, 13 reserve divisions, Thorn–Tilsit[9]
   1901/02: 16 active corps, 11½ reserve divisions, Thorn–Tilsit
   1902/03: 9 active corps, 9 reserve divisions, Thorn–Tilsit[10]
   From 1903/04 on [1904/05, 1905/06] there was only a small *Ostaufmarsch*.
   [13]
   1906/07: I, XX, XVII active corps　　= 　6½ active divisions
   　　　　　1 active brigade
   　　　　　I, V, VI reserve corps　　　= 　7 reserve divisions
   　　　　　3rd Reserve Division
   　　　　　7 Landwehr brigades　　　　= 　3½ Landwehr divisions
   　　　　　(2nd, 70th, 6th, 5th, 17th,　　17 divisions
   　　　　　22nd, 23rd)

   Because the main emphasis of our strategy was seen to be in the west, and also because of the difficult terrain, Count Schlieffen moved further and further away from an offensive into Russia. In his later discussion of the deployment it was his desire to avoid everything that could lead to communicating the German deployment plan to Austria, as our deployment was entirely dependent on the circumstances. He did, however, want to gain a clear appreciation of the Austrian deployment.
   On the initiative of Count Schlieffen, in May 1904 Major von Bülow presented the Feldzeugmeister a map on which was shown the Austrian deployment and the Russian forces and asked to confirm it. It was thus possible to entirely avoid discussing the German deployment. The map was [14] altered according to the information provided by the Feldzeugmeister and then presented to him a second time.
   In this manner the conduct of the operation came to be discussed: 1st and 2nd Armies as always attacking to the north, Group B of the 3rd Army towards the south-west. There was uncertainty concerning the employment of Group A of the 3rd Army, which was dependent on the conduct of Rumania.
   The military attaché is of the opinion that no one in Austria thinks about a war with Russia. Neither Austria nor Germany have points of friction with Russia. Germany desires a rapprochement with Russia because of England.

---

[5] For *Aufmarsch* II.
[6] 19 divisions. The locations are not completely clear. The text is poorly typed. The left flank is at Lötzen in the middle of the Masurian lakes.
[7] 22 divisions.
[8] 22 divisions. The left flank is at Bischofsburg in central East Prussia.
[9] 45 divisions along the entire East Prussian border.
[10] 27 divisions.

Austria's military preparations are therefore primarily directed against Italy. The deployment is presumably on the line Triest–Trient.

[Hand-written in lower left margin:
For 1 possible reduction
1. Clarification of the *casus foederis*
2. How was the general deployment with the older planned strength (18 divisions) with Landsturm, and later with 17 divisions, conducted on the Russian border until the Russian intent was established? It is simply not possible to discuss operations yet.
3. What will Austria do? (Also in relation to Italy.)]

Part II

SCHLIEFFEN'S *GENERALSTABSREISEN*[1]

---

[1] Zuber, *Inventing the Schlieffen Plan*, pp. 145–206.

4

1894 Ost: Tannenberg[2]

The exercise took place from 15 to 22 June. There were thirty-seven participants, six of whom were at the disposal of the exercise director. The German side had 17 players, and was led by Generalleutnant von Mikusch-Buchberg to 19 June, when Generalmajor Freiherr von Falkenhausen assumed command. Two generals commanded corps or army detachments. The Russian side had 13 players. Generalmajor von Sick commanded the Narew Army and Colonel Freiherr von Gayl the Niemen Army. There were three colonels, three lieutenant colonels, 11 majors and 10 captains who played corps and division commanders. The participants were billeted in the towns appropriate to the play of the problem. The exercise was conducted with maps and on the terrain: no troop units were involved. Communications between the players and the exercise director was by telegraph or in writing. The description of the exercise is 48 pages long and included four maps and five sketches. The description included the general situation, the orders and events for each day, and the exercise critique.

The 1894 Generalstabsreise *Ost was the template for the Battle of Tannenberg in August 1914.*

German Situation

A war between Russia and France on the one side against Germany and Austria on the other began with a Russian cavalry raid into Prussia on the right side of the Vistula. The enemy forces were driven out of Prussia, but only after the Prussian rail system had been largely destroyed. Aside from the line Dirschau–Königsberg, no significant stretches of the rail line were operational.

After the expulsion of the Russian cavalry, I Corps, the 1st Infantry Division and 1st Cavalry Division assembled between Angerburg and Insterburg, XVII Corps, 35th Reserve Division and 3rd Cavalry Division at Soldau. [The Germans repair some of the rail lines and the Russians attack I Corps, which withdrew towards Marienburg. To support I Corps, III and V Corps were moved by rail to assembly areas east of Marienburg.] The enemy army had considerably weakened itself to cover Lötzen, Königsberg and the Landwehr of the 1st Infantry Division, which had retreated behind the Deime, but was still estimated to be at least four corps and two cavalry divisions strong.

---

[2] Generalstab des Heeres, *Die Grossen Generalstabsreisen – Ost – aus den Jahren 1891–1905* (Berlin, 1938), pp. 1–50.

The enemy Narew Army (supposedly four corps and two to three cavalry divisions) had reached . . . Mlawa . . . by 15 June . . . .

In the meantime, II Corps and the 4th Cavalry Division had assembled at Thorn, 9th and 11th Reserve Divisions at Graudenz, 3rd and 5th Cavalry Divisions at Marienwerder.

[6] [German commander's analysis of the situation]: On 15 June the inner wings of two Russian armies, which were of about equal strength, were separated by five day's march . . . . [7] The most important consideration for us is to exploit the temporary division of the two Russian armies and if possible defeat them individually. We must execute this operation quickly, before the expected enemy reserve formations can arrive, probably in 5 to 8 days.

The deployment of our forces does not permit a concentration of sufficient strength against the Niemen Army. Even by bringing up the two reserve divisions at Marienwerder, we can assemble only nine infantry and reserve divisions and one cavalry division . . . against the enemy force estimated at the minimum to include of eight infantry and two to three cavalry divisions. We would not have sufficient superiority to be reasonably certain of victory. At the same time the Narew Army would reach Deutsch Eylau, and if we did not completely defeat the Niemen Army our situation would become extremely critical.

In addition, the Narew Army is at this time the more dangerous to us, both because its route of march threatens the flanks and communications of our corps to the north and as well as due to its proximity. The situation therefore requires that we turn against the Narew Army.

We can assemble 13 infantry and reserve divisions and 3 cavalry divisions and attack on 18 June from the line Strasbourg–Deutsch Eylau over the Drewenz to the east [against the enemy left flank]. If the enemy continues his advance, we will already engage his left flank on 18 June and his main body on the 19th. If the enemy remains stationary at Gilgenberg–Lautenburg, we will engage him there on the 19th.

Three infantry and reserve divisions [8] and one cavalry division will oppose the Niemen Army. These will not be able to defend, but will be able to delay the enemy advance so that on the 19th it will be no farther than east of the line Narien–Mahrung–Eising See [NW of Allenstein].

This solution was used as the basis of the exercise for the German side.

Of three other solutions, two also decided to attack the Narew Army. They differed only in the direction of attack of the left wing and in the strength of the forces that would be left against the Niemen Army.

[Generalmajor Freiherr von Hausen says that the solution above might well not work]: The hilly, cross-compartmented, heavily forested terrain severely restricts mobility and makes moving and deploying large units very difficult. This means that success in a decisive battle is doubtful.

[9] Defeat in this battle could lead to the complete destruction of the army, for a retreat over the Vistula under such conditions must cause it to dissolve.

The other solution is to withdraw over the Vistula and move the battlefield to the left side of the river. Initially, this sacrifices considerable terrain, which however does not compare to the advantages that are gained.

If the German army succeeds in drawing the enemy to the lower Vistula, the

Russian army will be forced to take time-consuming measures. It cannot risk crossing the river below [north of] Thorn, so it will have to turn around and cross to the west bank above [east of] Thorn . . . .

The Germans will then move to Bromberg–Nackel [west of Thorn] and, according to circumstances, seek a decisive battle against an enemy that has been weakened by the need to watch Graudenz and Thorn.

[10] Russian Situation

Russia, allied with France, began the war with Austria and Germany by launching a raid with six cavalry divisions into Prussia and two into Posen and Silesia, before their enemy had even begun his mobilization . . . . It could assume that the enemy deployment . . . had been significantly delayed and pushed to the west.

In order to exploit this success, the 1st and 2nd Armies were to cross the German border as soon as possible, defeat the enemy forces standing to the right of the Vistula as completely as possible and continue the attack across the river.

The 1st Army deployed with I Corps in southern Kurland, II, III and IV Corps on the Niemen between Kowno and Grodno and V and VI Corps at Bialystock.

The 2nd Army (VII, VIII, IX, X Corps) deployed on the Narew downstream [south-west] from Lomza . . . .

Total strength: 22 infantry, 7 reserve divisions, 2 light infantry brigades = 30 infantry divisions . . . [11] 11 cavalry divisions.

[13] [There was no Russian army group commander.] Intent of the 1st (Niemen) Army commander: The Niemen Army will continue a rapid march towards the Vistula, generally on Marienburg–Marienwerder, defeat the enemy forces on this side of the river and if possible push them into the Frisches Haff . . . .

It is nevertheless possible that the troop movements on the Dirschau–Bromberg rail line signal strong enemy troop concentrations on the right bank of the Vistula, and that the Germans will attempt to defeat our armies while they are several days apart and separated by unfavorable terrain.

If their objective is the Niemen Army, it becomes even more important not to be defeated in isolation, as the advance of the Narew Army threatens the enemy line of retreat.

On the other hand, if the Narew Army is threatened, quick assistance from the Niemen Army is called for.

In general, it is unlikely that the enemy will offer serious resistance on this side of the Vistula, unless the situation on the other fronts changes, or the enemy is considerably stronger than the reports have led us to believe.

This strength – not counting reserve and Landwehr formations – must be calculated at five active corps (I, II, V, XVIII, possibly III). If this is correct, then the enemy has good chances of success only when we attempt to cross the Vistula. The bridgeheads of Graudenz, Fordon and Thorn, which lie close to one another, and behind which we must look for the enemy main body, give the enemy the ability to use a favorable opportunity to cross from one bank of the Vistula to the other. No matter how safe our advance to the Vistula seems at this moment, given the current balance of forces it is not certain if we will be able to cross the river at all.

[14] Intent of the 2nd (Narew) Army commander: The mission of the 1st and 2nd Russian armies is to decisively defeat the enemy forces on the right bank of the Vistula. To this point, each army has been opposed by a single enemy corps. In addition, rail movements have been reported through Dirschau, supposedly in the direction of Königsberg, and through Bromberg to Thorn. If the enemy continues to move troops to the right bank of the Vistula, given the current situation that can only mean that he intends to assume the offensive to exploit the separation of the two Russian armies and attack one with superior force. If such an attack is planned, it is to be expected in the next few days, or it will be made too late. It is not certain which army would be attacked . . . .

Everything else [except for troop movements on the undamaged Königsberg rail line] argues for the probability of an attack on the Narew Army. It is closer. Since the swamps of the Narew river are to its rear, it can withdraw less easily. It is more dangerous to his communications. And he can use all the Vistula river crossings to concentrate against it . . . . Of the 30 divisions allocated for the operation in East Prussia only 16 are in the front line, divided into two equal groups, their inner flanks separated by five day's march, [15] the Niemen army on a front two day's march long, the Narew Army three. The Russian armies must strive to link up, to bring the reserve divisions forward and in the meantime to avoid a decisive engagement.

Conduct of the Exercise

[20] Due to the decisions of the commander of the German army, 13 infantry and reserve divisions and 3 cavalry divisions were committed to the attack against enemy forces initially numbering 8 infantry and 3 reserve divisions, while only 3 infantry and reserve divisions and 1 cavalry division opposed the 8 infantry divisions and 2 cavalry divisions of the Niemen Army.

[23] [17 July] [The Niemen Army commander] did not believe that there were strong enemy forces to the west of the Vistula; he had no reports concerning movements behind the enemy front. [24] The commander of the Narew Army, who also did not have any information concerning movements behind the enemy lines, assumed that the enemy *Schwerpunkt* lay opposite the Niemen Army. He was prepared to link up with this army using two corps east of Osterode. His immediate intent was to attack the enemy to his front, who was withdrawing.

[The Germans attack the Narew Army.]

[29] [19 June] The troops [of the Narew Army] were completely exhausted by their exertions, and stationary vehicles blocked the roads. The crossing at Soldau was completely blocked and could only be cleared after many hours of work.

Therefore, in spite of the [Russians'] early start, the enemy caught up with all the corps and they all suffered casualties, some heavy. The [Russian] VIII Corps found the crossing at Zielun destroyed and enemy artillery in position south of the town. It was soon attacked on its western flank and routed. Due to enemy pressure north of Soldau the retreat over the Soldau crossing turned into a panic, which engulfed the [Russian] 15th and 18th Infantry Divisions, which were attacked from Lauterburg and also found their assigned crossings destroyed. At Hohendorf the

[Russian] 17th Infantry Division and the X Corps were in the process of occupying their assigned positions when the approach of strong enemy columns from Heinrichsdorf and Borchersdorf made itself felt. Taking heavy casualties, the divisions retreated to the crossings at Kurkau and Solodau, closely pursued by enemy troops. Because the VII Corps was already crossing, and the enemy was attacking not only from Borchersdorf, but his artillery to the north-west was also holding the crossing under fire, all the units here dissolved in chaos. Thousands of prisoners fell into enemy hands.... The Narew Army dropped out of the remainder of the exercise.... On 19 June the German troops exploited the success of the preceding day and gained a decisive victory.

[38] Schlieffen's Exercise Critique

The deployment of an army is determined by the peacetime stationing of the units, the rail net and the international boundaries towards which the deployment is directed. These three factors allow a general determination of the deployment of every army. This is particularly true for Russia, with its simple and widely dispersed rail net. On the basis of some not very complicated calculations we can say with a high degree of certainty that the Russians will deploy against Germany with an army on the Niemen and another on the Narew.

[39] Another consideration is important. In the last 15 years Russia has made astonishing progress in its preparation for war and in improving its mobilization. Nevertheless, it has not been able to overcome the immense extent of the country and the great distances involved. The reserve divisions, which are supposed to receive the reservists of the eastern provinces, have weak cadres, will be very late in reaching combat readiness and arrive on our border even later. If we leave the initiative to the Russians, they will attack us only very late, with their united forces. However, alliance considerations may cause them to attack before all their forces are concentrated.

That was assumed to have been the case here. Russia took the offensive with two armies (10 corps in total), while one corps and seven reserve divisions had not yet arrived. During the advance it became necessary to detach forces, so that by the beginning of the exercise of a total of 30 infantry divisions only 16 were available to conduct operations.

Faced with a Russian advance, the Germans could withdraw behind the Vistula. It would not be difficult to defend the river from Thorn to its mouth with 16 divisions against an equal-sized enemy force. The Russians probably would not even have attempted a crossing. They would have deployed to cross the river above Thorn. This would have offered favorable opportunities for counterattacks. In any case, it would have gained time. However, the time gained would only have meant delaying the battle. The Germans cannot expect significant reinforcements, while the Russians would be able to unite their armies and bring forward their entire strength. The Germans would then have to deal with a great united army, while now they are opposed by two smaller armies, whose telegraphic communications in addition can be seriously interrupted on German territory by Landsturm and other detachments. It is obvious that this situation must be exploited. The Germans must attempt to first decisively defeat one of the Russian armies, and then turn on the other. There could be no question as to which army should be attacked first. [40] Due to its direction of march, the Narew Army was the more dangerous. It was also the army against which it was the easiest to mass the largest part of the German troops. Once the German commander decided to attack the Narew Army, he had to concentrate as many troops for this purpose as possible. No division could be used for another purpose unless it was absolutely necessary. For this reason, I can only approve of the concentration of all German forces, with the exception of I Corps, 1st Reserve Division and 1st Cavalry Division, against the Narew Army. This was 13 infantry and reserve divisions and 3 cavalry divisions. If these massed on the line Deutsch Eylau–Strasbourg, and they succeeded in defeating the enemy, they would drive him back to the east, that is to say in the direction from which he can expect the quickest support from the Niemen Army. This would not help the Germans much. The Narew Army must be decisively beaten and completely divided from the Niemen Army. This could be accomplished by an envelopment of the enemy right flank . . . .

The news which reached both Russian commanders by 15 June had to have convinced them that the reported German reinforcements, which had in part already crossed the Vistula, meant that the Germans intended to take the offensive. It was not possible to delay uniting the two Russian armies any further. This could not be accomplished towards the center, for they would have to move into the lake district. Nor was it possible towards the north, because the defile between Preussisch Holland and Saalfeld did not offer enough room for one massed army. It could only be done towards the south, where the enemy attack was also to be expected and where the Russians could themselves most effectively meet the enemy. The Niemen Army therefore needed to march to the south and the Narew Army . . . . [41] needed to march to the right to close up with the Niemen Army, after having pushed back the enemy forces immediately to its front over a general line Gilgenberg–Lautenburg.

This was similar to the initial intentions of the Narew Army. He changed his mind because the leader of the Niemen Army thought that a German offensive was impossible and wanted to quickly advance to the Vistula. The Narew Army had no other choice than to advance also . . . .

From the position of the two Russian armies it could be seen that if the Narew Army continued its advance, it could be destroyed. If it stopped, it could delay the catastrophe. But if it retreated to the east, while the Niemen Army moved to the south-west, the Germans would be put in an very unpleasant position.

In the meantime, the leader of the Narew Army had formed the opinion that the German offensive was oriented against the Niemen Army, and that his mission was to fix the enemy troops to his front and march to the right, to the aid of the Niemen Army, with the rest . . . .

[43] It was only necessary for the Germans to advance with all corps in the direction of Soldau town, to cross the Soldau river with the cavalry divisions and II Corps, take the crossings there away from the Russians and place them in a catastrophic position.

[49] The art of leadership for modern armies is considerably changed from what it was in the past. A commander can no longer direct armies with the use of

adjutants and couriers. The extent of armies has become too great. [50] A specific order for the battle will not always be issued. Instead of an attack order there will at the minimum be a movement order, and not one that leads to the battlefield, but orders which move the army from the assembly area to contact with the enemy. If everything proceeds smoothly and normally, the corps will have to do no more when they make contact with the enemy than to deploy and attack. The direction of the march will determine the form of the attack that the army commander intends to take place, such as envelopment or breakthrough. It will be rare when everything can be foreseen so clearly that such a simple course of events were probable. Many situations may arise at one level or another that will make a sudden change from the initial plan necessary. It will not be possible to obtain an order from the army commander for this change. In addition, telegraphic communications, relay riders, etc. will fail. It will be necessary for a corps commander or subordinate leader to make an independent decision. The army commander must sufficiently explain his concept to the corps and other commanders, in order that their decisions are made in accordance with it. Subordinate commanders must keep continually aware of the course of the entire operation and of the intent of the army commander.

Since the battle cannot be immediately controlled by the army commander, it is hardly possible to attain the decision by bringing forward reserves which have been held to the rear. The lines are too long to bring the reserves to the decisive point in time and the field of battle is too broad to recognize the decisive point, unless it is determined by the operations plan itself.

In a modern envelopment battle the enveloping wing itself constitutes the reserve. At Königgrätz the 2nd Army is to be considered the decisive reserve, at Gravelotte the XII Corps and in this exercise on 18 June III and V German Corps. It is beyond the power of the army commander to direct these reserves. In order to do so he would have to go to their location himself. As a rule, the mission, which Napoleon filled by leading his Guard forward, now falls to the senior commander on the spot. The decision of the battle rests on his understanding of the general situation, in order to commit his troops at the proper place.

5

1901 Ost[3]

Fifty-four pages, with four maps and six sketches. Time is now measured in mobilization days. There were twenty-four participants, including Major Freitag-Loringhoven as the German 4th Army commander and Lieutenant-colonel Steuben as the Narew Army commander.

On the strategic level, Schlieffen showed how the German army would use rail mobility to defeat the French and then transfer forces to counterattack in the east.

[177] German Situation

In a war between the Dual Alliance and the Triple Alliance, Germany deployed 22 active corps, 12 reserve divisions[4] and 7 cavalry divisions against France, 6 active corps, 4 reserve divisions and 4 cavalry divisions against Russia. France attacked early through Luxembourg and Belgium. Russia obviously waited for the completion of its slower deployment and attacked across the German border from the Niemen only on the 24th day of mobilization, from the Narew on the 29th day. The German army deployed the 1st Army (I, II, II Corps, 1st, 5th Reserve Divisions, 1st and 4th Cavalry Divisions) on the Angerapp, the 2nd Army (V, XVII; XX Corps, 6th and 35th Reserve Divisions, 2nd and 5th Cavalry Divisions) on the Soldau and Neide. Both withdrew in front of the superior Russian forces (Niemen Army, 6 corps, 8 reserve divisions, 3 cavalry divisions 1 light infantry brigade; Narew Army, 6 corps 4 cavalry divisions, 1 light infantry brigade).[5]

The enemy had closed off Königsberg on both side of the Pregel and was continuing the advance. [On the 33rd day the Niemen Army was at Bartenstein–Rastenburg, the Narew Army at Deutsch Eylau–Allenstein.]

In the meantime, on the 23rd day of mobilization the German army in the west won a decisive victory on the left bank of the Rhine near the Belgian border. Orders were issued immediately to transport by rail 9 corps and 3 cavalry divisions to the east.

The Austrians in Galicia crossed the Russian border on the 20th day of mobilization. Part of the Austrian army turned towards the Russian South-West

---

[3] Generalstab des Heeres, *Generalstabsreisen Ost*, 175–230.
[4] 56 divisions in the west, 16 divisions in the east.
[5] Niemen Army, 20 divisions, Narew Army 12 divisions, 32 divisions total, a 2:1 Russian superiority.

[178] Army, part against the Bug Army. The latter was driven on both banks of the Bug to the general area of Brest.

[Eight German corps will arrive on 34th day of mobilization, one on 35th, German 3rd Army with four corps in the area of Marienburg–Marienwerder, 4th Army with five corps at Graudenz–Thorn.]

[181] Russian Situation

France attacked into Luxembourg and Belgium against the German army in the west on the 12th day of mobilization. Russia waited until the deployment of both armies that were to be directed against Germany was complete, including the reserve divisions .... [182] The report arrived from Paris that the French had suffered a decisive defeat on the 23rd day of mobilization, and that only an energetic offensive by the Russians could assist them. In the last few days the Russians had received reports of the rail movement of German troops from the west to the east. It was not possible to ascertain reliable information concerning their strength.

[184–222] 33rd–42nd Mobilization Day

[The Russian Niemen Army continued its advance against the German 2nd Army, while the Narew Army advanced south-west on Graudenz and Thorn. The attack of the German 3rd Army on the 34th day caught the Narew Army completely by surprise, and would have destroyed two corps had Schlieffen not stopped the German advance in the interests of later problem play. At the same time the German 1st Army attempted unsuccessfully to sortie from Fortress Königsberg. Three German armies, from north to south, 2nd, 3rd and 4th, advanced from the Vistula to the east. However, on the 38th day the Niemen Army defeated the German 2nd Army and was then able to send forces against the left flank of the German 3rd Army to the south. By the 41st day the Narew Army had turned the 3rd Army's open flank which would have resulted "in a catastrophe of the worst kind for the Germans".]

[222] Schlieffen's Exercise Critique

In a war between the Dual and Triple Alliances, the most important factor for the latter is the numerical superiority of its enemies. Austria has great problems to overcome with its deployment and will be late reaching readiness for operations. Italy will fix only relatively weak French forces on its border.

Germany has the advantage, in that it lies in the middle between France and Russia and separates these allies from each other. It sacrifices this advantage as soon as it divides its army and thereby becomes numerically inferior to both of its enemies.

Germany must therefore attempt to first defeat one of its enemies, while it occupies the other. When one enemy is defeated, it must use its rail mobility to create a numerical superiority on the other front and defeat that enemy.

The first blow must be conducted with full force, and a truly decisive battle must take place. A Solferino is of no use to us: we must win a Sedan, or at least a Königgrätz.

A German advance against the French fortresses does not appear wise in a two-front war. We must wait for the enemy, who will eventually advance [223] out of his protective walls. This is what the Germans did in this case, and they won a decisive victory over the French.

The situation in the *Generalstabsreise* follows these developments.

[230] We must hold firmly to one principle. We must conduct enveloping attacks against the enemy's line of retreat, for in a two-front war we require complete victories!

6

2nd 1902 *Ost*[6]

Not included in the Generalstabsreisen Ost *book. Approximately 27 pages of text hand-written in Standard script. Found in the archives at Munich and Dresden.*

This exercise took place at a time when Schlieffen was planning for a strong Ostaufmarsch: 27 divisions in 1902/03 according to Dommes. Nevertheless, Schlieffen did not play an invasion of Russia, but once again a counter-offensive in East Prussia. In the west, the German forces remained in their mobilization stations, waiting to move by rail to counterattack against a French advance. In keeping with his proposals for a levée en masse *in East Prussia, Schlieffen also employed eight non-existent Landwehr divisions.*

Russian Situation

Russia deployed a part of its army opposite Austria, another part against Germany (see annex). During the mobilization period the Russian cavalry attacked into East and West Prussia from various directions. It succeeded in devastating parts of the border areas and cutting the rail lines in many places. But it was finally driven entirely out of German territory.

Due to the long duration of the Russian deployment, the Germans will have time to repair their rail lines. It can therefore be assumed that, as we believe, the Germans will complete their deployment with six to seven active corps and an appropriate number of reserve divisions in a timely manner, though they will also be prevented from launching their intended offensive. It is not possible to determine what position they have occupied, because the borders are strongly covered by Landwehr and Landsturm. The reports which we have been able to receive indicate that part of the enemy forces are behind the Angerapp, another in the area of Ortelsburg.

The fortifications of Königsberg extend to the Deime and from Tapaiu up the Pregel. Fortress Boyen [at Lötzen] and the Vistula fortifications are armed and have received their garrisons.

The Supreme Commander of the Russian forces against Germany received the mission to attack as soon as the deployment had been completed.

How will the three Russian armies advance?

---

[6] Kriegsarchiv Munich, Generalstab 1235. Also in the Sächsisches Hauptstaatsarchiv Dresden, GS XII AK, KA(P) 9195.

German Situation

In a war between the Triple Alliance against the Dual Alliance, Germany committed

against Russia:
9 active corps
8 reserve divisions
[26 infantry and reserve divisions total]
9 Landwehr divisions
4 cavalry divisions

initially awaiting instructions [in their mobilization stations]:
11 active corps
8 reserve divisions
1 light infantry brigade
7 cavalry divisions . . . .

It is known that Russia had deployed part of its forces against Germany on the Niemen between Kowno and Grondo and part between Bialystock and Warsaw. It is not known how the forces are allocated between these two fronts.

Schlieffen's Exercise Critique

In the given situation a weaker German army was opposed to a stronger Russian force. The ratio between the two, aside from Landwehr and Landsturm troops, was 3:5. Nevertheless, the mission for the Germans was to defeat the Russians.

In such circumstances it is advantageous if the enemy divides his forces. The Russians were forced to do so because they deployed on two fronts, one in Poland on the Narew, one on the Niemen or to the west of that river. This deployment was due to the peacetime concentration of forces in Poland as well as to the necessity to protect a principal line of communications, the Petersburg–Warsaw rail line. It can also be assumed that there is a detachment between the two at Bialystock.

In spite of their separation, by advancing the Russians would soon unite, were this not prevented by the Masurian lakes.

The roads leading through the lakes are blocked by Fortress Boyen and the newly built fortifications at Schimonken, Nikolaiken, etc. [in the Masurian lake district]. However, the latter are not very strong. It was therefore assumed that the defiles were also blocked by field [2] fortifications that had been built on the water line between the Löwentin and Spirding lakes. It was also assumed that fortified bridgeheads had been built east of Lötzen on the line of lakes from Possessere, Kruglanken, etc.

In this way one could count on the fact that the Russians would divide their forces, with one part advancing on Angerburg–Wehlau, the other on Gross Puppen [halfway between Johannisburg and Ortelsburg] and eastwards, with a separation of 80 kilometers. How strong each part would be could not be determined in advance, and it was unlikely that cavalry would be able to give any reliable information on it.

Schlieffen's Generalstabsreisen: 2nd 1902 Ost

This separation would last only for a few days during the Russian advance, for it is easy to link up both to the east and the west of the chain of lakes. If this separation is to be exploited, the time available for the attack is short.

The question is, which half should be attacked first, the northern or the southern? Initially, it appears the simplest to attack the southern wing from Thorn–Graudenz. The deployment there is relatively easy, the lines of communication are secure. However, if they have even the slightest suspicion that the enemy is at Thorn, it is unlikely that the Russians will advance in the manner that they did in this exercise. Since they deploy with their left wing at Warsaw, they will in any case find support for it on the Vistula and oppose the German advance frontally. A German success would only push them back to their strong defensive line.

[3] A more effective attack would be against the northern group. It can be attacked in the front, on the right with the protection of the Memel river, and perhaps from the lakes against the left flank. If the German left wing were defeated while attempting to envelop the enemy, it would fall into a very dangerous situation and ran the risk of being forced into the Haff and the swampy area in front of it. This attack therefore involves great risk. Without taking risks, it will hardly be possible to defeat a stronger enemy.

Having taken the decision to attack the northern army group, it is self-evident that the main body had to be assembled against it. Something had to be done to occupy and delay the southern group. There was a suitable position between Soldau and Neidenburg and then on to the lake district on the upper Alle. This was naturally strong to the front, which could be considerably increased through field fortifications. It could be outflanked or enveloped to the north only with difficulty and considerable loss of time. Finally, measures needed to be taken to protect the province, the rail lines and the lines of communications. This could only be accomplished by posting troops between Allenstein and the Masurian lake district as well as between Soldau and Thorn.

In this situation the German army in the East consisted of:

9 active army corps . . .
4 cavalry divisions . . .
8 reserve divisions . . . [4] to which were assigned artillery excess to the normal corps tables of organization . . .
8 Landwehr divisions [with no artillery] . . . and 17 Landsturm battalions.

Of these troops, seven corps were deployed from Lötzen behind the Angerapp to Labiau, a corps and two reserve divisions at Tilsit, three Landwehr divisions occupied the fortifications on the Masurian Lakes while five Landwehr divisions held the Soldau–Neidenburg position. A corps and six reserve divisions were between Soldau and Thorn. The Landwehr divisions occupied the defiles between Allenstein and Rudczanny. Such a deployment could not be conducted by rail alone. Foot marches were necessary to reach the assigned areas. This required time, which is available if the Russians first cross the border on the 26th day of mobilization.

The Russians had in total 11 corps [each corps with 32 infantry battalions, 7 or 8 battalions stronger than its German counterpart] . . . and eight reserve divisions [with 16 infantry battalions, 5 or 6 battalions stronger than its German counterpart] . . . one of which was left at Warsaw. [Russian field force of 29 active and reserve divisions.]

These troop masses were divided into three armies. One with five corps and three reserve divisions was to advance to the north of the Masurian lakes, the other two with three army corps each and a total of four reserve divisions to the south. The Russians assumed that they would succeed in conducting a concentric attack against the German forces that were presumed to be behind the Angerapp and in the area of Ortelsburg, force them into the Samland [5] and then to capitulate. This plan did not count on the fact that the Germans would not remain stationary in order to await the consequences of the Russian operation, but on the contrary that they would maneuver. [Schlieffen discussed errors in the advance of Russian V Corps, 1st (Niemen) Army.]

The Germans had initially hoped that the Russians would attack the position on the Angerapp, and while the Russians were bleeding in vain attacks, [6] the Germans could attack the Russians in the flank and rear with several corps. They soon recognized that the Russians were not going to allow themselves to be drawn into this combination.

The left-wing German cavalry corps threw back a Russian cavalry division and was thereby able to screen the advance of the German left wing for a time, but this could not succeed permanently. The Russians suspended the advance on the Angerapp as soon as the German flank attack was noticeable. The German commander then decided to advance with the entire army. Five corps were to attack the Russians in front and three in the flank, while the Russians had only four corps at hand. The result of the following battle seemed beyond all doubt as soon as one looks at the situation map.

[The German VII and VIII Corps and Cavalry Corps destroy the Russian 2nd Corps, the German V and VI Corps defeat the Russian 3rd Corps. The Russian commander orders a withdrawal.]

[7] Whoever breaks off the fight declares himself to have been beaten. If the infantry has already been committed to combat and is under enemy fire, it will suffer serious losses during the withdrawal. The Russian retreat continued throughout the entire night, so that the losses increased. A new position was occupied behind the Przerosl–Filipowo sector and the rear guards were instructed to oppose the enemy advance.

Many armies have enjoyed a similarly favorable situation as the Germans did after their victories on the 28th, and have not continued the pursuit on the next day, but rather remained stationary on the battlefield. Not all victorious generals have acted like General von Goeben at St. Quentin, who ordered his troops to pursue the beaten enemy for nearly 40 kilometers. Now it was absolutely necessary to follow this famous example. The defeated enemy must be completely destroyed before the Germans turned to other missions. This was all the more easy to do, since three to four divisions were completely fresh and had not been in combat, and these divisions were located on the wing [8] which would naturally conduct the principal part of the pursuit.

On the evening of the 29th the German advance guards re-established contact with the enemy, who as on the previous day felt that his flank was threatened. The

Russians had no choice but to again conduct a night march to escape from the threatening envelopment....

On the 30th the Russians halted after another exhausting night march, only on that afternoon to again consider themselves threatened with encirclement and to conduct yet another night march to escape destruction. On the morning of the 31st they were on the level of Lozdzieje. They had entered a lake district, in which almost the entire army was restricted to using one road through Sereje. The situation permitted the pursued no rest and must lead to their complete dissolution and destruction. There was another night march followed by the crossing of the Niemen the next day over one bridge erected at Kryksztany, while the enemy exerted pressure on the flanks and rear. The enemy cavalry had already crossed downstream and was on the right bank. Nothing further need be expected from this army for a fairly long time.

[9] This significant German success was due to the fact that the Russians had divided their forces and that the Germans had concentrated as many troops as they were able against one part. It cannot be overlooked that the Russians could have considerably reinforced their 1st Army (for example with the 6th and 7th Corps) and thereby at the least made the German victory considerably more difficult.

On the 29th the Germans had already turned their 4th Army around and marched in the direction of Schippenbeil. On the 31st, of the 3rd Army only the VI Corps and the advance guards of the other corps continued the pursuit, while the mass of the corps (II, III, IV, V) also turned around in the direction of Darkehemen–Lötzen [to the south-west in the direction of the Narew Army].

In the meantime the Russian 2nd and 3rd Armies had been given a direction of march south around the Masurian lakes generally towards Ortelsburg–Mlawa, obviously with the intention of attacking the enemy, who was reported first at Ortelsburg, then at Soldau–Neidenburg. The report of the advance of enemy forces from the line Thorn–Strasbourg reinforced them in their opinion, that the enemy main body was to be sought on the southern front, and that to the north on the Angerapp there were no significant enemy forces....

[10] The events of the 28th opened the eyes of the Russian Supreme Commander concerning the actual situation. The enemy main body had gained a victory in the north. There could be nothing more than second-rate troops on the southern front. So much was clear: the Russian 2nd and 3rd Armies must go to the place where the enemy main body was. Its advance must force the enemy to break off the pursuit of the 1st Army and then, with whatever support it could provide, fight a decisive battle. There was still some doubt as to whether they should first attempt to defeat the opposing, second-rate enemy forces in order to gain complete security on this side. An analysis of the opposing situations on the 28th made it clear that such an operation would require far too much time, especially since the enemy could be expected to withdraw. On the other hand, the 6th, 7th, 8th, 9th and 11th Corps could turn on the 29th and march in a northeasterly direction, without the German 1st and 2nd Armies being able to seriously hinder this movement. The 10th Corps, four reserve divisions and a light infantry brigade should suffice to provide the protection for the left flank. The Russian Supreme Commander reached a different conclusion. He wanted to cut off the withdrawal of the enemy forces that had advanced east from the Angerapp by means of a march west of the Masurian lakes

and force them to fight with a reversed front. If the Germans were defeated, they would be destroyed. But if the Russians were defeated the same [11] fate also awaited them. By marching south of the Masurian lakes the Germans would have been forced to accept battle with very unfavorable lines of communication, while the Russian route of withdrawal to the south would have stood open. In addition, the march to the west of the Masurian lakes cost time and gave the Germans room to continue the pursuit of the 1st Army and literally forced the second-rate German 1st and 2nd Armies to be at their most effective in the decision.

Without cover for the left flank and rear the march to the west of the Masurian lakes could not be conducted. Therefore the 2nd Army, with the addition of the 9th and 11th Corps, was ordered to conduct the march, covered by the 3rd Army (10th Corps, four reserve divisions, and a light infantry brigade). It was not strong enough for this mission, and had to withdraw continually in the face of superior enemy forces. Finally, it got into the extremely unfavorable terrain between Orzyc and Omuleh and was completely encircled.

In the meantime the 2nd Russian Army had advanced, evidently hesitantly and uncertain as to what was to be done, delayed on the left and the right by German Landwehr divisions in secure positions. Of these, only the 1st had engaged in operations against the Russian 3rd Army. The rest followed the Russian 2nd Army as soon as it had marched past them. A certain amount of caution in this case was indicated. It was not out of the question that the 2nd Army could suddenly turn around, overrun the Landwehr divisions, free the 3rd Army [12] from its awkward position and by so doing establish the freedom of action and security necessary for its operations against the German forces approaching from the north. This caution was observed by the 2nd, 3rd, 4th and 5th Landwehr Divisions. They moved by bounds, from defile to defile, and always sought out a position of great defensive strength. On the other hand the 7th and 8th Landwehr Divisions believed they could pursue impetuously, without consideration for the insufficient cohesion of their troops and without heeding the enemy troops on their flanks, attempting to inflict a defeat on the enemy through a bold independent attack. They were enlightened concerning their error in the severest manner by the 6th Russian Corps. Apart from the considerable losses that they suffered, the Russian victory presumably weakened the German barrier to the south . . . .

On the 34th day both sides were, in general, drawn up in battle formation. Both leaders intended to envelop the enemy western flank . . . . [13] Due to the fact that both sides were shifting their enveloping wings to the west, the eastern wings lost all support from the terrain, so that there was also a danger to both sides of being enveloped here, as well as the possibility of enveloping the enemy. Since in a battle it will be difficult to establish where the enemy flank is, one would do well either to make the defensive flank strong enough to be able to parry an envelopment, or to refuse it so far that it cannot be enveloped . . . . The 4th German Army, which was also informed of the enemy advance, stopped at the generally favorable position at Massaunen–Dietrichsdorf–Laggarben–Fitzendorf. It knew that the Russians had to attack in order to free themselves from an untenable position in which there were enemy forces to the front, right flank and rear. They could therefore exploit the advantages of the defensive. [Schlieffen then relates the tactical details of the battle.]

[16] ... the entire German IX Corps advanced against the Russian left wing. This, in conjunction with the breakthrough of the German 10th Division at Barten determined the victory for the Germans.

The Russian retreat led them towards new enemies. The 2nd, 3rd, 4th and 5th Landwehr Divisions had advanced and had occupied all the roads in the enemy rear between Sorquitten and Rothfließ. The routes through the Masurian Lakes between Schimonken and Rudczanny were blocked by the 6th and 7th Landwehr Divisions. Only one road through Sensburg, Peitschendorf and Friedrichshof to Myszyniec was still open, but it was not adequate for an army of five corps . . . . The retreat could not be conducted without combat. The fight was, to be sure, only against Landwehr troops, but if the Landwehr was able to resist only for a short time this would be sufficient to allow the pursuing German forces to arrive.

The brilliant German success was due in the first case thanks to the envelopment of the Russian left wing by the German IX Corps. But this envelopment was made possible by the fact that the other corps of the 4th Army waited for the attack of superior enemy forces on a relatively broad front. The 3rd Army, [17] which attacked with weak forces in an exaggerated expectation of victory, had to withdraw and through this withdrawal put the result of the battle in question. Nevertheless, the attack had the advantage that three enemy divisions were drawn to the right flank, and a gap was created which allowed a breakthrough by the 8th and 10th Divisions.

The victory would have been much more certain had two corps not been kept from the battlefield. First the II Corps, which in advancing through Lötzen on the 34th day found its way blocked by the Russian VI Corps in strong positions at Rhein as well as Orlen and Sturlack. On the next day the Russian corps pulled a division out of the position in order to have as many troops as possible for the expected decisive battle. In spite of this weakening of the Russian position the II Corps attack, although reinforced by the 6th Landwehr Division, would have expended a great deal of effort for nothing. The corps should have followed its opponent's example and left only enough forces in front of the Russian position to prevent the enemy from advancing out of it, and hurried to the battlefield with the rest through Kamoniken, where there were only four Russian battalions, or through Rhein, where there was only one . . . .

The other corps that was missing at the decisive battle was the Ersatz Corps. It had been formed out of 24 ersatz battalions and the ersatz squadrons and ersatz batteries available in East and West Prussia. One can only approve of this measure. If a part [18] of the homeland is made into a battlefield, all ersatz and garrison troops of the province, in so far as they are capable, must be committed. They should then actually be employed in the field and not merely moved out of the fortresses. The newly formed Ersatz Corps was assembled in Allenstein. This location may have been suitable for this purpose. However, as the Russian army moved farther to the north, the corps should have also moved parallel to it on the left bank of the Alle. On the 35th day it could have been moved into position through Bartenstein . . . .

[Schlieffen then critiqued the employment of cavalry on both sides.]

Rations for the [20] troops in such operations remains an important question. In spite of their daring movements the Germans had their very effective rail system behind them, so that their ration supply was surely feasible and at worst the supply of the reserve divisions on the right flank would have posed problems. On the other hand, ration supply for the Russians during both their retreat over the Niemen as well as the advance of the 2nd Army to the north (with the Landwehr Divisions standing in the Russian rear) would have been extremely doubtful.

7

1903 Ost[7]

Sixty-three typed pages long, with one map and nine sketches. Twenty-six participants.
Faced with a simultaneous Franco-Russian attack on the 18th day of mobilization, Schlieffen played a Westaufmarsch *followed by a massive rail movement from west to east and a surprise counterattack.*

[234] Russian Situation

The French and Russians had agreed that in a war against the Triple Alliance, both powers would attack into Germany as soon as possible with all available forces and would not put down their arms until the demands of both allies had been fulfilled.

In accordance with this, both France and Russia crossed the German border almost simultaneously on the 18th day of mobilization. It soon became evident that France was opposed by the far stronger portion of the enemy forces, while Russia was faced only with the German I, II, V, VI, XVII Corps and their respective reserve and Landwehr divisions, which were stationary along the border. According to all reports, serious German resistance was only to be expected behind the fortified stretch of the Vistula between Thorn and Marienburg. The Niemen army was to move against this front, while the Narew Army crossed the Vistula between Warsaw and Wloclawek in order to attack the enemy position from the south. [The Niemen Army consisted of 6 corps, a reserve corps and two reserve divisions – 16 divisions; the Narew Army consisted of 5 corps and 2 reserve corps – 14 divisions – with the Guard Corps arriving.]

[235] On the 29th mobilization day a message arrived from St. Petersburg, saying that on the 27th day the French army in Lorraine had been forced to retreat. It had withdrawn behind the Meuse and the Moselle in order to resume the offensive as soon as possible. The Germans had taken very heavy losses and were following only tentatively. It was now important for the Russian army to relieve the pressure on its ally through a determined advance.

[236] The South-West Army had been attacked by the Austrians, but was defending itself successfully, supported by the Vohlynian fortress triangle (Lutzk, Rowno, Dubno). The Austrians had not conducted serious operations against the Bug Army, which was generally on the line Lublin–Cholm [on the east side of the Bug].

---

[7] Generalstab des Heeres, *Generalstabsreisen Ost*, 231–308.

[236–41][The Russian army group commander decided on the 29th mobilization day to defeat the German forces in the east before the German reinforcements arrived, presumably on the 34th day of mobilization. By the 32nd day of mobilization, the Niemen Army was a day's march east of the Vistula, the Narew Army was crossing the border south of Thorn.]

[241] German Situation

... By the 27th day of mobilization the situation in the west has been decided to the degree that the French army, which had attacked into Alsace-Lorraine, had suffered heavy casualties and had been forced to withdraw behind its fortified lines on the Meuse and the Moselle. This did not mean an end to the war. France would attack again, and begin the battle once more, as soon as it had recovered. [242] But a short pause would ensue, and the Germans intended to use this to turn with the greatest possible strength against the Russian armies which had broken into East Prussia.

Eleven corps, the greatest number that could be moved by rail from the west to the east in a reasonably short period of time, were to reinforce the seven corps already on the Russian border (I, II, V, VI, XVII, XX, XXII–XX and XXII being made up out of units excess to normal tables of organization) in order to attack with at least local numerical superiority.

The fortifications on the Vistula make it appear likely to the Russians that the Germans will assemble their main body to defend between Thorn and Marienburg. The strength of this position makes it prudent for the Russians not to limit themselves to a frontal attack, but to support it with an envelopment of the German right. Therefore, the Niemen Army should advance through East Prussia directly against the river line, while the Narew Army crosses to the left bank of the Vistula at and below Warsaw and then crosses over the Netze between Thorn and Posen in order to conduct a concentric attack with the Niemen Army.

If the Russians adopt this plan, their forces will remain divided for a considerable period. The question is, which of these the Germans, who may be assumed to have assembled behind the Vistula, can attack with the greatest chance of success. An attack on the enveloping Narew Army, using the Vistula, Netze and Warthe, the numerous lakes between these rivers and the fortresses of Thorn and Posen, offers without doubt favorable prospects. It would be far more effective to attack the Niemen Army, if this can be done with a deeper and more extensive envelopment of its right flank.

To accomplish this, the four corps on the left bank of the Vistula (II, V, VI, XXII) were assembled at Marienburg–Elbing, as soon as there were enough reserve, Landwehr and Landsturm troops on hand to cover the borders of the provinces of Posen and Silesia.[8] The three corps on the right bank of the Vistula (I, XVII, XX) were ordered to withdraw in front of the advancing Russian forces without allow-

---

[8] On page 302 Schlieffen says that these corps would initially have been better employed in the west.

ing themselves to become engaged in combat, with I Corps going to Königsberg and the other two to the Vistula. Five corps (Guard, Guard Reserve, III, IV, IX) would be moved by rail from the west to the same place.[9] [243] From the very first four reserve divisions (1st, 5th, 6th, 17th, assembled in I and II Reserve Corps) would be moved to Königsberg. For the attack on the Russian forces on the right side of the Vistula the Germans would have 12 corps and 4 reserve divisions = 14 corps available. To this could be added as desired some of the nine reserve divisions to be assembled in the districts of Thorn, Bromberg, Schneidemuhl and Posen (Guard, 3rd, 7th, 9th, 18th, 19th, 23rd, 24th, 35th, assembled into III, IV, IX, and XII Reserve Corps, 35th Reserve Division remains independent).

The remaining corps from the west are to off-load [along the border between Posen and Breslau]. As soon as they are prepared to march, their mission is to advance to the east with the right wing directed at Warsaw, in order as far as possible to attack the Narew Army, which has crossed to the left bank of the Vistula, on the left flank.

[244] The first elements of these corps will arrive on the evening of the 30th day of mobilization, the last on the evening of the 34th or morning of the 35th, the combat trains can be expected on the 36th, the field trains on the 37th.

[246] The intent of the commander of the German army in the East on the 32nd mobilization day was: Envelopment of both enemy wings; destruction of the enemy force by cutting off his line of retreat over the Narew and Vistula.

[247–300][The German left wing started the attack on the 32nd day, with the 5th Army successfully breaking out of Königsberg, while the 4th Army crossed the Nogat. On the 33rd day the Austrians attacked with two armies of three corps each against Lublin–Kholm. By the 34th day the Russian situation was becoming critical. The German 4th and 5th Armies were enveloping the Russian right at an operational depth. The German 3rd Army was assembling on the Russian right and the German 1st Army was unopposed on the Russian left. Both the Niemen and Narew Armies began to withdraw to the south while the Russians moved troops west from Warsaw to try to shore up their open left flank. The Niemen Army was unable to get away. It was fixed in place by frontal attacks while the German 3rd and 4th armies crushed its flanks and German cavalry closed it off to the rear. On the 37th day it was completely encircled north-west of Soldau and by the 38th day it was annihilated. The Narew Army lived only slightly longer. At the end of the exercise on the 40th day it was being encircled to the west of Warsaw, with the German 1st and 2nd Armies to the front while the 3rd Army turned its right flank. The Narew Army's rear area was also infested with German cavalry. At the same time, the Austrians had taken Brest-Litovsk.]

Schlieffen's Exercise Critique

[301] The question is, what was Germany to do? If it acted in the east as it had done in the west, and driven the enemy behind the Narew, the Vistula, or some other line,

---

[9] On page 302 Schlieffen says that this was the limit of the German rail capacity in this sector.

it would have soon seen itself forced to send at least some of the corps back to the west to oppose the renewed French advance. The Russians would have used this to renew their advance. After a time, we would have again needed to send troops from the west to the east. This back-and-forth movement of German troops, pushing the enemy back here and there, then a renewed enemy advance, is the sort of strategy which must lead eventually to the complete exhaustion of the German army.

Such a war on two fronts can only be brought to an end by the most complete annihilation of one enemy, then the other, and not by throwing back one enemy or the other.

[302] The means of destroying the enemy are well-known to us from military history. Frederick the Great attempted to do so repeatedly. Napoleon did so in 1800, 1805, 1806 and 1807, and would have done the same in 1809 if Berthier or, one can also say, his presumption, had not ruined it. The Allies used it in 1813 to break Napoleon's rule. The immortal Field Marshal von Moltke built his success on the same method in August and September 1870.

It consists of maneuvering all, or at least the largest portion, of the army into the enemy flank or rear and forcing him to accept battle with a reversed front and making him retreat in the least favorable direction. If this attack is conducted from two sides, as it was at Leipzig, Gravelotte and Sedan, it will, or at least can, lead to the encirclement of the enemy army.

8

1st 1904 *West*[10]

Hand-written in Standard style, twenty-one pages of text, seven maps. The Bundesarchiv obtained this exercise from the East Germans.

In spite of a German deployment similar to the 'Schlieffen plan', the decisive battle is fought in Lorraine.

[3] French Situation

From the 7th mobilization day on, reports gradually reached the French headquarters of German troops unloading on the Hohes Venn, Eifel, Moselle and Nahe rail lines as well as further south on the Saar. Later, strong concentrations were reported between Cologne and Wesel. From the 10th mobilization day, strong German columns were reported advancing from the lower Rhine towards the Meuse below Liège. The heads of the German columns are seen at Aachen and those of the troops unloaded in the Hohes Venn and Eifel appear to the south along the Belgian and Luxembourg borders . . . . There are relatively few troops in the upper Alsace.

[3–6] German Situation

Belgium has mobilized. Its army is thought to have deployed behind the strong Meuse position Liège–Namur. The left wing of the French army is thought to have taken position opposite Luxembourg and Belgium. [French forces are advancing on Metz, the Saar, the Donon and the Vosges.]

[German army includes 26 active corps, 16 reserve corps (84 divisions) and 14 Landwehr divisions.]

Schlieffen's Exercise Critique

[7] It is well-known that the French have barricaded their entire border opposite Germany along the line Epinal–Toul–Verdun–Montmédy with fortresses and

---

[10] BA-MA PH 3/659. 'Foerster' is written with blue pencil on the cover in the upper right-hand corner, and 1474 in the lower right corner. PH3/660 has the exercise narrative, but no maps.

The first text page of the 1st 1904 *Generalstabsreise West*, BA-MA PH 3/659

Sperrforts. The two gaps which they have left open do not facilitate our attack. The one between Epinal and Toul will be blocked by a naturally very strong position: the Moselle and the Madon constitute two obstacles one behind the other. The greatest part of the army is assembled here. The other gap between the Verdun and Montmédy can be easily blocked behind the Loison, and whoever attacks here must be conscious of being enveloped by a French attack [from Verdun] through Belgium and Luxembourg.

Given this situation, Britons and Americans who have studied the problem, as practical people with few scruples, have assumed that it is self-evident that the Germans will attack the French through Belgium. The Swiss have happily agreed in the hopes that in this way they will avoid damage to their own country. The Belgians have drawn a practical conclusion from the question. Earlier, so long as they only felt threatened by the French, they limited themselves to Antwerp. They would withdraw there and wait until the British or the Germans liberated them. In the current state of affairs they have fortified Liège–Namur, naturally against both neighbors, for the most part against Germany.

The French have not considered the matter with the same enthusiasm as the less involved nations. They credit us with such a high offensive spirit that we will attack straight at their fortresses. They hope that the offensive will fail, and then they will attack us in the flank. Since this will hardly be possible except through Belgium and Luxembourg, it can therefore be [8] said that all the nations that have anything to do with the question expect the violation of Belgian neutrality to be a given fact. We would therefore be permitted at least to examine the matter more closely and academically.

When a march through Belgium is considered, the first question is the envelopment of the French defensive position. It may be imagined that a part of the German army will attack the front and another part will advance around Verdun with the right wing in the area of Mézières. If this latter attack succeeds, it cannot be said that the French must vacate their position. On the contrary, they will stand fast, and then initially the Germans would have only succeeded in dividing their army. One part of the German army is to the east, the other to the west of the French position. The French, on the contrary, are united on the west side. The result of the operation would hardly be favorable for the Germans. Another possibility is to completely go around the French position and march around Verdun with the entire German army [9] or at least with the larger portion of it. In other words, one does not attack the front Verdun–Belfort, but rather the front Verdun–Lille, for it will be necessary to extend the flank this far in order to gain enough space for free maneuver. There are fortifications on this new front, but not so strong or so difficult to overcome as on the front facing us. Many of the smaller forts would be taken without difficulty and the fortresses can be bypassed. The lines of communication would not be unfavorable. The line Meuse–Sambre is on the direct line between Berlin and Paris. If it is possible at any point to establish a connection between the German and French rail nets, then it is through the use of Belgian rail system. These advantages are fraught with serious disadvantages. The width of northern Belgium is so great and the march through it takes so long that the French have time for all possible counter-measures. There can be no question of achieving surprise. In addition, it is not possible to march across Belgium on such an extended

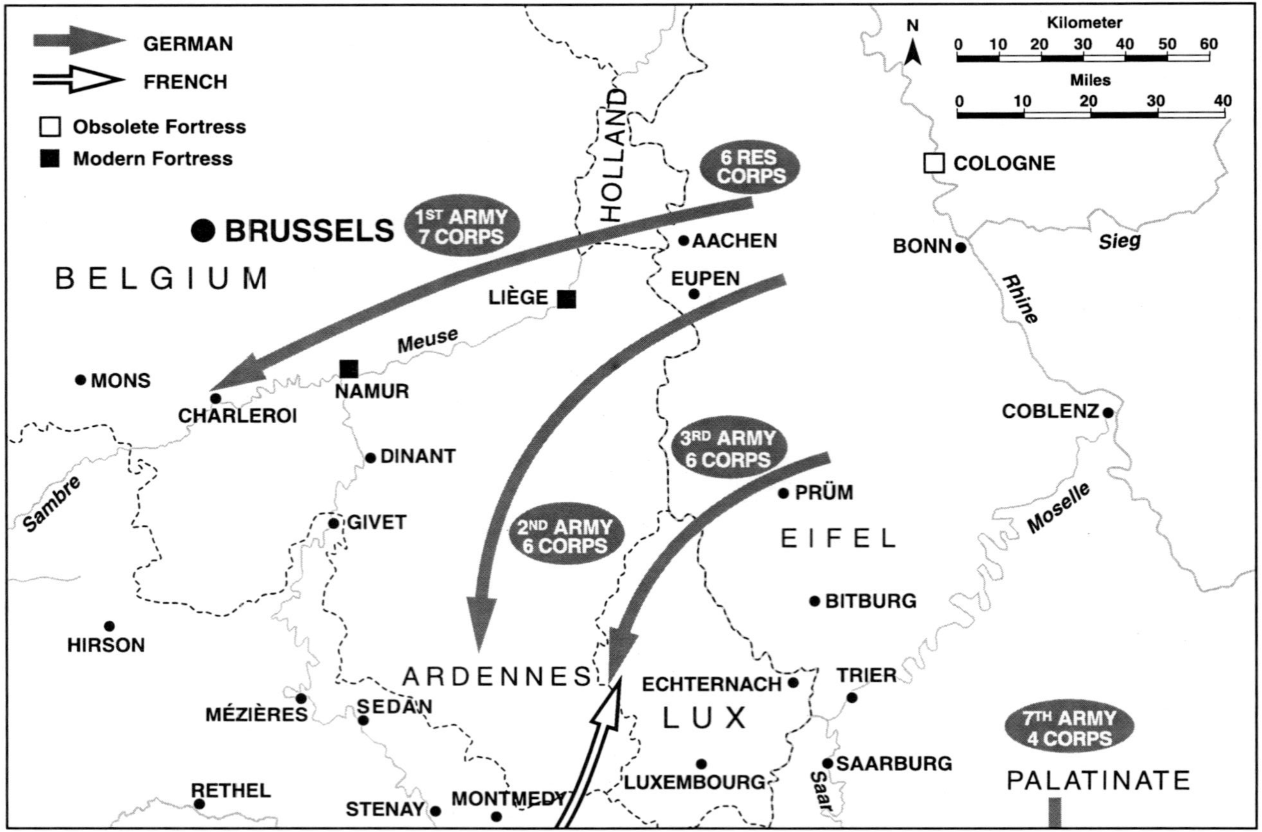

GERMAN
FRENCH
Obsolete Fortress
Modern Fortress
N
Kilometer
0 10 20 30 40 50 60
Miles
0 10 20 30 40
COLOGNE
BRUSSELS
BELGIUM
HOLLAND
1ST ARMY 7 CORPS
6 RES CORPS
AACHEN
EUPEN
LIÈGE
Meuse
NAMUR
MONS
CHARLEROI
DINANT
Sambre
GIVET
2ND ARMY 6 CORPS
3RD ARMY 6 CORPS
PRÜM
EIFEL
BITBURG
BONN
Sieg
Rhine
COBLENZ
Moselle
HIRSON
ARDENNES
MÉZIÈRES
SEDAN
ECHTERNACH
LUX
TRIER
7TH ARMY 4 CORPS
SAARBURG
LUXEMBOURG
Saar
PALATINATE
RETHEL
STENAY
MONTMEDY

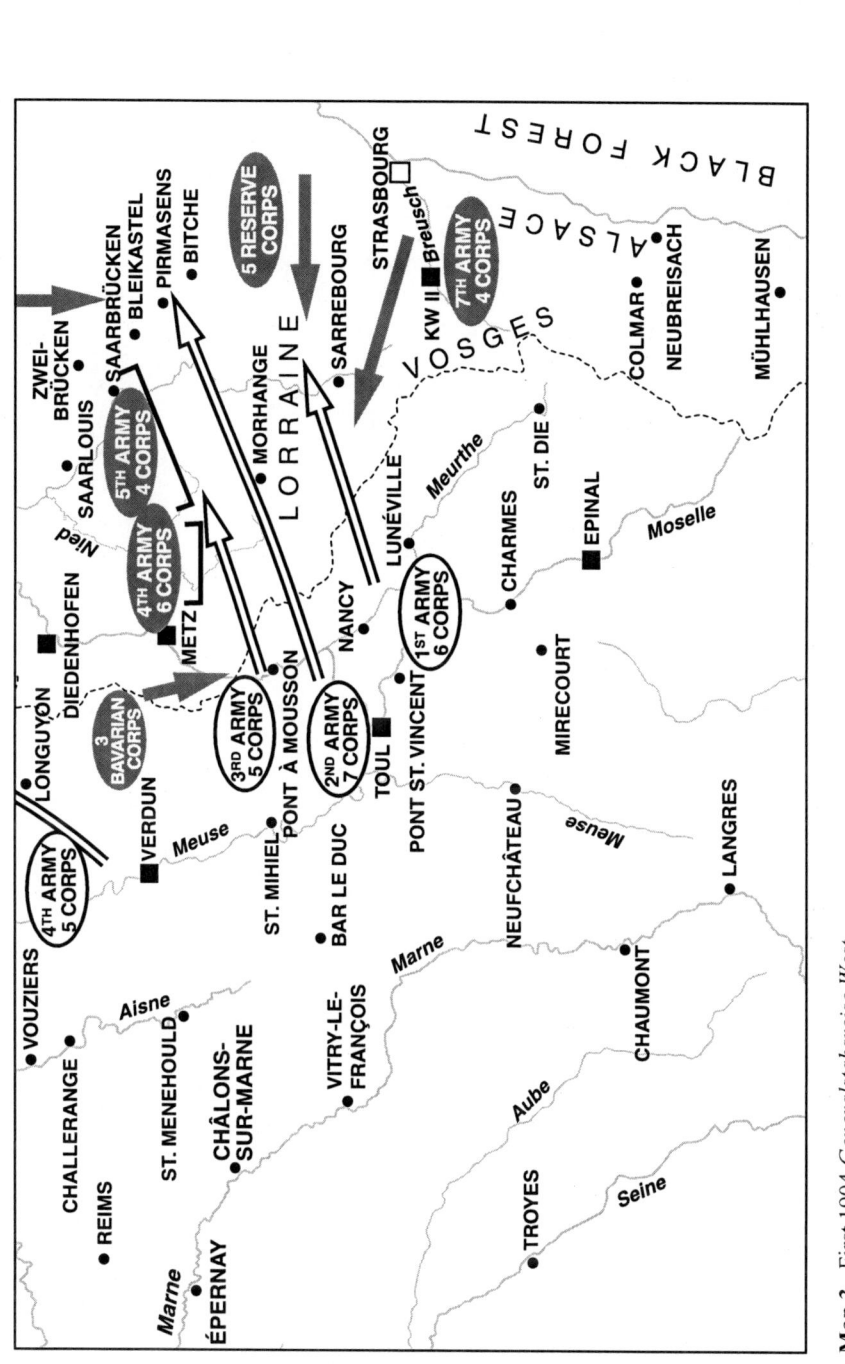

Map 3 First 1904 *Generalstabsreise West*

front without violating Dutch territory. Further, it is not possible to execute the deployment so that it takes place solely along the Rhine north of the Moselle. Rather, the deployment must include the rail lines that extend as far as Strasbourg. In so doing, the deployed German army literally offers its left flank to the French.

I have asked a number of officers [10] to develop a French operations plan under the precondition that the French, who have begun their deployment very early, hear that the Germans are conducting their deployment on the lower Rhine. They will therefore remain under no doubt that the Germans would advance through Belgium. Many officers decided to allow the French rail deployment to run to its conclusion, at least for the combat troops, and then conduct a new deployment towards the second front. Several officers wanted to go from this second deployment immediately over to the counterattack. Others preferred to take up one defensive position or another at Reims–Verdun. In any case this double deployment, which must be followed by a third for the supply trains, is a very complicated undertaking, and it is very questionable if it would succeed.

Other officers wanted to attack the German left flank, which they expected to be at Saarbrücken. I think that this is a thoroughly healthy idea. If Metz is not considered[11] and a French attack is postulated from their assumed deployment, as shown on the map, the result is Leuthen on a grand scale. The Germans will of course have to turn to the south, even as the Austrians had to do. But such a movement generally does not proceed optimally and in good order, even as it did not at Leuthen, and the attacker has the advantage, even if he is not numerically the stronger.

However, the situation will be changed when Metz and Strasbourg are taken into consideration. I do not mean a Metz and Strasbourg that are to be besieged and [11] defended, but rather a Metz and Strasbourg in which armies are assembled and through which they march in order to attack the enemy by surprise. If this assumption is made, then the situation is fundamentally different. First, the French will not be expressly forced to do so, but they will be induced to divide their forces and send one part to the east and the other part to the west of Metz, because they will not have enough room east of Metz, because they will want to cover their left flank, or for other reasons. This already causes an advantage for us. Another advantage lies in the fact that the French must cover their advance against Metz, where an army can be assembled, as well as against Strasbourg and the Rhine, where another army, if only of reserve units, can also be assembled. If they do this, they will so weaken themselves that they will not have enough strength to defend against an attack from the north. If they do not cover these fortresses adequately, they will be enveloped from the left or the right or perhaps from both sides. All of the operations plans that were submitted to me which propose to attack the German left flank suffer more or less from inadequate protection for the flanks. If the enemy does not make too many errors, these plans must lead to an envelopment of their uncovered flanks. Even the plan that was used in this exercise must suffer this fate. The author's

---

[11] The first modern fortifications at Metz would not be completed until late 1904, and even this constituted only the torso of a complete fortress.

name will not be mentioned. The officer, who did not agree with the plan, but attempted to execute it to the best of his ability, still could not correct its inherent errors.

[12] The French therefore advanced with 14 active corps, 4 reserve corps and 2 reserve divisions, together 40 infantry divisions (two corps had three divisions) and four cavalry divisions between Metz and Strasbourg. Five active corps, 7 reserve divisions (18 infantry divisions) and 2 cavalry divisions accompanied this movement along the left bank of the Moselle. Two active corps, 2 reserve corps and a cavalry division were assembled further to the west [66 infantry divisions]. Belgium and Holland, threatened by Germany, sought French assistance and placed their armies at French disposal. The French army thereby grew by eight infantry divisions and three cavalry divisions [74 infantry divisions grant total]. A massive force of far more than a million infantrymen was poised against the left flank of the widely extended German army. To oppose this the Germans must draw as many corps as possible towards their left flank and assemble them so as to find support on their right from Metz. The reserve corps, which naturally deployed on the Rhine, threatened the enemy right flank. The important thing was for the northern wings of both fronts to link up, to prevent an enemy breakthrough, and at the appropriate moment to advance with strong southern wings. The 3rd, 4th and 5th Armies conducted this mission in an appropriate fashion. They gradually formed a bow with a strong right wing which extended from the south of Metz to Bitche. The Reserve Army did not conform to the concept of the operation. Instead of moving with the right wing (II Bavarian Reserve Corps) through the mountains to link up with [13] left wing of the 6th Army (XVIII Corps), holding back the left wing (XII Reserve Corps) at Hagenau– Brumath, the exact opposite was done. The left flank was advanced, the right held back and the enemy was, completely unnecessarily, given the chance to gain an advantage. The 7th Army also forgot its principal mission: envelopment of the enemy left wing, for which three corps (XIII Reserve, I Bavarian and XIV) were immediately available and could even be reinforced. It turned the main body towards Strasbourg, although this fortress was strong enough to protect itself for a considerable time.

On the eastern front 15 active corps and 6 reserve corps, in total 40 infantry divisions and 4 cavalry divisions, opposed the French. In the number of divisions there gave a small superiority over the opposing French forces. In actual numbers of troops the German infantry was not inconsiderably weaker. Both sides were probably equal in field artillery. Only the heavy artillery added a considerable weight to the scales for the Germans. Eight active corps, three reserve corps and five cavalry divisions advanced between the Meuse and the Moselle. Two reserve corps were detached against the Dutch.

The gentlemen will ask where all the reserve corps came from. If we want to march through Belgium, many tasks arise, such as the occupation of Belgium, and covering both Belgian fortresses and [14] the Dutch. We must also have reserve troops available so that when we enter France we can cover the flanks and the French fortresses must be surrounded. More reserve units were formed than previously, not in our imaginations, but rather according to reality, the principle being: that when you want to win, you can never be strong enough. [Schlieffen then discussed the details of the battle near Strasbourg.]

[16] The events [French defeat] at Strasbourg and Molsheim, the proximity of Metz and the reports that the enemy was on the Saar, convinced the French not to advance any further, but to wait for the enemy attack in a defensive position. Due to its length, the position that they chose could not be uniformly favorable. In part, as we have been able to establish, it was very advantageous for the defender, in other places less so. But even in the areas suitable for the defense, with careful reconnaissance the attacker could bring batteries into position during the night. The infantry will always find folds in the ground which will cover its advance. In any case, there will always be covered positions for the heavy field howitzers, with their maximum range of 6,000 meters, from which they can fire effectively. In addition, in such a long position there will always be a gap somewhere. The precondition for finding such gaps is that the position be attacked along its entire length, and that the frontal attack not be delayed until the envelopment is effective, as is often the case. On the map for the evening of the 19th mobilization day (1:200,000) the position is displayed with more detail. Ten French corps are defending, ten German corps are ready to attack. The only German superiority rests in the superior allocation of the forces and in the form of the attack, which is prepared to conduct an envelopment. [The next section discussed indecisive combat in the northern Vosges.]

[17] Through a misunderstanding or perhaps just by chance there was a gap generally in the centre of the French position. The XIX Corps penetrated here and, continuing the advance, struck the French 3rd Reserve Corps, that is, a corps with little artillery and above all inferior in combat power. It could therefore be assumed that this reserve corps would have been forced back and the gap would have become wider. The German penetration would have pressed against the newly created interior flanks, thereby creating a normal breakthrough. The report of this breakthrough caused the commander of the neighboring (3rd) army [18] to send a corps which he had in reserve in support, not to the corps that was being forced back, but to its neighbor. It was supposed to conduct a flank attack here, although there was nowhere a flank to be seen that could have been attacked. It is not clear what occurred, but when an entire corps advances on a three-kilometer front to conduct an attack, it can only do so in masses. There are examples in military history, for example at Wörth, where advancing skirmisher lines have been forced back by the appearance of massed troops. Given such examples, it is possible to concede that this corps made a certain impression. It would soon have fallen apart under the fire of the enemy batteries and attacks on both flanks. Little would probably have remained of this corps and it can only be regretted that such an unfortunate use had been found for it, although it could have been of great utility elsewhere.

The decisive battle took place on the French left flank. They had chosen to make the Wallersberg the anchor for the position. Once it was fortified, it exercised a remarkable magic influence on all the commanders. I don't think it was of much advantage. Given the great masses of artillery which the Germans could deploy here, the little ridge would have been deluged with shells and I do not believe that the defenders would have been able to hold for very long. In any case, this was not of considerable importance. An entire German army passed by the French left flank. [19] Three active corps and a reserve corps were able to advance south of the Wallersberg. They were initially only delayed by the 68th Reserve Division, which was at Louvigny. However, no matter how strong this position was or how bravely they fought, they could not stand long against the vast superiority of the German artillery and the far more numerous German infantry. They were broken into fragments and had to retreat. The 54th Reserve Division, which extended the front of the 3rd Army, could not materially improve its position. Both it and the army were attacked in the front while the three Bavarian corps swung one after the other against the French left flank. The corps on the far right flank was to have marched to Château-Salins, but did not reach its goal that day. The next morning it was opposed by the 18th French Corps, which it defeated, so that the victor was able to close the bow at Château-Salins. The French wanted to hold their position on the Wallersberg, but this steadfastness became their downfall. Because they stood fast, they were completely cut off and were lost. The others finally decided to withdraw in order to occupy a new position behind the Seille. However, the German cavalry was already south of the river, and their artillery dominated the crossing points. The trains, supply columns, baggage and vehicles, which had to cross the river in order to retreat, were thereby brought to a halt. Streets and crossing points were soon completely blocked. The withdrawing army therefore came to a halt on the Seille [20] and the pursuing Germans soon caught up with them.

The French right wing was in an even worse position. Here, as has been said, a German corps (19th) had broken through the gap between the French 5th Corps and 3rd Reserve Corps, pushed back the right flank of the latter and the left flank of the former and with it pushed the right flank of the French 2nd Army in a south-easterly direction. In addition there were the retreating columns of the 1st Army.

The commander of the German 7th Army had recognized days previously that it was not necessary to stay at Strasbourg with his corps, and that it was much more important to initiate the pursuit, which must begin soon, in a timely manner. He sent his corps to Schirmeck and beyond on one road and on the day after the battle (21st) had already turned at Saarburg and Cirey in order to bar any retreat route for the French right wing. The situation of the 1st French Army thereby became desperate.

In the meantime the French had also advanced on the left bank of the Moselle. The German mission here was obviously to prevent the enemy from crossing over the Moselle north of Diedenhofen, in order to take part in the battle from there. That was initially difficult, because the right flank of the 3rd Army and the 2nd Army were very far to the rear. It was therefore initially important to hold on the Moselle with the left flank of the 3rd Army, in order to prevent the French from bypassing this front, and to wait until the other corps had completed their turning movement and approach march.

[21] Miraculously, the commander of the 3rd Army was ordered to give up the completely correct position he occupied and to advance with his left wing leading. This order was probably motivated by the desire to gain a favorable position for the left wing of the 3rd Army, and the Ulzette River seemed to offer such a position. This river might constitute a good frontal obstacle but its orientation offered the enemy a clear route to the left flank of the 3rd Army. The left-wing corps was defeated, as was the division that came to its assistance. The entire army was forced

to fall back behind the Sauer. Only the difficulty the French experienced following over this river saved this German wing. It won enough time to deploy on a new front and was able to defend in place the next day. It was almost unsuccessful in doing this too, for French columns were advancing against the entire front of the 2nd and 3rd Armies and the Belgian army was advancing against their right flank. The French could have won a complete victory if the corps of its extreme left wing (14th, 15th Corps, 39th Reserve Corps) had been moved from the start further by rail and not left too far to the rear as they were now. The report of the defeat on the right bank of the Moselle and the simultaneous appearance of the German 1st Army north of the Sambre convinced the French commander to pull back the 4th and 5th Armies. Had he not done so, the German 1st Army would have advanced into his rear from one side and several corps from the German 4th and 5th Armies would have done so from the other.

[22] The German operation has provided the proof that a French attack against the left wing of a German Army marching through Belgium is not easy to execute. It would have been more difficult for the Germans to have solved their problem had the French not divided their forces, but had attacked to the east of Metz [between Metz and Strasbourg] with at the minimum their main body. The reinforcements that would have been gained for the decisive battle would admittedly for the most part have been used to cover the flanks. In spite of the great numbers of troops the French were not guaranteed the victory. The question is, how could the now unopposed German troops on the left bank of the Moselle enter the battle.

In considering the German movements, one must be convinced of the necessity that the Army commanders make the Supreme Commander's plan their own and that one concept must motivate the entire army. The arbitrary and uncontrolled movements on the German wing at Strasbourg betray no evidence of a unified concept.

The principal objective must be to envelop the enemy. Then it is necessary to avoid being enveloped oneself. The first principle was neglected. As far as the second, the enemy was given all the advantages possible . . . .

[23] Many officers recognized the importance of Metz for the operation. However, there was also no lack of officers who believed that they could block the influence of the place on enemy operations with one or two reserve divisions. It was hardly possible to perceive from the measures of the commanders that Strasbourg and the upper Rhine fortresses could influence the fate of the armies. The French made a long flank march parallel to the Rhine from Belfort to Molsheim without feeling the least bit uneasy. The Germans seem to have regarded it of more importance to protect Strasbourg from any enemy contact than to sortie from there with full force against the unprotected French right flank.

The defensive is the stronger form of war. Therefore it is usual for the party which perceives itself to be the weaker to take refuge in a defensive position. This is the beginning of the end, unless there are forces outside the defensive position which can effect a relief. If this is not the case, in the end even the best position will be made untenable by being outflanked or enveloped. If the envelopment is to succeed, it must be conducted in conjunction with a frontal attack. The frontal attack must not wait for the envelopment. Rather, the flank attack must meet an enemy who has been fixed in place to the front.

In every age there have been prophets who would oppose the firing line with masses, the bullet with the bayonet. Prague, Waterloo, the Alma and Königgrätz bear testimony to that. A few weeks ago [24] a massed Russian rifle regiment was shot down by encircling Japanese troops. Nevertheless, one commander wanted to commit a closed-up mass of 32 battalions against the concentrated fire of enemy batteries and infantry.

In order to assist the attack we have received effective support in the form of the heavy and light field howitzer.

Part III

THE GREAT 1905 WAR GAME[1]

Thirty-six pages, typed, with seventeen maps, which in Freiburg were not in the file with the text but were found in Schlieffen's papers. The Bavarian Kriegsarchiv also has a complete copy.

From 1896 to 1905 Schlieffen held an annual winter wargame. This is the only one to survive, though a summary of the 1897 war game is in Wilhelm Groener's papers.[2]

This is the culminating point of the Schlieffen doctrine, which exploited Germany's interior position and the mobility of her rail net to counterattack against the advancing French and Russian armies.[3]

Chief of the General Staff of the Army   Berlin, 23 December 1905

    J. Nr. 13083 Z

War Game November/December 1905

    Exercise Critique

        Secret!

The situation on which this war game is based is the same that appeared months ago in the *France militaire* and later the *Matin*, from which it was picked up by all the newspapers. It concerned war between Germany on the one side and England, France and Russia on the other. As unlikely, or better yet, impossible that such a war will ever take place, it offers enough interest for us to concern ourselves with it. Fundamentally, it presents nothing new. For about 20 years we have lived in the expectation of war on two fronts. It has been said again and again for 40 years that in addition to a theatre of war in the east and one in the west a third in the north would be added. For a considerable period it has not been believed likely that the Italians would lend us worthwhile assistance and tie down significant French forces on the Alpine front. On the other hand, we can assume, as in the past, that the Austrians will keep a part of the Russian army occupied. Therefore, we will have to fight against the entire French army, without detachments against Italy, as well

---

[1] BA-MA PH 3/646 Schlußbesprechung Kriegsspiel November–Dezember 1905. Maps BA-MA N43/133 Nachlaß Schlieffen. Also Kriegsarchiv Munich Generalstab 1237.
[2] Zuber, *Inventing the Schlieffen Plan*, pp. 156ff.
[3] ibid., pp. 206–12.

as all the European forces of the British army in addition to a significant part of the Russian army.

The most interesting, if not the most important, question, is [2] how Britain would participate in the war, and if its army, as some say, would land in Jutland, where it would feel a bit lonely, or, as others would maintain, in one of the Channel ports, in order to play the unenviable role of an auxiliary army. The participants of this war game decided the question in favor of Dunkirk and Calais. The three English corps therefore only provide reinforcement for the French army. Our enemies are thereby reduced to two: one English–French, whose line and reserve troops, without counting the other arms, consist of 1,300,000 infantrymen, and Russia, whose armies committed against Germany can be numbered at 500,000 infantrymen.

To conduct an offensive against both and march with one army on Moscow and another on Paris would in the best case very quickly put us in a situation that Clausewitz characterized as "strategic emaciation". Even an offensive against one enemy alone, whether into the swamps and forests of Poland and Lithuania or into the maze of French fortresses, would require so many forces and so much time that too little would be left over for a defensive against the other. It is advisable to wait for our enemies to advance, and attack the first to cross our borders, then turn on the other. The enemy can thwart this plan by crossing our borders in the east and west simultaneously. The question then is, should we [3] concentrate the strongest possible forces and first engage the stronger or the weaker enemy? There are many points for and against both courses of action.

The choice fell on the east, because there was a greater possibility not only of defeating the Russian army, but of completely smashing it, in order to turn against France with greater freedom of action. Even this plan could not be realized to the desired extent. The number of corps that could be transported on the few rail lines leading to the small strip of German territory east of the Vistula is limited. It was possible, aside from fortress garrisons, Landwehr and Landsturm troops, to make available for the eastern theatre of war only 13 active corps and 12 reserve divisions with 456,000 infantrymen. This resulted in an inferiority in rifle strength to the Russians' 11½ active corps and 10 reserve divisions (500,000 infantrymen), and a small superiority in corps, divisions and guns, but one which certainly was not sufficient to insure the defeat and destruction of the enemy. However, such assurance was absolutely necessary. We could not conduct war in the Manchurian manner, pushing the enemy slowly from position to position, sitting for months inactively opposite each other, until both adversaries were exhausted and decided to make peace. Rather, we need to eliminate one enemy in the shortest possible time in order to be free to turn on the other. [4]

The theatre of war offers us two advantages. The first accrues to us from the Masurian lakes. They extend from Angerburg to the south of Johannisburg and form an obstacle about 75 kilometers long. The principal road which leads between them is blocked by Fortress Boyen at Lötzen. The remaining roads can be blocked to the east as well as the west by field fortifications. To some degree two fortresses are formed between the Löwentinsee and Spirdingsee and between these and the Niedersee, which can be considered to be occupied by Landwehr and Landsturm and equipped with heavy artillery.

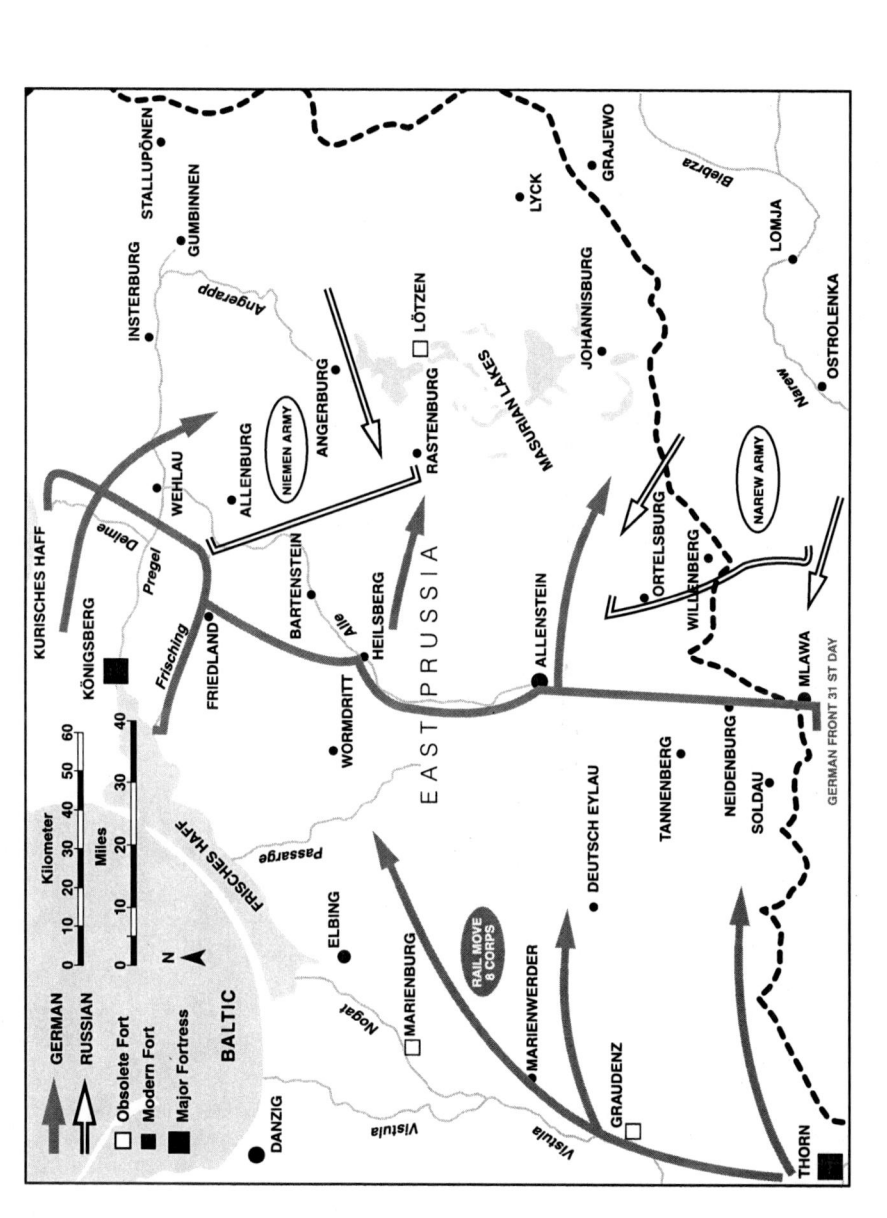

Map 4 November–December 1905 *Kriegspiel Ost*

The Russians, who advanced with one army (18 divisions) from the Niemen and another (14½ divisions) from the Narew, could first link up on the west side of the lakes. This gave the Germans the opportunity to advance beyond the lake barrier and attack either the Niemen or the Narew Army in the flank, or attack one of the Russian armies on the west side of the lakes with superior forces before it could unite with the other.

The other advantage comes from the fortress of Königsberg, although admittedly not Königsberg in its current condition. This Königsberg can be rendered harmless by a few reserve troops. Even a Königsberg with the planned extension north to the sea is not of any value worth mentioning. For our current needs a fortress is necessary in which an army is based and from which an army can sortie. The extent [5] of such a fortress is established by nature in the course of the Deime, the Pregel and the Frisching. We cannot expect that the engineers will construct armored fortresses on this 80-kilometer-long line, but this is completely unnecessary. If, as was the case here, we are given four weeks time, we can supplement what nature has provided, to the degree that the Russians will not be able to immediately push into the fortress. In it an army can be assembled that can advance either across the Deime or the Frisching against the flank of the Niemen Army, which must march with the centre of mass between Insterburg and Angerburg on Friedland–Rastenburg and beyond.

Practically everyone who has been given leadership of the Russian armies has advanced with the Niemen Army in this manner and with the Narew Army around the south end of the lakes in a northerly or northeasterly direction, with the happy prospect of destroying the Germans, who they assumed have deployed behind the lakes or the Alle, with a concentric attack. They have been regularly deceived. The Germans have not waited in place for the completion of this envelopment. They have withdrawn and have used the opportunity presented them to attack the left flank of the Narew Army in a most effective manner.

From all this, the offensive options for the Germans, aside from a frontal attack, are: 1. against the right flank of the Niemen Army; 2. against the left flank of the Narew Army; 3. against the inner flanks of one or [6] both west of the lakes, before they can link up. There is not enough time for a similar attack east of the lakes.

To cover the deployment on the right bank of the Vistula:
I Reserve Corps (1st and 35th Reserve Divisions) was at Tilsit
The I Corps Landwehr behind the Inster
I Corps behind the Angerapp
Guard and 1st Cavalry Divisions were pushed forward to the border
I Corps Landwehr held the Masurian lake fortifications
XX, XVII and VI Corps were along the border between the lakes and Lautenburg [east of Soldau]
The Landwehr and Landsturm of XVII Corps as well as the 2nd, 5th, and 8th Cavalry Divisions were behind the Drewenz [north-east of Thorn]
7th, 9th and 11th Reserve Divisions to the south of Königsberg (aside from the normal wartime garrison)
II Corps on the left bank of the Vistula at Fordon–Graudenz
V Corps at Thorn.
As soon as the Russian advance was recognized, the following forces were

deployed by rail [on a line extending from the Deime through Allenstein to the west of Soldau]:

    Guard Corps to Labiau [behind the Deime]

    X Corps to Königsberg with a further forward movement to Tapiau north of the Pregel

    2nd Guard Reserve and 19th Reserve Divisions to Löwenhagen and Tapiau [east of Königsberg]

    Guard Reserve Corps to Mehlsack [between Königsberg and Allenstein]

    IV Corps, Allenstein

    XIX Corps, Osterode [west of Allenstein]

    III Corps, Deutsch Eylau [7] 5th and 6th Reserve Divisions following

    XII Corps, Strasburg [west of Soldau], followed by 23rd and 24th Reserve Divisions

    II and V Corps and the 3rd Reserve Division were also marching to the east.

The Russian Niemen Army advanced on six roads with its right wing along the Pregel in the direction of Friedland, the left wing through Angerburg in the direction of Rastenburg.

The Narew Army sought to link up with the Niemen Army, with its right wing moving in the direction of Sensburg [west of Lötzen] and its left wing covered against envelopment by a pronounced left echelon, moving forwards towards the north in a sort of "half column". When the Russian commander was absent for a short time his deputy came to the opinion that this left flank was too far to the rear and pushed it forwards. He thereby exposed his left flank to the German right flank (XII, V, VI German Corps) which was marching on Mlawa and Soldau. He would surely have suffered a defeat had not the Russian commander returned and pulled it back again. This measure was surely justified. But he was certainly being too careful in moving the three corps of the left wing behind the Orzyc and thereby bringing the entire forward movement of the army to a halt. The few crossings over the swampy banks of the Orzyc could have been blocked with far fewer troops and the left flank of the Narew Army would have thereby been adequately covered. As a consequence, the two armies could not link up [8] so that the Germans, as we shall see, pushed between them and forced the Narew Army to retreat.

This withdrawal made any envelopment of the left flank of the Narew Army impossible. Now it was only a question of a northern envelopment or a breakthrough. In order for one or the other to succeed, the enemy front had to be attacked, and in order to accomplish this the Germans had to first of all establish their own front. To this point little of the kind had been accomplished. The Germans attempted to construct a front as quickly as possible on the general line Mlawa–Allenstein–Heilsberg–Friedlend, which would receive the withdrawing I, XVII and XX Corps and the corps disembarking from their rail transport as well as the reserve divisions moving from the south of Königsberg. In spite of the difficulties which lay in the withdrawal of some units and the advance of the others, these movements succeeded thanks to the slow advance of the Niemen Army and the suspension of forward movement or retrograde movements of the Narew Army. The German movements were completed by the 30th day of mobilization.

On the 31st day both sides ran into each other. The right flank of the Niemen Army at this time remained practically uncovered. The entire area north of the

Pregel was left free for the enemy. Originally, three reserve divisions were assigned to cover the right flank. They could have been employed to block the Deime line or, as Napoleon probably would have done, followed the right wing deeply echelloned. [9]

The commander of the Niemen Army chose another method. He sent these three reserve divisions individually and in pieces to those places where enemy cavalry or infantry had recently been reported. In a short time one and one-half divisions were in part defeated, in part broken up, one division was committed to the front line and only a half division remained to cover a flank about 40 kilometers long.

There was no obstacle worth mentioning to the march from the north on the Pregel and Iser of the I Reserve, Guard and X Corps and a division formed out of ersatz units. The few Russian troops which held the bridges could not offer serious resistance.

While on the 32nd day the Niemen Army was engaged against roughly equal forces, its commander learned that early that morning the enemy had crossed the Pregel at several places and threatened his rear. In my opinion under these circumstances he had no other choice than to pull as many troops as possible out of the front line and throw them against the advancing enemy, while standing on the defensive in the original front line. The commander chose another method. He held two brigades in reserve and sent only two and one-half divisions against the enemy in his rear, which could hardly be able to attain a complete victory, and wanted to continue the attack with the main body of his army against the stronger enemy to his front. Since he felt he was too weak to accomplish this on the [10] entire front, he massed his remaining forces into three or four groups, which were so far separated from each other that the enemy was able to easily envelop and defeat them.

In real combat operations no commander could have conducted such a maneuver. The truth is that if one is going to follow the example of General Kuropatkin and pull out individual units in order to protect the flank, one may easily reduce the combat power of the front and be defeated.

Therefore on the evening of the 32nd day the individual groups of the Niemen Army also had to withdraw in front of the enemy counterattack.

The commander now intended during the night to take a position behind the Alle and the Omet in order to renew the battle, while at the same time once again withdrawing forces from the front line to engage the enemy forces which had appeared in his rear. Even though the position behind the Alle and the Omet did not appear unfavorable, all the necessary measures could not be executed by the defeated and completely exhausted army in the few available hours of darkness. Even if one assumed this to be possible, it was demonstrated one further time with convincing power that such a position, sought out in great haste, will nevertheless always be turned or enveloped on one of the flanks. Further, the divisions and brigades pulled in equally great haste out of the line and sent to the rearward front were not able to conduct either a coordinated attack [11] or defense. In any case both opponents wanted to hold two long lines in the east and west. The Russians could not completely occupy either one or the other. The Germans broke in through the gaps. The Russian position began to collapse. All the routes of escape were closed to the Russians.

On the 31st day the Narew Army also made contact and fought a battle, which was continued on the 32nd. The Russians held a long line generally from Przasnyßcz–Chorzele–Willenberg–Ortelsburg to the Große Schobensee and from the northern tip of this lake with the front to the north-west to Krummendorf [generally a bow from Willenberg to the Masurian lakes]. This [right] flank held by the Russian 18th and 6th Corps was attacked by superior German forces in the front and on the right flank and pushed back. The front line was thereby also rendered untenable over the long term. It nevertheless had to be held until the 6th and 18th Corps had reached the level of Ortelsburg. The withdrawal was thereby rendered extremely difficult. Nevertheless, because the measures for the withdrawal were made in an appropriate fashion, it could have been conducted without serious losses, had not, in spite of all the precautions, a subordinate commander neglected to occupy a crossing over the Orzyc. The Germans pushed across it on the 32nd and 33rd and on the 34th were able with brigade groups to block the withdrawal roads to the Narew, which ran through numerous defiles between the rivers and swamps, and to delay the Russians until the pursuing forces caught up with them.

[12] On the eastern wing the German 24th Division succeeded in reaching the crossing over the Skrwa at Dudy–Pußczanskie [in Russian territory south of the Masurian lakes] by the shortest road before the Russian 18th Corps and thereby permanently denied the enemy the crossing over the river. Through these two movements, four Russian corps were completely cut off.

The 6th Russian Corps was attacked during its march through Kovno [south of Johannisburg] by the German IV Corps, which had advanced from Johannisburg, and the German 40th Division, and could only continue the march after taking heavy losses while being pursued by the enemy.

One corps and three reserve divisions as well as four cavalry divisions escaped largely unscathed across the Narew at Ostrolenka and Rozan.

A large portion of the Russian army had been destroyed. The remnants were not able to undertake any operations against the victor. They probably would have sought refuge in Warsaw.

On the 35th day several corps that were located immediately near the rail lines could begin movement. A part of the German forces was needed to guard prisoner transports and police up the battlefield. Other units marched to appropriate rail stations to load for rail transport.

There is no reason to believe that the operation against the Niemen Army portrayed here would not succeed in wartime. It is only necessary that the envelopment be conducted with adequate forces and in the greatest possible breadth. Of course, an obstacle [13] like the Masurian lakes is necessary to conduct a complete encirclement of the enemy army. It is more doubtful if the encirclement of the largest part of the Narew Army would have succeeded, or if many commanders would have trusted their luck and pressed on across the Orzyc at Budki and into the unknown in the swamp and river area north of the Narew. Even if none had done so, the Russian retreat through an area that they themselves had intentionally left undeveloped would have been disastrous. The army would have crossed the Narew only after having taken very heavy casualties and would not have been able to resume operations for a considerable time.

In a future war we will have to contend with long positions reinforced with field fortifications. The ability of a few troops in a more or less dug-in position to resist far superior enemy forces will easily lead to an increase in the incidence of positional warfare. The Russo-Japanese War has demonstrated that. Over in Manchuria it may be possible for the opposing sides to sit for months in invulnerable positions. In western Europe we cannot allow ourselves the luxury of waging war in this manner. The machine, with its thousand wheels which provides the livelihood for millions, cannot be brought to a halt for long. We cannot fight twelve-day battles, moving from position to position, for one or two years, until both sides, completely fought out and exhausted, sue for peace and accept the other's conditions. We must seek to quickly defeat and destroy the enemy.

The long lines offer some prospect that we will find gaps through which the attacker can conduct a breakthrough. The Battle at Shaho provides an example, which however did not lead to a decisive victory.

In this war game it happened that a breakthrough was quite possible, if the undefended bridge at Budki was used, and that this breakthrough could lead to a significant success.

In general, however, we will time and again be required to conduct an envelopment: but not an envelopment with a division, and not one to push in an enemy wing, but rather a deep envelopment prepared well in advance and conducted with strong forces. We must advance against a wing with a Napoleonic *battalion carrée* of 100,000 and more men, so that not only the enemy flank is threatened, but also the enemy rear.

In this war game an envelopment of the right flank of the Niemen Army with somewhat over three corps can give an example of how such an operation should be conceived. However, this turned out to be weak, because of the relatively weak forces available. Nevertheless, it provides a point of reference.

It would be a gross mistake to rely on the envelopment alone. It must be conducted in conjunction with a powerful frontal attack, even when the desired number of units for the frontal attack is not available. And it must further be coupled with an unremitting pursuit. [15]

In this case the encirclement of the enemy was made easier by the Masurian lakes. Indeed, on other battlefields a similarly effective obstacle can be found, if not one identical to this. Too much reliance cannot be placed on such obstacles. It is more important to commit every unit to close every gap that the enemy, in his distress and despair, may use to find an escape.

In the west the small German army had no choice but to wait and see where the enemy, who was twice as strong, would make his attack.

Initially the borders, or more to the point, the rail lines, had to be secured. For this reason Landwehr brigades and cavalry divisions were pushed up to the Belgian border along the Meuse and the Moselle.

In the enlarged Metz, besides the wartime garrison, there was XVI Corps, the 43rd Infantry Division and nine Landwehr brigades.

The principal front between Metz and Saarburg was covered by two corps, two reserve divisions and a cavalry division.

XV Corps was in Strasbourg.

The 14th and 28th Reserve Divisions were in the upper Alsace.

A number of Landwehr brigades covered the upper Rhine.

Behind this were the three northern army corps and their reserve corps assembled behind the right wing at Cologne and Aachen.

[16] The XXI, XIII Corps and the three Bavarian Corps as well as a number of reserve divisions remained in their corps mobilization areas prepared to move by rail.

It was learned as early as during the deployment period, from observation posts established on the Belgian-French border, that a strong enemy army would assemble at Lille and that this would be joined by three British corps that would land in Calais. Several armies deployed along the Belgian border between Verdun and Maubeuge. But in addition, not insignificant forces seemed to have been pushed forward over the upper Moselle and to the Vosges.

Therefore, it was highly probable that the French intended to march through Belgium on both banks of the Meuse.

The Field Marshal [Moltke] explained the characteristics of this march through Belgium 50 years ago. The French could not continue their march over the Rhine, but must swing to the right towards the Moselle. If they were not disturbed in this movement, it was possible to calculate exactly when they would reach the line Verdun–Coblenz. If they succeeded in crossing the Moselle, they would be surrounded on two sides by the Rhine and the Moselle, and find themselves in an uncomfortable position between Metz, Strasbourg and Mainz.

The march through Belgium, as it was planned by the French, [17] is therefore subject to many difficulties, without being compensated by the prospect of great success. Such an advance only appeared possible if another French army went across the upper Moselle and supported the main army by swinging to the left against the line Metz–Saarburg. The French troops which were reported moving over the Moselle and against the Vosges appeared to intend to do something of this sort.

Therefore, first of all, these troops must be thrown back. The right bank of the Moselle had to be kept free and secure as an operational base and in order to be able to deploy the forces expected from the east. Therefore, the uncommitted corps, except for the ones near Cologne and Aachen, were brought forward in the following manner:

XIII and XXI to Strasbourg

II Bavarian to Saarburg

16th and 43rd Divisions to the south of Metz

I and III Bavarian to the area near Hüningen, where they linked up with the XIV Corps which had withdrawn over the Rhine.

The Germans wanted to conduct an enveloping attack from this deployment, but the French preceded them and advanced with several columns from Belfort over the Vosges as well as against Strasbourg. It was therefore possible for the Germans to advance with elements from Strasbourg up the Rhine valley and with other elements across the Rhine at Hüningen and Istein, where bridgeheads had been established, and then down the Rhine valley.

[18] The enemy forces, which for the most part consisted of territorial and reserve divisions, were pressed together in the narrow Rhine valley from the north and south and destroyed in a few days. Even though these were second- and

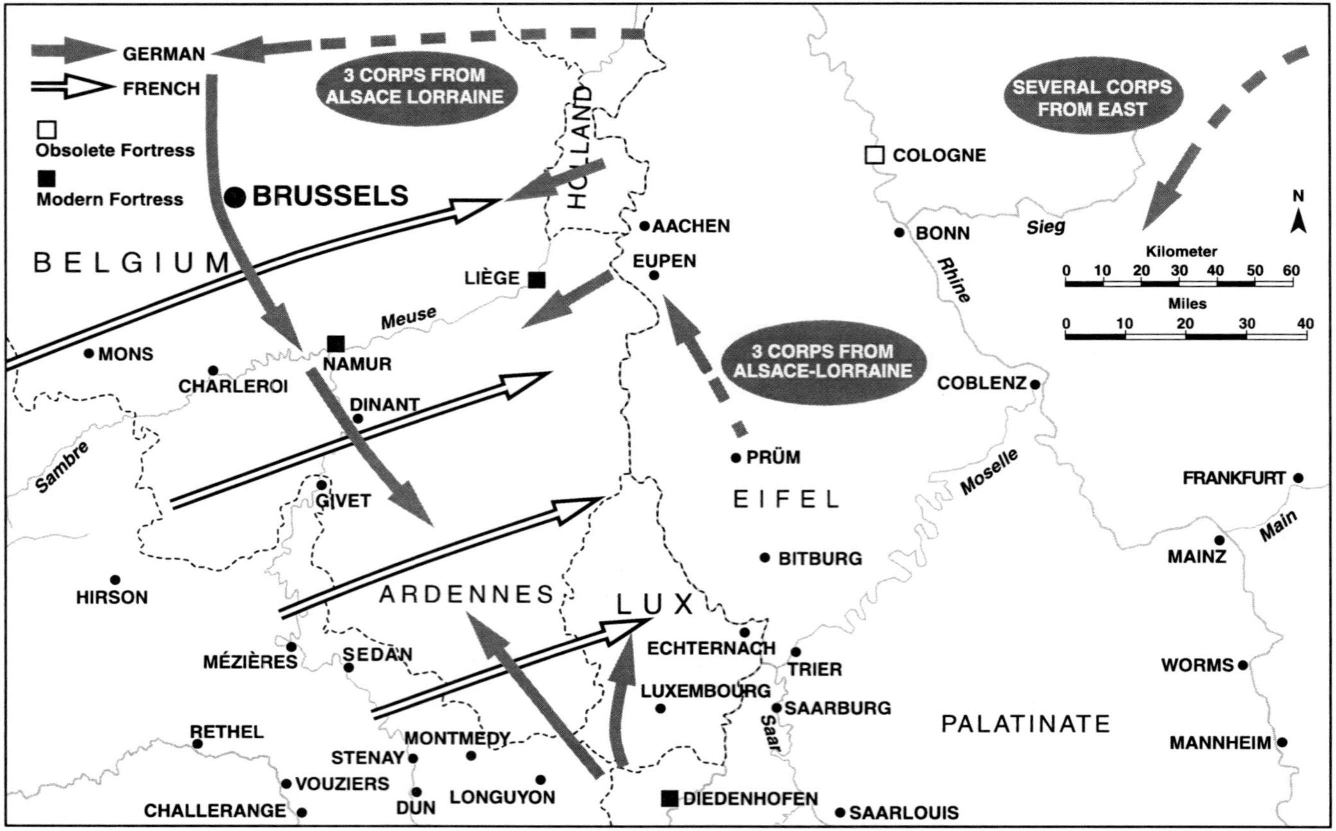
GERMAN
FRENCH
Obsolete Fortress
Modern Fortress
3 CORPS FROM ALSACE LORRAINE
SEVERAL CORPS FROM EAST
3 CORPS FROM ALSACE-LORRAINE
BRUSSELS
BELGIUM
HOLLAND
COLOGNE
AACHEN
BONN
Sieg
Rhine
EUPEN
LIÈGE
Meuse
MONS
NAMUR
CHARLEROI
DINANT
Sambre
GIVET
PRÜM
EIFEL
COBLENZ
Moselle
FRANKFURT
Main
MAINZ
BITBURG
HIRSON
ARDENNES
LUX
ECHTERNACH
TRIER
MÉZIÈRES
SEDAN
LUXEMBOURG
SAARBURG
Saar
WORMS
PALATINATE
MANNHEIM
RETHEL
MONTMEDY
STENAY
VOUZIERS
DUN
LONGUYON
DIEDENHOFEN
SAARLOUIS
CHALLERANGE
N
Kilometer
0 10 20 30 40 50 60
Miles
0 10 20 30 40

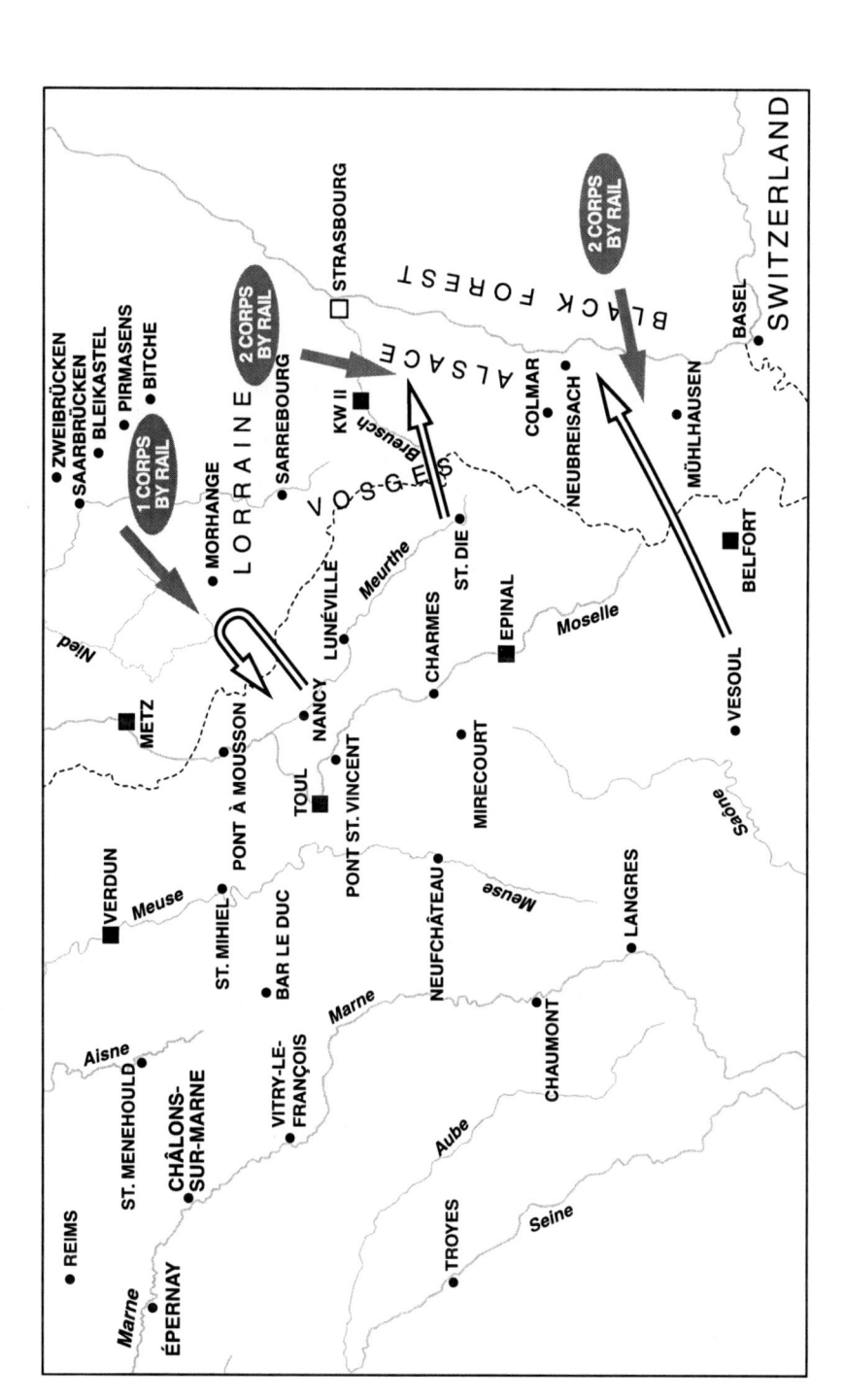

Map 5 November–December 1905 *Kriegspiel West*

third-rate troops, the enemy strength was reduced by twelve divisions at the very beginning of the campaign. The Germans had gained the *première victoire* (first victory) that the French had always desired, and in a brilliant fashion. This victory would have raised morale in Germany even as it lowered morale in France.

The German right wing between Saarburg and Metz threw the opposing enemy force back over the Moselle, so that the entire right bank of the Moselle fell into German hands.

It was now a question as to whether the Germans should exploit their victory by a pursuit across the Moselle between Toul and Epinal. In all probability the attempt to cross the Moselle would have failed due to the strength of the Moselle position. If it nevertheless succeeded, the Germans could in truth advance on Paris without having a significant [terrain] obstacle to their front. But they would have then been opposed by the entire Franco-British army under unfavorable conditions and with a poor line of retreat.

From the information to this point the conclusion seemed certain that the French intended an envelopment to the north and their entry into Belgium would soon be confirmed.

Under these circumstances the question was, whether the Germans [19] should wait behind the Moselle for the enemy attack. The defense of this river line seemed not unfavorable, for it could be combined with an attack across the Rhine against the enemy left flank. Yet it was not wise to sacrifice the entire left bank of the Moselle and the Rhine to the enemy and wait inactively as a large piece of German territory was devastated.

In spite of the limited forces available, the Germans had to attack, and there were plenty of opportunities to do so.

During their entire advance and maneuver to the right, the French left flank was threatened from Antwerp, from both banks of the Meuse and from the Rhine between Cologne and Coblenz. The attack must therefore be conducted against the French left flank. This must become increasingly effective as the French proceeded further to the west and exposed not only their flank but also their rear.

The Germans therefore decided to send as many corps as possible by rail to Antwerp, with the remainder going to Cologne to reinforce the corps already there (VII, VIII, IX). On the three (although only one-tracked) rail lines three corps could be moved to Antwerp by the 33rd day, three more by the 37th.

This movement had to be secured. For that reason the Belgians were asked to occupy the line of the Dyle and the Demer between Mecheln and Diest with their five divisions. The four Dutch divisions would extend this position beyond Hasselt and link up with the German [20] reserve corps so that the entire stretch between Mecheln and Liège was covered.

The question is, would Belgium and Holland comply with these requests?

By crossing the Belgian border France violated the neutrality of its northern neighbor. In order to preserve its independence, Belgium must defend its neutrality. In the enemy of France it found its natural ally. Holland acted in a similar manner. Its neutrality had not yet been violated, but must be if the French continued their advance. They would do well to add their strength in good time in conjunction to that of Belgium and Germany in order to maintain their independence. For there could be no doubt that if France and England emerged victorious in a war against

Germany both small states would become part of the booty, while in case of a German victory they could expect significantly more favorable conditions. Their own interests called Belgium and Holland to Germany's side. Of course it cannot therefore be said that in fact they will follow this call. The question as to which side appears more likely to emerge victorious must also have an influence in the choice of which side to take, and given the number of its enemies, Germany's chances do not look very good. For all that we can assume that both threatened states would make the wiser and healthier decision.

[21] The opposing side estimated that the value of the Belgian and Dutch troops was very low. Admittedly, the military system in both states was very much like that of a militia. Nevertheless, the Belgian officer corps enjoyed a good reputation, and as for the Dutch soldier, his temperament was suited to holding out in defensive positions. Both armies were initially assigned this easier form of combat.

It would later be shown that their opponents were also not of particularly high military value. They consisted above all of French reserve divisions, whose troops were well advanced in years and appeared little suited to particularly heroic deeds, as well as British troops, of whom Field Marshal Lord Roberts, who must understand what he is talking about, said in a public speech that they were poorly prepared for combat and that it would be the "height of insanity" to want to commit them to a continental war. Therefore the two opponents were about evenly matched.

[Schlieffen then described the strengths of the Belgian and Dutch defensive position.]

[22] The position could not immediately be enveloped. On the contrary, the attacker ran the danger of being outflanked. He marched into the envelopment, into a dead-end street. By the conduct of their offensive the Allies themselves increased the difficulties offered by the situation and the state of the defensive position. They advanced into the restricted area allowed by the fortress [Antwerp] and the defensive position with six French and three British corps, six reserve divisions and a territorial division, little concerned by the threat to both flanks. In disregard of the experience already provided by older wars, not to mention the experience made in South Africa and East Asia, they thought to overpower the devastating fire of the dug-in enemy with mass attacks and numerical superiority. They got the worst of the engagement. Gradually it became clear to them that in this manner with the 26 divisions of their left wing (4th Army, British and 2nd Reserve Army) they could not conduct the planned operations.

In the meantime the French 1st, 2nd and 3rd Armies continued their right wheel and on the 30th and 31st days reached the line Verdun–Liège. Further advance meant tearing the army into two parts. Either the 1st, 2nd and 3rd Armies swung farther to the south, which would leave the left wing alone north of the Meuse, or the 2nd [23] and 3rd Armies would swing to the left, to go around to the east of Liège, and open the way across the Meuse at and below Maastricht for the left wing. Then the 1st Army and 1st Reserve Army, etc., would be left with an entirely different mission, namely covering the Moselle.

The last alternative was to evacuate the north bank of the Meuse, which would hardly have improved the situation. The enemy would have followed to Liège–Namur and extended their right flank along the Meuse beyond the latter fortress.

The French leader decided initially to advance in a northerly direction with the 2nd and 3rd Armies, screening Liège, in order to open the way across the Meuse for the 4th and British Armies, while the 1st and 1st Reserve Armies provided security towards the Moselle. Then a gap must arise between the northern and southern halves of the army, into which the enemy could penetrate from the Rhine. To defend against this, a 5th Army was to be formed from elements of the 1st and 4th.

In the meantime three German corps and two cavalry divisions arrived by rail transport and foot march behind the fortifications of Antwerp. As soon as they completed assembling, they were to advance against the left flank of the French 2nd Reserve Army, which had been identified in the area of Mecheln.

It is possible that the enemy would have noticed this movement. Experience shows that in war a large number of reports arrive and are distributed, and an even larger number of rumors. In this case too a mass of reports and rumors would have spread concerning the position of the enemy army which had shown itself on the right bank of the Moselle. [24] One would have heard that the enemy army stood behind the Moselle, that part of it had been transported to the east, that it was assembling at Cologne, that it had been sent to the Netherlands and finally that it was also moving to Antwerp. It would have been impossible to base further decisions on one of these reports with any certainty, even as the Field Marshal [Moltke] objected to marching to the north after the first newspaper reports of MacMahon's maneuver [towards Metz in late August 1870]. Before such a step is taken, it is necessary to be certain, in order to avoid committing oneself to a completely useless operation. Every leader forms a picture of the probable enemy intentions. Reports that do not confirm this picture are initially rejected and he will maintain his estimate of the enemy for as long as possible. It was so unlikely that German corps would be transported to Antwerp, that when it was reported to the French leader that 100,000 men had already entered Brussels, he initially did not believe it.

The German leader believed that he could not wait for the second wave of three corps to arrive before conducting his attack. The secret could not be kept that long. If the French discovered the German intent, they could take adequate countermeasures to prevent a sortie from Antwerp. If the attack were only conducted by three German corps, supported to be sure by elements of the Belgians, there was a risk that the French could withdraw overwhelming forces from the 4th, 3rd and 2nd Armies and counterattack, even to the [25] south of Namur. Since the Germans could know nothing of the formation of the French 5th Army which was then in progress, and since they considered the 4th Army to be engaged, they therefore saw a particular danger in the 2nd and 3rd Armies, whose presence had been reported by the Landwehr and cavalry which had been pushed forward to the Belgian border. As soon as they received word of the German advance from Antwerp, they could turn around against these weaker forces. It appeared very important to the Germans to hold both of these armies in place so far as possible. In spite of their lack of adequate strength the German commander therefore ordered the three corps (VII, VIII, IX) which had assembled from the beginning to the south-west of Cologne to advance against the two French armies. The three corps moved by rail to Cologne after the battle in the south (XIII, XIV, XXI) should follow as quickly as possible,

The Great 1905 War Game   181

echelloned to the south. On the 32nd day the first three corps made contact with the French between Montjoie and Prüm. On the following day they intended to attack.

By chance, three fateful actions occurred on this (33rd) day:

1.) The French 2nd and 3rd Armies attacked the VII, VIII, IX Corps of the German 4th Army.
2.) Three corps (14th, 15th, 19th) of the French 4th Army marched off to join the formation of the 5th Army on the Meuse.
3.) The German 1st Army with three corps (XI, XV [Reserve], XVI) [moved by rail] and three Belgian divisions advanced against the left wing of the French 2nd Reserve Army.

It appeared that the first operation would destroy the Germans. [26] Instead, it was a complete French failure. Although the French had seven and one-half corps available, their advance massed them so closely together that they did not outflank the three German corps either to the right or left. The German corps saw that they had fulfilled their mission of attracting the enemy's attention and were then able to withdraw almost undisturbed. This withdrawal brought the Germans into terrain on the confluence of the Urft with the Roer which was very favorable for the defense and very unsuitable for the offensive. Here, between the two rivers and the Hohes Venn, with two German corps to their front, four and one-half French corps were so pressed together that they were rendered practically immobile. The French right wing attempted a deep envelopment of the German flank with two corps, but were defeated in detail by the arriving three German corps (XIV, XV, XXI) of the 2nd echelon [from Alsace]. It was touch and go. By the 36th day the seven and one-half French corps had not been encircled by the numerically far inferior German 4th Army, but they were nevertheless completely wrecked. They were saved only by the arrival of the French 5th Army, which caused the Germans to call off their enveloping maneuver (36th day). In such cases it is absolutely necessary that elements of two armies do not advance under different commands, but that an unified command be established.

The movement of the three French corps of the 4th Army (14th, 15th, 19th) did not completely succeed. The 3rd [4th?] Army had the mission of blocking off Liège on the right bank of the Meuse. It accomplished this mission in a more than adequate manner in the sector between [27] the Vesdre and the Ourthe, but in a completely unsatisfactory manner in the sector between the Ourthe and the Meuse. A German reserve corps advanced in the latter sector and forced the French 19th Corps to swing to the left, which permitted only the other two corps (14th, 15th) to continue the march over the Meuse.

The Germans had expected that they would break out of Antwerp somehow. Blockading this massive fortress required so many forces that in all probability there would be gaps. No one had foreseen that the break-out from Antwerp would be as easy and simple as was actually the case. The 2nd Reserve Army, which had the mission of blockading Antwerp, interpreted this mission to require it to block a side door, which was very difficult to use anyway, but not to block off the big front main entrance. In addition, they chose their position in such a manner that they extended their flank precisely in the direction of an attack from Antwerp. If this attack occurred, their rear was immediately exposed to all sorts of danger. It was therefore not surprising that the mere appearance of three Belgian divisions caused the left-most divisions of the 2nd Reserve Army to abandon their exposed positions. In the prevailing circumstances the withdrawal had to turn into a costly defeat and a panic flight as soon as the Belgians, who had two cavalry divisions in the area, conducted any sort of pursuit. It must therefore be assumed that the Belgians had followed closely and that the three reserve divisions (52nd, 60th, [28] Zouaves) would be thrown disintegrating and in confusion over the Dyle with their left wing at Louvain. It was now advisable for the French to first withdraw the reserve divisions from immediate contact with the enemy, to considerably reinforce the front to the west from the rear, and then to go over to the attack. The question is, would these measures have succeeded, given the enemy superiority and the support which he received from Namur. Nevertheless, these measures would have been appropriate in a situation in which the French would not decide to immediately evacuate the left bank of the Meuse, which could hardly be held in any case.

The measures which the French actually adopted were in part infeasible, in part completely inadequate. The defeated and disintegrating reserve divisions were to conduct a flank march in the face of the enemy, extend the French front and prevent a further envelopment. Individual divisions were brought forward from the rear to reinforce the threatened flank. In order to execute this mission they had to conduct long marches of up to 40 kilometers and they naturally arrived too late. This procedure was repeated in the following days. The Germans and the Belgians continually lengthened their front by drawing the divisions freed up from the Dyle and Demer position to the left flank, while at the same time extending the right wing to the south. In this manner they constantly extended their front considerably beyond that of the enemy. The French continually observed the same [29] procedure. They attempted to extend their front by flank marches and by moving individual divisions forward, without success. They continually saw themselves outflanked. After they had thoroughly weakened their eastern front by withdrawing troops, the Germans advanced here also, moving around Liège. Both French fronts pulled further and further back and with this rearward movement gradually approached each other. The northern wing also withdrew before the flanking fire. The circle became continually tighter. On the 36th day the encirclement was complete.

To this point the French commander had not considered the conditions north of the Meuse to be threatening. He believed that he had to deal with an unimportant enemy who could finally be thrown back without difficulty. The reports that he received on the 36th forced him to recognize the seriousness of the situation. A decision was necessary. Had he previously underestimated his enemy, now according to the laws of psychology he went in the other direction and overestimated him. He decided to withdraw to the French Meuse (principally with the 2nd Army), and with the 3rd and 5th Armies to the Belgian Meuse, covering the Moselle with the 1st Army. If the conditions are considered more closely, this retreat would have been very difficult to execute. Given the situation, it was not at all necessary. Admittedly, the French had twice taken heavy casualties – on the upper Rhine and north of the Meuse, which involved for the large part only troops of lower quality: reserve and territorial divisions, as well as the British army. [30] Only two divisions of the active French army had been lost on the upper Rhine and two corps to the north of the Meuse. The French still had 19 complete active corps in place, considerably more than the Germans could possibly have, even under the most optimistic calculations. The French also enjoyed all the advantages of the interior lines, though they could not concentrate on this inner position much farther if they wanted to avoid the logical conclusion: encirclement on the battlefield.

It did not have to come this far. The opportunity presented itself to deploy a strong army with its front to the west, in order that the enemy, who had just obtained a success north of the Meuse and now appeared in the process of advancing over the Meuse and through Namur, could be thrown back and the 4th Army and the British be relieved. Further, the 2nd Army and the right wing of the 3rd Army had to be withdrawn from their unhappy situation in order to be able to go over to the offensive themselves, or at least prevent the enemy forces opposite them from continuing their advance. The 1st Army must make a serious effort to throw the unimportant enemy forces to its front over the Moselle and take up positions so that no enemy forces could cross the river or sortie out of Metz.

There were completely adequate forces available for all of these missions, especially if the current composition of the armies was not considered sacrosanct.

The measures ordered by the French commander met these requirements, insofar as the 3rd and 5th Armies [31] were to be massed against the enemy main body and the 1st Army was given the mission of defending on the Moselle. The withdrawal ordered for the 2nd Army, however, made the success of the other operations questionable, even more so because there was a change of commanders, and the new commander put his principal emphasis in the retreat in the southwesterly direction, and then still other unpleasant circumstances were added.

During the initial blockade of Liège the sector between the Meuse and the Ourthe had been neglected. After the 34th day it was secured by two corps (3rd and 19th). The commander of the 4th Army had withdrawn one of these divisions (37th) to support the forces north of the Meuse, without being able thereby to avert the impending catastrophe. The other division of the 19th corps, (38th) was sent to oppose the advance of the Germans from Namur and succumbed to the numerically superior enemy. The 3rd Corps, instead of withdrawing in good time over the Ourthe, stayed with its front facing Liège and waited until the Germans (XI and XVI Corps) appeared in its rear. Thus its destruction was unavoidable. The number of available French corps was thereby reduced from 19 to 17 and the attack against the German forces advancing across the Meuse made more difficult.

Nevertheless, the German situation was by no means brilliant.

Their 2nd and 3rd Armies were for the most part occupied north of the Meuse with the defeated and still encircled enemy armies. The 4th Army was opposed by superior enemy [32] forces. The troops at Metz and on the Moselle were so weak that they could accomplish nothing. Reinforcements from the east would not arrive for several days. On the 37th day the 1st Army was still widely dispersed. However, the three divisions of the second echelon were moved first from Antwerp to Brussels, the last trains being sent immediately on to Namur and Charleroi. The army first had to be assembled in order to advance with six active corps and a reserve corps. This was no doubt the minimum strength that an army could be given that had the mission of advancing against a far superior enemy whose location and movements were both unknown. Once the army began to execute this mission, it had all of France in its rear and must be prepared at the minimum to be attacked from this direction by hastily assembled territorial divisions.

Originally the Germans had hoped to move several reserve divisions by rail to provide protection for the rear. The priority given to rail transportation from the east prevented this. If one or two corps were diverted to protect the rear, it appeared that the completion of the 1st Army mission was impossible. There remained only a cavalry division available to provide a degree of security against surprise in the rear. Gradually, as many troops as possible were withdrawn from the encircling army in order to be able to later follow the 1st Army.

As early as the 38th day the XV Reserve and XI and XVI active Corps [33] made contact with the enemy, who had occupied a position on the right bank of the Ourthe from the Amblève to beyond Durbuy and then to Marche, and who were not to be easily thrown out of it. The movement of the German 1st Army continued with the intention of reaching the area of Semois where possible with the right flank, while avoiding the forested area to the greatest degree possible, and awaiting the enemy attack in relatively favorable terrain. The French route to the west would thereby be blocked. Cavalry divisions with machine guns attempted to prevent the French from swinging wide over the Semois by blocking the few and difficult crossing points. From the east the 4th Army pushed the French 2nd Army back, until the French were forced by the barriers erected in its path to stop and defend itself against its pursuers. This completed the encirclement here as well.

In the meantime, the French 4th Army, the British Army and the 2nd Reserve Army had surrendered. Initially four Belgian-German divisions could advance to the Meuse and then over it. It was high time that the German 1st Army received this support. The French had committed their last reserve, the light infantry detachments which were guarding the highest Alpine Valleys on the Italian border, formed them into a corps, moved them by rail to Maubeuge, and then sent them through Givet into the rear of the 1st Army. Two divisions of the two right-wing corps (II and III Bavarian) [moved by rail from the upper Alsace] had to turn around and confront this new enemy long enough until the [34] four divisions moving from the north could complete their defeat.

The French 1st Army conceived of its mission as one of offering determined resistance on the Alzette and west of Diedenhofen. They would have done better to withdraw as soon as the 2nd Army reached the level of their left flank. Because they stood fast, their left flank was turned by the I Bavarian Corps, their right by elements of the corps arriving just then from the east and they were thereby at the least put in a very difficult situation.

This part of the war game offered the opportunity to show that a smaller army can defeat a larger one. It will hardly be able to do so if it moves directly against the front of the numerically superior enemy. It will simply be gobbled up. On the contrary, the smaller force must advance against the enemy in the most sensitive direction, seek to attack his flank and rear and force the surprised enemy to quickly change his front. When the smaller force does this, it places itself in the greatest danger and undertakes a significant risk, for its flank and rear are also threatened to the highest degree. This requires a determined commander, with iron character, a stiff-necked determination to win and troops who are clear that it is a question of life or death. And yet, these factors alone do not bring victory. It is also necessary that the enemy, surprised by the suddenness of the attack, becomes more or less confused and he is ruined by his hasty decisions, hastily executed.

[35] At Leuthen the Austrians believed that they would be attacked on their right flank. But the attack took place against their left. However, according to the drill manuals there was still enough time to conduct a left wheel. Had the Austrians done this, with their great numerical superiority they would have surely defeated the "Parade of the Potsdam Guard". But the turn failed. In their haste and hurry they only formed a deep, disorganized mob, into which the thin Prussian line fired continually at the word of command. The disorganized mob was defeated by the thin orderly line. This is true in all similar cases, and if one considers the map for each individual day of the war game, one must say that analogous conditions applied here too.

I want to mention one further thing. It has often been said that these war games are far too broad and too wide, and that lieutenant-colonels have no business leading armies. That is certainly true so long as they are lieutenant- colonels. Fortunately, they have the ambition to someday command an army, or if they are more modest in their goals, to be the commanding general of a corps, or to stand at the side of one as the corps chief of the staff. In wartime these corps will hardly operate independently. They will be part of an army, and the army an element of a group of armies. The corps will know nothing of the army and army group relations which determine their missions. The difficulties grow with the size of the [36] armies. Napoleon failed to some degree because his marshals did not act according to his concepts. If one follows the events of 1870, step by step one comes upon the errors of subordinate leaders. It has been reported that in Manchuria neither the Russian leaders nor the Russian General Staff understood either how to lead armies or the corps within the armies. Gentlemen, if you confidentially ask the commanders in this war game, you would hear: this or that subordinate didn't understand my instructions at all and acted in a completely different manner than I wanted. Another, it will be said, ruined everything for me, etc. It is an art for the supreme commander to make his ideas and his intent understandable to his subordinates. And it is an art for subordinates to grasp the overall situation, understand the supreme commander's intent and implement it in an appropriate manner. This art must be learned. A means for doing so is the war game. This means is imperfect, but nevertheless offers the possibility to place oneself mentally in a position within a great army and in the missions of the corps operating within it and then act in accordance with the intent of the supreme commander as well as in the interests of the whole.

In such war games annoyance and irritation are almost unavoidable. Hopefully the gentlemen present will find these acceptable, when they consider the objective, which is to train leaders for war. It is therefore irrelevant if one officer or another emerged as the victor. It is more important that he was presented with the requirement to make as many difficult and important decisions as possible.

Part IV

THE 'SCHLIEFFEN PLAN'[1]

This translation is based on what appears to be the final copy of the 'Schlieffen Plan' Denkschrift. It escaped the destruction of Potsam because the various copies of the Denkschrift *were among the few documents that had been transferred entirely out of the area. The original version was dated December 1905, though apparently written in January 1906, after Schlieffen had retired. There is also a supplement dated February 1906 concerning British intervention on the continent. Both are hand-written in two or more hands, and apparently cobbled together from the parts of several drafts. The last version is dated 1911 and typed, and includes Moltke's marginal comments, though there are still corrections of numerous typographical errors, and one section, which had been forgotten, was inserted, hand-written, in the margin. The maps referred to in the margin were almost certainly drawn in 1911. Map 6, which shows the great arrows sweeping to the west of Paris, has been widely reproduced. The 'Schlieffen Plan' was then in the possession of Schlieffen's daughters from 1913 to 1931.*

The original copies of the Schlieffen plan were 'discovered' by Gerhard Ritter in the early 1950s among the documents that the American army had seized and brought to the United States after the war. Ritter first published them in German in 1956 (and in English in 1958), along with an immensely influential commentary which criticized the plan for being too militaristic.[2]

Berlin, December 1905

[in left margin]
War against France

In a war against Germany, initially France will presumably limit itself to the defensive, in particular so long as it cannot count on effective support from Russia.

For this purpose it has long since prepared a defensive position, in large part of permanent fortifications, in which the great fortresses of Belfort, Epinal, Toul and

---

[1] BA-MA *Nachlass* Schlieffen N43/138; Zuber, *Inventing the Schlieffen Plan*, pp. 44–6, 212–19.
[2] G. Ritter, *The Schlieffen Plan: Critique of a Myth* (New York, 1958). The translation here is my own.

Verdun form the principal centers of resistance. This position can be adequately occupied by the large French army and poses great difficulties for the attacker.

Marginal comment by General von Moltke: "Whether France adopts an offensive or a defensive strategy will be determined fundamentally by the *casus belli*. If Germany begins the war, France will probably be on the defensive. If France desires war and brings it about, in all likelihood they will conduct it offensively. If France wants to recover her lost provinces, she must march into them, hence operate offensively. I do not regard it as entirely certain that France under all circumstances will be on the defensive. The border fortifications, which were built shortly after the 1870/71 war, certainly emphasize the defensive idea. However, this does not correspond either to the traditional, inherently offensive, spirit of the French nation or to the current teachings and doctrine of the French army."

[2] [In the left margin]
France:
995 battalions
444 squadrons
705 batteries. Without territorial troops and fortress garrisons.

Germany:
971 battalions
504 squadrons
801 batteries. Without Landwehr, Landsturm, and fortress garrisons.

This attack will not be directed against the great fortresses, for taking them would require a large siege apparatus, considerable time and large numbers of troops, the more so because it is impossible to invest them on all sides and the siege can only be conducted from one direction. The attacker on the contrary will advance against the zones between the fortresses. Two of these (Belfort–Epinal and Toul–Verdun) are filled with intermediate forts (*Sperrforts*) which, however, are not of much significance. It is more important that the terrain in these zones offers very strong positions, with one position lying behind another, their flanks protected from envelopment by the fortresses while at the same time the fortresses threaten the flanks of the attacker.

An attack on the right flank of the Moselle front (Fort Ballon de Severance) [north of Belfort] offers the greatest prospects of success. However, not enough preparation has been made to overcome the terrain difficulties here. Even when this has been accomplished, the campaign will hardly be opened with the siege of the "Ballon de Severance". However, the capture of this fort may be important at a later period in the war.

Nancy, which is protected primarily by field fortifications, is easy to envelop and to bombard with artillery, and can be attacked with a chance of success. However, once the city and the heights behind it have been taken (Foret de Haye), one runs directly into the fortress of Toul. An attack on Nancy offers almost only the advantage that in order to save the capital of Lorraine from occupation, the French [3] might decide to come out of their fortifications and fight in the open field. However, then their fortifications are so close to their rear, that if they are defeated they will suffer no significant damage and the victor will gain no great success. It is the same as defeating a sortie from a fortress, which causes the besieger and the besieged the same number of casualties, but leaves the situation for both sided unchanged.

Comment by General von Moltke [in the left margin]: "I regard it as absolutely certain that the French will not allow Nancy to be bombarded without a battle. The army high command would never dare to do so because of public opinion."

A frontal attack on the Belfort–Verdun position therefore has little chance of success. An envelopment from the south can only take place after a successful campaign against Switzerland and the capture of the Jura fortifications, both time-consuming operations, during which the French will not be idle.

Comment by General von Moltke [in the left margin]: "These can only be conducted in conjunction with a simultaneous offensive against the front."

Against an envelopment to the north the French intend to occupy a position on the Meuse between Verdun and Mézières. Their real resistance is not supposed to take place here, but behind the Aisne generally between Ste. Menehould and Rethel. They also appear to intend to hold an intermediate position behind the Aire. If the German envelopment is extended farther, it comes up against a position on high ground whose principal strongpoints are the fortresses of Reims, Laon and La Fère.
Map 1 [in the left margin]
Therefore, the Germans are opposed by:
  1.) the Belfort, Epinal, Toul, Verdun position, extended along the Meuse to Mézières. Troops will be pushed forward to the Vosges, to Nancy on the Meurthe and on the *Côtes Lorraines* between Toul and Verdun.
  2.) the intermediate position on the Aire
  3.) the position on the Aisne [4]
  4.) the position Reims–Le Fère.
An attack on these many strong positions could not be conducted with much confidence. An envelopment from the north-west against the flanks at Mézières, La Fère and across the Oise against the rear of the position seems to be more promising than a frontal attack combined with an attack against the left wing.

In order to conduct this attack, the Belgian-French border on the left bank of the Meuse with the fortifications Hirson, Maubeuge, three small *Sperrforts*, Lille and Dunkirk, must be taken and to be able to come so far the neutrality of Luxembourg, Belgium and Holland must be violated.

The violation of the neutrality of Luxembourg will have no significant repercussions aside from protests. The Dutch regard France, in alliance with England, to be no less an enemy than Germany. It will be possible to reach an agreement with them.

Comment by General von Moltke [in the left margin]: "If our diplomacy can accomplish this, it will be a great advantage. We need the Dutch railroads. Holland as an ally would be of incalculable value."

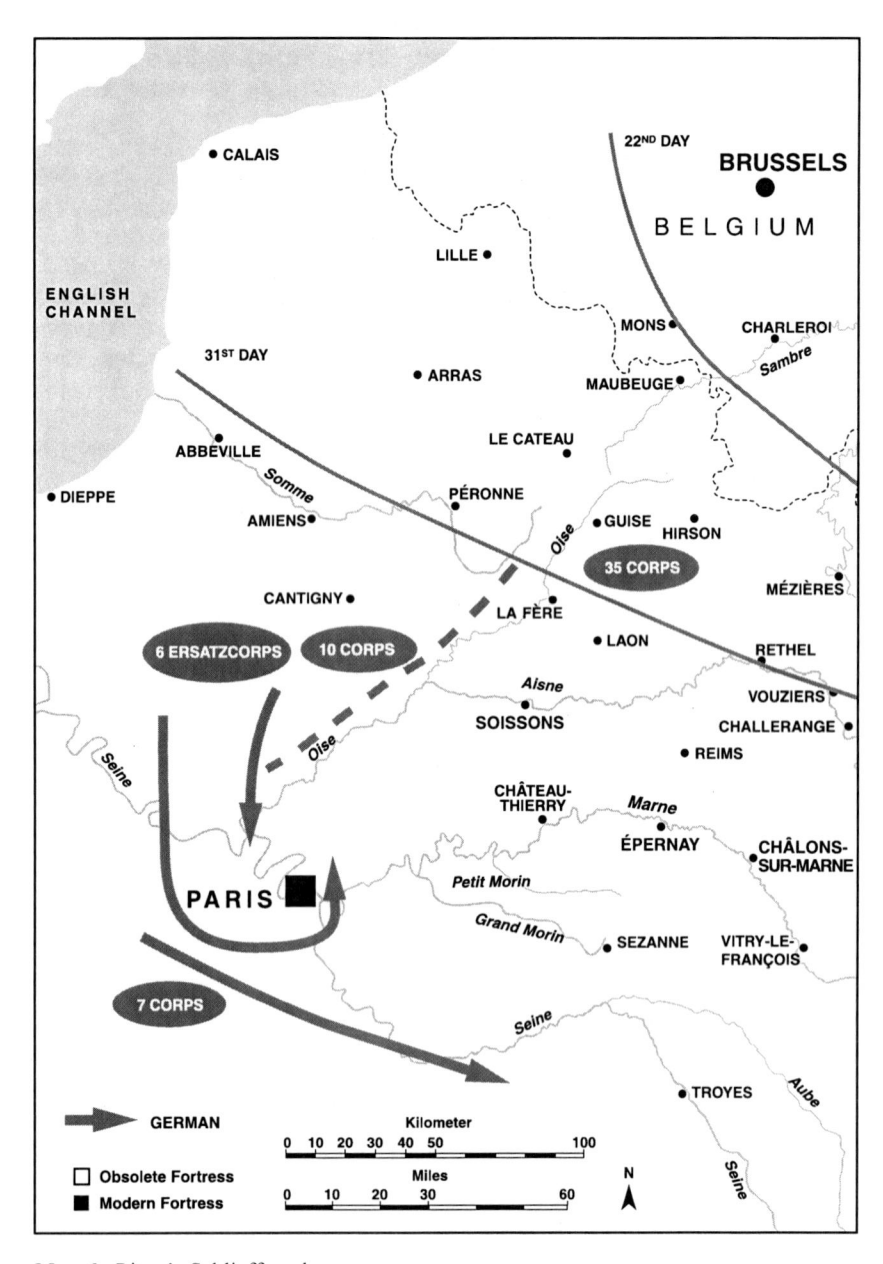

Map 6 Ritter's Schlieffen plan

The 'Schlieffen Plan' 191

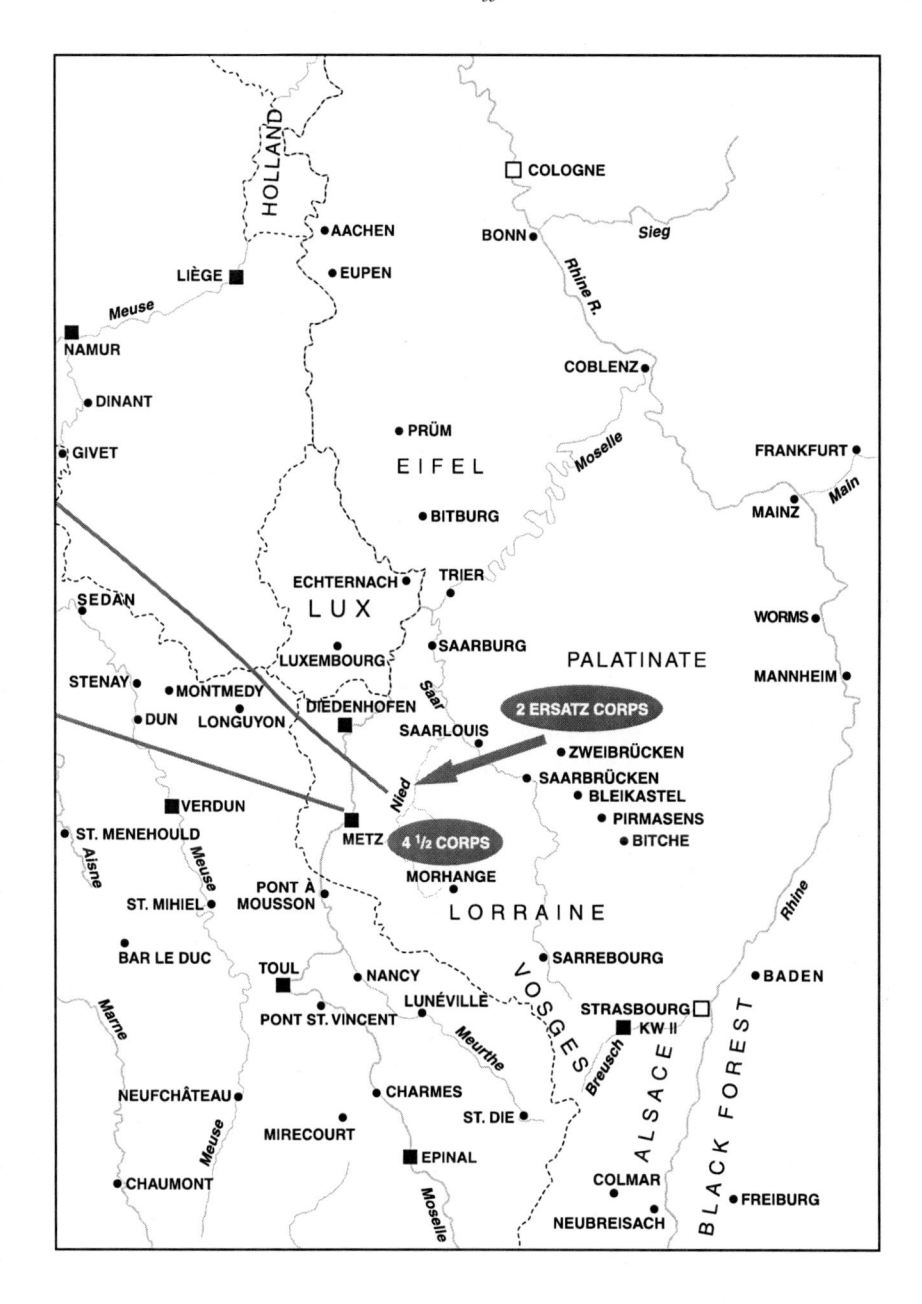

Belgium will presumably resist. Given a German advance north of the Meuse, its army will retreat to Antwerp according to plan and must be kept there, if possible also to the north by blocking the Schelde in order to cut the sea communications with England. An observation force will be adequate for Liège and Namur, which will receive only weak garrisons. The citadel of Huy will be taken or rendered harmless.

[In the left margin]
5 divisions [probably referring to the Belgian army]
Comment by General von Moltke: "A blockade of Antwerp would be followed as quickly as possible by a formal siege."
3 corps [probably referring to the force blockading Antwerp]

If the Germans advance while blockading Antwerp, Liège and Namur, they will find that the Franco-Belgian border in front of them is not so extensively and thoroughly fortified [5] as is the border with Germany. If the French want to defend here, they must move their armies and corps from the original front to the threatened one, along with the reserve forces, such as the corps on the Alpine border. We can hope that they will not entirely succeed. They would probably abandon the attempt to occupy such an extensive position and take the offensive against the impending invasion with all the troops that they could assemble. Whether they attack or defend, it is not unlikely that the two sides will make contact in the vicinity of the Mézières–Dunkirk border, and for this battle the German mission is to be as strong as possible. If this battle does not occur and the French should remain behind the Aisne, a strong German right wing would be of great value for the succeeding operations.

Comment by General von Moltke [in the left margin]: "Liège and Namur have no intrinsic value. They are, to be sure, weakly garrisoned, but robust fortified places. They block the Meuse rail line, and we cannot count on using it during the war. It is of exceptional importance to take at least Liège as early as possible, in order to have the use of the rail line."

If we want to attack the French positions at Mézières, Rethel, La Fère and beyond in the rear, it appears expedient to advance through Belgium solely on the left bank of the Meuse, swing to the left at Namur and deploy for the attack. There are not enough roads for a march on such a small front and moreover not enough rail lines to deploy the troops in such a manner. The conditions which the rail net imposes leads to a deployment of the German army which extends principally on the line Metz–Wesel. Here 23 active corps [6] 12½ reserve corps and 8 cavalry divisions will be assembled, initially to make a left wheel, moving against the line Verdun–Dunkirk. In so doing the reserve corps of the northern wing will cover the right flank, principally against Antwerp, the reserve corps of the southern wing will cover the left flank against an enemy advance from the line Toul–Verdun on the left bank of the Moselle. The attack would therefore not be directed exclusively against the flanks, but also against the left part of the front.

Three and one-half active corps, one and one-half reserve corps and three cavalry divisions remain on the right bank of the Moselle. Initially, they will draw the largest number of enemy forces towards themselves and away from reinforcing the northern front by attacking Nancy. Later, they will support the operation by covering the left flank or by reinforcing the right wing.

Metz will form the strongpoint for the protection of the left flank: not the current Metz, also not the Metz as is to be expanded by the last plan, but a Metz consisting largely of field fortifications, whose perimeter will generally follow the course of the Moselle, the Saar and the Nied, which will include a strong garrison of Landwehr troops and heavy artillery and which will be capable of drawing off a considerable part of the enemy forces.

Map 2 [in the left margin]

The German army should attempt to win the battle through an envelopment with the right wing. Therefore it should be made as strong as possible. For this purpose eight active corps and five cavalry divisions should cross the Meuse below [north of] [7] Liège on six roads and advance in the direction of Brussels–Namur. A ninth active corps (XVIII) should join them after crossing the Meuse above [west of] Liège. In addition it must render harmless the citadel of Huy, in whose area it has to cross the Meuse.

Seven reserve corps follow the nine active corps, the majority of which will blockade Antwerp, while the rest will initially further cover the right flank.

In addition there remains the option of a reinforcement by two active corps from the left bank of the Moselle, which can be brought up by rail (German and Belgian) as soon as the lines are free and put back into operation. These may be decisive.

Six active corps and a cavalry division, followed by a reserve division, will march towards the Meuse between Mézières and Namur. When these have crossed the river, 15–17 corps will be united on the left bank of the Meuse.

Eight active corps and two cavalry divisions will advance on the Meuse between Mézières and Verdun. Five reserve corps, supported by Metz, will cover the left flank.

Ten Landwehr brigades follow to the north of the Meuse, six to the south, six are part of the wartime garrison of Metz, three and one-half on the upper Rhine and one in lower Alsace.

It can be assumed that the German deployment will be completed undisturbed. At the most it might be necessary to move back the debarkation of the reserve corps on the extreme left wing, which now takes place on and behind the Saar above Saarbrücken. The advance of the entire army left [north] of the Moselle [8] will be conducted according to plan. It is completely uncertain whether the French army will march against us on the left [north] or the right [east] bank or both banks of the Meuse, or if and where it will wait for our attack. In any case it is important to pass through the defile between Brussels and Namur <u>before</u> making contact with the enemy, so that the eight corps can complete their deployment undisturbed. It is therefore important to accelerate the advance of the German right as much as possible. Since a left wheel will be conducted, the further the unit is to the left, the slower will be its advance.

The German armies advancing on the right bank of the Meuse [in the Ardennes] must be prepared every day to make contact with the enemy, even on this side of the river. At all times they must be able to establish a front which is at least adequate to conduct a defense even against a superior enemy. This will be made more difficult by the fortresses of Longwy and Montmedy, which should be taken if possible or at least rendered harmless, and by the hilly wooded terrain which extends south of the Semois, as well as the extensive woods to the north of this river. The army commanders must exercise continual vigilance and a suitable allocation of routes of march, which is that much the easier to attain since the daily marches can be kept short. The troops will only be able to accomplish their missions if they have trained for combat in woods and hilly terrain.

When the Germans have broken through the French belt of fortifications on the left bank of the Meuse, either [9] after winning a battle on Belgian territory or after a successful attack on the fortified position, or finally without having encountered any serious resistance, according to plan they will turn against the left flank of the French positions at Mézières, Rethel and La Fère. The French will probably soon abandon their forward position on the Meuse at Mézières–Verdun. But the French will also not wait motionless for the attack on their left flank in their positions on the Aisne and between Reims and La Fère. On the contrary, they will seek out a new position or conduct a counterattack. The latter is for us the more desirable. Assuming that the two corps have been brought forward from the right bank of the Moselle, the Germans will have united their forces as well as is possible in the given circumstances. They are marching in close formation. Their left wing is appropriately supported, their right is strong. It is not likely that the French, who first had to assemble their corps, will have put their entire army in such good order. The enemy envelopment through Belgium would have put them in such a situation that they will have resorted to hasty measures and more or less unjustified detachments. After the Germans have passed by the Belgian and the French fortresses on the northern border as well as the unfavorable terrain in the Ardennes, their situation must be seen as being the more favorable. Their situation will be less favorable if the French wait for the enemy attack in a prepared position or behind a river.

It is not impossible that a army which has been beaten in Belgium or northern France [10] will withdraw behind the Somme, which is connected by a canal with the Oise at La Fère, and renew its resistance there. This would lead to a march by the German right wing on Amiens or even on Abbeville.

However, this is not very likely. The German advance against the Meuse at Verdun–Mézières and farther to the west in the direction of Hirson will hold the French in place in their positions behind the Aisne and between Reims and La Fère. These positions, however, cannot be held when the Germans advance from the area of Lille–Maubeuge directly against their left flank and rear. The French must cover this flank or they must fall back behind the Marne or the Seine. They will do the latter only very reluctantly. They will hardly decide to give up northern France without serious combat. Therefore, if they cannot save their honor with a counter-offensive, they will probably prefer to form a defensive flank behind the Oise between La Fère and Paris, rather than surrender a great rich region, its beautiful fortresses and the north front of Paris. It can hardly be said that a position behind the Oise is impossible. Since the main front Belfort–Verdun needs only to be weakly held, the available forces are adequate for the defense of the Aisne and Oise. The position on the Oise is supposed to be weak to the front, but it is supported on the left by such a colossal fortress as [11] Paris. If the position is broken in the front, the defender would retreat behind the Marne or the Seine. The victor must be satisfied with blockading Paris first on the northern front, then on still other fronts, and finds himself forced to continue the attack with considerably weakened forces against a numerically superior enemy. In order to bring the enemy out of his new position, it will be necessary to go around the left flank, which is supported by Paris, and thereby once again commit considerable forces for blockading the west and south fronts of the giant fortress.

One thing is clear. If the French do not do us the favor (*Liebesdienst*) of attacking, and we have to move against the positions on the Aisne, Reims-La Fère and the Oise, we will be forced – regardless of whether the enemy holds the Aisne–Oise etc. positions or if they fall back behind the Marne or the Seine – to pursue them with one part of our forces, and to go around to the south of Paris with another force and encircle the fortress. We would therefore do well to prepare beforehand to cross the Seine below the confluence with the Oise [north of Paris] and to first blockade Paris on the west and south sides. These preparations can be made any way that you like: it will soon become clear that we will be too weak to continue the operation in this direction. We will have the same experience as that of all previous conquerors, that offensive warfare both requires and uses up very strong forces, [12] that these forces continually become weaker even as those of the defender become stronger, and that this is especially true in a land that bristles with fortresses.

The active army corps must be retained untouched to be used in battle and cannot be used for rear-area protection, for sieges and for blockading fortresses.

Map 4 [in the left margin]

When the Germans have reached the Oise, their rear area extends on the right to the sea and to the Seine below Paris. Its forward boundary is the Oise and the Aisne up to the Meuse below Verdun. The boundaries of the rear area from that point to the Rhine depend on the progress that the French might have made on the right bank of the Moselle. The rear area includes Luxembourg, Belgium, part of Holland and northern France. In this extensive area, numerous fortresses must be besieged, blockaded or observed. In so doing, the 7½ reserve corps and 16 Landwehr brigades available on the left bank of the Moselle will all be committed, with the possible exception of two and one-half reserve corps and two Landwehr brigades, which are absolutely necessary to reinforce the front and cover the flanks of the main body.

Footnote [in the left margin]: (It is not possible under any circumstances to leave an army behind to cover against a landing by the British at Dunkirk, Calais, Boulogne, etc. If the British land and advance, the Germans will halt, if necessary go over to the defensive, send enough corps to defeat the British and then in turn continue the operation against the French.)

We can reckon with:
Five reserve corps to blockade Antwerp (perhaps not enough)
to observe
Liège   2 Landwehr brigades
Namur   2
Maubeuge   2

Lille	3
Dunkirk	3
Mézières Givet Hirson	1
Longwy Montmedy	1

Above all the rail lines, insofar as they are necessary for supplying the army, have to be secured. The large cities, the heavily populated and highly industrialized provinces of Belgium and north-west France must be occupied. The entire area must provide the army a secure base. To accomplish this the Landsturm must be brought forward. If the law does not allow such a measure, on mobilization the law must be changed as soon as possible.

Even more troops must be obtained. We have just as many ersatz battalions as infantry regiments. From these battalions and the remaining troops from the reserve, if necessary from the Landwehr too, we must form fourth battalions as we did in 1866, and from these and ersatz batteries create divisions and corps, as we did in 1866. It is possible to create eight corps in this fashion. We cannot wait to raise these new formations until the need for them has become painfully evident, when the operation has been brought to a halt, but rather immediately after the mobilization of the other units.

[14] Therefore, first of all we have to bring the Landsturm forward to occupy the entire rear area from Belfort to Maastricht, etc. We must also bring forward the Landwehr remaining in the fortresses. And we must create at least eight corps. That is the absolute minimum that our duty demands we accomplish. We invented universal military service and the nation in arms and have proven to the other nations the necessity of implementing these institutions. But having brought our sworn enemies to the point of infinitely increasing the size of their armies, we have relaxed our own efforts. We still point with pride to our large population, to the masses of our people that are available to us, but not all of the useable manpower of these masses is trained and equipped. The fact that France, with 39 million inhabitants, can raise 995 battalions for the field army, while Germany with 56 million can raise only 971 speaks clearly.

The greatest need is for the eight corps with or behind the right wing. How many we can move there depends on the capacity of the rail lines. Those corps which cannot be moved through Belgium and northern France to the left bank of the Meuse and the Sambre must be brought south of Liège–Namur to the Meuse between Verdun and Mézières. If this is also not entirely possible, the remaining units can be used as necessary at Metz and on the right bank of the Moselle.

We must figure that we have available for the advance to the position on the Aisne–Oise–Paris, etc. [15]

active corps	25
reserve corps	2½
newly formed corps	6

33½ corps

Of these, more than ⅓ will be committed for the envelopment of Paris, with 7 corps conducting the actual envelopment while the 6 newly formed corps blockade the west and south sides of Paris. The concept for the advance and the attack on the position is shown in Map 3.[3]

If the enemy stands fast, the attack will be conducted on the entire line, in particular from two sides against La Fère, which is isolated. Following a success here the attack will be continued to Laon and against Reims, which is open to the west. All along the line the corps will advance from position to position according to the principles of formal siege warfare. They will seek to close with the enemy by day and by night, moving forward, digging in, moving forward again, digging in again. They will use all the means of modern technology that are available to weaken the enemy in his field fortifications. The attack can never be allowed to come to a halt as it did in East Asia.

France must be considered to be a great fortress. The part of the outer enceinte from Belfort to Verdun is almost invulnerable, but in the section Mézières–Maubeuge–Lille–Dunkirk the fortifications are full of gaps and at this time almost unoccupied. We must seek to penetrate into the fortress here. If we succeed, a second [16] enceinte will appear, or at least the piece of one, namely the position from Verdun behind the Aisne–Reims and La Fère. This piece of the enceinte can however be enveloped to the south. + [Comment by General von Moltke in the left margin: "+north"] The fortress builder probably expected a German attack from the south of the Meuse–Sambre, but not from the north of this river line. It will be too late to remedy the deficiency by extending the fortified line Reims–La Fère through Peronne along the Somme. The defender can only meet the impending envelopment with an offensive around the left wing of the position at La Fère. This counterattack, which may be accompanied by an advance from the entire Verdun–La Fère front, will hopefully fail. The defeated defender can then still seek to hold the Oise between La Fère and Paris. The suitability of this river line for the defense has been questioned. If this doubt is justified, or if the French dispense with the defense of the Oise and allow the Germans to cross the river with sufficient forces, the second enceinte Verdun–La Fère is no longer tenable. The entire position of La Fère, Laon and Reims (which is open to the west) on high ground which is oriented towards an attack from the north-east, would be taken and the Aisne position would have to be abandoned. The Meuse forts between Verdun and Toul, which have a limited defensive capability against an attack from the west, would be sacrificed. Verdun and Toul would become isolated fortresses. The entire French fortress system directed against Germany would be in danger of collapse. It is therefore doubtful if, in spite of all of its deficiencies as a defensive position, the French would not seek to hold the Oise, [17] and the question is, could they not defend it successfully? In this case, Paris must be enveloped to the south. This will also be necessary if the French fall back from the Oise and the Aisne behind

---

[3] Page 23 of the hand-written original says "the attached map" ("der anliegenden Karte") with "the attached" scratched out and "3" written in above "map". "Map 3" is also written in the left margin of the hand-written copy, but not in the typed copy.

the Marne, the Seine, etc. If we allow them to fall back further in this direction, it will lead to an endless war. The attempt must be made by all means to attack the French left flank to force them in an easterly direction against the Moselle fortresses, the Jura and Switzerland.

[Hand-written in Roman script – not Schlieffen's Standard script – in the left margin: The fundamental point for the course of the entire operation is to form a strong right wing and win the battles with this wing, then in continual pursuit with this same strong right wing force the enemy time and again to withdraw.]

If the right wing is to be made strong, this can only be done at the expense of the left, which will therefore probably have the mission of fighting against numerically superior forces.

The exertions for the right wing must be very great if it is to succeed. However, in general the roads that will be used are very good. Given the numerous villages, the billeting for the troops will be adequate, unless the corps of the right wing have to march in such a massed formation that even the densest civilian population is not sufficient to provide quarters for the troops.

On the other hand, there can hardly be a lack of rations. Belgium and northern France are rich and can provide much. If placed under the appropriate pressure they can also obtain supplies from external sources to make up for any possible shortfalls.

An increase in demands on their resources may perhaps move the Belgians to cease hostile actions and surrender their fortresses, in return for the advantages that an uninterested third party can gain in a battle between two enemies.

[18] At the beginning of the campaign three active corps, one reserve corps and three cavalry divisions on the right bank of the Moselle should attack Nancy. Whether this attack succeeds or not is largely dependent on whether the French restrict themselves to the defensive or if they, true to their doctrine, go over to the counterattack. If the latter, the principal purpose of the attack on Nancy, engaging the greatest possible number of enemy forces on the French eastern front, will have been attained. The more troops that the French commit to the counterattack, the better it is for the Germans. The Germans must not allow themselves to become engaged in serious combat, but have the mission of drawing the strongest possible enemy forces after them and fix them with the help of the expanded Metz. There can hardly be any danger for the German forces isolated on the right bank of the Moselle. On the other hand, it would be damaging for the German main body if the army on the right bank of the Moselle enjoyed numerical superiority [over the French]. The goal is to fix the greatest number of French forces with the fewest number of German.

If the French do not counterattack, two corps must be moved as soon as possible to the furthest German wing in Belgium. The most important thing is to be strong on this wing. We can look forward to the decision with a clear conscience, when we have 25 corps available on the left bank of the Moselle for the battle, in which we cannot be strong enough.

The few troops which remain on the on the right bank of the Moselle, specifically [19]

1 active corps
1 reserve corps
30th Reserve Division (Strasbourg)
possibly two newly formed corps
Landwehr brigades on the upper Rhine and from Metz, if these are not attacked
59th Landwehr Brigade (upper Alsace)
six light infantry battalions in the Vosges

must be reinforced as much as possible. The fortress garrisons still provide resources with which to form new units. The south German Landsturm can also be employed to cover the country left of the Rhine, blockade Belfort, etc. A new army must be formed with the mission of advancing between Belfort and Nancy, while the five reserve corps of the left wing and two Landwehr brigades isolate Verdun and attack the *Côtes Lorraines*.

If, during the course of the deployment, the French hear that the Germans are massing on the lower Rhine and the Dutch and Belgian borders, they will not doubt that the enemy intent is to advance on Paris, and probably refrain either from advancing with all or the principal part of their forces between Strasbourg and Metz, or from conducting an all-out attack across the upper Rhine into [south] Germany. This would be the equivalent of the garrison leaving the fortress at the same time that the siege should be opened. In spite of that, if they do one or the other, this could only be welcome to the Germans. Their mission would thereby be made easier. It would be the most advantageous for the Germans if the French would choose to invade south Germany by way of [20] Switzerland. This would be a means for us to obtain an ally, which we need very much, who would occupy a part of the enemy forces.

In all of these cases, it would be advisable for the Germans to change their plan as little as possible. In the meantime the lower Moselle between Trier and Coblenz must be secured, the section between the Moselle and the Meuse at Diedenhofen blocked. The German army would attempt to reach the general line Coblenz–La Fère, with a reserve on the right flank. The right bank of the Rhine upstream from Coblenz will be occupied from the rear. The right wing will attack.
Map 5 and 5a [in the left margin]

If the French cross over the upper Rhine, we will defend the Black Forest. Troops being moved forward from the rear will be assembled on the Main and the Iller.

If the Germans persist in their operation, they can be assured that the French will quickly turn around, and indeed not to the north of Metz, but rather to the south in the direction from which they perceive that the greatest danger threatens. It is therefore imperative that the Germans be as strong as possible on the right wing, for here the decisive battle is to be expected.
Map 6: map of the overall operation [in the left margin]

Count Schlieffen

Berlin, February 1906

[21] In case of a war between Germany and France, if the British want to land in Antwerp with no more than 100,000 men, this can hardly occur in the first days of mobilization. Although the activation of their three corps may be well prepared, their army organization and their military system will present so many obstacles to its implementation that the sudden appearance of the British forces in the great Belgian fortress is hardy credible. But if they land relatively early and leave the fortress to attack the Germans, they will also soon find that the few roads that lead through the peat moors of northern Belgium and southern Holland to the north and east fronts of Antwerp have been occupied. If they choose the southern front between Netze and Dyle as the sally port for their attack, they will run into the eight German corps which crossed the Meuse below Liège.

Map 7 [in the left margin]

The continued German advance blocks off one more section of the fortress front after another. Each attempt by the united British and Belgians to throw back a blockading corps will fail because of the support that this corps will receive from the advancing German army. Until the left-wing corps completes the blockade on the left bank of the Schelde, there will always be a number of German corps prepared to intervene in a fight.

The terrain in front of most of the fortress is [22] not favorable for the development of a British and Belgian sortie: they must struggle to deploy through defiles. The sections of the fortress perimeter which might facilitate a sortie will be reduced if the Belgians execute the planned inundations.

If the British and the Belgians want to advance from Antwerp to the attack, they must undertake battles that will be just as futile as the numerous French sorties at Metz and Paris [in 1870/71]. It is of course necessary that during their advance the corps conducting the blockade prepare field fortifications daily and are continually aware of the possibility of an attack. They must push forward as close as possible to the enemy works and then improve the defensive strength of their field fortifications until they are invulnerable. The right and left flanks will attempt to approach the Schelde as closely as possible and close the fortresses' last escape route over water with batteries and sea mines.

The prospect is not unfounded that if the British land at Antwerp, they and the Belgians will both will be shut in there. They are the most surely accommodated in the fortress, far better than on their island, where they pose a significant threat and a continual danger to the Germans.

The small fortress of Termonde makes a blockade of Antwerp not a little more difficult. Nevertheless, it is neither strong nor well maintained and its artillery at least can be rendered harmless with the assistance of the heavy artillery of the nearest [active army] corps. Then it will be possible to draw the Antwerp blockade line between Termonde and Rugelmonde.

[23] The battle for Antwerp will be more difficult if the French succeed in reaching the line Namur–Antwerp ahead of us, and in conjunction with the British and the Belgians block the further advance on the left bank of the Meuse. Then an envelopment with the right wing will be impossible. The plan must be changed. An advance by our allied enemies north of Namur–Liège can also be blocked. If

A page from the original hand-written January 1906 Schlieffen plan, BA-MA *Nachlass* Schlieffen N 43/137, page 23

they want to throw us back, they must advance on the right bank of the Meuse and thereby they will not be able to avoid exposing their right wing to a German attack.
Map 8 [in the left margin]

If the French arrive later, the possibility presents itself for the Germans to fight a battle in two directions, to be precise, with one front towards Antwerp and the other towards Hirson, Maubeuge–Lille.
Map 9 [in the left margin]

The French, according to their frequently repeated intent, want to advance in deep masses. The words of the immortal Field Marshal will then prove true, that a small front runs the risk of being enveloped, while the broad front, if only it guards against an enemy breakthrough, promises great success.

The British have also been credited with the intent of landing not in Antwerp but at Esbjerg [Denmark]. Sometimes their plan then would be to appear at a very early date on the coast of Jutland, other times they would delay their operation until the German and French forces were completely engaged. [24] Germany would be completely denuded of troops and this condition will supposedly be used for a march on Berlin, possibly with the support of several French corps.

As far as the first case is concerned, if a British army landed in the north while the German deployment was in progress, the Germans would not complete their deployment. The corps which had still not deployed would be halted and sent against the new enemy in order to destroy them with a greatly superior force. The French would have no other choice than to move to assist their ally, that is, leave their fortresses and defensive positions and go over to the attack. Then we have the prospect of a war on the left bank of the Rhine, with all the advantages which have been so convincing to us on various occasions [war games and General Staff rides].

If the British wait for a favorable moment to conduct their landing, they will hardly find it before the first battle. If the Germans win this battle, the British will probably abandon their hopeless operation. This battle therefore determines a great deal, and it would be a grave error to absent from it an army, a corps or a division on a far-away future battlefield, when it might bring the decision against the French.

Nevertheless, if the British conduct their landing after we have completed our deployment, whether it is before or after the battle, we must assemble all forces still in Germany, and they are still considerable, and crush the British invaders. [25]

However, it is necessary to establish a command and control system for the homeland forces.

Count Schlieffen

[26] General von Moltke's Comments Concerning the *Denkschrift*

[Moltke made six marginal comments in the first five of the 25 pages of the typed text. In the last 20 pages he made none at all. In his concluding comments, Moltke first pointed out that Germany would have to fight a two-front war, not "War against France". His intent in moving through Belgium is to "meet the enemy in the open field". The disadvantage of advancing through Belgium is that the defeated French can withdraw to the interior of the country.

He then focused entirely on the relatively minor question, considering that he was deploying an army of over 2 million men and 87 infantry divisions, of Dutch neutrality and his project for a *coup de main* against Liège with six under-strength brigades: quite an anti-climax. In doing so, he passed over in silence the quite substantial parts of the *Denkschrift* which concerned raising new units and using the Landsturm in combat operations. The *coup de main* on Liège was a complete failure, both in concept and execution. On the other hand, in the event, a largely intact Liège did not present a effective obstacle to the 1st German Army's crossing of the Meuse.]

It can be assumed with complete certainty that the next war will be a two-front war. France is the most dangerous enemy and the first prepared to fight. We must deal with them very soon after the conclusion of the deployment. If we succeed in quickly and decisively defeating the French, we will then also free up troops for use against the Russians. I agree with the fundamental concept of beginning the war with a powerful offensive into France, initially remaining on the defensive with weak forces against Russia. In order to obtain a quick decision against France, the attack cannot be directed exclusively against their strongly fortified eastern border. If the French army remains, as we assume, on the defensive behind these fortifications, there is no prospect of quickly conducting a breakthrough. Even a successful breakthrough would expose the German army, or elements of it, to flank attacks from two sides. If we want to meet the enemy in the open field, we must go around the border fortifications. This is only possible either by means of an advance through Switzerland or Belgium. The first presents great difficulties and, given the defended mountain roads, would require considerable time. However, this envelopment of the French fortifications would have the advantage that, were it successful, the French army would be forced to the north. An advance through Belgium would force the French into the interior of the country. Nevertheless, it is preferable because the advance will be faster here, and the weak Belgian forces can be dispersed without difficulty, [2] unless they retreat without a fight into Antwerp, which then must be blockaded.

It is naturally important that during an advance through Belgium the German right wing be made as strong as possible. But I cannot agree that in order to conduct the envelopment Dutch as well as Belgian neutrality must be violated. A hostile Holland in our rear could have fatal consequences for the advance of the Germany army to the west, especially if the British should use the violation of Belgian neutrality to join the war against us. If Holland remains neutral, it secures our rear, for if Britain has declared war against us because we have violated Belgian neutrality, it will not in turn be able to violate Dutch neutrality. It cannot break the same law that it has used to declare war on us.

In addition, it is of the greatest importance for us to have in Holland a land whose neutrality allows it to export and import. It must remain our wind-pipe, in order that we can breathe.

As uncomfortable as it may be, the advance through Belgium must be conducted without violating Dutch territory. We will essentially be able to do so only if Liège is in our possession. [3] This fortress must therefore be taken immediately. I consider it possible to do so by a *coup de main*. The forward forts of the fortress are so poorly sited that they have no observation over the intervening terrain and cannot cover them by direct fire. I have had reconnaissance conducted of all the avenues of approach which lead between the forts to the centre of the city, which is not protected by a wall. It is possible to advance in several columns without being observed by the forts. Once our troops have penetrated into the city, I do not believe that the forts will shell them; they will presumably capitulate. The most important factors are exact prior preparation and surprise. The operation is feasible only if the attack is conducted before the Belgians dig in between the forts. It must therefore take place immediately after the declaration of war with units at peacetime strength. There is probably no example in military history of taking a modern fortress by *coup de main*. But it can succeed, and it must be tried, for the possession of Liège is the *conditio sine qua non* for us. It is a daring act whose success promises great consequences. In any case the heaviest artillery will be ready, so that in case the *coup de main* fails the fortress can be taken with an abbreviated siege. I believe that the lack of an inner wall will cause the fortress to fall into our hands.

The possibility of conducting the advance through Belgium without crossing Dutch territory rests on the success of the *coup de main*. The deployment of the army must be organized in an appropriate manner.

(Troop list for the *coup de main*, heavy artillery. Mobilization. Preparatory work.)

B. 1911   v. M.

Part V

MOLTKE'S WAR PLANNING

9

Moltke's 1908 *Generalstabsreise West*[1]

Helmuth von Moltke (the younger) became Schlieffen's successor as Chief of the Great General Staff in January 1906. The Reichsarchiv made practically none of his war planning available to the public. His 1906 and 1908 Generalstabsreisen West *were obtained by the Bundesarchiv-Militärarchiv from the Militärarchiv der DDR (the East German military archive) after the fall of the Wall and first published in summarized form in 1999.*[2]

In spite of many points of difference the 1908 Generalstabsreise West *is the surviving German exercise which most closely approximates the situation in August 1914.*

Thirty-six pages of text, typed, and eight maps.

Situation for Red [France]:
    War between France and Germany. England is allied with France and has promised the French vigorous support.
    Russia has not yet declared war. It can be expected that Germany will leave strong forces on their eastern border against them.
    The French mobilization proceeded according to plan and the deployment, as Map 1 shows, has begun.
    There are German outposts everywhere opposite the border security detachments in Alsace and Lorraine. Considerable German cavalry has been sighted between Saarburg and Metz. Further to the north, on the 1st mobilization day the Germans moved from Trier into Luxembourg and occupied the city and the rail system. According to a report from Belgium, enemy cavalry has been reported on the border between St. Vith and Aachen.
    The French High Command prepared far in advance for the destruction by agents, etc., of the rail lines most important for the German deployment. The goal was to execute the demolitions when the deployment was expected to begin.
    Up to the 8th day of mobilization reports had reached Paris of extensive demolitions that had been successfully carried out to numerous Rhine bridges, multiple structures on the Eifel and Nahe rail lines as well as in Lorraine. There were specific reports concerning: the destruction of the [2] Rhine bridges at Duisburg and Düsseldorf, the Hohe–Venn rail line south-east of Aachen, the Eifel

---

[1] Große Generalstabsreise West 1908, BA-MA PH3/664. For commentary see Zuber, *Inventing the Schlieffen Plan*, pp. 228–32.
[2] T. Zuber 'The Schlieffen Plan Reconsidered' in: *War in History* Vol. 6 No. 3 (1999).

line west of Brühl (reports arriving from Holland and Belgium) and concerning the destruction of the rail station at Beningen, south-west of Saarbrücken.

According to reports received by carrier pigeon from agents in Mayen and Bingen troops have begun to unload east of Coblenz.

[Pages 2 and 3 then describe the French deployment. The French organize a covering force army of three corps including eight infantry divisions and eight cavalry divisions. The deployment of the active army is completed by the 9th day of mobilization, except for 19th Corps from Africa which is ready on the 10th day. Each of the four armies receives 15 batteries of heavy artillery. The four groups of reserve divisions contain four divisions, except for the 2nd, which has only three. The 1st, 2nd and 4th groups of reserve divisions are deployed by the 10th day, the 3rd by the 11th. The XIV and XV Corps from the Alps can arrive in Belfort by the 12th day, the four reserve divisions by the 15th, or at Neufchâteau by the 14th and 16th, or at Laon by the 15th and 17th. The 10 territorial divisions can deploy by the 18th.]

Requirement: How does the French command intend to conduct the operation? The Red commander's solution:

The only way that the successful destruction of the German rail lines can be exploited is by an immediate offensive, because the offensive of the enemy right wing will be delayed.

Because it is not in the French interest to be the first to violate [4] Belgian neutrality, and because the nearest enemy forces are in Lorraine and the French army is massed on this front, it is indicated that the offensive be conducted into Lorraine. [This is followed by a list of troop movements necessary to conduct the offensive.]

The best place for the British army to land is Antwerp, which is available only if the Germans have entered Belgium and therefore the Belgians have decided to join the British and French. If the British transport fleet is ready to sail before the Germans have violated Belgian neutrality, the British must land in Calais and Boulogne.

Order of Battle:

Alsace Detachment: XIX Corps, 14th ID (VII Corps), 8th Cav., 58th and 66th RD.

1st Army: VII Corps (minus 14th ID), XIII, XVI Corps, 2nd Col. D, 2nd Cav., 63rd and 67th RD.

2nd Army: V, VIII, IX, XII, XVII, XVIII, XX Corps, 1st, 6th, 7th Cav., 55th, 59th, 62nd, Zouave RD.

3rd Army: III, IV, VI, X Corps, 3rd and 5th Cav., 61st and 68th RD.

4th Army: I, II, XI, Colonial Corps, 4th Cav., 51st, 52nd, 53rd, 54th, 60th, 77th, 78th, 79th RD. [5]

Army Reserve: XIV, XV Corps.

Assignment of territorial divisions to be determined.

The operations should be conducted in the following manner: The Alsace Detachment, 1st, 2nd and 3rd Armies should cross the border into Germany and Luxembourg on the 11th mobilization day. The Alsace Detachment will enter

Alsace, 1st and 2nd Armies Lorraine, the former in the direction of the right bank of the Saar, the latter in the direction of Saarburg–Metz, 3rd Army will move north of Metz in the direction of Luxembourg. 4th Army remains on this side of the Belgian border along the Meuse . . . .

The Alsace Detachment should occupy Alsace to Schettstadt, observe Idstein and lay siege to Neu Breisach.

The 1st and 2nd Armies should seek out and defeat the enemy in Lorraine. 2nd Army will also blockade the east side of Metz.

3rd Army will secure the west side of Metz, thereby supporting the advance of the 1st and 2nd Armies.

The employment of the 4th Army is contingent on whether the Germans cross the Belgian border. If they do not do so, the corps of the 4th Army will follow through Luxembourg to cover the flank of the 3rd Army; otherwise the 4th Army still has the mission of covering the left flank of the 3rd Army.

The employment of the British army is dependent on where they will assemble.

[6]

On the 8th mobilization day Belgium declared that she felt threatened by the German deployment and offered France an alliance.[3] After the successful rail sabotage and the French decision to assume the offensive became known, Britain promised immediate intervention by its army on the continent. The British army (six ID . . . one Cav . . . .) will land as of the 13th day in Antwerp and be ready for movement on the 15th day.

<u>Requirement</u>: Does this news call for any changes in the concept of the operation of the French Supreme Command?

The French commander stated: If it had been clear from the very beginning that England and Belgium would take part in the war <u>against</u> Germany, the best solution would have been to remain on the defensive with weak forces (six corps, ten reserve divisions) on the fortified right wing from Belfort to Verdun. The main body (15 corps, 9 reserve divisions) would deploy between Verdun and Maubeuge in order to attack in conjunction with the Belgian and British armies on the line Diedenhofen–Liège.

On the 8th day of mobilization, however, the French deployment is so far advanced that a change would only cause disorder. The plan for an offensive into Lorraine must be adhered to. Since consideration for Belgian neutrality is no longer an issue, the left wing (4th French, Belgian, British armies) can follow the main attack as a second echelon.

A certain amount of danger arises through the fact that the British army will only to ready to move on the 15th day. Between Luxembourg and Aachen strong German forces [7] are to be expected, which may be stronger than the French 4th and the Belgian armies. The left flank of the 3rd Army must however be protected. Therefore the advance of the left flank will be retained.

The Belgian government has agreed to assemble the Belgian army by the evening of the 10th day at Namur to link up with the 4th Army. The XIV Corps was prepared to advance through Reims to Givet.

---

[3] That is, before the Germans had violated Belgian neutrality.

[Map 2 shows French deployment on 10th mobilization day.]

Reports received to this point: the Germans have evidently sent no troops to the upper Alsace. On the other hand significant German forces are apparently in Lorraine and between Aachen and Cologne. Other reports are indicated on the map.

The French commander directs the execution of his plan on the 11th mobilization day [this is followed by specific orders to the armies].

The British army will be ready in Antwerp for operations on the 15th day. It was requested to advance on an axis Huy–Liège. It is desirable to delay the decision on this part of the front until the British army can be engaged. [8]

Situation for Blue [Germany]:

War between Germany and France. England is allied with France and has promised the French vigorous support.

Germany has left an army on its eastern borders as cover against Russia [overall deployment was probably 64 divisions in the west and about 11 in the east], the German coasts are guarded by reserve and Landwehr troops.

The German *Westheer* was to deploy with the main body along the border from north of Aachen to Metz, with weaker forces between Metz and the Vosges, as well as on the upper Rhine. The intent of the deployment was to attack through Belgium and Luxembourg.

The mobilization proceeded smoothly, the border security deployed according to plan, the cavalry divisions and the mixed brigades sent forward to cover the deployment arrived at their destinations. The IX Corps moved into Luxembourg from Trier.

The deployment had just begun when bridges and rail installations were destroyed by agents, etc., whose actions had obviously been planned by the enemy far in advance.

To the 8th mobilization day the following demolitions had been reported to the *Oberste Heeresleitung* [OHL, the German Supreme Headquarters]: the rail bridges over the Rhine at Duisburg, Düsseldorf and Coblenz, the Hohes–Venn rail line south-east of Aachen, the Eifel rail line and the line on the left side of the Rhine in the area of Brühl, the Nahe rail line near Oberstein, the rail station at Bingen [9] south of Saarbrücken.

After coordination between the Chief of the Field Rail System (Chef des Feldeisenbahnwesens) with the officials controlling the debarkation rail stations (Ausladekommissaren) and the rail line commandants (Linien-Kommandanten) the debarkation rail stations were changed, as shown in map 3 and the debarkation table . . . .

In Lorraine and Alsace there are French outposts opposite the German border security. There is nothing in the reports received to this time that would indicate that the French deployment will be other than as expected.

[Order of battle was contained in map 3. Three Landwehr brigades were attached to the 1st and 2nd Armies, two to the 3rd, 4th and 5th Armies, one to the 6th, and three Landwehr brigades and a regiment were sent to the upper Alsace.][10]

Point and date of arrival movement table

	debarkation point	combat troops	trains
		[mobilization day]	
1st Army:			
I	Duisburg	10	16
II	Erkelenz	11	15
III	west of Elberfeld	9	14
I R	Mühlheim (Ruhr)	14	16
2nd Army:			
V	south-west of Düsseldorf	8	12
IV	east of Aachen	10	12
VI	south-west of Cologne	10	13
VII	east of Bonn	10	13
II R	Düren	11	13
18 RD	east of Cologne	12	13
3rd Army:			
VIII	west of Cologne	13	15
IX	Geroldstein	9	11
X	Neuwied	13	16
III R	north of Brühl	13	14
IV R	St. Gaorshausen	11	12
17 RD	north-west of Cologne	15	16
4th Army:			
XI	Luxembourg	10	14
XII	Kirn	10	15
XIII	Ober-Lahnstein	10	16
V R	½ east of Coblenz	11	15
	½ north of Trier		
VI R	½ west of Limburg	13	15
	½ west of Kreuznach	14	16
[11] 5th Army:			
XIV	Saarburg (Rhineland)	10	15
XV	Merfig	10	14
XVI	north-east of Busendorf	11	16
XVII	south of Küsel	10	14
VII R	½ Saarlouis	14	15
	½ Homburg	13	14
6th Army:			
XVIII	Metz	6	8
XIX	Bolchen	12	16
XX	west of Saargemünd	9	14
7th Army			
XXI	Forbach	10	12
XXII	north-east of Saarburg in Lorraine	8	9
XXIII	Colmar	8	11
VIII R	Bensdorf	12	13

Requirement: Will new orders have to be issued before the conclusion of the deployment? What is the Blue commander's concept of the operation?

The Blue commander's estimate of the situation was:

The strength of the two parties (without the British) is about equal. The delay in the Blue right wing reaching operational readiness due to the rail demolitions [12] leads to a later march into Belgium, so that the violation of Belgian neutrality falls to the French, if they decide to take the offensive north of Metz. This is probable, for otherwise the rail demolitions were pointless and because popular opinion supports the exploitation of this success. It cannot be assumed that Belgium would not limit itself in this case to armed neutrality. Nevertheless, Germany must calculate that Belgium will be an enemy.

If Red decides to take the offensive through Belgium–Luxembourg, it can use the four days it has gained through the rail demolitions to shift its armies to the north by rail and foot march. By the 13th day of mobilization the Red 2nd, 3rd and 4th Armies and the 2nd, 3rd and 4th Groups of Reserve Divisions could have reached the line Liège–Verdun. At this time the Blue 1st and 2nd Armies (without I Reserve corps) would stand ready north of the line Montjoie–Euskirchen, the 4th, 5th, and 6th Armies (without VI Reserve Corps and ½ V Reserve corps) on the Moselle and north of Trier. The 3rd Army would have only IX Corps in the Eifel, but in two to three days could expect the arrival of a further four active corps.

The French offensive will therefore not meet a numerically inferior enemy. Rather, Blue is deployed to the north of Metz with strong wings, the middle pulled somewhat back, prepared for an attack from the Trier–Metz area towards the northwest.

If Red decides to conduct an offensive between Metz and Strasbourg or over the upper Rhine, the Blue 3rd and 4th Armies are better positioned for an offensive between the Moselle and the Rhine than if they had reached the area to the north of Trier on a broad front on the 12th day of mobilization.

Therefore, no reason exists to make changes [13] in the deployment. The troops of the 1st to 4th Armies have only to concentrate forward.

The decision should be sought where the enemy main force is to be found. Recognizing this in a timely fashion is difficult.

If the enemy remains on the defensive, it is necessary to adhere to the plan for the offensive through Belgium, whereby both the right wing north of Liège–Namur and the left wing between Sedan and Metz are to be made strong.

If the enemy conducts an offensive between Metz and Strasbourg it is planned that the 7th Army will withdraw along the Rhine and the 3rd to 6th Armies will attack over the line Metz–Coblenz with a strong right wing towards the southeasterly direction, covered by the 1st and 2nd Armies to the north of Metz.

The French offensive to the north of Metz is the more likely, whereby the left wing should not extend past Maastricht. This will be met with an offensive by the 1st to 6th Armies, whereby it must be left open whether the decision will be reached on the right wing with the 1st and 2nd Armies or on the left wing through a breakthrough by the 4th and 5th Armies, which the 6th Army is to cover in connection with Metz.

A premature advance before the armies are completely assembled is rejected.

To the 10th day of mobilization the Blue situation developed as follows: Belgium has joined France and England.

[Reports of contact with French cavalry all along the front. A dirigible reported French columns at Landres, Etain and marching through Thiaucourt on Pont à Mousson. A number of units will not meet their scheduled arrival times. In 1st Army, II Corps and I R; 2nd Army, II R; 3rd Army VIII and X Corps, III R and IV R, 17th and 18th Reserve divisions; 4th Army, V Corps and VI R; 5th Army, XVI Corps and VII R; 6th Army, XIX Corps; 7th Army, VIII R. The Blue commander nevertheless does not change his deployment plan. Corps in place are given the mission of covering the arrival of the later corps.]

[16] General von Moltke critiqued the first decisions and orders of both commanders as follows:
"During the days that we have ridden through this beautiful country, which we have won by the sword and which we once again may have to defend with the sword, we have been removed from the events of the larger world, even more or less from the reports of the political events that fill the newspapers. We have lived in a self-made world of war, which indeed only exists in our imagination and whose battles are only fought on the map, but which one day could become reality. When we now return from this imaginary world into the circle of our accustomed daily life, we will again have before our eyes a world filled with political accommodation and tension, of hopes and fears. We will look on with amazement as states that for ages have stood in irreconcilable opposition, now reconciled extend their hands to each other, as republican France joins with liberal Britain, and as absolutistic Russia joins as the third member of the alliance. All of this takes place under the motto of securing the European peace, which no one threatens.

If one objectively considers this remarkable revaluation of all previous political values, it appears to me that in the loud assurances of peaceful intent there is to be heard an undertone of the revaluation of this old word. For in all of this readiness to promote peace, the motto is no longer *si vis pacem, para bellum* [if you desire peace, prepare for war][17] rather *si vis bellum, para pacem* [if you desire war, prepare for peace]. Even more forcefully than before, our duty requires us to prepare for the moment in which out of all this concern for peace, war is born. We want to look at that moment in the decisive hour which must determine the existence or the extinction (*Sein oder Nichtsein*) of the German people, calmly and firmly straight in the eye, and we want to be judged as to whether we have wasted the time we have used on this ride, which was valuable as preparation for that moment.

Occasionally during our discussions I have addressed the idea that an operational war game played in general outline, as the one we have played in this ride, cannot give a realistic picture of events in war. It is built up out of an entire series of unnatural and arbitrary situations. It does not consider the ability of the troops and presumes command and control systems that are incorrect. Above all the daily contact between all commanders gives a knowledge of the daily events in the entire theatre of war and thereby an overview of the general situation that in reality could never be counted on. If this were to be changed, the exercise would have to go into far greater detail. However, this would require time which is not available. In 14 exercise days we would be able to play only a very few operational days.

This unnaturalness is not harmful, if we continually keep in mind that what we are doing is not real war [18] with flesh and blood, but only the skeleton of one.

The value of such an operational war game is that the commanders become used to operating with great masses and learn to fit their actions into the overall framework. Further, that the consequences of the operational decisions become evident and the commanders are forced to adjust to the results of a situation formed by cause and effect.

We have no practical experience with leading our modern mass armies and we must therefore seek to develop a generally clear idea of it through the use of theory.

I have based this ride on a situation – a war with Germany against France and Britain – as it would probably appear to us. It is not important what will cause it. It could arise due to French desire for revenge or out of British concern for our growing battle fleet: we will always have to count on a war against both states. It was assumed that Russia had not yet declared her intentions. The Germans were therefore required to leave an army in the east opposite them. The other states were not addressed in the military situation. According to the political constellation of the Great Powers one could calculate that Austria would initially display a benevolent neutrality towards Germany and Italy benevolent neutrality towards France. We can assume that Holland, Switzerland and Denmark would be absolutely neutral while it could be calculated that Belgium would probably ally with France.

[19] In the west, active and reserve troops, Germany could employ 800 battalions, 409 squadrons, 657 batteries, and 105 heavy batteries. These were opposed by:

France	966 battalions	398 squadrons	622 batteries	75 heavy batteries
Britain	77	56	60	18
Belgium	68	44	34	–
Total	1111	498	716	93
a superiority of	311	81	59	

The French commander was given a deployment that was based on the peacetime stationing of the French troops and the capacity of the French rail net. Behind a covering force army stood four armies (active army troops) in the first line, with four groups of reserve troops in the second line. It is a defensive deployment, deeply echelonned, but which at the same time facilitates the offensive or a displacement of forces along the front.

It was assumed that the French High Command had planned far in advance for agents, etc., to destroy the rail lines most important for the German deployment.

In order to delay the Germans for the longest possible period of time, the goal was to conduct the demolitions in conjunction with the expected beginning of the German deployment.

The French plan succeeded surprisingly well. It will be objected that these numerous demolitions could not occur. However, we have reports that the French actually [20] are recruiting agents for this purpose. Nevertheless, such extensive demolitions can only be conducted if we are guilty of criminal negligence. I had also originally intended to take as a basis a smaller number of demolitions. The result of the calculations that I had ordered showed that these did not result in a serious disruption of our deployment. This result is very comforting for our real-world situation. They forced me to base our exercise here on the scale of demolitions used in the initial situation.

On the 5th day, Paris was informed of the general extent of the rail demolitions and had also learned that the Germans had begun disembarking troops on the right bank of the Rhine.

At this time there could have been no reports of the German deployment, which had just begun. It was clear that the rail demolitions must considerably delay the German army from attaining operational readiness. Given the average distance from the Rhine to the border one could calculate a delay of about four days. The intent of the French commander was to exploit this advantage. He believed that he could do so only by going as quickly as possible over to the offensive in the hopes of engaging the Germans before they had completed their deployment.

The French commander could see no advantages in the defensive, only a delay in fighting the decisive battle. The advantage that the French [21] had gained should be exploited by attacking.

The hoped-for cooperation of the Belgian army and the additional strength of the British seemed to him to favor an operation in which the right wing, based on the defenses from Verdun to Belfort, would limit itself to the defensive with weaker forces (6 active corps, 10 reserve divisions), with the main body deploying between Verdun and Maubeuge. From here, possibly in conjunction with the Belgians and the British, they could attack from the line Diedenhofen–Liège.

Two objections argued successfully against the conduct of this operation. First, from the outset it required the violation of Belgian neutrality, which they would rather leave to the Germans. Second, the prerequisite was a deployment specifically designed for this operation. Changing the deployment as of the evening of the 8th day seemed too risky.

It was preferable to allow the original deployment to continue in order to go over to the offensive as quickly as possible, with the initial objective being the strong German forces which were reportedly in Lorraine.

The French army was reorganized for the advance . . . ."

General von Moltke then described the intent and initial orders of the Red commander as given on pages 6 and 7 above. He then continued:

"The French commander recognized that there was some anxiety concerning the advance of the French left wing. The strength of the German forces [22] at Aachen was unknown. It had to be calculated that until the British would arrive the French would be outnumbered. The separation which Metz–Diedenhofen imposed on the French offensive was particularly unfavorable. From the very beginning this meant that they unnecessarily had to renounce the advantage which it is imperative to strive for, of having decisive superiority on one part of the theatre of war. Many studies have shown that there is so little prospect of an attack with all forces between Metz and Strasbourg gaining this superiority that it cannot be advocated. It may therefore very well be asked if it were not advisable to shift forces to the north for the planned offensive. I instructed that such a movement be worked out.

The result was that a second deployment in the general line Verdun–Huy by the 14th mobilization could be executed very easily. All the corps except two, which move by rail, conducted foot marches. The movement was even less risky because the Germans, due to the delay in being ready to march, were not in a position to disturb it. On the 15th day the mass of the French army could have advanced from the line Verdun–Huy while the Belgians and the British joined in to the north of the Belgian Meuse."

General von Moltke now discussed the Blue situation, emphasizing that due to the rail demolitions the situation for the 3rd and 4th Armies, large portions of which had been required to disembark on the right bank of the Rhine, [23] had become particularly unfavorable. He added the following to the estimate of the situation of the Blue commander related above:

"The German operations plan was simple. It aimed at seeking a decision where the enemy main body was presumed to be. The French operations plan was just as simple: attack the nearest enemy with all available forces.

A good plan will usually be simple. It was in 1870 too: advance on Paris with the intention attacking and defeating the enemy forces that must oppose this advance. It is not possible to plan beyond the first battle."

General von Moltke now described the situation on the 10th . . . and commented:

"The grouping of the cavalry divisions is characteristic: nine German divisions are opposed by eight French and two Belgian. While the French divisions are distributed across the entire front, the Germans satisfied themselves with four divisions south of Luxembourg and employed five in front of the right wing, where they are opposed by only one French and two Belgian. It is not difficult to recognize that in the restricted space in front of the centre of the armies the cavalry divisions will have only a limited scope for operations, while for the German divisions on the right wing a broad field opens up for their activity."

[24] Blue operations, 11th day:
[Details of cavalry operations and reconnaissance reports. No enemy troops in southern Belgium to Ciney–Recogne.]
The 1st Army moved up to the border north of Geilenkirchen, 2nd Army reached the line Aachen–Schleiden . . . .
[Situation in centre and Lorraine largely unchanged.]
It was recognized from this that the enemy was advancing with strong forces on both sides of Metz into Luxembourg and Lorraine and also into the upper Alsace . . . .

[The Blue commander ordered 2nd Army to march south, echelonned to the right to reach Eupen–Blankenheim by the 12th. 1st Army would follow 2nd in echelon right over the line Geilenkirchen–Jülich. Other armies move only individual corps. [25] There is a requirement to present an operations order for the 6th Army.]

[26] General von Moltke's critique of the 6th Army operations:
"Unfortunately the great importance that Fortress Metz must have for these movements was not recognized. XIX and XVIII Corps were directed to march to

the east of the fortress and were sent frontally against the enemy. The most important purpose of the fortifications of Metz–Diedenhofen is to cooperate in offensive operations by facilitating the undisturbed assembly and deployment of entire armies. If the resulting advantages are exploited, that is, if the corps designated to conduct a flank attack are moved through the fortress, the attack obtains an entirely different effect. In the present case the fortress was used only as Germany's shield, not as her sword."

The Blue situation on the evening of the 12th mobilization day . . . . There was currently no enemy threat to the northern wing . . . . There were no enemy forces in southern Belgium as far as the Meuse. However, nothing was known concerning the Belgian army. But strong enemy forces were advancing on both sides of the Moselle [27] . . . . [Superior enemy forces in front of XX, XXI, VIII Reserve and XXII Corps of the 6th and 7th Armies.] In case of a defeat [of the 6th and 7th Armies] the 5th Army on the Moselle would also find itself in a difficult situation. It was not yet possible to count on effective intervention by the 1st, 2nd and 3rd Armies. [1st Army reaches Aachen, 2nd Army Malmedy–Büdersheim, joined by 3rd Army. 4th Army to assemble east of Metz. Considerable reassignment of corps between 4th, 5th and 7th Armies. [28] 6th Army withdraws behind the German Nied. Moltke approved of the withdrawal, but said that it did not suffer heavy casualties only because the French were forced to cover their left flank against Metz.] [29] [14th day. Deadlock east of Metz for the remainder of the exercise.]

General von Moltke commented on the battle for the new German position as follows:

"Nine French corps are now attacking eight and one-half German corps in a strong position. On their left the Germans still have one and one-half surplus corps, but their last elements will only arrive on the 16th.

The French were superior in infantry, the Germans in artillery. It was not possible to envelop the German right wing due to the influence of the eastern fortresses [Metz–Diedenhofen] and the mobile reserve of Metz, the envelopment of the continually lengthening German left wing was made difficult by the Vosges. Therefore only a [30] frontal breakthrough remained. Massing troops for such an attack finds its limits in the amount of available deployment area, for only the infantryman who can shoot is of any value. The front was 75 kilometers long. Therefore there were three German and four French infantrymen per meter of front.

At St. Privat there were 10 Frenchmen and 15 Germans per meter. Therefore, today we calculate with considerably larger deployment areas. Nevertheless, the extent of the fronts that we have postulated in our situation are considerably smaller than in Manchuria, where they calculated with two men per meter.

In the German position, which was being continually reinforced, as well as in front of it, the forces on both sides were being fixed in place. They were given no further operational employment. However, it would still have been possible to pull units out of the line. Proof of this comes from the use of the I Siberian Corps in the battle of Mukden, which was intended to block the Japanese envelopment."

To this point, the Red situation was not described in detail because it called for no new decisions. The Red 3rd and 4th Armies conducted their movements in accordance with the initial directives.

On the 12th, the Red 3rd Army, which had come up to the level of Luxembourg, received the order to attack the enemy Moselle line downstream from Diedenhofen in order to assist the advance of 1st and 2nd Armies.

[31] General von Moltke said:

"The attack met four corps in a strong position and could not succeed. Crossing such a broad and deep river such as the Moselle is always a difficult matter. The maxim, that river crossings always succeed, is not applicable when such a short part of the river is involved as it was here."

A short summary of the remainder of the ride is adequate, as there were no important decisions made.

On the evening of the 14th, Blue ordered the 1st, 2nd and 3rd Armies to continue the march [south-east]. [The lead two corps of the 3rd Army were attached to 4th Army] which was to attack on the entire front [to the west] in the direction of Luxembourg–Esch.

Red ordered the 3rd Army to renew the attack against the Moselle line on the 13th . . . . The attack of the Blue 4th Army succeeded through strong pressure on both flanks. Red took heavy casualties and had to abandon the Moselle line and retreat in the direction of and to the south of Luxembourg . . . .

[Moltke criticized the failure of a Blue cavalry division to fit its operations into those of the rest of the army.] [32]

[For the 16th, Blue ordered the 1st, 2nd and 3rd Armies to continue the march. The 2nd Army would attack on the 17th, with 3rd Army joining in. 4th Army was to continue the attack to the west. 5th Army was to begin advancing. 6th and 7th Armies received no orders.]

For the 16th, Red ordered the 3rd Army to withdraw . . . . 4th Army was to cease its advance and shift to the right, the Belgians were to operate in unison with the 4th Army. 1st and 2nd Armies received no new orders.

The 16th day: in the face of an enveloping attack by the Blue 5th Army the Red 1st Army bent its [right] wing back to the line Mutterhausen–Saargemund. The withdrawal of the Red 3rd Army succeeded; Blue followed but did not attack further. The 3rd and 4th Divisions of the advancing Belgian Army were attacked and defeated by the Blue I and II Corps north of Durbuy. The British army continued the march in the direction of Tienen–Sint Truiden.

On the 17th, Blue wanted to further exploit the successes of the 16th. [33] The 1st and 4th Armies were to continue the advance, 2nd and 3rd to stop in order to be able to conduct a coordinated attack on the 18th. The 5th Army was to continue the attack in Lorraine.

For the 17th, Red ordered that the 1st Army was to remain on the defensive, 2nd and 3rd Armies were to attack, 4th Army to delay . . . .

Of the British divisions, only the 1st had reached the immediate vicinity of Namur, the last (6th) was still to the west of Hasselt. Ten Landwehr brigades [!] were marching up the right bank of the Meuse against the British with I Reserve Corps approaching from the east of Liège.

The Blue 1st Army was south-east of Givet, the Belgian army and the Red XIV Corps were enveloped. The 2nd Blue Army was from the west of St. Hubert to the east of Bastnach, front to the south-west. The 3rd Army was between Wiltz and Diekirch, the 17th and 18th Reserve Divisions still had not arrived. There were no enemy forces in front of the left wing of the 2nd Army or the 3rd Army. The Blue 4th and the Red 3rd Armies stood opposite each other on the line Diekirch–Luxembourg–Esch. In Lorraine the right flank of the Red 1st Army had bent back to Lutzelstein. The lead division of the Red XIX Corps, coming from Alsace, had only reached Alberschweiler and could not prevent the envelopment of the Red right wing by the Blue XXIII Corps, ½VI Reserve corps and IV Reserve Corps, which had reached Bitsch.

This resulted in a picture at the end of the ride that we know from many others, which shows:

The Red operation has failed, withdrawal is unavoidable and will not be accomplished without serious losses. But Blue has not obtained a complete success. [34] The mass of the Red Army will be able to escape behind the fortress front and therefore it will be necessary for Blue to conduct another difficult campaign.

General von Moltke closed the ride with the comment that the French could not hold their ground and that it would be necessary for them to make new operational decisions. He returned once more to the battle of Lorraine and noted that:

"The following forces were either engaged or in the immediate vicinity and prepared to engage:

	French	Germans	
12th	305,000 infantrymen	150,000 infantrymen	2:1
13th	305,000	175,000	12:7
14th	321,000	212,000	4:3
15th	345,000	237,000	7:5
16th	397,000	287,000	4:3

The ratio of French to Germans in infantry was therefore initially 2:1, but improved for the Germans until it was 4:3. The Germans had a superiority of about 250 guns.

In spite of their great superiority in infantry I decided that the French attack east of Metz would be unsuccessful, which may have astonished some officers. I did so in order to illustrate a point.

I wanted here to emphasize once again that in my opinion no success can be expected from a purely frontal attack.

The French were not entirely able to make effective use of their numerical superiority.

On the evening of the 17th day there were, in active and [35] reserve infantry:

Allies	Germans
approaching	
77,000 British	- - - - -

in the theatre of operations in Belgium	
483,000	500,000
(including 48,000 Belgians)	

in the theatre of operations in Lorraine	
397,000	287,000
in Alsace	
76,000	- - - - -
in the rear	
30,000	13,000
(two reserve divisions)	one reserve division in rail movement

On the French side 231,000 men were not actively engaged with the enemy, on the German side only 13,000. The art of bringing all available troops to the battlefield is the criterion for generalship. That the French were not able to do this successfully during the play of the problem is a consequence of the speed of the exercise.

[36] A future war will not proceed this quickly. It can, however, be assumed that the first decisive battle will occur very early. It will presumably decide the entire campaign. But afterwards we will have to reckon with a long war in enemy territory."

Part VI

THE GERMAN WAR PLAN IN AUGUST 1914[1]

Moltke's instructions to the Army commanders (Aufmarschanweisungen) *were not published by the Reichsarchiv in the official history or anywhere else. The original documents were then destroyed in the bombing of Potsdam in 1945. Nevertheless, three of the* Aufmarschanweisungen *survived elsewhere. The Bavarian Kriegsarchiv has the original* Aufmarschanweisungen *for the 6th and 7th Armies, as well as the estimate of the situation* (Lagebeurteilung) *of the Army Chief of Staff, Krafft von Dellmensingen. The US Army captured the 5th Army's* Aufmarschanweisung *at the end of the First World War and an English translation of it is in the archive at Freiburg.*

---

[1] Zuber, *Inventing the Schlieffen Plan*, pp. 258–63.

10

6th Army *Aufmarschanweisung*[2]

[Hand-written, almost surely by a General Staff officer. The main document, minus the annexes, is 30 pages long. The 7th Army *Aufmarschanweisung* differs from that of the 6th Army only in minor details.]

Secret!
Deployment   1914/15

<u>6th Army</u>
Army Headquarters Munich

Deployment Orders
for
Headquarters 6th Army

[The *Aufmarschanweisung* is organized in 54 consecutively numbered paragraphs. Usually only the title of each paragraph has been translated.]

I. Introductory Information

1. Deployment plans will be distributed to:
Army headquarters
Corps headquarters
Reserve corps headquarters
(parts I, II, and III will also be given to their advance parties)
Higher [Corps] cavalry commanders
Cavalry division commanders
The Governors of Metz and Strasbourg
The Higher Landwehr Commander 2 for special duty
The commanders of mixed Landwehr brigades – but only the necessary sections of Part II
The commanders of disembarking stations

---

[2] Aufmarschanweisung für Oberkommando der 6. Armee, Kriegsarchiv Munich, AOK 6, Bund 369 Nr. 45. A typed copy of both the 6th and 7th Army *Aufmarschanweisungen* is also in the papers of the Chief of Staff of the 6th Army, Krafft von Dellmensingen, Kriegsarchiv Munich *Nachlass* 145.

2. Parts I, II, and III of the deployment orders are identical except for the handwritten entries in Part II; each headquarters receives only the necessary sections of Parts IV and V.

3. The deployment orders and all extracts are <u>Top Secret</u>. Subordinate headquarters are to receive in written form only the information that is <u>absolutely necessary</u>.

4. Cavalry reconnaissance squadrons are to be briefed <u>orally</u>. They are not permitted to receive written extracts – or extracts from the Army Signal Instructions.

5. The higher cavalry commanders and commanders of cavalry divisions will <u>destroy</u> their <u>deployment material</u> before the commencement of hostilities.

II. Information Concerning the Deployment

6. Order of Battle
7. Deployment assembly areas
8. Lines of communication
9. Time of arrival

III. General Instructions

10. Border and rail security in deployment assembly areas
11. Defense against enemy air reconnaissance is to be continually observed in the deployment assembly area. Enemy aircraft and aviators are to be destroyed.

German aircraft will be identified in an annex to be published. All troops are to be instructed in these markings immediately upon arrival of the deployment orders . . . .

12.–14. Debarkation
15.–17. Billeting
18.–25. Command and control; reporting; communications instructions.
26.–31. Forward movement; lines of communication in enemy territory.
32. Supply
33.–35. Miscellaneous.

IV. Special Instructions

36. <u>Holland</u> is <u>not expected to be a belligerent</u>. The behavior of <u>Belgium</u> is <u>questionable</u>. Until the relationship between our two states has been clarified, security against Belgian military measures, including air reconnaissance, will be taken.

It is <u>not unlikely</u> that the <u>British</u> Army will intervene. It can move through Holland, land at Antwerp or immediately seek to link up with the French Army with a landing at Calais–Dunkirk.

37. Initially, it is forbidden to <u>enter neutral territory</u>. This restriction is

August 1914: 6th Army Aufmarschanweisung

immediately no longer effective as soon as neutral territory is entered by enemy troops or overflown by enemy aircraft.

The territory of Luxembourg is excepted from this order; it can be entered immediately.

Crossing the Swiss border is forbidden. Commercial and private movement across the border is to be controlled according to the agreements made by the XIV Corps in peacetime. XIV Corps has been so advised.

38. The German deployment against France is based on the following intent:

The main body of the German Army is to advance through Belgium and Luxembourg into France. The concept for the advance – provided that the available information concerning the French deployment is correct (see Annex 19b) – is a wheeling movement with the 5th Army maintaining contact with the pivot at Diedenhofen–Metz.

Protection for the left flank of the main body of the army is to be provided by the forces deploying south-east of Metz in Alsace and Lorraine (6th and 7th Armies, Higher Cavalry Commander 3 – HKK3) as well as the fortresses of Diedenhofen and Metz.

The general intent of the *Oberste Heeresleitung* [OHL, the German Supreme Command] is to be transmitted only to the Army headquarters; it is not otherwise to be made known.

39.–40. Border and rail security in Alsace-Lorraine.

41. HKK3 has the mission, supported by the border security forces, of conducting reconnaissance towards St. Mihiel and beyond Pont à Mousson–Lunéville–Blâmont–Baccarat. For specifics see Annex 22.

42. A position consisting of field fortifications will be built by civilian labor between Metz and the Saar – the *"Niedstellung"* – and will be occupied by five Landwehr brigades of the 5th Army as well as two Landwehr brigades and eight 10cm batteries of the Fortress Metz. The commander of the *Niedstellung* is the Higher Landwehr Commander 2 (XVI Corps). The *Niedstellung* is subordinate to the Governor of Metz. The Fortresses Diedenhofen and Metz are directly subordinate to the Commander, 5th Army.[3] At the commencement of the advance by the 5th Army (see paragraph 43) the OHL may, as circumstances require, direct other command relationships.

43. The deployment assembly area of the 5th Army has great depth. This will facilitate intervention of the 5th Army in any combat south-east of Metz during the deployment period. The 5th Army has been instructed to maintain a deep formation in the assembly area, with the lead elements approximately on the line Bettemberg–Diedenhofen, until the OHL orders the advance (see paragraph 38). The further advance of the 5th Army will be conducted in a pronounced left echelon with the right wing probably moving through Mamer to Arlon while the left wing maintains contact with Diedenhofen. The 5th Army will maintain coordination with the 4th Army and be continually prepared to swing to the south.

Higher Cavalry Commander 4 (3rd and 6th Cavalry Divisions) will conduct reconnaissance to the front of 5th Army with the left flank between Verdun and Metz and the right flank in the direction of St. Mihiel (see paragraph 41).

---

[3] Largely in order to facilitate the 5th Army's deployment into Lorraine.

44. The forces deploying south-east of Metz in Alsace and Lorraine
Higher Cavalry Commander 3 (see paragraph 39)
6th Army (III Bavarian, II Bavarian, XXI, I Bavarian, I Bavarian Reserve Corps and Fortress Bitsch) and
7th Army (XV, XIV, XIV Reserve Corps and presumably two Italian cavalry divisions, as well as Fortress Strasbourg with Fortresses Kaiser Wilhelm II, Neubreisach and the upper Rhine fortresses)
will be placed under the command of the senior of the two Army commanders. The mission of the Joint Commander is to advance against the Moselle below Frouard and the Meurthe in order to fix the French forces here in place and prevent their transport to the French left wing, in addition to taking Fort Manonviller.
This mission may no longer be valid if the French advance in order to attack with superior forces between Metz and the Vosges. If the forces in Alsace and Lorraine are thereby forced to withdraw, their movements are to be directed so that they prevent a threat to the left flank of the German main body by a French envelopment of the *Niedstellung*. If necessary the 6th Army will detach forces to reinforce the *Niedstellung*.
If the 6th and 7th Armies are not opposed by superior enemy forces, it may be possible that elements of the 6th Army and of the Higher Cavalry Commander 3 will be engaged through or to the south of Metz on the left bank of the Moselle. The degree to which this possibility influences the structure of the advance against the Moselle and the Meurthe must be determined by the Joint Commander.
Continual coordination will be maintained with the 5th Army Headquarters.
45. If the French offensive extends into the upper Alsace, this is not unfavorable for the overall operation as long as the enemy does not advance beyond the Fortress Kaiser Wilhelm II–*Breuschstellung*–Strasbourg. Holding this line and the area west of Fortress Kaiser Wilhhelm II is chiefly the mission of the Governor of Strasbourg.
46. The protection of the Upper Alsace and southern Baden during the deployment is the mission of the Commander of the 7th Army . . . .
The mission of the Commander of the 7th Army in the Upper Alsace and southern Baden is *temporary*. The Joint Commander of the troops in Alsace–Lorraine must take into consideration that as many units of the 7th Army as possible are to be moved to conduct operations in immediate conjunction with the 6th Army . . . .
If necessary, rail-transport assets are to be requested in a timely fashion from the Chief of the Field Rail System. The two Italian cavalry divisions will presumably arrive on the 5th mobilization day in Strasbourg.
47. Covering the upper Alsace cannot lead to the sacrifice of the 7th Army, or elements of it, to superior enemy forces which may attack early from Belfort in conjunction with a French offensive between Metz and the Vosges (see paragraph 24) and thereby give the French the opportunity for a cheap success. It is much more important to throw back an early offensive by weak French forces, in order that the province is not left unprotected against any enemy operation. The 7th Army must therefore decide whether the French offensive is a limited attack by inferior French forces or a planned offensive by strong French forces from and to the north of Belfort.

August 1914: 6th Army Aufmarschanweisung

If it is recognized that the French are advancing with superior forces into the upper Alsace, all resources in the province (all rail material, public funds) are to be denied to the enemy. The troops are to be moved back to Strasbourg (XV Corps) and to the right bank of the Rhine (XIV Corps) (see Annex 21, XV Corps, paragraph 3 and XIV Corps paragraph 3). The Rhine bridges and the rail lines on the <u>left</u> bank of the Rhine are to be <u>thoroughly</u> destroyed. The cooperation of the Line Commandants Z (Strasbourg) and F (Karlsruhe) is to be assured.

By this time at the latest the largest possible part of the 7th Army is to be made available for immediate cooperation with the 6th Army. In which direction this will occur, and whether by rail march or foot march, must be decided by the situation of the 6th Army.

After the evacuation of the upper Alsace it will be necessary to <u>protect southern Baden</u>. Whether the Landwehr units which have the principal responsibility for this will be adequate, or whether they will need reinforcements from garrison troops in the XIV Corps area or finally by the elements of the XIV Reserve Corps, is to be determined. In case of necessity the headquarters, 7th Army can utilize all the XIV Corps ersatz troops.

[The rest of the paragraph orders that the command and control relationships in the upper Alsace be determined. In addition, it assigns units to the protection of the Rhine bridges, defense of the upper Rhine and rail lines on the right bank in case the line of the Rhine has been lost.]

48. Engineer equipment park at Germersheim.
49. Passenger vehicles excess to XIV Corps needs are to be turned over to the covering force in the upper Rhine.
50. [2nd Heavy Tractor Park is directed to tow the 2nd Heavy Coastal Mortar Battery.]
51. [Espionage in Switzerland and the upper Alsace.]
52. In the period from the 5th to the 10th mobilization days the 1st and 2nd Italian Cavalry Divisions will arrive in Strasbourg. Initially they will be attached to the 7th Army. It is desirable that they cooperate with the German army-level cavalry in Lorraine (HKK 3). It may be requested that they be disembarked further forward.

Further, presumably as of the 17th mobilization day an Italian army (three active corps) will arrive on the upper Rhine.

53. [Assignment of a German liaison officer to the Italian cavalry divisions. Distribution of Italian–German military dictionaries.]
54. [Repeats paragraph 52 concerning arrival of an Italian army.]

11

5th Army *Aufmarschanweisung*[4]

IV. Special Instructions

38. The following plan forms the basis of the German concentration against France: The main force of the German army will advance on France through Belgium and Luxembourg. Its advance – so far as the available information regarding the French concentration (see Appendix 19b) proves to be correct – is planned as a wheel with the holding of the pivot Diedenhofen–Metz by the 5th Army. The right flank of the armies (main force) sets the pace for the advance of the wheel. The movements of the interior armies will be so regulated that the cohesion of the army and the contact with Metz–Diedenhofen will not be lost. The roads designated for the advance are to be seen from Appendix 5.

The protection of the left flank of the main forces of the army – in connection with the fortresses of Diedenhofen and Metz – is to be taken over by the forces concentrating to the south-east of Metz (6th and 7th Armies, Higher Cavalry Commander 3) (see Par. 42).

The general plan of the Supreme Army Command is to be made known only to the army Headquarters; it is not to be divulged further.

39. The VIII.A.C. of the 4th Army will enter the Grand Duchy of Luxembourg after the announcement of mobilization in order to secure the roads there.

The 50th Mixed Infantry Brigade (xvi) [probably actually a Landwehr brigade] at Frisingen, and, south-east of Luxembourg, the Higher Cavalry Commander 4 (3. and 6. Cav. Divs. as well as the attached Jäger Batls. 5 (v) and 6 (vi) are placed under the VIII.A.C. for frontier and road defense.

The Higher Cavalry Commander 4 has orders, supported by the detachments in the line Luxembourg–Diedenhofen–Metz, to reconnoiter toward the Maas [Meuse] sector Mezieres–Mouzon–Stenay–Verdun–St. Mihiel.

The XVII. and VI. Army Corps of the 4th Army are directed, without further indication to push their troops into the Grand Duchy of Luxembourg and to relieve the covering force troops of the VIII. Army Corps and of the Higher Cavalry Commander 4. With a view to security against a possible swift advance of the

---

[4] BA-MA 3/284. English translation of the 5th Army *Aufmarschanweisung* captured by the US Army at the end of the First World War. The translation was given at some later time to the Germans, perhaps after the Second World War. The translation is poor. The Army translator sometimes did not make the effort to understand what he was translating, unthinkingly used dictionary definitions for words and preserved the German word order and sentence construction. It was not possible, however, to clean up his work.

French, the Commander of the 4. Army is recommended not to cross the Alzette with his main forces for the present.

40. The XVI. Army Corps, under which the 53. Mixed Inf. Brig. (xiii), at Gr. Hettingen is placed for the frontier defense, has instructions to assemble its concentration area as the 5. and 6. Armies arrive.

The Government of Metz and the Military Command Diedenhofen are placed directly under the 5th Army.

41. On the Nied, between Metz and the Saar, the "Nied position", a fortified field position, will be constructed by labor troops. The peacetime preparations have been made by the Hq. XVI.A.C. For the direction of the work, the Pionier Regt. 20 (xvi) is placed at his disposal. The Hq. 5. Army will have the use of this regiment only after the completion of the work.

The Nied position is under the 5. Army, unless circumstances after the commencement of the advance (see Par. 44) result in another disposition of the command.

As Commander of the Nied position, the Higher Landwehr Commander 2 (xvi) is announced; he is placed under the Governor of the Fortress Metz. The alerting of this chain of command is delegated to the Hq. 5. Army. The XVI. Army Corps is directed to send to the Commander of the Nied Position five passenger automobiles which have become surplus in the frontier defense. (Compare Par. 10b).

For the occupation of the Nied position the Mixed Landwehr Brigades of the 5. Army (see Par. 9), as well as two Landw. Brigs. and eight 10cm Canon batteries of the Fortress Metz, are to be used. The first billeting of the Landwehr Brigades is to be arranged by the Hq. 5. Army.

42. [Mission of the forces in Alsace-Lorraine.]

43. The concentration area of the 5. Army has a narrow front and great depth. Thus the participation of parts of the 5. Army in engagements south-east of Metz during the concentration is facilitated, but on the other hand the formation of march columns for the intended advance north of Metz will be rendered more difficult.

44. The beginning of the general advance of the German main forces will be ordered by the General Headquarters.

The Higher Cavalry Comdr. 4 with attached Jäger Bns. will then come directly under the G.H.Q. and will receive orders, while continuing the reconnaissance toward the Maas [Meuse] Sector Mezieres–Mouson–Stenay–Verdun–St. Mihiel, to move on Carignan and Damvillers. It must ascertain whether the Maas below Verdun is strongly occupied, or whether from there via Verdun, or between Verdun and Metz, French forces are advancing against the 4. and 5. Armies. The Higher Cavalry Commander 4 is directed to keep the Hdqrs. 5. Army informed through reports; its reports are to be transmitted without delay to the General Headquarters (comp. Par. 28).

The 4. Army (VI., VIII., XVIII.A.C., VIII., XVIII.R.Cs.) will take up the advance toward the Maas with the right flank on Fumay and the left flank on Attart (north of Arlon)–Neufchateau, and in addition be at all times ready to incline to the south – toward the Semois – to the support of the 5. Army.

Upon the ordering of the general advance of the German main forces by General Headquarters, the 5. Army has the task of holding the pivot Diedenhofen–Metz with connection to the 4. Army (see Par. 38). For this purpose the 5. Army has at first while maintaining the deep echelonement, to place itself in readiness for the advance with its first troops in the approximate line Bettenberg–Diedenhofen.

The 4. Army is directed, upon request, to clear the road in front of the right flank of the 5. Army (Mallingen–Rodemachern–Bettemberg) and the territory southwest of that road. For the dividing line between the armies in the advance see Appendix 5.

The further advance of the 5. Army is to follow, with strong echelonement to the left, with the right flank from Bettemberg via Mamer–Arlon upon Florenville south of Chiny, while the left flank maintains connection with Diedenhofen. The right wing of the 5. Army and the left flank of the 4. Army must operate in mutual agreement.

In order to ward off a French counterattack undertaken with strong forces from the direction of Verdun, the deployment of the 5. Army in a position with the front towards the south-west or the south may become necessary at any time. For this are required timely reconnaissance of the ground and precautionary preparation of all the resources offered by Metz and Diedenhofen for the construction and defense of a fortified field position. The fortress-motor-truck park established in Metz can be employed by agreement with the Government, to the extent to which they can be spared from the work of labor troops and the construction of the Nied position.

Circumstances must decide as to the bringing up of the Metz main reserve.

For the further progress of the advance, the taking of Longwy and Montmedy will probably fall to the 5. Army (see App. 25, 26).

45. The airships P. III and P. IV belonging to the war garrison of Metz are placed initially at the disposal of the XVI.A.C.

12

6th Army Evaluation of the Situation[1]

Eighteen pages personally hand-written in Standard script by the Chief of Staff of the 6th (Bavarian) Army, Krafft von Dellemensingen.
In the German army, written evaluations of the situation were taught at the General Staff school and were the norm at the army level. We can be practically certain that not only did all of the army commanders or their chiefs of staff write a Lagebeurteilung *such as this one and submitted it for Moltke's approval, but that Moltke himself wrote his evaluation of the situation. All have been lost except for Krafft's.*
Even at the army group level, the principal concern is with operations. Strategy is dependent on enemy actions and the results of combat. There is no mention of the 'Schlieffen plan'.[2]

Mission of the 6th and 7th Armies.
Initial estimate of the situation
and intentions. Copy

First draft, based on the deployment plan, written from 2 to 5 August 1914. (Submitted in somewhat altered form to the Great General Staff)
1) Operational readiness. According to the movement table the combat troops and an adequate portion of the unit trains will be available:

II Bavarian Corps	10th mobilization day, evening
I Bavarian Corps	11th
III Bavarian Corps	11th (minus part of combat trains)
XXI Corps	10th
I Bavarian Reserve	12th
5th Landwehr Brigade	11th
Siege units	11th

The four first-line units are therefore operationally ready on the evening of the 11th; the I Bavarian Reserve on the evening of the 13th [12th?]. The advance can

---
[1] Krafft von Dellmensingen, 'Erste Beurteilung der Lage', Kriegsarchiv Munich, *Nachlass Dellmensingen* 145.
[2] Zuber, *op. cit.*, pp. 260–3.

therefore begin at the earliest on the 13th mobilization day. Even then the lines of communication are not entirely ready.

2) In addition to its own units, Headquarters, 6th Army will be responsible for the overall command of the 6th and 7th Armies in Alsace-Lorraine.

3) The overall mission culminates in the protection of the left flank of the German army.

[2] There are three possible scenarios in the deployment instructions:

a) The 6th and 7th Armies are to advance against the Moselle below Frouard and the Meurthe to fix the French forces deployed there and prevent their movement against the decisive wing.

b) If the enemy comes against us with a great offensive between Metz and Strasbourg, withdraw and prevent either a breakthrough or envelopment of the *Niedstellung*, which consists of field fortifications.

c) If no strong enemy forces are met on the Meurthe, send elements across to the west bank of the Moselle at or to the south of Metz to engage in the battle there.

Beforehand and parallel to this, the 7th Army has the temporary mission of protecting the upper Alsace against incursions by weaker French forces. It is to withdraw before a strong enemy offensive and send as many forces as possible to cooperate with the 6th Army.

In all of these cases it must be remembered that the group of forces in Alsace-Lorraine is charged with the defense of the army flank and has under all circumstances the duty of giving the decisive wing the time (and unrestricted opportunity for its attacks) – or, in case the mass of the French army advances against Alsace-Lorraine – to give it the time [3] to swing to the south-east and come to support.

All considerations must be subordinated to this purpose. Under no circumstances can the Army Group allow itself to be defeated, it is the shield that the OHL holds in front of the left flank.

4) The first mission of the 6th Army, in which the 7th Army should also participate – holding the enemy – has the character of a demonstration: demonstration of an attack. It must be conducted in such a way that it can be transformed without difficulty into its opposite, a withdrawal in the face of an enemy attack.

At the same time, care is to be taken that elements of the army can be moved quickly to the Moselle at and to the south of Metz.

The mission is therefore somewhat complicated. But it must be solved.

Case a. The offensive against the Moselle and the Meurthe cannot be conducted in an unlimited manner, as an offensive would be if it sought a decision. It must nevertheless attempt to give the appearance of a great, powerful offensive against the line Toul–Epinal. Whether it will have this effect or not is, of course, not certain. The enemy will assuredly gain enough information during the deployment period to determine which corps are in Alsace-Lorraine. If no new forces appear during our advance, he will have no doubts concerning our strength. Notwithstanding, the attempt must be made, in order to at least [4] prevent the enemy forces from leaving Lorraine outright.

Above all, in order to feign great strength the offensive must be conducted on a broad front. The front can be over-extended without causing concern. If the 6th Army advances on a line from Pont à Mousson–Baccarat it will cover 70 kilometers, much farther that if it were to fight a decisive battle. For our purpose

August 1914: 6th Army Evaluation of the Situation 233

here even this extent is permissible. The broad front requires the units be deployed in multiple columns, in order that all the roads are occupied by advancing troops. This is best suited to give the enemy the impression of an attack in great strength. Perhaps we can also lengthen the columns by special means (narrower march formations).

Dispersing the units in multiple small columns will at the same time make it easier to break contact with superior enemy forces and transition to a withdrawal.

Advance guards pushed far forward and provided with strong artillery, attacking boldly, will be the fastest method of clarifying the situation. Considerable separation from the main body (5–10 kilometers) will best prevent the main body from becoming involved in a battle with superior enemy forces.

Of course, it will be difficult to maintain unity of action between the various columns. Larger columns would, however, be harder to turn around and get away. In any case the army cavalry must be active in order to protect the rear guards from being outflanked. [5] Perhaps it would be most effective to put the rear guards with the army cavalry under the control of HKK 3.

In order to be able to transition quickly from the offensive to a withdrawal it is also necessary that the army rear area be kept clear – therefore the trains and other relatively immobile units and installations (heaviest artillery, dumps, hospitals, etc.) must be held far to the rear.[3]

<u>Case b.</u> If the enemy advances against us with much superior forces, the army will initially withdraw without offering serious resistance. The army cavalry and the rear guards will delay the enemy. In view of the 6th Army's separate mission to cooperate with the defense of the Nied between the Nied and the Vosges, the army will be withdrawn to the Saar. It will defend there until the 6th and 7th Armies, together with elements of the decisive wing, go over to the counterattack. Resistance by the rear guards must provide the time necessary to prepare the Saar line for defense – (bring up the engineer equipment park at Germersheim). The farther the enemy advances towards the Saar and the Nied, the more his flanks are threatened and attacked all the more effectively from Metz and Strasbourg.

It is necessary that the rear guards maintain contact with the enemy while withdrawing, in order to immediately [6] recognize changes in enemy activities, but not endanger the units by engaging in premature costly battles to buy time.

This movement must provide the time necessary for the decisive group to bring up sufficient forces for the counterattack. The enemy offensive must also be brought to a halt on the Nied and Saar in order to prevent him from gaining any significant advantage. We must intend to defend the Saar for a considerable time. Our resistance on the upper Saar and east of the Donon (on the Donon massif and on the Breusch) must be particularly well prepared and determined, because the enemy will attack here first against our most sensitive spot. It is possible that it will be a question of withdrawing for several days. In the most unfavorable case, the French will begin a major attack only when we have crossed the Meurthe: our right flank would have to fall back about 75 kilometers (Junéville–Saarbrücken) or three marches, the left only two.

---

[3] This would also make any offensive more difficult.

Troop leaders must take the men into their confidence concerning the purpose of this withdrawal, so that it does not damage morale. During the withdrawal the army must be prepared at any time to deploy towards the enemy, in order to fix him if he either no longer follows us or withdraws.

The 6th Army cannot allow itself under any circumstances to be pushed away from contact with the *Niedstellung*. It must also hold the Saar from below Saargemund to the mouth of the Nied.

[7] The mission of the left wing of the 6th Army and the 7th Army will be to prevent the Saar position from being rolled up from Saarburg–Pfalzburg as well as on the Donon flank. Contact from there through Molsheim to the *Breuschstellung* must be assured.

If we succeed in holding the line Metz–Nied–Saar–Pfalzburg–Donon–Molsheim–Strasbourg long enough, the conditions for a transition to the offensive are favorable. We can assume that within this bow an enemy who has been brought to a standstill will be very restricted in employing his units and have great difficulty defending against an attack from three sides. The goal of such an attack must be to destroy the enemy through envelopment.

Defending the entire Saar to the mouth of the Nied requires individual corps to hold extended frontages. It is therefore even more important to delay the enemy advance in order gain enough time to improve the position, for which, unfortunately, no special labor or materials are available as they are for the *Niedstellung*.

Case c. The movement of elements of the 6th and 7th Armies to Metz and the south of Metz in case no strong enemy forces are found in French Lorraine requires swinging towards the right flank. We can prepare for this only if during the advance the 6th Army holds its right flank back and pushes the left flank forwards. In any case the right flank is the nearest to the enemy, while the left needs two marches to reach the Meurthe (implementation, see p. 15).

[8] The left flank must thus move out first. Therefore, the right flank cannot remain inactive. Here, very early the advance guards of the III Bavarian Corps must attack sharply, but only in order to attract the enemy's attention: the main body will be held back. Support against enemy field fortifications will be provided by the mobile and heavy artillery reserves of Metz. The advance guards, beginning on the right flank, would gradually reach the line Pont à Mousson–Position de Nancy–Lunéville–Meurthe. The main bodies must then be brought forward so that when they have reached this line they are equidistant from each other.

In addition, the march to the north-west can be prepared by moving the I Bavarian Reserve Corps from the second line to the west wing of the army.

4) Initially, the role of the 7th Army is determined by the mission of protecting the upper Alsace.

a) If there is no French attack into the upper Rhine valley the 7th Army will then take part in the offensive against the Meurthe.

For that purpose, together with the 6th Army, the XV Corps will advance either north or south of the Donon towards the line Raon l'Etape–St. Die, XIV Corps towards the line St. Die–Gerardmer, while the XIV Reserve Corps takes over the protection of the Rhine valley to the south.

b) If a weak enemy incursion into the upper Rhine valley has been thrown back, this is an indicator that the enemy will hardly commit strong forces in an offensive either in the Rhine valley or between Metz and Strasbourg. [9] Then the priority for the 7th Army will be cooperation with the 6th Army. The 7th Army will then probably be employed for an offensive on the left bank of the Moselle.

The execution of the operation will be completely dependent on the development of the situation to that time. Linking up with the 6th Army or moving through Metz can then either take place by foot-march towards the front, along the enemy fortress front in the general direction past Lunéville to Pont à Mousson, or by rail march.

Bringing the 7th Army forward by foot-march would take a considerable time, especially for the southern elements. The army thereby continually runs the risk of being delayed by an enemy attack from the French fortress front. Therefore, if at all possible elements of the 7th Army which are the furthest away must be moved by rail.

c) If the French conduct an offensive with strong forces into the upper Rhine valley, it is clear that they intend to conduct a major offensive in Lorraine. Then plainly the portion of the deployment instructions comes into force which concerns the evacuation of the upper Alsace by rail or foot-march for the purpose of cooperating with the 6th Army, and for the thorough destruction of the rail lines. From this point the 7th Army would assume the defense of the fortified Breusch line, the Donon and the high ground around Saarburg and Pfalzburg, in cooperation with the 6th Army, which would be pulled back to the Saar.

As soon as possible, and in conjunction with the reinforcements moving through Metz, a resumption of the advance will be considered, [10] if at all possible, south of the Donon against the flank and rear of the enemy forces that have pushed into Lorraine. All troops conducting the defense of the upper Rhine and all mobilized ersatz formations that can be assembled in the area will participate from the Rhine.

5) Individual Aspects of the Execution of the Mission
a. Advance against the Moselle and the Meurthe.

During the advance the right flank very quickly comes up against the Position de Nancy, the middle and left against Fort Manonviller.

It is doubtful whether the reinforced position on the high ground between Pont à Mousson and Amance can be taken. It has been prepared for weeks in the same manner given to the wartime expansion of permanent fortifications. An army can deploy behind it.

However, if the impression is to be given that the Germans are conducting a serious offensive to the south of Nancy, these fortifications cannot be left idle. The position must be sealed off and the enemy forces east of the Moselle pushed into the most restricted space possible.

The forward parts of the position must therefore be taken where possible. It is questionable if the resources available to a corps are adequate. Therefore the support of the heavy and reserve artillery from Metz must be obtained. In no case can the cooperation of XVI Corps be counted on. A serious move against the Position de Nancy can only take place after a very thorough artillery preparation. [11] No strong infantry forces will be employed for this purpose. On the front Ste. Génevive (south-east of Pont à Mousson)–Jeandelaincourt–Amance weaker forces must be employed so that enough units are available for the remaining, wide, front. Admittedly, this thinly held front poses a danger: the enemy could see it as an opportunity to attack here. We must always be prepared for this. Precisely for this reason, the bulk of the troops engaging this position must be carefully held back and allow the heavy artillery to do the talking.

It would be desirable if the III Bavarian Corps could move through Jeandelaincourt more to the south, and the I Bavarian Corps could also be brought over to the western wing, because an enemy attack to the north, against Metz, is less likely and German reinforcements can be brought there the most quickly. The best troops would therefore be opposite the more threatened east front of the Position de Nancy. This would also make the task of the II Bavarian Corps easier, which has a broad front and only one completely combat-capable unit (4th Infantry Division and a Bavarian reserve infantry division). The I Bavarian Reserve Corps would be on the strongest portion of the front while at the same time being closest to the *Niedstellung*. It would be able to reinforce the garrison of the position if necessary, as provided in the deployment orders. The more difficult missions would be reserved for the active corps. Two active corps would therefore stand with their main bodies near Metz, so that at any time they could be quickly thrown onto the west bank.

Shifting the I Bavarian Reserve Corps requires three short marches, and presumably could still be conducted in time. Admittedly, [12] the corps would have to move through the rear echelons of the II and III Bavarian Corps. The difficulty of doing so may be reduced in that the combat trains of the I Bavarian Reserve Corps are attached immediately to the combat units, while the II and III Bavarian Corps can move their combat trains more to the east behind their corps. The field trains of the I Bavarian Reserve Corps remain in their deployment area billets until the roads are clear and they can follow their Corps along the northern border of the deployment assembly area.

I therefore consider that the I Bavarian Reserve Corps is best employed on the western wing.

If this is not desired, I Bavarian Reserve Corps could also be inserted between the III and II Bavarian Corps or between the II Bavarian and XXI Corps. Movement would be simpler in the latter case. The Corps could no longer be considered the army reserve and would be presented with missions which at the beginning of hostilities would be more suitable for an active corps. The army formation would be less favorable for a march to the Moselle at Metz.

Or the I Bavarian Reserve Corps can remain as army reserve.

In that case, the advance would be conducted in the following manner:

III Bavarian Corps would move towards the line Landremont–Mont Toulon–Leyr; detachments move against Pont à Mousson and Dieulouard.

II Bavarian Corps sends detachments with heavy artillery towards the line Leyr–Amance, under the overall command of the III Bavarian Corps.

Common mission: roll up the Position de Nancy. The main body of II Bavarian Corps advances against the line St. Nicholas du Port–Luneville (excluded); security against Nancy.

I Bavarian Corps through Blâmont–Cirey to Chenevières–[13] Baccarat.

The *Denkschriften* and plans for an attack on Manonviller demonstrate that an attack on the north side is difficult but easier on the east, south-east and south sides. Therefore the attack on the fort will be assigned to the I Bavarian Corps. XXI Corps will provide heavy artillery.

August 1914: 6th Army Evaluation of the Situation

If the I Bavarian Reserve Corps is sent to the western wing, it can move in two columns through Falkenberg–Budry and through Bellingen–Moncheux to Pont à Mousson–Noményi. For two days of the march it can act as army reserve. III and II Bavarian Corps would then shift accordingly to the east.

From the 7th Army: XV Corps moves on Raon l'Etape–St. Dié. No determination can be made concerning the employment of the rest of the army.

Initially, HKK3 remains to the front and then conducts a rearward passage through the advancing troops. This presents the opportunity to give HKK 3 a rest. If the enemy withdraws beyond the Moselle and the Meurthe, only the cavalry will follow.

From this deployment the cavalry can easily withdraw to the Saar.

b. If the Army has to withdraw to the Saar, the front that has to be defended is 80 kilometers long.

Five corps are far too few to do so. We must strive to assure that in all cases the XV Corps [14] takes part in the defense of the Saar. If it participated in the offensive, it should attempt to move back on the west side of the Donon. XIV and XIV Reserve Corps, can, according to need, form the left flank to the east or to both sides of the Donon.

The following could be considered for the first position on the Saar:

I Bavarian Reserve Corps: reinforcing the garrison on the Nied and cutting off the angle Busendorf–Saarlouis
III Bavarian Corps: Saarlouis–Saarbrücken (excluded)
II Bavarian Corps: Saarbrücken–Saargemünd (excluded)
XXI Corps: Saargemünd–Lorenzen (included)
I Bavarian, XV Corps: Lorenzen–Pfalzburg–Lutzelburg
XIV Reserve Corps, Bavarian Landwehr with the 7th Army: Donon–Breusch–Strasbourg
5th Bavarian Landwehr Brigade: Army reserve at Zweibrücken
Local reserves – a mixed infantry brigade each:
    from III Bavarian Corps, Hensweiler
    II Bavarian Corps, St. Ingbert
    XXI Corps, Rohrbach
    I Bavarian Corps, Tieffenbach
    XV Corps, east of Pfalzburg.

The general trace of the position has already been reconnoitered by us once during a *Grosse Generalstabsreise*.

HKK 3 acts in coordination with the rear guards of the corps (common orders?) and protects them from envelopment. Both prepare to substantially delay the enemy. Maintain close contact with the enemy! If he no longer follows or withdraws, immediately pursue and stay on his heels! The overall situation will decide whether the army will follow or marches to the Moselle.

[15] When the enemy approaches closer to the *Niedstellung* the cavalry divisions must be separated. The Italians (if they are actually there!) and the 7th Cavalry division to the east wing, east or west of the Vosges, Bavarian and 8th Cavalry Division on the west wing south of Metz, forming the outer enveloping columns of the German counterattack.

c. Movement to the Moselle at Metz

The conduct of this maneuver is very dependent on the point in time in which it is initiated and then on the formation that the army is in.

A pure march to the flank can be made easier if the two right-wing corps (I Bavarian Reserve and III Bavarian or III and II Bavarian) turn immediately and make room to the north-west. These are the first units that would be ready to engage on the west bank.

The remaining corps must make a right turn and follow. They cannot be deployed in long, deep march columns one next to the other, but would march better in many small parallel columns behind each other, with the trains accompanying them on the north flank (schematic sketch attached). In this manner, in four days the march can be made from Baccarat to the Moselle. New deployment to the east of Metz. Thereby each corps can also turn its front quickly and unhindered to the south. Leaving a special covering force (I Bavarian Reserve, III Bavarian Corps) south of Metz for the flank march would [16] delay engaging the army on the west bank and appears unnecessary. Fortress Metz must perform this service. It will be able to inspire the enemy with that much respect. If necessary the flank march will be conducted farther from the enemy.

Forces from the fortress will insure that the Moselle crossings at Metz and to the south are secured early and are kept open. Earliest possible use of all of the available mobile units and support from the fort. Operational control of the fortress will be requested at once.

Movement of the 7th Army is dependent on the situation. XIV and XIV Reserve Corps will probably move by rail; XV and the corps of the 6th Army probably by foot-march.

d. If the French attack very early between Metz and Strasbourg, possibly from the 10th mobilization day, and reach the border on the 11th or 12th mobilization day, the deployment cannot be conducted according to plan.

The troops that have already disembarked must immediately move back to the protection of the Saar, covered by the border security and the cavalry, and further disembarkments moved behind the river. Order of battle as in b.

This possibility, as well as case b requires caution in establishing the location of magazines, rear-area installations and the like forwards of the Saar and Nied. Here, everything must remain mobile.

[17] Initial Orders

1.) Estimate of the situation to the Great General Staff – Request for attachment of heavy artillery – Metz mobile and fortress artillery reserve, etc. – for the Position de Nancy. Operational control of the Fortresses of Metz and Germersheim.

2.) Directives to the corps of the 6th Army and to the 7th Army concerning the first operations. Meetings.

3.) Establish the initial line of resistance for the forward troops of the 6th army. Field fortifications! Line: Buchy–Delme–Château Salins–Marsal–Geistkirch–Maizieres–Avricourt.

4.) Reconnoiter rearward lines of resistance and the Saar position (in my deployment map light green) [Krafft then gives eight possible successive positions, the last as far back as Saarbrücken–Pfalzburg]

[18] 5.) Instructions to the corps and rear-area units concerning mobility of elements between the front line and the Saar.

6.) Plan for demolition of rail and roads in case of withdrawal in Lorraine and Alsace.

7.) Order of the day to the corps and 7th Army.

8.) Coordination with 5th Army concerning intent, especially movement of supply units in a withdrawal!

(signed) Krafft

13

Wenninger's Description of the German War Plan[1]

At the beginning of the Great War, Generalleutnant Karl Ritter von Wenninger was the Bavarian military representative to the Imperial government in Berlin. As such, he sent frequent reports to Munich. His report of 7 September 1914 gives probably the only clear statement of the intent of the German war plan that has survived. Wenninger was later killed in action on a personal reconnaissance to the front lines. In 1933 his reports became the source of a heated controversy between the Bavarian Kriegsarchiv and the Reichsarchiv.[2]

Wenninger's description of the German war plan bears little resemblance to the 'Schlieffen plan'. First, he says that the final concept was adopted in 1909, not 1905. This date corresponds, oddly enough, to that given by the official history, which says that Moltke developed the concept for the final plan beginning in 1909 (Volume I, pp. 62–6). Wenninger then goes on to say that the intent of the German war plan was not to push the French into Switzerland with a strong right wing, but to conduct a double envelopment of the Verdun–Toul fortress complex, with the left wing of the German army attacking through the 'Trouée de Charmes' between Toul and Epinal. This is very much like Beseler's 1900 Operationsstudie *described by Dieckmann.*

Review: As I hear, until now Schlieffen's operations plan (*Schlieffen'sche Operationsplan*) of 1909 had been executed without significant changes, even beyond the first contact with the enemy. One glitch only occurred because the 6th and 7th Armies, contrary to Schlieffen's assumption, were not able to advance because the famous gap at Charmes was in reality no gap at all. Instead, both armies encountered here a continuous fortress-like line constructed in peacetime 150 kilometers in length Toul–Nancy–Epinal–Belfort. The *Oberste Heeresleitung* was initially very incredulous and only reluctantly came to terms with these disturbing facts. It was written on the last page of Schlieffen's plan (*Schlieffen'schen Entwurf*) that the northern and southern halves of the army would swing together in the middle to produce the greatest Cannae in world history "on the Catalaunian

---

[1] Kriegsarchiv Munich, Altreguister Abt. III Bd. 5 Bayerischer Mil. Bevollmächtigter 18. Bericht, 7 Sept 1914.
[2] Zuber, *Inventing the Schlieffen Plan*, pp. 296–8.

fields".³ Painfully, this had to be abandoned. An expedient now had to be found from its [OHL's] own resources.

---

³ The "Catalaunian fields" was a reference to the battle of Châlons (actually *campi Catalauni* near Troyes) in June 451 in which Aëtius defeated the Huns. A certain amount of hyperbole was involved here. Had the Germans actually been able to close the sack around the Verdun–Toul fortress complex a great many French troops would have been surrounded – the garrisons of the two great fortresses and the *Sperrforts* were not insignificant. Nevertheless, it would have been unlikely that the Germans could have caught a very large portion of the French field army in the trap.

Part VII

THE BIRTH OF THE SCHLIEFFEN PLAN

14

The Development of the German Operational Concept[1]

Wilhelm Groener was lieutenant-colonel and the head of the rail section in the General Staff in 1914. He therefore developed the rail plan for the strategic deployment of the German army and planned for the rail support of operations. He rose through his bureaucratic talents in the rear area – and not as a combat leader – to be Ludendorff's replacement as de facto *head of the German army in October 1918. He became one of the leading proponents of the infallibility of the Schlieffen plan.*[2]

The following request from Colonel von Mertz to Groener and his detailed response were found in Groener's papers at the Bundesarchiv-Militärarchiv. Von Mertz asked Groener to evaluate a secret history of German war planning (now lost) that had been written in 1919 by an anonymous officer/historian working for the General Staff. This document arrived at conclusions that would have destroyed Groener's concept of the 1905 'Schlieffen plan' Denkschrift.[3]

Reichsarchiv   Berlin, 11 October 1919
Nr. 5 Secret
Secret!
                        Generalleutnant (inactive) Groener
                                  Excellency

    I have the honor of requesting to submit to Your Excellency for your examination a *Denkschrift*, written here [Reichsarchiv], concerning "The Development of the Operational Concept for a Two-Front War from 1871 to 1914".
    I would be particularly thankful for an evaluation of the description in the *Denkschrift* concerning the planning and intent of Generaloberst von Moltke and for any information on the questions it raises.
    This work is to be considered preliminary to the official history of the World War.

---

[1] Die Entwicklung des Operativen Gedankens im Zweifrontenkrieg von 1871 bis 1914, Oktober 1919, BA-MA *Nachlaß* Groener N46/41. I would like to thank Frau and Herr R. Erben for helping me decipher Groener's Standard script handwriting.
[2] See Zuber, *Inventing the Schlieffen Plan*, pp. 36–8.
[3] *ibid.*, pp. 291–5.

If Your Excellency agrees, permit me to transmit the *Denkschrift* by registered mail.

(signed) Mertz[4]

Draft

[From Groener]
To the Reichsarchiv
Colonel von Mertz

[Four pages, in extremely small and poorly written Standard script, with even smaller marginal notes. All pages have numerous corrections, the original text of the third page is almost entirely blacked out.

Groener makes repeated references to Schlieffen's operational concept without ever defining exactly what it was. Indeed, Groener's understanding of the actual 'Schlieffen plan' seems weak. He was, nevertheless, convinced that it was the perfect plan.]

I read the *Denkschrift* concerning the development of the operational concept since 1871 with great interest. I ask that the marginal comments that I have made be considered merely as an expression of my interest in the matter. As is well known, I acknowledge that I am an enthusiastic supporter of the teachings of Count Schlieffen. In 1912, when the question was raised if *Aufmarsch* II was to be continued, as Chief of the Rail Section I supported the so-called Great *Westaufmarsch* in the strongest terms possible.

In addition, after 1910 the Rail section conducted planning for shifting units from the left to the right wing. Even during the deployment period, empty wagons for a total of nine corps were attached to locomotives and positioned on both sides of the Rhine. This type of rail movement was practiced in peacetime war games with the Line Commanders.

In order to compensate for the fact that the German forces were significantly weaker than those required for the execution of Schlieffen's operational concept, as soon as I became the Chief of the Rail Section I formulated a plan for a major expansion of our rail net, thereby increasing the speed of our deployment, in order to reach the operational readiness of our deployment three to four days sooner. The execution of this plan was overtaken by the war. During the war the speed of the trains prescribed by the military rail schedule was increased as well as the completion of important elements of the rail expansion plan (Rhine bridge at Remagen and double-tracking [?] of the Moselle rail bridge was begun).

In my estimation, it was particularly important for the execution of the operational concept from the very beginning that on the right wing rail debarquements provided a deep deployment. Count Schlieffen, if I am not mistaken, maybe in 1905, expressly approved this in a briefing by the Chief of the Rail Section. Later, many voices were loudly raised in opposition to the depth of the deployment.

---

[4] Bavarian officer, service in General Staff of 6th Army in 1914 and thereafter at OHL. 1919 appointed President of the Reichsarchiv by Groener. Herrmann, *Reichsarchiv*, 565.

The Birth of the Schlieffen Plan

[2] In reading the *Denkschrift* the question forced itself upon me, as to whether General von Moltke was aware that because of the changes in Schlieffen's deployment the operational concept had been blurred. I would like to believe that even in August and the beginning of September 1914 he thought he was acting according to Schlieffen's intentions. Even the decision to break through between Toul and Epinal, which according to my notes and my recollection entered the thoughts of the OHL on 27 August, appears to me to have been considered Schlieffen's strategy. This is confirmed by a comment made at that time by Lieutenant Colonel von Dommes, said to be a particular confidant of Moltke's, to whom I characterized the breakthrough between Toul and Epinal as "the greatest sin against the spirit of the departed Schlieffen". The ideas of the *Oberste Heeresleitung* from 23 August developed within an unclear picture of the situation. Because of the exaggerated reports from the armies of victories this [picture] became completely false and brought forth fatal decisions which no longer corresponded to the operational concept. According to my observations, there was never a conscious deviation from it [Schlieffen's operational concept]. It was psychologically understandable that this belief in victory led them stumbling in the wrong direction. The recognition that they were on the wrong path, that the operational thread had been lost, came only slowly and too late. If I am not mistaken, the dawn of recognition can be read in the OHL order of 5 September. But even then they thought victory was in their grasp. General von Moltke has been reproached for allowing the reins of the leadership of the army to drag on the ground. Certainly, that's how it appeared in retrospect. According to my personal impressions, the concern was not pull too hard on the reins of a victorious army. In addition, the Chief of the Operations section had adopted the practice, as he said, that the operations must be conducted with brute force.

[The rest of this paragraph is a virtually illegible marginal comment. The original text opposite is completely scratched out. The translation is therefore not certain.]

In the 4 September order [for 5 September] I think that with a bit less brutality and instructions more in Schlieffen's sense, Moltke could have gained a great success. I was of the opinion that the heedless attack of the 4th and 5th Armies was not appropriate to the concept of the operation and I expressed this to Tappen.

In making these comments concerning the *Denkschrift*, I thereby want to reinforce the question of whether the cause of the failure of the operation in 1914 is to be sought primarily as the result of the blurring of the operational concept before or [two illegible words] of the operational concept during the conduct of the operations themselves. What cannot be [determined] here is that because the concept had already been distorted, the danger existed that it would become even less clear. Due to a lack of healthy skepticism in the *Oberste Heeresleitung*, self-deception crept even more easily into their heads and increased the danger. To comprehend the psychological factors, the period between 31 August and 7 September appears to be particularly important. On 31 August there was a spark of recognition that our right flank was seriously threatened from Paris, which disappeared on 3 September, reappeared again on 5 September and was only on 7 September fully clear.

[3] In conclusion I would only like to be permitted a question. What intent is the *Denkschrift* pursuing? Is it merely to establish the cold historical basis of how the operational concept developed, or should it demonstrate the military necessity of marching through Belgium as the prerequisite for victory in a two-front war?

[The original *Denkschrift* "The Development of the Operational Concept for a Two-Front War from 1871 to 1914" has not survived. The document in Groener's *Nachlaß* consists of his comments to specific parts of the paper. Groener presents his, often unfounded, opinion on all of German strategy. Curiously, Groener's own comments are typed and his summary of the part of the *Denkschrift* he is referring to is written in Groener's miserable Standard script, sometimes on the body of the page and sometimes in the margins. Groener is clearly preparing the ground for his 'Schlieffen plan' project. This is a *Streitschrift* and its descriptions of the deployment plans must be treated accordingly. In spite of its many deficiencies, this is one of the few documents that describes the German war planning.]

[4] [Handwritten] <u>Comments on the *Denkschrift* from the Military History Section concerning the "Development of the Operational Concept in a Two-Front War from 1871 to 1914"</u>

[From the *Denkschrift*. Handwritten] Re: *Denkschrift* by Field Marshal von Moltke immediately after 1871 pointed out the possibility of a simultaneous war with France and Russia. It said that there was a need to consider <u>in good time</u> to provide for the <u>means</u> to conduct the <u>defense</u>.

[Groener's comment. Typed.] Was anything said about these means, then or later? In my opinion, given such a combination there were only two effective remedies:
a) military training for the <u>entire</u> male population.
b) massive expansion of the rail net.
Neither was done adequately. The erroneous idea of the necessity to maintain the longer period of conscription stood in opposition to a). The principal obstacle to b) is to be seen in the failure of Bismarck's plans for the Imperial railways. In my opinion both points now require further historical research and enlightenment and can hardly be separated from operational thought.

[*Denkschrift*] Germany would never conduct an aggressive war or a war of conquest in order to defend itself.

[Groener] There can be no doubt that the <u>initial</u> bud in the political development that led first to the political and then to the military encirclement of Germany is to be sought in the results of the 1870/71 war. In his time Bismarck would not hear of preventive war because he hoped that through clever foreign policy he could prevent the most dangerous combinations. After his successors as Chancellor failed <u>here,</u> the most important thing was <u>solely</u> to break the ring that had been created <u>politically</u> through <u>military</u> means, at a time that was the most favorable for us and for which the preparations had to be <u>planned,</u> with the creation of the largest number of forces possible, but <u>without</u> transmitting a threat to the outside. [5] Bismarck would surely have approved of <u>this</u> kind of preventive war. In doing so, the responsibility for "attack" <u>had to</u> be pushed onto to the enemy. This was the mission of the political leader of the Empire. (Compare this to the concept for the operation against Liège, which made it impossible for the political leader to blame the attack on the enemy.)

[*Denkschrift*] Moltke's 1877 *Denkschrift* advocated the assembly of our main body in the west in order to bring about an immediate decision. It would not have been possible to continue the pursuit to Paris. It must be left to diplomacy to see if it could conclude peace on this side, if only on the basis of the *status quo ante*.

[Groener] It is questionable whether even Bismarck himself could have succeeded in accomplishing this. Preferable to this idea of the strategist was that of the statesman to delay the establishment of the Entente between France and Russia as long as possible. This must unfailingly come to pass as soon as the German Empire had exceeded a certain level of political and economic development and was thereby tempted to go beyond its previously purely continental politics – the Orient – and otherwise to pursue *Weltpolitik*.

The Russian-Turkish War and the Congress of Berlin can hardly be passed over in the development of the operational concept. In my opinion, after the Congress of Berlin the Russians were a threat because the results of the Russian-Turkish war were inadequate for Russia's power position in the Orient and gave Pan-Slavism the most powerful impulse. Even though Bismarck's brilliant restraint in the Eastern policy itself and his Reinsurance Treaty prevented the dangerous coalition for a decade – the danger for us grew greater and greater. This was probably reflected in the [6] operational thought of the 1879 and 1880 *Denkschriften*.

[*Denkschrift*] Moltke planned an offensive against Russia, initially a defensive against France.

Denkschriften of 1879 and 1880. In them, it was said that the Vosges formed a shield for a part of the front.

[Groener] This protection was questionable if the French, thanks to their superior rail net, advanced early from two sides – from Epinal and Belfort. On the other hand, it was possible for an army that maneuvered skillfully to attack and defeat the advancing French as they emerged from the gap at Belfort or from the Vosges. The double-tracked rail line in the upper Alsace was particularly suitable for this purpose. In case the French attacked with superior forces, the only defensive possibility was, in my opinion, the line of the Rhine. (The upper Rhine was particularly favorable for the defense).

[*Denkschrift*] In the same *Denkschrift*: As long as Metz and Strasbourg held out, Lorraine and Alsace could be invaded by the enemy, but not conquered.

[Groener] Whether Metz and Strasbourg could have long played the roles intended at that time is questionable.

[7] [*Denkschrift*] In the same *Denkschrift*: If Austria is in a war against Russian and another Power, it has to make peace! "Possibly" observation against Italy.

[Groener] Wasn't it to be expected that if the campaign in the east were dragged out (a danger that could easily occur, given the vast spaces) that Italy would turn against Austria?

[*Denkschrift*] Up to his retirement (in 1888), Moltke advocated the offensive against Russia.

[Groener] The plan at this time for an offensive against Russia suffered from one great deficiency: the preparations for the expansion of the lines of communication were just being formulated. There was a lack of railway troops. The field railway system with locomotives was just being formed, but was still a very shaky supply system. However, the Vistula and the Niemen could have been of some help. Fast and decisive operations were hardly to be expected, given the transportation routes of the time.

[*Denkschrift*] Increase in forces through Italian units north of the Alps.

[Groener] What advantage did Italy gain from a defensive in the west? What were the conditions of the military treaties with Italy? They could have attempted to seize Nizza and Savoy. They would have gained support for this from a German offensive.

[8] [*Denkschrift*] The question was the siege of Belfort, if possible by the additional Italian units.

[Groener] For what purpose? Probably to keep it as the victor's prize.

[*Denkschrift*] In 1886/87 Waldersee thought that the impulse for war came from France. Waldersee also thought that the Germans and the French would advance simultaneously.

[Groener] Was this assumption justified?

[*Denkschrift*] Waldersee recommended an offensive with the main body in the west.

An offensive blow in the east in spite of the limited strength.

[Groener] In what direction was this [eastern] offensive blow to be made and with what operational goal? Or, if superior enemy forces were encountered, was it to be only a demonstration with an immediate withdrawal?

[*Denkschrift*] After 1888 Waldersee thought that the impulse for war was now coming from Russia. France would join in, if not immediately, then in a short time.

[Groener] Are there any statements and opinions from Prince Bismarck concerning the question of the impulse for the beginning of the war, that is, probably, "declaration of war" or "commencement of hostilities"? It would be very interesting to study the development of the operational concept in conjunction with the opinions and [9] intentions of the political leadership.

[*Denkschrift*] In the east, Waldersee's recommendation was to conduct an initial, perhaps short, offensive in conjunction with the Austrians to bring a decision there as early as possible.

[Groener] As an operational concept, isn't this a half-measure? Does not such a half-measure easily lead three steps forward and two steps back?

[*Denkschrift*] Moltke: It was more likely that the French, as the originators of the war, would have to take the initiative and, pressured by public opinion, would seek a decision.

[Groener] This sentence can be turned to our disadvantage. By this line of reasoning, because we took the military initiative in 1914, we could be held responsible for causing the war.

[*Denkschrift*] Re: Moltke's opinion concerning strategic defensive in the west. He recommended that strong forces be assembled behind both wings.

[Groener] According to the exact wording of the preceding text these echelons on the wings were termed "tactical", for envelopments on the battlefield, not as operational groups intended to strike deep into the rear of the invading French forces. Would it not have been more effective, unless the French did us the favor of attacking between Metz and the Vosges, to make the front very weak and assemble [10] two offensive groups astride the lower Saar (from Saarbrücken) as well as between Pfalzburg and Wasselnheim? [Both are west of Strasbourg.] The strong group on the lower Saar would simultaneously have been favorably placed in case of a French advance through Belgium that presumably did not threaten Antwerp but was directed against Aachen–Trier. The historians must seek to determine whether in those days Britain would have turned against France because of the violation of Belgian neutrality. If the French marched through Belgium, in my opinion the important question was if it was not necessary to move the troops in Alsace by rail to the lower Rhine (Cologne–Düsseldorf–Bonn) in order to conduct a combined offensive from the lower Saar and Cologne. The central position behind the Main between Mainz and Frankfurt was indeed the requisite expedient in case the French advanced with their main body against the middle Rhine. It offered the possibility of offensive operations in case the French crossed the Rhine between Mainz and Strasbourg. It was unfavorable only in the case where the French advanced with their main body against the lower Rhine. However, then we could attempt to conduct offensive action over the middle Rhine.

[*Denkschrift*] In his October 1884 *Denkschrift* Count Waldersee's position to Moltke's view was, among other things, that it would probably be the most appropriate to mass on our right flank.

[Groener] Does this mean, no withdrawal whatsoever behind the Rhine, but rather operate west of the Rhine in the Rhine province with the Moselle to the rear? Possible withdrawal to Cologne? This idea frequently played a role in Count Schlieffen's studies.

[*Denkschrift*] In Waldersee's opinion when the French crossed over the Moselle and Seille valleys there would perhaps be moments which could be used to go over to the attack. Waldersee did not want to make accepting combat forwards of the Saar a "firm arrangement". Moltke approved of this reservation.

[Groener] Why not [attack the French] while they are crossing over the Saar? In doing so, striking deep into the rear would be more likely to succeed. Compare this to the battles of the 6th and 7th Armies, though under very different circumstances.

[*Denkschrift*] Moltke and Waldersee were so convinced of the advantages offered by a defensive in the west that they wanted to retain this form of warfare even in the case of a war with France alone, without simultaneous Russian participation.

[Groener] Stated in this lapidary form, this is very critical of our advance in 1914.

[*Denkschrift*] Moltke: If the Meurthe has been reached from Nancy to Luneville, the Mortagne and the Moselle present new positions behind which the enemy must surely attack us. The French will not abandon such valuable areas without a fight. The strategic offensive requires them to attack tactically.

[Groener] This seems questionable to me. Why would the French not defend against our attack behind the Moselle line Toul–Epinal? [12] During this period of time that was surely the best line for a French strategic defensive. Difficult to envelop on both wings, very strong in front.

[*Denkschrift*] Moltke's thoughts concerning an offensive against Russia. He said: the Podolian and Volhynian armies will have difficulty coming together at all against the Austrians.

[Groener] Is this substantiated by the condition of the rail nets on both sides?

[*Denkschrift*] Waldersee's operations plan against Russia 1890. Deviation from Moltke's plan. Moltke agreed on 30 March 1890. The question was one of deploying the German forces in East Prussia somewhat farther to the north. Weak detachments from Soldau to Pultusk. Main body in two equally strong groups from the line Ortelsburg–Lyck and from Gumbinnen and offensive in the direction of Lomza–Bialystock, also against the Niemen above Kowno.

[Groener] The changes of 1890 did not mean a change in the operational concept, but rather in my opinion a stronger concentration of forces on the outermost wings, therefore an even stronger emphasis on the operational concept.

[*Denkschrift*] General comments concerning Moltke's and Waldersee's *Denkschriften*.

[Groener] The entire development means therefore that the legacy of Moltke and Waldersee was avowal of an attack in the east and defense in the west. This operational concept stayed in force as [13] *Aufmarsch* II.

[*Denkschrift*] Schlieffen in agreement with the Chief of the Austrian General Staff, Freiherr von Beck. August 1892.

[Groener] The German deployment in Silesia at that time was a sort of episode in the development of the operational concept, which remarkably was repeated in Ludendorff's decision in the fall of 1915 [sic: 1914] to advance from Silesia on Warsaw.

[*Denkschrift*] 1894. In order to win, we needed to be stronger where the main opposing forces meet. We only had the prospect of being so, if we determined where the operation was to take place. Not if we waited passively in a position to see what the enemy would do to us.

[Groener] This is the new idea in the operational concept!

[*Denkschrift*] 1894. Attack on Nancy. Precondition for an offensive against Toul–Verdun or against the Moselle below Epinal (1st Army ready north-west of Metz.) When the 2nd Army, with 120–144 heavy guns, attacks Nancy, its right flank must be covered in the area of Pont à Mousson by the 1st Army Detachment. The left flank will be covered by the 3rd Army on the Meurthe at Lunéville. The 4th Army crosses the Vosges, initially to reach the Vosges between Baccarat and St. Dié. The 2nd Army Detachment covers the upper Alsace and provides security against Belfort.

[Groener] The *Denkschrift* of 1894 recommended a purely frontal attack against superior enemy forces. It attempted to compensate for the deficiencies of such an operation by strongly echelloning both flanks. The Cannae-concept has not yet been born. These are old ideas, but will be fertilized by a new bud, [14] which will grow from year to year, become larger and ripen into the strategic Cannae-concept. 1894 was a careful exploration towards the great offensive.

[*Denkschrift*] West army 1899/1900 echelonned on the line Liège–Trier–Saarbrücken–Saarburg–Strasbourg. *Aufmarsch* II for 1899/1900?? For the first time in 1900/01 the west corps were retained in their garrisons, ready for rail movement, in order to be sent to attack the enemy left flank by surprise. The French could attack wherever they wanted: the moment would come when their left flank would lose secure support.

[Groener] This *Aufmarsch* was my particular responsibility within Rail Section IIa and gave me forthwith the occasion to make a thorough personal study of rail operations and to work them out in war games and other studies. Before this time the Rail Section limited itself to unprepared movements of smaller troop units – divisions – for tactical purposes. In the following years Count Schlieffen frequently gave the Rail Section problems for rail operations.

[*Denkschrift*] 1905 *Denkschrift*. However, perhaps an increased demand on Belgian resources would also induce the Belgians to refrain from hostile actions and surrender their fortresses. In return it would gain all the advantages that accrue to a third party which is not involved in a war between two others. [A direct quote from pages 17 and 18 of the Schlieffen plan *Denkschrift*.]

[Groener] This is not entirely clear to me! It is not very likely that the Belgians would have surrendered Antwerp. However, I don't think it was out of the question that King Leopold could have attempted to stay out of the war. [15] A great deal of skill on the part of the political leader of Belgium would have been required to stay neutral in a war between Britain and Germany, which Leopold's successor surely did not possess.

When you read Schlieffen's 1905 *Denkschrift*, its enough to make you cry out of rage and shame over our stupidity in 1914. If the leadership had not memorized it, they needed only to have put this breviary for victory in their pocket and then pulled it out!

[*Denkschrift*] Moltke thought that Schlieffen's 1905 *Denkschrift* applied only in case Germany and France were at war, but not when the Triple Alliance would be involved in a war between Russia and Austria.

[Groener] The political situation could have been anything you like: there was no other way to conduct the offensive against France and Britain than the one recommended by Schlieffen.

[*Denkschrift*] Moltke did not accept Schlieffen's opinion that perhaps Russia would hesitate to enter East Prussia if the defenders had withdrawn.

[Groener] This is certainly true. However, it is not the core of the question. [16] If Moltke felt that he needed more troops for East Prussia, then he first had to make the right wing strong and weaken the left wing for the benefit of the east, not the other way around, as actually occurred.

[*Denkschrift*] Moltke: The war would be decided in the battle against France. The Republic is our most dangerous opponent, but we can hope to gain a quick decision here.

[Groener] A great victory only through a very strong right wing.

[*Denkschrift*] Moltke's letter to Conrad von Hötzendorff: If the French advance in the west, the decision can come in the first three weeks. If the French stay on the defensive behind their border fortifications, within four weeks.

[Groener] Tranquilizers for Conrad! Moltke intended with this letter to calm the Austrians because we had few forces in the east. It is to be evaluated accordingly.

[17] [*Denkschrift*] The author [of this *Denkschrift*] assumed that Moltke's intent was not the complete destruction of the Franco-British armies but rather to gain the most complete victory as possible in the first battle in order to get some breathing space on this side and free up adequate forces for the other side.

[Groener] This appears to me to be a too far-reaching assumption. What do you call "the most complete victory as possible"? An "ordinary" victory, one which sacrificed the decisive effect of the operational concept.

[*Denkschrift*] Moltke did not want to abandon the land east of the Vistula to be overrun by the Russian forces, and went beyond the quantity of troops that Schlieffen felt was necessary to protect the east, at the expense of the forces to be employed with the main body in the west.

[Groener] You can look at this however you like. These considerations are all too human and perfectly understandable. Persons in influential circles pointed out his [Moltke's] duty not to expose the heartland of the Prussian monarchy to a Russian invasion. (Similar considerations were operative in the critical days of 1914, when the senior administrator in East Prussia appealed to the Kaiser for help, which led to a further weakening of the right wing.) The same psychological influences were operative in the question of reinforcing the troops in Alsace-Lorraine. We were not concerned here with old Prussian lands, but rather with the victor's prize from 1870/71, behind which lay the south German monarchies. It was not thought possible to reward their good conduct in the last decades by abandoning them to a French invasion. All of these were fine upstanding intentions, but not the operational considerations of a strategist.

[18] [*Denkschrift*] 1912: The ersatz divisions that were not needed in the east were reserved for use as necessary in the west or to reinforce coast defense. (In 1912 the forces in the east were again reduced, from 13 divisions to 9, compensated by establishing an ersatz army of 6 divisions there.)

[Groener] In fact, the creation of the ersatz divisions did nothing to contribute to strengthening the operational concept. Experiments were made with Schlieffen's 1905 deployment. Nothing better could be found. Nevertheless, it could not be fully admitted that the great man was right. They fell back on lesser solutions, lost the great idea and wandered – exactly as in the political policy – into a strategy of half-measures, without really noticing they had done so.

[*Denkschrift*] The author of this *Denkschrift* said that due to the dangerous development of the political situation it had become continually more difficult for Moltke to retain the great and bold concept of his predecessor.

[Groener] It was therefore even more necessary to remain true to the operational concept on which the offensive in the west was based.

[*Denkschrift*] Moltke did not let any opportunity slip by to make the Foreign Office aware of the importance of holding Rumania in the alliance.

[Groener] There was, in my opinion, only one means of keeping Rumania in the alliance: complete alteration of the operational concept. Defensive in the west, in the east a great strategic Cannae in the direction of Kiev with German troops on the Austrian right flank. To accomplish this, intensive expansion of the Galician rail system was necessary, which would have taken years.

[19] [*Denkschrift*] In the spring of 1914 the Italians, through [the Chief of the Italian General Staff] Zuccari agreed in an official governmental statement that three corps and two cavalry divisions would be sent immediately to the upper Rhine to support Germany.

[Groener] At Easter 1914 I was in Vienna for the negotiations with the Italian Lieutenant-colonel Fiatri [?] concerning the transportation of the Italian troops to Alsace. I was also present at the negotiations with Zuccari and Montanari. On both occasions I had the personal impression that the Italians were <u>very</u> reserved. I never believed that the Italian troop transports would take place. Zuccari and Montanari may have been personally loyal to us, but the Italian promises were very conditional. They requested the attachment of German troops and above all heavy artillery and were very little satisfied with the mission intended for the Italian army of advancing against Epinal and the forts of the upper Moselle.

[*Denkschrift*] According to all the information assembled by the General Staff it became continually more likely that the French and British would also enter Belgium and that the Belgians would go over to their side.

[Groener] In my opinion there was no doubt of it. It was only a question of who would actually enter Belgian territory <u>first</u>. In addition, the King of Belgium was supposed to have gotten wind of our plan.

[20] [*Denkschrift*] Moltke could not decide to go through Holland.
[Groener] The violation of Dutch neutrality was naturally dangerous, if the right wing was no longer made as strong as Schlieffen wanted.

[*Denkschrift*] Moltke wanted to use Dutch neutrality in order to import and export.
[Groener] In particular, the Foreign Office was counting on it, so that shortly before the war they expressed the expectation that the Americans would supply us through Holland.

[*Denkschrift*] The author of the *Denkschrift* praised Moltke's decision not to march through Holland.
[Groener] This may be useful for public opinion, but it meant a reduction in the operational concept.

[*Denkschrift*] *Coup de main* against Liège.
[Groener] Politically, this plan had serious consequences. The *coup de main* had to be conducted at once during the first days [of mobilization]. The wound-up [21] clock had to run smoothly. The statesman was shoved aside precisely in the days in which policies in the Bismarckian sense would have been in the position to push the responsibility for the declaration of war and being the first to enter Belgian terrain onto the enemy. Entering Holland according to Schlieffen's plan (*Schlieffen'schen Plan*) left time for the diplomatic prelude to the war. However, Bethmann, Jagow and Co. would not have been able to pull it off.
I think the principal credit for Liège (preparation and conduct) is to be given to General Ludendorff.

[*Denkschrift*] Deviation from Schlieffen's distribution of forces: weakening the right, strengthening the left.
[Groener] The greatest danger lay in this deviation! In order to be able to make the left flank stronger, the deep envelopment through Dutch territory had to be cancelled. Why did the left flank have to be made stronger? Because – see my comments on page [17] – <u>German territory</u> was not to be surrendered to a French invasion!! In my opinion this idea played a significant role in the period after Schlieffen. [22] I cannot say with certainty who it originated with. In fact, this dilution of the operational concept was fatal for us in 1914: see the *Aufmarschanweisungen* for the 6th and 7th Armies. If the French broke into Alsace and Lorraine, we should not have prevented them from doing so, but have refused [bent back] our flank and not allowed ourselves to be fixed in place. <u>The deeper</u> that the French drove forward, the further they removed themselves from their rail lines and could no longer be thrown against the north wing.

[*Denkschrift*] Movement of the 7th Army across the northern Vosges to join the 6th.

[Groener] Instead of putting it on trains and sending it to Aachen (with the greatest number of trains possible) to allow it to serve as the operational reserve on the right wing.

[*Denkschrift*] A tactical success in Lorriane would have assisted the operations of the right wing.

[Groener] In this way, neither the left nor the right wing was strong enough. In the best case, the left wing would be standing in front of the French fortress line.

[*Denkschrift*] The author of the *Denkschrift* contended that the destruction of the enemy in Lorraine could be counted on only if the French ran into the sack.

[Groener] In 1914 this sack wasn't even opened. If I recall correctly, in this matter the *Aufmarschanweisungen* were not very clear and definite.

G. 17 Nov 1919
My comments typed

Part VIII

THE SCHLIEFFEN PLAN DEBATE 1919–1930

15

1919: Hans Delbrück Criticizes the German War Plan[1]

Hans Delbrück, editor of the prestigious journal the Preußische Jahrbücher *and author of the groundbreaking military history,* The History of the Art of War within the Framework of Political History, *contended that the Germans used the wrong war plan in 1914. The Germans should have defended in the west and attacked in the east, as, he said, the great elder Moltke had planned to do. This set off a battle concerning German strategy which continues to this day.*[2]

[272] When Germans point out that it was Russian mobilization that forced war upon us, foreigners ask: Why didn't you satisfy yourselves by answering mobilization [273] with mobilization? Why did we immediately have to declare war? It would surely have been possible to negotiate after having mobilized. In Germany it is often said that after the Russians had mobilized, war was in any case unavoidable, but we should not have declared war. Rather we should have waited until it arrived. The Cossacks would have crossed the border soon enough and begun the war. Through our hasty declaration of war we unnecessarily put ourselves in a bad light. This argument does not consider our war plan. The *Oberste Heeresleitung* intended to march as fast as possible through Belgium into France. The plan was to defeat France before the Russian masses could arrive, and then, when they did arrive, turn around to meet them. Therefore, Germany could not wait until France declared war on us, but was forced by the war plan to declare war on France. But we could not declare war on France until it had been decided that we were at war with Russia. It was the war plan that forced us, by our quick declaration of war on Russia, to take on the evil appearance of having maliciously started the war. [Delbrück said that this wasn't discussed during the war so as not to give the impression that the German war plan had failed.] Today we must be clear that not only did we already suffer a defeat on 9 September 1914 that was decisive for the outcome of the war, but that this military defeat also had fateful moral consequences: that we have not been able to clear ourselves of the charge made by the world that we frivolously began the war.

---

[1] Hans Delbrück 'Die deutsche Kriegserklärung 1914 und der Einmarsch in Belgien' in *Preußische Jahrbücher* Band 175 Januar bis März 1919, pp. 271–80.
[2] Zuber, *Inventing the Schlieffen Plan*, pp. 1–32.

Was this war plan of the Great General Staff correctly thought out, appropriate to the situation and the only one possible? Now that we can see the situation and the strength of both sides, it is clear that it was based on false assumptions. It was calculated that the Russians would only be able to enter Germany in six weeks,[3] while they drove into East Prussia with two large armies in hardly three weeks. We did not succeed in overrunning the French, who were assisted by the British with their small but excellent army. On the contrary, our rush forwards appeared more and more as though we had [274] fallen into a trap and it was not we who were preparing a Cannae for the French, but the French for us. [As proof, Delbrück then mentioned two French articles in 1912 and 1913 that had predicted that the Germans would march through Belgium.] Our pressure was so strong that the French government had already left the capital. But what use is such a success, if we didn't obtain the final victory? When, before the war is over, we roll back from the culmination point of our success? . . . . The French recognized our strategic idea and thought it could not be executed. Were they right? Was it at all reasonable to hope that we could have beaten down our western opponent within six weeks, in order to turn unconcerned to the east? [Delbrück said that some assert that military victory was impossible, even if the Germans had taken Paris and Calais.] Therefore, from the very beginning we had the wrong war plan. The French army was much better, the French people much tougher and the British more willing and able to aid the French than we had assumed. In addition, it is completely clear that the Great General Staff seriously underestimated the moral contradiction which our conduct caused in the world: our sudden declaration of war, our march through neutral Belgium, the terrible severity with which we beat down the popular resistance against us. It is a part of that which the world calls our militarism: it was the military calculation that the march through Belgium was correct and the political consequences were not considered further. However, they became of completely immeasurable importance. There is no doubt that without our march into Belgium, Britain still would have taken the French side. Their Balance of Power principle unconditionally demanded it. But without our march into Belgium a very strong peace party in Britain would have asserted itself from the very beginning and weakened their will to make war. Conscription, which in the event was only voted because half of Parliament [275] abstained, would never have been instituted. America's passionate partisanship from the very beginning and finally its entry into the war would never have occurred without our march into Belgium.

The long-prepared war plan of the Great General Staff was therefore very questionable from the beginning, and there was another plan. This would have been, to restrict ourselves in the west to defending our borders and conduct the offensive against Russia. This was the idea of the elder Moltke. It was intended to advance

---

[3] This assertion is commonly made, and it must be suspected that Delbrück is the source. Delbrück does not say where he got his information. There is no indication from the surviving German intelligence documents that the German army thought that the Russians could not attack for six weeks. On the contrary, Schlieffen's exercises never postulated a Russian attack later than four weeks. Since 1911 the army was telling the Chancellor and the Reichstag that the Russians were not to be underestimated and that they were continually getting stronger while their mobilization was getting faster.

from East Prussia quickly into Poland on the other side of the Vistula, presumably at the same time as the Austrians from Galicia, envelop the great Russian army in Poland, cut it off and force it to surrender at Warsaw. This plan was dropped because certain indicators pointed to a Russian withdrawal in the face of our attack, which would result in us hitting only air. Events have shown that the Russians had no intention of withdrawing, that we could have conducted the attack, and the great success we enjoyed in the summer of 1915 could have been attained in the fall of 1914. However, would this success have been enough to give us a lasting superiority? Was it not quite possible that the Russians would have quickly noticed the approach of our masses and withdrawn without taking significant losses and reached a position in the east, where they would be reinforced by their countless reserves, until they brought our advance to a halt and we were then really exposed to overpowering pressure both in the east and west?

This is the consideration that caused the Chief of the General Staff and the Kaiser to decide for the west offensive, in spite of all their misgivings. It would therefore be presumptuous to want to criticize them for it. The factors that were finally decisive, particularly the French power of resistance, were of a moral nature, and it is beyond human ability to estimate those with certainty. [Delbrück said he argued repeatedly against underestimating the French army before the war, and that he was disconsolate when he heard that the Germans had invaded Belgium. However, he said that the chaotic French parliament might have interfered enough with the army leadership to make the German attack successful. He then compared Germany's situation in 1914 to that of Frederick the Great in 1757. [276] Due to the number of Germany's enemies and Austro-Hungarian military weakness, the German situation was desperate.] Objectively, it can be said today that it would have been better if Germany had followed a strategy from the very beginning with the political goal of the *status quo* [*ante*]. But who will blame a proud, aspiring nation and army, full of its own power, that such restraint was a moral impossibility. So they decided to bet everything on a shattering blow to the west, accepted all the odious moral consequences, which were unavoidable – and failed.

[Delbrück pointed out that German attempts to justify the violation of Belgian neutrality by maintaining that Belgium was already in collusion with the Entente were unsuccessful. The only right the Germans had was self-defense, and Bethmann-Hollweg was correct when he based Germany's actions on it.]

[277] Our hope of salvation against this enemy numerical superiority could only be sought in our superior speed. That was not first recognized at the beginning of the war, but years before, since the time that Britain went over to our enemies. One thing followed another with terrible consistency. As soon as the Russians mobilized, we had to attack. In order to attack (at least such was the belief of the army leadership) we had to make the first blow against France. In order to do that, we had to declare war and take on the appearance of being breakers of the peace. In order to execute this war plan we had to march through Belgium and perpetrate an injustice on the Belgians. Finally, in order to complete the march through Belgium, we had to suppress a guerrilla war, which could not be done without several individual acts of cruelty. This once again touched off the enmity and hate of all peoples against us.

In this entire chain of events, political as well as military, where is there personal guilt? Our guilt lies in nothing else than the fact that we had the illusion that the German people was called upon to be equal to the other great peoples of the world, and therefore could gain colonies, take Turkey under our protection and build a fleet.

[278] We attempted to do nothing more. In the process, we stepped in the path of the ambitions of other nations. Finally, because we, of all the states, were the best organized, most powerful and therefore the most feared, all of them united against us, and this superiority caused our defeat. [Delbrück then discussed what he felt were the German mistakes before and during the war. But he contended that neither Bethmann-Hollweg nor the Emperor were responsible for starting the war.]

[281] It remains that it was nothing other than the Russian general mobilization that both caused the war as well as our sudden declaration of war and everything else that followed.

16

1920: Kuhl Reveals the Schlieffen Plan[1]

Hermannn von Kuhl was largely responsible for writing the pre-war German intelligence estimate in the west. During the Marne campaign he was the Chief of Staff of the right-wing 1st Army, which failed to destroy the BEF at Mons and Le Cateau and was forced to retreat from the Marne.
In 1920 Kuhl gave the first public description of the Schlieffen plan.[2] Kuhl maintained that it was failure to follow the Schlieffen plan, and not errors in the pre-war intelligence estimate or by the leadership of the 1st Army, which led to the retreat from the Marne in 1914.[3]

[894] It is not possible here to relate the course of the Marne campaign, even in general outline. This will only present in summary form the most important reasons that caused the failure of the Marne campaign in order to prove – contrary to many accounts that appeared after the fact – that in 1914 we did not attempt the impossible and that we could have gained the palm of victory.

It is clear to everyone that the battle of the Marne formed a turning point in the World War. In my opinion, losing the battle by no means meant that the war was lost, but we had to give up the hope of a quick victory. This was the goal of the operations plan of Count Schlieffen. While the left flank in Lorraine remained on the defensive, practically the entire mass of the German army, linked up on the left with Metz–Diedenhofen, would conduct a great turning movement, swinging like a giant roller through Belgium and northern France, enveloping any possible French position. In the meanwhile, the Russians were to be delayed by weak forces until the decision had been reached in the French theatre and it was possible to send reinforcements to the east. We decided to rely on mobile warfare. Count Schlieffen believed that a long, drawn-out war had to be avoided. It was not possible to conduct a war of attrition. [Kuhl said that the French and British had short-war strategies too.] Of course, in 1890 Field Marshal von Moltke had pointed out that the next war might be a seven- or even a thirty-year war. In the last years before the war our General Staff had pointed out the possibility of a long war and the necessity for an economic, industrial and financial operations plan. [Kuhl quoted Ludendorff's

---

[1] Hermann von Kuhl 'Warum mißlang der Marnefeldzug1914?' in: *Deutsches Offizierblatt* 21. Dezember 1920, pp. 894–5, 21. Januar 1921, pp. 38–9.
[2] See also H. von Kuhl, *Der deutsche Generalstab in Vorbereitung und Durchführung des Weltkrieges* (Berlin, 1920).
[3] Zuber, *op. cit.*, pp. 258–60, 267–91, 295–99.

Denkschrift of 1 November 1912, which Ludendorff had already published.] A long war, however, appeared to be so difficult that everything had to be done to reach a quick decision.

It has been argued that the General Staff did not recognize that the Schlieffen plan was no longer suitable. The use of barbed wire and the spade, modern weapons and explosives meant that there was an entirely new means of waging war. A quick decision had become unlikely. The march through Belgium has been called a "desperation measure" and the intent of defeating the French before the Russians could intervene criticized as over-extension of our strength.

I am of the opinion that we could have reached a decision in France in 1914 and the plan of Count Schlieffen must have led to victory, if only we had held on to it and consistently executed it.

In 1914 we went to war with the best army that Germany has ever had. In mobile warfare it was superior to all others. We believed that this was the principal reason why we would succeed. The marches made by the 1st Army in August and September 1914 are unprecedented in all of military history. [Kuhl cited the marches of IX Corps from 7 to 9 September 1914 and Foch's praise for the German army of 1914.]

It is a widely held error that in August 1914 Joffre avoided a decision and drew us after him, until we fell into the trap he had set for us on the Marne. On the contrary, it is known that the French operations plan sought to reach a decision through the offensive as soon as the deployment had been completed. Yet it is not possible to discern a great, clear objective. Joffre retained his offensive concept after the Germans began their advance into Belgium, but quickly became dependent on the German operation. He sought to reach a decision through a general counter-offensive. From Mühlhausen to Mons he was defeated on the entire front in the last third of August in a series of great battles. Our operations plan proved itself to be far superior to that of the French. Joffre had to admit in his report to his War Minister that "his offensive had failed". "Our corps, in spite of the numerical superiority that we possessed, did not display the offensive characteristics in the open field which we had expected after our initial successes. We have therefore been forced to go over to the defensive".

[Kuhl described the consequences to the French army from their defeat in the Battle of the Frontiers: the necessity to retreat, perhaps as far as Langres, and especially the lowering of French morale. The British lost confidence in French leadership.]

[895] This was the enemy situation before the Battle of the Marne began. One comes to the conclusion that a second great defeat would have completely broken the power of the enemy. [Kuhl said that Joffre and one French historian agreed.]

Why did we not succeed in winning this second victory? This question arises continually among the German people. The veil that concealed the individual events has now been raised. The causes of the unfavorable result of the battle of the Marne in September 1914 are now undeniably clear.

Before the war a shift in our deployment took place. In the expectation of a strong French attack in Lorraine the German left wing in Alsace-Lorraine was strengthened at the expense of the main body on the right, which was to conduct the great envelopment through Belgium. While Count Schlieffen wanted to leave, besides fortress garrisons and Landwehr on the upper Rhine, only 3[1/2] active corps, 1 reserve corps and 3 cavalry divisions in Alsace-Lorraine, of which two corps were to be sent later as quickly as possible by rail to the right wing, in 1914 8 corps of the 6th and 7th Armies deployed in Alsace-Lorraine. The mission of the two armies was expanded appropriately. They were to advance against the Moselle and Meurthe in order to fix the French forces assembled here or, if the French advanced to attack with strong forces, withdraw in front of them in order that, initially using Metz and the *Niedstellung*, they could be attacked concentrically and defeated. This marked a deviation in the operational intent of Generaloberst von Moltke from that of Count Schlieffen. The latter desired a French counterattack into Lorraine. The envelopment through Belgium was to be continued unchanged. Count Schlieffen assumed that the French would turn around. In this case, Generaloberst von Moltke wanted to defeat the enemy in Lorraine.

Schlieffen's plan was preferable. It was simplicity itself. The central idea was rigorously executed. The course of events in September 1914 demonstrated that Schlieffen was right. We would have done better to have concentrated our forces more on the decisive right wing from the very beginning and weakened the 6th and 7th Armies, while at the same time restricting their mission. The forces that could not be moved in the first echelon with the right wing of the German army, which was restricted due to the projecting southern point of the Dutch province of Limburg, must follow as a second echelon. Landwehr and Landsturm were to follow in a third echelon, to observe and besiege fortresses and secure the lines of communication and the rear areas.

After the French attack had been defeated in the Battle of Lorraine from the 20th to the 22nd of August, the strength of the left wing in Lorraine encouraged the *Oberste Heeresleitung* to make the fatal decision to continue the pursuit with the entire force in order to break through on the upper Moselle. The attempt failed due to the natural strength of the position, which was supported on the wings, on one side by Toul–Nancy and by Epinal on the other. While on 4 September, immediately before the beginning of the Battle of the Marne, the Germans again attempted to conduct a strong attack on Nancy, on the French side a withdrawal of forces from the Moselle to the other fronts had already begun on 1 September. It would have been better if, immediately after the battle in Lorraine, on about 23 August, we had restricted ourselves to the defensive in Lorraine and sent a number of corps to Aachen by rail, to follow the right wing as a strong second echelon. On 27 August, as the *Oberste Heeresleitung* made new operational decisions, and even on 30 August, when the difficulty of the breakthrough on the upper Moselle began to be recognized, it would have been possible to move corps by rail, not as before to Aachen, but to Luxembourg, and to march them from there, while conducting a general shift of the front to the right. Instead even the available ersatz divisions were moved to the left wing. At the end of August two corps were moved from the right wing to the eastern front in the mistaken idea that the great decision in the west had had already been reached in our favor.

Therefore our strength on the right wing was not adequate to envelop the enemy wherever he stood, as Count Schlieffen wanted. The further the offensive proceeded into enemy territory, the more forces that had to be detached to secure the lines of communication and besiege enemy fortresses. Speed was to replace what we were losing in strength. It was necessary to do too much in a hurry. The operation oscillated back and forth between contradictions. First the right wing was to swing wide in the direction of the lower Seine below Paris. Finally it was to swing to the south-east, leaving Paris on the right. At this moment the flank attack struck from Paris.

[38] A great difficulty for the *Oberste Heeresleitung* lay in the fact that it had to conduct war on two widely separated fronts. The question may be raised, if the OHL should not have remained in Berlin and named a supreme commander in the west, in the same manner as the later *Oberbefehlshaber Ost*. This meant self-denial. The decision was to fall in the west. It is understandable that the Chief of the General Staff wanted to conduct the operations here himself. Then he should not have remained in Coblenz and later in Luxembourg, where he moved from Coblenz on 30 July. Here, during the decisive days, he was too far from the focus of the operations. Long, hand-written orders, brought by vehicle from Coblenz or Luxembourg to the farthest wing of the army, were often out of date when they arrived. During the entire campaign to the end of the Battle of the Marne neither the Chief of the General Staff nor the Chief of the Operations section nor the *Generalquartiermeister* [*de facto* Moltke's chief of staff] were ever at the headquarters of the 1st Army on the right flank. There were no face-to-face discussions.

In addition, the electronic communications between the OHL and the furthest Army headquarters were extremely poor. The signal units were too weak and not adequately provided with the newest equipment. Only occasionally could the 1st Army establish telephone communications using the rear echelon telegraph lines. Electronic communication with the 1st Army was almost exclusively by radio telegraph. Headquarters 1st Army had two stations with different equipment, one of which was supposed to maintain communications with OHL, the other with the headquarters of the 2nd Army. In the latter case, considerable delays arose. This explains why in the decisive moments before the battle of the Marne important reports from the 1st Army needed 24 hours to come to the attention of OHL. It is clear that because of this, firm leadership, as would have been necessary in these difficult operations, was impossible.

In order to coordinate the operation, the OHL frequently resorted to the expedient of subordinating one army to another or instructing neighboring armies to cooperate with each other. Both measures proved to be unsuitable. For this reason the French 5th Army was not destroyed at Namur on 23 August, which had been quite feasible, as well as at St. Quentin on 29 August. The German 3rd Army was continually pulled hither and yon by cries for help from its neighbors.

[Kuhl said that the solution to the command and control problems would have been the establishment of Army Group Headquarters.]

The enemy attack in the battle of the Marne struck the right wing of the army in an unfavorable situation. The 1st Army had moved too far forward. According to OHL instructions of 27 August the right wing, the 1st Army, was to advance to the Seine below Paris. It appeared as though the Schlieffen plan was to be executed in its entirety. However, it was quickly evident that such a deep envelopment could not be conducted, due to the allocation of forces that resulted from the deployment and the subsequent measures taken by OHL. A few days after it was issued, the order of 27 August was overtaken by events. Even though the order was not cancelled, the Army, following the natural impulse, swung to the south. With the agreement of OHL and the 2nd Army, on 30 August the 1st Army turned left towards the Oise, in order to exploit the success gained by the 2nd Army at St. Quentin and envelop the French left wing. To further realize this idea, OHL ordered the entire right wing to turn left, in order to drive the French in a south-easterly direction away from Paris. According to the reports of the 2nd Army the enemy had once again been decisively defeated. It was hoped to outflank him not only with the right but also the left, from the upper Moselle, and encircle him. To do so the right flank had to go past the east side of Paris and cross the Marne. It was too weak to do so: there was insufficient protection against Paris. The left was not able to cross the Moselle. OHL's plan failed. Of course, the 1st Army's mission had been to follow in echelon behind the 2nd Army and protect the right flank. When the order arrived, however, the 1st Army, because of the preceding movements, was far in front of the 2nd. In order to follow in echelon, it would have had to remain stationary for two to three days. Then forcing the French to the south-east would have been out of the question. The 2nd Army had fallen behind. Even if it reached the enemy, it could only attack him frontally. Only the 1st Army, which outflanked the enemy, was capable of pushing him back. According to the reports of the 2nd Army, the enemy was streaming to the rear in complete disorder. The 1st Army decided, contrary to orders, to exploit its forward position and make a last attempt to reach the French left flank and envelop it.[4] It attempted to cover its right flank by echelloning the army. No offensive was to be expected from the British. The French troops that had appeared previously on the right flank had been dispersed.

Unexpectedly, on the morning of 6 September the Franco-British offensive began along the entire front and from Paris against our right flank. It had not been betrayed by any indicator, prisoner statement, or newspaper report. The enemy decided on this course of action at the last moment. The first warning came from a bold attack by the IV Reserve Corps, which had been pushed forward by the 1st Army as flank protection towards Paris, against the French 6th Army which had been assembled north-east of Paris prepared to counterattack. Suddenly the situation cleared. We were standing before a serious crisis.

How did this sudden enemy change occur? Joffre had wanted to continue the withdrawal behind the Seine, when Gallieni, the Governor of Paris, learned from air reconnaissance during the day on 3 September that the German columns, which had previously been marching on Paris, had swung to the south-east. He recognized the favorable opportunity to attack the German right wing from Paris with Maunoury's newly formed 6th Army and on 4 September convinced Joffre to attack. While the French right wing in the Vosges and on the Moselle remained on the defensive, the entire line from Verdun to Paris was to turn around and go over

---

[4] It failed to even find the French flank: the French had either withdrawn to the south or into Paris.

to the attack, while the 6th Army attacked the German right from the north-east of Paris.

The premature collision of the 6th Army with the IV Reserve corps forestalled surprise. The 6th Army had not completely assembled and proved too weak for the decisive mission assigned it. The British had obviously failed. Generaloberst von Kluck threw the 1st Army quickly around to the west in such a manner that the French 6th Army, instead of outflanking the Germans, was itself outflanked. But in doing so a large gap appeared on the Marne from Ourcq to Montmirail between the 1st and 2nd Armies, which was supposed to be filled by two cavalry corps and later one and one-half infantry divisions. The British entered this gap only very cautiously. But the right flank of von Bülow's 2nd Army could be enveloped by the 5th French Army and had to be bent back. At noon on 9 August the situation was as follows: the German 1st Army had won a complete victory over the French 6th Army, whose left wing had been enveloped and turned. It was only a question of a last push in order to throw the enemy back into Paris. In the gap between the 1st and 2nd Armies the British were feeling their way slowly over the Marne with their lead elements. The bent-back right flank of the 2nd Army [39] had not been attacked, but was threatened by the advance of the French 5th Army. On the left flank of the 2nd Army and the right flank of the 3rd a brilliant victory had been won at Fère Champenoise. The right flank of Foch's 9th Army had been defeated and was in retreat, the Army Headquarters had fled to the rear. Further pursuit threatened the rear of the French 5th Army to its left, while the British were in danger of losing their lines of communications because of Generaloberst von Kluck's victory. It was to be expected that they would retreat. On the eastern part of the battlefield (German 4th and 5th Armies, French 3rd and 4th Armies) no decision was being reached in frontal battles.

Therefore, at noon on 9 September there was a crisis on both sides. It was touch and go. Whoever wanted to master the crisis in his favor had to have the stronger nerves. Certainly it was a risk for us to fight the battle through to a decision. But the prize was worth it.

We didn't take the risk. On the afternoon of 9 September Generaloberst von Bülow took the decision to withdraw behind the Marne. He was moved to do so by an inaccurate, unfavorable appreciation of the situation of both the 1st Army and of his own right wing, so that there seemed to be a danger of a breakthrough between the 1st and 2nd Armies. Today it can easily be said that the 2nd Army situation did not require it to withdraw.

Even less so for the 1st Army. Lieutenant-colonel Hentsch, who visited the armies by order of OHL, agreed on the morning of 9 September with Generaloberst von Bülow's decision, and then went that afternoon to the headquarters of the 1st Army, where in spite of the exceptionally favorable situation he gave the order to withdraw in the name of the *Oberste Heeresleitung*. There was considerable disagreement over his mission and the manner in which he carried it out, but they are now quite clear. When Lieutenant-colonel Hentsch was dispatched, OHL thought that it was essential that the right wing stand fast. However, for the contingency that the withdrawal had already been ordered by the Army Headquarters, Lieutenant-colonel Hentsch was to act to coordinate their movements. The 1st Army was then to withdraw in the direction of Soissons. This eventuality had now occurred. The 2nd Army had decided to withdraw. Lieutenant-colonel Hentsch was therefore justified in giving the 1st Army the order to withdraw to Soissons. There was no other way to establish cooperation. Generaloberst von Kluck had to comply with these orders, once it had been established that the 2nd Army had begun its withdrawal during the afternoon and the 1st Army was isolated. The details of this depressing tragedy cannot be given here.

Early on 10 September the French were happily surprised to see the unexpected German withdrawal. That was "The Miracle of the Marne". Schlieffen's concept of the envelopment and the quick decision had failed. The reasons are now clear. It must be acknowledged that it could and must have happened otherwise and that in 1914 the German army did not attempt anything that was not within its power. The troops never failed and made the impossible possible. It was the leadership that failed.

17

1921: Delbrück Criticizes the Schlieffen Plan[1]

In spite of his assertion that he had access to the General Staff's archives, Delbrück obviously had not seen the real text of the Schlieffen plan Denkschrift *or any of Schlieffen's war games in the west. His evaluation of the plan is also dominated by his vendetta against Ludendorff. Nevertheless, relying largely on published material, Delbrück's critique is perceptive.*[2]

The starting point for all examination of strategic planning in the World War is the plan of Count Schlieffen. It is supposed to have consisted of the following. The German army would initially stay on the defensive against the Russians and attack the French with the maximum possible forces. Because the front against France was too short and too well fortified, it would be bypassed by going through Belgium. In order to make this envelopment as effective as possible, our left flank in Alsace would be kept weak. The right wing, which would conduct the envelopment, would be made as strong as possible. "Only make the right wing strong" Schlieffen is supposed to have cried out in his death throes.

The point of contention is, did we fail because the plan was not carried out properly in both form and spirit, or because it was incorrectly conceived from the beginning? Tirpitz accused the General Staff of "Absolute confidence in the recipe for victory (*Siegesrezept*) of the dead Schlieffen". Others complain on the contrary that his successor sinned against Schlieffen's spirit by spoiling his brilliant plan.[In a footnote Delbrück cited Kuhl, *Der Marnefeldzug 1914* and Foerster, *Graf Schlieffen und der Weltkrieg*.]

After a comparison of the various publications and the General Staff archival documents I have come to the view that the equally famous and criticized Schlieffen plan in practical terms never existed at all. What Schlieffen bequeathed and was used in 1914 was an idea, but not a plan.

Schlieffen's plan for an advance through Belgium and an envelopment of the enemy left wing was based on the premise that Russia, which at the time seemed to have dissolved in anarchy as a consequence of defeat in Manchuria and the revolution, had very little military capability. Schlieffen was always clear that however great the victory was against France, we would nevertheless not be able

---

[1] Hans Delbrück, 'Die strategische Grundfrage des Weltkrieges' in *Preußische Jahrbücher* 183. Band Januar bis März 1921, pp. 289–308.
[2] Zuber, *op. cit.*, pp. 8–32.

to transfer the army from there [290] and move it against the Russians.[3] He pointed out that even after a total victory like 1870 at Sedan, the German army was not free. We would actually not have been able to spare a single man from a continuation of the war against France. Schlieffen therefore wanted to establish an army against the Russians from the very beginning. But how large should this army be? Schlieffen thought that he could get by with about six active corps. Six active corps!

That was reasonable in 1906, but would no longer work in 1914, after Russia, with its astounding powers of rejuvenation, had completely built up its massive military forces again. In 1914 the war strength of the combined Central Powers was 3½ million men, of its united enemies 6,200,000 men, of which almost 3½ million were Russians. (According to Kuhl, p. 7. Before the parliamentary committee of inquiry Count Monteglas calculated 135 German and Austrian infantry divisions against 215 enemy, which were considerably larger than ours. England was credited with only 6 divisions.) How were something short of 1½ million Austrians supposed to withstand these 3½ million, plus 300,000 Serbs, if we deployed only 6 corps on our eastern border, at the most 240,000 men?

It could be pointed out that Hindenburg with about six corps actually did defeat a Russian army at Tannenburg and thereby threw back their entire northern front. (This includes troops that were not involved in the battle. Without these there were only 10 divisions.) But that brought only momentary and local relief. Immediately afterwards the Austrians lost the battles of Lemberg and Galicia. Division after division had to be sent from the west front to the east. The army in the west was too weak to complete its mission.

Even Count Schlieffen could not escape from the changes in the situation which occurred during his lifetime. Although he was no longer on active duty after 1906, he continued to think about the great problem. Even in December 1912 he wrote down his observations that included several possibilities, in particular considering a breakthrough in the French front in addition to the envelopment. The entire French front was to be attacked simultaneously. The German front was to be extended with the right wing reaching to the sea. However the individual aspects are evaluated, even Lieutenant-colonel Foerster, who published the notes, adds that there were naturally not enough German troops for such an immense operation. [291] And thereby the principal question, how we were to defend ourselves against the numerically superior Russian forces, and whether the operation in France could be conducted quickly enough in order to send part of the army to the east, is not even mentioned.

From the point of view of the World War of 1914, the Schlieffen ideas in 1912 as well as in 1905 are actually nothing more than ideas, which can stimulate thought, but not plans that can be made better or were badly executed.

Moltke actually went to the field in 1914 with a significantly different basic plan. True, he retained the march through Belgium and the envelopment of the enemy

---

[3] Schlieffen never reached any such conclusion. In fact, most of his east-front war games were based on the premise that on about the 25th day of mobilization the Germans would be able to transfer significant forces from the west to the east.

left wing, but he did not want to extend our front to the sea. Rather, he hoped that the French would allow themselves to be drawn into an offensive in Lorraine. Then they would be outflanked by short swings from the right and the left and defeated. This idea appears in the 1909/10 *Aufmarschanweisungen*. Their spiritual father can be considered to be Colonel Ludendorff, who had become the Chief of the Deployment Section on 10 April 1908. The left wing (7th Army) was reinforced, and while Count Schlieffen had wanted to abandon all of Alsace south of Strasbourg, it was now decided to cover the area against a French invasion and for this purpose two corps were deployed on the upper Rhine. The *Aufmarschanweisung* states that the 7th Army was initially to be held back on the Rhine, ready to assist on the left flank of the 6th Army (in Lorraine) or to be transported to some other theater. In the following years this idea was developed further. The 7th Army received further reinforcements, and in case the French did not conduct the expected attack in Lorraine, the 6th and 7th Armies were themselves to assume the offensive "in order to deceive the enemy by advancing between the Moselle and the Meurthe and prevent him from transferring his forces to the left wing. In the next year the offensive concept was again reinforced by the instruction to take Fort Manonviller, for which siege equipment was made available. The result is that all forces were no longer employed in the right wing, as Count Schlieffen had intended, but that the troops were almost uniformly distributed along the entire front. Only after the expected victory in Lorraine were troops to be transported behind our front from the left wing to the right. A large rail apparatus was made available for this purpose.

This plan has been criticized for being too complicated. It pursued two goals at the same time: victory in Lorraine and the envelopment with the right wing through [292] Belgium. Covering southern Alsace and Baden seemed petty, for it subtracted several corps from the tactical decision. But it appears to me that some things can well be said in favor of the plan. Generalleutnant von Tappen has said that more corps than were actually used could not be accommodated on the right wing. Kuhl, in contrast, said that the extra corps could have followed as another echelon. On the other hand, it was possible that the advance through Belgium would be stalled in the defile between Antwerp and Namur, while the French undertook a powerful offensive in Lorraine. Then the excessive strength on the right wing would appear to be a mistake. The two corps on the upper Rhine covered not only the province, but also, if it actually came to a great battle in Lorraine, the left flank of the armies fighting there. Was it also so certain that the precondition for the great turning movement of the northern wing, the *coup de main* against Liège, would really succeed?

General von Stein wrote in his memoirs, quite correctly, "The deployment in the west did not predispose us to a particular operation. The enemy could precede us, his rail net made this appear likely." After the first deployment the course of a campaign is always uncertain, as Field Marshal von Moltke said repeatedly. Finally, it appears to me that it is not impossible that Ludendorff's plan stands in connection with the changes in the situation in the east . Neither the General Staff documents nor the statements of the persons concerned say anything about it, but the course of events themselves allow some sort of conclusion. The real strategic problem lay not only in defeating the French, but in that whether this victory would be fast and great enough to allow sufficient forces to be turned against the Russians in time. It may have been considered that, although the plan was built on uncertain preconditions and was complicated, it also offered the chance of a quicker and far greater victory.

On 21 August General von Moltke appeared with shining eyes among the officers of his staff and told them that a great victory had been gained in Lorraine. It was decided to send no fewer than six corps to the east.

The picture changed quickly. The victory in Lorraine proved to be only a moderate success. Several French corps had indeed been smashed, but the main body was intact. Instead of six corps, only two could be sent to the east, but the lack of these two corps already weakened the right wing so much that the planned [293] envelopment failed and we had to retreat from the Marne. The intended reinforcement of the right wing by the left from behind the front (7th Army) came too late.

General von Kuhl explains in his latest book on the Marne campaign that in spite of all this we could have won the campaign had it not been for certain mistakes made by the OHL as well as by individual army commanders. Critics had long been concerned with these errors. Who was guilty? This investigation is naturally of significant interest for military history. For world history it is hardly necessary to come to a conclusion concerning it. What is decided, if the guilty party is named Moltke or Hentsch or Bülow? Kuhl proves in his book that we would have won a complete victory had Generaloberst von Bülow not withdrawn, without actual necessity, because of the gap between him and Kluck. It is possible that he is right. It is also probably true that earlier and at other places mistakes were made and favorable opportunities were not exploited. But in war there is no such thing as faultless leadership. Frederick the Great, Napoleon and Gneisenau made enough mistakes as well. In the campaign of 1815 the three greatest generals of the age, Napoleon, Wellington and Gneisenau, were present. The distinguished British Field Marshal Wolseley once wrote a book where he showed that all three continually made one mistake after the other and showed themselves to be quite mediocre leaders. [Delbrück then listed various mistakes made in 1815.] If one allows Napoleon to operate as subsequent critics think was the optimal manner, the same principle must be permitted to his opponents, and then where are we? [More on 1815.][294] In war it isn't the leader who makes no mistakes who wins, but the one who makes one mistake fewer than his opponent. The argument that we could have won on the Marne, had no mistakes been made, interesting as it may be from the critical point of view, must from a higher perspective be rejected. If the war plan was correct, we should have won even if there were mistakes, indeed serious mistakes. Of course, there are limits. The mistakes cannot be too much worse than those the enemy makes. Were the mistakes made by OHL and the army commanders really so severe? It has been contended that the command and control system functioned inadequately: army group headquarters should have been formed. Quite true, but not abnormal, given the lack of experience with the direction of such unheard-of masses. Two army corps were sent too soon to the east. Quite true, but it was believed that victory in the west was already assured. Generaloberst von Bülow, under the influence of Lieutenant-colonel Hentsch, sent from OHL and a particular confidant of Moltke, began to retreat, although it was not absolutely necessary. Perhaps. But the army headquarters had the impression that its army (2nd) had been reduced to "cinders" and must be preserved or a catastrophe would result. Who could say for certain that a catastrophe would not have occurred? [Delbrück then compared 1914 with the mistakes made in 1866. In spite of those, the Germans beat the Austrians because of the superiority of the Prussian troops and Moltke's brilliant campaign plan.] We lost the Marne campaign because, given the force ratio, even moderate friction and deficiencies in our leadership must give the enemy superiority. We were therefore too weak. The French had as many divisions in the field as we did (79) and the six British and six Belgian divisions in addition. The six ersatz divisions that we brought up could only re-establish parity, but not give us superiority. We can see that we were near to victory, [295] but that does not prove that we were strong enough. It can only mean, and does mean in this case, that the enemy's mistakes allowed us to come so far in spite of our weakness. The French were surprised by our advance. They expected us to march through Belgium, but not as deeply as we did. They had not counted on the fact that we would use our reserve corps in the first line. In spite of the immense advantage that we gained thereby, because we completely upset the French operations plan, we finally failed because we did not have sufficient forces. Therefore, the war plan was wrong. The way things turned out, the original Schlieffen plan of 1905 – and here Kuhl and Foerster are sure to agree – had a better chance of succeeding than Moltke's revision. But the conclusion, which Schlieffen made himself, namely that after winning a victory we could not send sufficient forces quickly enough against the Russians, remains true. No remedy for this was found between 1905 and 1914.

Now we understand why Generaloberst von Moltke was so unwilling and hesitant to come to the decision for war, and why on 30 July, two days before our mobilization, he wrote this despairing marginal note, that we must be "ruined" and "bleed to death", and why Tirpitz could write in his *Memoirs* that it was impossible that the Imperial leadership wanted to bring on a war, because we were convinced from the start that we would not win.

The question is, was an alternative war plan feasible? It was impossible that even Napoleon could win against the immense numerical superiority of Blücher and Wellington. Nevertheless, military criticism has not blamed him for heroically daring to challenge his fate, for this alternative was the one of all the possibilities that offered him the greatest chance of success. If the French Emperor had waited until the Russians and Austrians arrived, he would probably have had to lay down his arms without a battle. Was the situation in 1914 similar? Our military critics, Kuhl, Foerster, Müller-Löbnitz, the anonymous "General Staff officer", are agreed that the idea of first attacking the western enemy and defeating him, was obviously the correct one.

[Delbrück quoted Foerster and the anonymous officer. He then referred to the campaigns of Frederick the Great in Austria, which Delbrück said show that, rather than trying to destroy the enemy in one campaign, Friedrich preferred attrition warfare. Since the General Staff had a faulty appreciation of Frederick's strategy, it was unaware of the advantages of attrition warfare.]

Debate: Delbrück Criticizes the Schlieffen Plan

[297] [Kuhl said that if the Germans had won on the Marne, Paris and Verdun would probably have fallen. The Germans would have regrouped for a further offensive. Delbrück replied that "without a doubt" the British would have instated conscription, the Americans would have declared war on Germany. Both, one way or the other, would have sent "gigantic" armies to France. The enemy simply could not have been defeated by offensive warfare. [298] Delbrück then returned to what he said was the example of Frederick the Great in the Seven Years' war.]

In so doing, naturally I do not lay claim to having seen all of these things either before or during the war as I do today. Not only did I not have the information that was available to the General Staff, but I also still consider myself to be a historian, not a military writer. However, I may assert that as a matter of principle I was in favor of an initial offensive against Russia and not against France, that I saw the march through Belgium, the attack on Verdun[4] and unrestricted submarine warfare with suspicion. But in public I naturally spoke very carefully. Today completely open historical-critical observations can only be of benefit in our internal struggles that we have to endure, and in our external struggles they can no longer do us harm.

The first consequence of the decision to forgo a quick decision and adopt an attritional strategy would have been far-reaching economic preparation for war.

[Delbrück repeated Moltke's famous statement in 1890 that the next war could last seven or thirty years, as well as Schlieffen's well-known statement that long wars would ruin modern societies.[5] He said that this meant that Schlieffen thought the next war would be short.[6]]

Because the General Staff was trained in this [Schlieffen's] doctrine, naturally no preparations in the opposite sense [for a long war] were made.[7]

[299] In addition, the question as to whether the advantage of a quicker mobilization should be used for an offensive to the east or the west comes into a different light. In 1914 it was decided to conduct an offensive against France because the Russians had the unlimited ability to withdraw and therefore no decision could be gained. That was suitable for a strategy of destroying the enemy. For a strategy of attrition it would have been more appropriate to satisfy ourselves with a great success against the forward Russian elements in Poland, Lithuania and Volhnya and stay on the defensive against France. Then the march through Belgium would have been unnecessary, and according to the most recent publications it appears very questionable if the British government would have succeeded in convincing public opinion at all, or at least so quickly, of the need to enter the

---

[4] In all three cases, Delbrück never wrote any such thing at the time.
[5] Delbrück failed to notice that these statements can both be true simultaneously.
[6] In fact, Schlieffen was saying that a long war would be ruinous.
[7] Economic policy was not the provenance of the General Staff, but principally of the Ministry of the Interior. In any case, the German people were not even willing to make the effort to utilize all of their available manpower in the army. Where were the resources to come from to prepare for a long war of attrition?

World War. Recently [Paul] Cambon, at that time French ambassador in London, published his memoirs of the first days of August 1914, which state that until the news of our entry into Belgium it was altogether doubtful whether public opinion would not decide for British neutrality. Statements of the Russian ambassador Benkendorff confirm this. Cambon was in complete despair over the stance of Sir Edward Grey and his feeble speech in the Commons.

[Delbrück said that if a march through Belgium and an invasion of France were unavoidable, then Germany should have used a strategy appropriate for an 18th century *Kabinettskrieg* and occupied northern France up to the Somme, as Frederick the Great occupied Saxony in 1756. If the Germans could have immediately sent troops to help the Austrians, Austria-Hungary might have held together longer and better. He then discusses the multitudinous mistakes made by Ludendorff, the standard bearer of the *Vernichtungsstrategie*, and the manner in which his 18th century strategy could still have won the war after the Battle of the Marne, with renewed references to Frederick the Great.]

18

1921: Foerster Defends the Schlieffen Plan[1]

Wolfgang Foerster was a General Staff historian who found employment in the Reichsarchiv. His was one of the first books to describe and defend the German war plan.[2]

Since all the documents were secret, Foerster was able to fabricate a dichotomy between Schlieffen's planning and Moltke's which did not exist.

[29] On retiring from active service, Count Schlieffen left an extensive *Denkschrift* with the title "War Against France" as his legacy to his successor. It was closely related to the *Westaufmarsch* prepared for that [1905/06] mobilization year and showed, on the basis of years of continual study that considered all possibilities, how the Master thought the operation from this deployment should best be conducted. The *Denkschrift*, as the title notes, was concerned not with the case of a multi-front war, but in consonance with the political situation at the time, with a war on the west front against France and – in the form of an addendum – against England. (The *Aufmarsch* plans of the German General Staff at the same time considered in addition, in the form of a second *Aufmarsch*, the unlikely case at the time of a two-front war – with the mass of the army in the west and a small part in the east. In the latter, 10 infantry divisions would deploy in the east.) Therefore the entire German army in the strength of 26 active corps, 13½ reserve corps, 11 cavalry divisions, 26½ Landwehr divisions [sic: brigades] was employed on the western front.[3] In addition, Count Schlieffen made it clear in the *Denkschrift* the absolute necessity of forming a minimum of eight new corps – ersatz corps – immediately on the conclusion of the mobilization, out of trained replacement troops, unutilized reservists, if necessary Landwehr men, and committing them into the operation as soon as possible. Further, he demanded the immediate mobilization of the Landwehr in the entire Empire and its operational employment in occupation duties in the rear area, which would continually expand in the course of the operation, as well as in protecting the lines of communication.

Count Schlieffen envisaged an attack on "the great fortress France". Not where it was almost invulnerable, on the eastern front Verdun–Belfort, but where there

---

[1] Wolfgang Foerster, *Graf Schlieffen und der Weltkrieg*, (Berlin, 1921, 2nd revised edition 1925).
[2] Zuber, *op. cit.*, pp. 29–31.
[3] This is the number of divisions – 80 – the 'Schlieffen plan' required. Somehow Foerster failed to mention that in 1905/06 the entire German army consisted of 72 divisions.

were gaps in the fortifications and where it was almost unmanned, on the north front Dunkirk–Lille–Maubeuge–Mézières. If this succeeded, it was then necessary to attack frontally the second uncompleted fortress line which lay behind it, which ran from Verdun behind the Aisne through Reims–Laon to La Fère, while the deeply echelonned [30] offensive mass of the right wing enveloped it from the north, directing its attack against the left flank and the rear of the enemy position.

In accordance with this concept the deployment was planned as follows: the mass of the *Westheer* – seven armies with 69 active or reserve divisions, 8 cavalry divisions, 22 Landwehr brigades, were to deploy in the Rhineland, with elements also in Lorraine and on the Saar. They would seek to conduct the decisive offensive by making a great left wheel with the pivot at Metz, initially against the line Dunkirk–Verdun. The eight ersatz corps would follow as soon as they were able. In Lorraine there was only one army with 10 active and reserve divisions, 3 cavalry divisions, 1 Landwehr brigade, in addition to the garrisons of Metz and Strasbourg. Three and one-half Landwehr brigades were to remain on the upper Rhine. The upper Alsace would remain unprotected. The force ratio between the right and left wings, in reference to active and reserve divisions, was about 7:1.[4] Within the right wing there were to be three large groups. By far the strongest with 30 divisions was again on the right wing, the weakest with 13 divisions in the middle, a third with 16 divisions on the left flank. Ten reserve divisions would follow the last.

The deployment of the right group (three armies) had its northern border in the area of Crefeld and extended in great depth to the rear, even beyond the Rhine. This was done in the first case to facilitate rail movement and then out of consideration for neutral Holland. The southern tip of this country, the province of Limburg, extends far to the south to the level of Aachen and put a barrier in the way of a march directly to the west. Purely for reasons of operational expediency the thought must come to mind of moving the extreme right wing through Dutch territory. Count Schlieffen had provided for this possibility – but only under the condition that German diplomacy succeeded in bringing Holland over to the Central Powers at the beginning of the war. He started from the premise that Britain was just as great a danger to the Dutch colonies as it was for the German, and that recognition of this would perhaps bring the Dutch government over to our side. (. . . The thought of a "rape" of Holland through German violation of Dutch neutrality was as far from Schlieffen's mind as it was from Moltke's.) If this did not occur, [31] the right wing, respecting Dutch neutrality, would move first to the south and then the west through the narrow bottleneck at and south of Liège. In any case it was important for the northern group to gain ground forwards quickly, in order to deploy its forces from the unavoidably deep formation to a broad one. This seemed certain, if after an opposed crossing of the Meuse against the Belgians we reached the defile between the fortresses of Antwerp and Namur with forced marches before making contact with the French and the British. At the same time, this made it necessary to initially screen Antwerp, where Schlieffen thought it was most likely that the British would land. This mission was intended for part or all of the rearward echelon of the northern group consisting of 10 reserve divisions.

[4] Eight of the divisions on the right wing did not exist.

The relatively weak middle group (two armies) of the great turning movement was initially assigned a purely east-west direction of march towards the Namur–Mézières section of the Meuse. Due to the left wheel, it had to make less strenuous marches. Still easier were those of the southern group (two armies) which, while maintaining contact with the pivot at Diedenhofen–Metz, was to swing forward to the Mézières–Verdun section of the Meuse. The southern group had to count on the possibility of an enemy attack from the direction of Verdun–Toul. This could occur early – therefore it was made strong for the defense – or only after a certain time had passed in the conduct of the operation. In the latter case a strong second echelon was attached as flank protection, which later, according to the progress of the general advance, had the mission of closing off Verdun. Therefore, precautions were taken that the great wheeling movement itself remained intact for the continuation of the operation in the open field.

If the defile between Antwerp and Namur had been transited before making contact with the French and the British, the question for the right wing was no longer one of the fastest possible movement. Its place was taken rather by the requirement to continue the wheeling movement of the enormous *batallion carrée*, aligned from right to left in space and time according to the drill-book command, "eyes right, contact on the left". Everything that opposed it was to be crushed by this thundering march. How Count Schlieffen envisaged this close-order forward movement is shown by his unfavorable critique of the conduct of some officers during the 2nd 1904 *Generalstabsreise West*, where he was the exercise director: "Everybody rushed forward, every man for himself, [32] attempting to reach the enemy as quickly as possible, although nobody really knew where he was. Considerably more use should have been made of the drill book, more "eyes right" and "contact left" as well as something from the methodical procedure of the Japanese, who in this situation very surely would not have advanced in this manner."[5] In the exercise critique of his operational war game in the spring of 1905, he said: "We must accustom ourselves to always lead the armies in a coordinated manner. I was often tempted to tell the army commanders: wouldn't you first like to have your people dress and cover [drill command to align a troop formation]? There was such confusion. It is true, the people who discovered aligned formations became great pedants, but in the beginning they only wanted to hold their forces together and employ them in a coordinated fashion." A reduction in the tempo of the forward movement was also indispensable out of consideration for the entire supply situation, which given more or less effective rail demolitions could be expected to present great difficulties.

If the advancing German forces met a British expeditionary force operating independently, or if it was attacked by such in the flank or rear, the Germans would

---

[5] When Foerster wrote this, the exercise critique of the 2nd 1904 *Generalstabsreise West* was still a classified document and was made accessible only to those with a "need to know" within the Reichsarchiv. Foerster wanted to exploit this situation to give the impression that the 1904 exercise was a dry run for the 'Schlieffen plan'. Since the fall of the Wall this document came into the hands of the Bundesarchiv (PH3/661). From reading the critique it is clear that the situation Schlieffen was describing in 1904 had nothing whatsoever to do with that in the 1905 *Denkschrift*. See Zuber, *op. cit.*, pp. 200–2.

stop and attack and deal with the enemy – if necessary with the assistance of rearward elements of the deeply echelonned right wing – and then the advance would be resumed. The French could do whatever they wanted: attack, stand fast or withdraw. Through continual and repeated pressure on their left wing and left flank they would gradually be pushed in an easterly direction against their Moselle fortifications, the Jura and Switzerland. The best thing for the Germans was a French counter-offensive. Their forces, quickly thrown together and not completely organized, would then meet a compact front that was secure on the left, strong on the right and which probably extended beyond their flank. "It is not likely", Schlieffen said, "that the French, who must first pull their corps together, would have been able to put their army in good order. The situation that the enemy envelopment through Belgium puts them in will cause haste and more or less unjustified detachments." This is exactly what happened to the French in 1914. But on the German side there was no closed front which overlapped the French flank. Continuing his line of thought, Schlieffen said that if the enemy chose to defend in successive positions, the envelopment on Amiens, if necessary on Abbéville, would push in his left flank. If he formed a defensive flank behind the Oise between Paris and La Fère, it would be attacked in front [33] according to the principles of siege warfare with the assistance of all technical means. It could hardly be hoped that this would have a decisive effect. This would rather be reserved to an operational envelopment west and south around Paris. Six ersatz corps were assigned to close off the west and south sides of the giant fortress. This operation would also be necessary if the enemy gave up the position behind the Oise to withdrew to the Marne or even the Seine.[6] But in the long term the enemy could not avoid a decisive battle. Out of consideration for his connection with Paris, the heart of the country, for the morale of his own troops, for public opinion and the conduct of his allies and the neutrals, he must eventually accept battle. Count Schlieffen's operational arrows therefore directed seven corps towards Auxerre–Troyes.

What mission did Count Schlieffen intend for the German left wing in Lorraine? It had intentionally been kept weak – ten divisions, aside from the garrisons of Metz and Strasbourg – and was nevertheless to fix the greatest number of enemy forces possible, in order to make the difficult task of the decisive right wing easier. How the enemy forces were to be fixed was primarily dependent on their conduct. If they were defensive-minded, Nancy was to be attacked. This offered the possibility that the French, in order to save the capital of Lorraine, would perhaps allow themselves to come out of their fortifications and counterattack. Such an operational success was completely adequate. The weak German forces could not allow themselves to become involved in a decisive battle in the open field. They must withdraw, pulling the enemy after them and hold them with the help of Metz, expanded with a great line of field fortifications on the line Moselle–German Nied–Saar. If the attack on Nancy did not achieve this goal and the enemy remained on the defensive, two corps were to be transferred immediately by rail behind the right wing, where the decision would be reached. It was also possible that the

---

[6] Foerster also fails to note that at this point Schlieffen says that even after the addition of six non-existent ersatz corps, the German army was still not strong enough to envelop Paris.

enemy for his part would take the offensive into Alsace-Lorraine from the beginning, perhaps even violating Swiss neutrality to invade south Germany. Schlieffen did not consider this likely because he did not believe that the garrison would leave Fortress France at the same time that the enemy began the assault at another threatened area. If this occurred nevertheless, it could only be welcome, for the forces that conducted this invasion of German territory would not be present at the great decisive battle. [34] If the German commander continued unerringly in the conduct of the operation with the mass of the German army moving through Belgium and Luxembourg, he would soon have the satisfaction that the enemy in Alsace-Lorraine and south Germany would not only stop, but quickly turn in the direction from which the greatest threat came. Then the moment would appear in which the strategic Cannae, beginning with the great envelopment of the enemy left wing, would come to its highest expression, as all of the German forces in Lorraine and Alsace, reinforced by the garrisons of Metz and Strasbourg, the reserve divisions that had to this point sealed off Verdun, the Landwehr brigades from the upper Rhine and new formations, went over to the attack against a front that the enemy had stripped of troops. In his mind's eye the strategist saw the complete encirclement of the enemy through double envelopment.[7]

Theoretically such or a similar supreme achievement was conceivable by means of an operational envelopment of the enemy's southern wing through Switzerland. If it succeeded, the strategic effect was even easier and quicker. The enemy would be driven from his strategic hinterland to the north, perhaps into Belgian territory. The Germans could avoid the violation of Belgian neutrality. Instead of that, Swiss neutrality must be violated, unless diplomacy succeeded in bringing the Swiss over to our side. That was unlikely. In that case it would have been necessary to break the resistance, which was not to be underestimated, of a warlike people determined to defend their rights and then cross the strongly fortified Jura under the most difficult terrain conditions. Supply and lines of communication for a million-man army must have proven exceedingly unfavorable. For good reason Count Schlieffen rejected this theoretical solution.

It would be a sin against Count Schlieffen's spirit if it were assumed that he intended that this legacy to his successor be considered a "recipe for victory", full and punctual adherence to which to some degree guaranteed victory over our western opponents. Count Schlieffen was well aware of the truth of Moltke's dictum "No operations plan is valid with any certainty beyond initial contact with the enemy main body. Only the layman believes to see in the course of a campaign the systematic execution of a previously planned idea, worked out beforehand in all particulars and maintained to the end." With his [35] 1905 operations plan he wanted nothing else than to express the operational concept for an offensive against our western opponents. This consisted of: the left flank of the enemy was to be operationally enveloped with a right wing which had been given overwhelming strength, through repeated pressure on his outer wing the enemy would be shaken, forced to withdraw and to give up his operational base, and finally, with the timely

---

[7] This double envelopment was not in the 1905 *Denkschrift* but was rather an embellishment by Foerster.

increase in this pressure, as well as pressure from the other side, he would be encircled. This was operationally the maximum that could be striven for. The purpose of this document was to present the proof of the possibility that it could be conducted.

The German 1914 *Westaufmarsch*

The assertion has been made against the 1905 Schlieffen *Denkschrift* that it required forces that at that time the Germans were not in a position to create. That is true insofar as according to the mobilization plan of the time Schlieffen treated a large number of reserve corps as though they were complete corps, though they were really only reinforced reserve divisions with a corps headquarters, and he created ersatz corps when in fact only very modest preparations had been made in this direction. In this sense his legacy is to be considered a plan for the future, which his successor was to strive for and complete if possible. This was not completely successful by the outbreak of the war, principally because the 1913 Army Bill did not come close to bringing the army the reinforcement that Ludendorff, its creator, had envisaged. Nevertheless, so much was accomplished that all the reserve corps had been expanded to complete corps and 6½ ersatz divisions had been created.

To gain a correct gauge for a comparison of Schlieffen's 1905 deployment and operations plan with that which was actually conducted in 1914, it also cannot be overlooked that unlike the 1905 plan, which was for a war only with the western powers, the 1914 plan concerned a two-front war. It was not possible for OHL to employ the entire field army in the west, leaving the east unprotected and Austria-Hungary initially to its own resources to fight the Russians. When Generaloberst [36] von Moltke assigned only nine infantry divisions, one cavalry division, one Landwehr corps and three Landwehr brigades to the east, he went below the minimum permissible force. He demonstrated to what degree he was convinced of the necessity of initially committing all available forces for the decisive battle in the west. Including the army reserve, which was not committed at once, but nevertheless in a timely manner (IX Reserve Corps, 6½ ersatz divisions, 2 Landwehr brigades) and the mobile reserves of the fortresses of Metz and Strasbourg, at the beginning of the war the Germans had 72 active and reserve divisions, 10 cavalry divisions, 6½ ersatz divisions and 19½ Landwehr brigades deployed in the west.

The question is, were these troops employed according to Schlieffen's concept?[8]

First the deployment itself. The force ratio between the two wings, that is the right, which was to conduct the great offensive through Belgium and Luxembourg and the left, which had the supporting mission in Alsace-Lorraine, showed a fundamental shift from Schlieffen's plan. Two armies were deployed in Alsace-

---

[8] The real question is, was this the *number* of divisions Schlieffen employed, and the answer is 80 active and reserve divisions and 16 ersatz divisions, 96 divisions in total. That is, in 1914 there were 24 divisions too few. See Zuber, *op. cit.*, pp. 35–6.

Lorraine and Baden – the 6th and 7th – with a total of 16 active and reserve divisions. To this was very quickly added the ersatz divisions, as soon as they were combat-effective, and the mobile reserves of Metz and Strasbourg, in total 24½ divisions, that is, nearly a third of the entire force. The deployment area of this wing of the army also displayed a significant extension as far as the upper Alsace and south Baden. The main body deployed in five armies in the Rhineland (all on the left bank), in Luxembourg and with its left flank also extending into Lorraine.

How can this conspicuous deviation from Schlieffen's allocation of forces be explained? Did this change in the appearance of the deployment also mean that there was a break with Schlieffen's concept? Numerous indicators, particularly those obtained by careful observation of the intellectual trends in the French officer corps and in the military literature, had caused Generaloberst von Moltke to believe that the enemy would begin the war with a strong offensive into Alsace-Lorraine. In contrast to Count Schlieffen, he thought that the upper Alsace should not immediately be given up without a fight, but that determined resistance would only be offered on the Breusch line and on the upper Rhine to protect south Germany. The 6th Army in Lorraine was initially to avoid a decisive battle and withdraw in the direction of the Saar and allow the enemy to advance as far as possible to the south of Metz. [37] Metz and the *Niedstellung*, which was occupied by Landwehr and heavy artillery, were to be reinforced by the 6th and if necessary the 5th Armies, in order to prevent the German right wing from being turned by means of an envelopment of the *Niedstellung*. At the same time, it was intended to bring the 7th Army, or at least strong elements of it, from the lower Alsace across the northern Vosges to the left flank of the 6th Army. In this way Generaloberst von Moltke hoped to decisively defeat the presumably superior enemy forces which had attacked towards the Saar with a double attack from the north and the south. If, contrary to expectations, the early enemy attack into Alsace-Lorraine did not materialize, it was the mission of the 6th and 7th Armies to advance against the Moselle below Fort Frouard and against the Meurthe to fix the enemy forces here and to prevent their possible transport to the left wing.

Aside from the protection of the upper Alsace, which in any case was only to consist of temporary resistance during the deployment period, it is evident that the operational mission of the German southern wing was the same for Moltke as for Schlieffen. The difference rested in the fact that Moltke's force was twice as strong as Schlieffen's and in the planned execution of the mission. Against an enemy offensive in Alsace-Lorraine, Schlieffen wanted to conduct a mobile defense only to win time, not allowing himself to become involved in serious combat. Moltke envisaged the conclusion of his operation as a decisive double envelopment against a superior enemy. If this succeeded, the success gained on this wing presumably would have significantly aided the movement of the right wing. Everything that the enemy committed to the decisive battle in Alsace-Lorraine would be absent from his defense against the German offensive through Belgium, and it did not seem to matter if in the beginning the right wing was a considerable number of corps weaker than Count Schlieffen had intended. After the victory, the immediate transfer of the main body of the 6th and 7th Armies by rail behind the right wing could continue to be the goal. The pre-positioning of a considerable quantity of empty rolling stock on both sides of the Rhine, even during the deployment, expressly provided for this option. With this distribution of units Moltke wanted to some degree to multiply his force, first winning in Lorraine and then immediately shifting most of the available units to and behind the decisive northern wing.[9] It also offered the possibility of moving strong forces through Metz to the other side of the Moselle and thereby reinforcing the attacking masses of the great turning movement. [38] However, these comments do not exhaust all elements of the critique. For the situation would be different if the results of the operation in Alsace-Lorraine were less decisive than envisaged by the strategist. And that could easily happen, for a decisive blow could only be counted on if the enemy ran into the sack that was being held open for him. As we have seen, Count Schlieffen thought that such a favorable situation for the Germans was unlikely and therefore did not initially commit strong forces in Alsace-Lorraine.[10] For so much was clear: an indecisive battle, or even merely a tactical success which did not prevent the enemy from conducting an orderly withdrawal to his strong fortress line but left him free to redeploy the troops here to other missions, could hardly be counted as a gain for the overall German operation, because it involved the employment of strong forces at a non-decisive place. Concerning this, Count Schlieffen said: "An attack on Nancy offers practically only the advantage that the French, in order to save the capital of Lorraine, might allow themselves to be drawn out of their fortifications and fight in the open field. If they do so, they have their protective line so close behind them that a defeat will do no great damage and will bring the victor no great advantage. It is like the defeat of a sortie from a fortress, which inflicts the same number of casualties on the besieger and the besieged, but leaves the situation largely unchanged."[11] In 1914 the situation was even more favorable for the French, because in the preceding years strong fortifications had been constructed around Nancy. On the other hand, since initially the 6th and 7th Armies were to conduct an offensive against the Moselle and the Meurthe, in order to fix the enemy in place if he did not attack, the danger arose that strong forces of our own would be committed in an operationally ineffective direction. Conducting a tactical offensive here precluded the free use of these forces for other missions. However the change in the allocation of forces for the *Westaufmarsch* is judged, Schlieffen's requirement that "as many French units as possible be fixed by the fewest number of German" was no longer observed. On the other hand, the possibility of operating in accordance with Schlieffen's concept from this deployment, although more difficult, was not impossible. Everything depended at a given moment of the presence of a powerful will at OHL making the decision to act in such a manner and then executing it, and not being diverted by the particular interests of the subordinate army commanders and the local tactical situation [39] in Alsace-Lorraine.

[9] This was impossible. By the time the 6th and 7th Armies detrained in Aachen, the right wing would have been 15 day's march ahead of them in central France. See Zuber, *op. cit.*, p. 269. Nor was such a move mentioned in Moltke's *Aufmarschanweisungen*.
[10] In every one of Schlieffen's surviving exercises, including those in 1904, the decisive battle was fought in Lorraine, with the exception of the November–December 1905 war game, which was largely fought in Belgium, though even here Schlieffen conducted a major counterattack in Lorraine. See Zuber, *op. cit.*, 191–211.
[11] As Schlieffen says, he is analyzing a German attack on Nancy, not a French attack into Lorraine.

.... Actually, the reasons for Moltke's instructions deviating from Schlieffen's plan should hereby have been adequately explained, but nevertheless the core reason has not yet been touched upon. This lay far more in an obvious difference between Schlieffen's and Moltke's estimate of the importance and effect of the march through Belgium. Count Schlieffen was the father of this idea, and it did not suddenly come to him, but rather it was poured into the gigantic mold as we now know it only after a gradual development over the years.[12] It thereby had gained a deep and unshakable persuasiveness for its creator. This strategist believed in the ability of the victorious power of his idea to defeat all opposition. His successor, whose character was entirely different, found a complete plan, thought through to the last details.[13] He had only to accept or reject it. Given General von Moltke's deep seriousness and sense of responsibility, accepting it was not easy for him. First because of the violation of Belgian neutrality associated with the plan, whose political consequences did not escape his keen and realistic perception for a second. Then there were the operational considerations. Initially he could accept only with great difficulty the idea that the right wing would march through Belgium into the complete unknown. He had no illusions about the fact that, given the length of time required for the approach march, strategic surprise could only be hoped for at the very beginning. The French could meet the German advance either through the massing of strong forces in the north or with a counter-offensive from the middle of their front.[14] And finally – and this appears the most remarkable – Moltke rated the effectiveness of an early French offensive into Alsace-Lorraine conducted with superior forces far more highly than did Schlieffen. The exercise critiques at their *Generalstabsreisen* give an indication of the difference in their opinions. In the summer of 1904 Count Schlieffen played a French offensive into Alsace-Lorraine and south Germany and noted at the end[15] "I think that in reality the French would not have carried out their plan. When they heard that the German forces were standing ready on the Belgian border to march on Paris, they would probably [40] have dropped their entire operation and in one way or another turned against the threatening invasion. On the other hand, it could be hoped that the Germans would stick to their plan." And in his operations plan of December 1905 he said "If the Germans continue their operation, they can be sure that if the French should invade the upper Alsace and Lorraine, they will turn quickly around, and not to the north, but to the south of Metz in the direction from which the greatest

---

[12] The idea of a German march through Belgium was common knowledge since the late 1870s, and according to German intelligence the French fully understood the idea of a German attack through Belgium coupled with a defense in Lorraine. See Zuber, *op. cit.*, pp. 79–81, 239–52.
[13] The hand-written version of the Schlieffen plan gives an entirely different impression. See Zuber, *op. cit.*, p. 45. Then there was the fact that Moltke was not fighting a one-front war and the problem of where he would find 24 more divisions.
[14] This contradicts the passage in which Schlieffen says strategic surprise will be so overwhelming that the French will not be able to mount a coherent defense.
[15] This comment does not come at the end of the critique, but near the beginning. Once again, Foerster would have us believe that in 1904 Schlieffen was working on the 'Schlieffen plan', while at the same time Foerster kept the text of the exercise critique in its entirety secret. In fact, in this exercise, the 2nd *Generalstabsreise West*, the German army was annihilated along the Moselle river. See Zuber, *op. cit.*, pp. 200–2.

danger threatens. It is therefore imperative that the German right wing be as strong as possible. For the decision is to be expected here." The exercise critique of Moltke's *Generalstabsreisen*, which are based on the same or a similar situation, sound differently.[16] In 1906 he said: "If the French main body advances in Lorraine, there is no purpose any longer in the German right wing marching through Belgium . . . . Then only one overriding thought is operative, to attack the French army with all available force and defeat it, wherever it is to be found. Here the decision was in Lorraine and for it all forces had to be moved there as quickly as possible." In 1912 he spoke in a similar vein: "From the moment in which the main body of the French army was recognized advancing between Metz and the Vosges, the advance of the German right wing was pointless . . . . The operation must be conducted, so that the German left wing opposed the French advance defensively while everything that was not necessary to defend against the Belgians and the British marched down in a southwesterly direction to attack through and to the west of Metz."[17] The fundamental idea that the destruction of the enemy army is the object of the German operation is incontestable and requires no elaboration. This demonstrates, however, that Moltke was not convinced, as Count Schlieffen was, of the effect and power of the march of the German right wing through Belgium to determine the course of the operation and the decisions of the enemy leadership.[18] Rather than by maintaining his own plan and thereby forcing the enemy to do his will, Moltke was under certain circumstances prepared to subordinate his will to the enemy's and allow the enemy to dictate where the decisive battle was to be fought. So our observations finally lead to the conclusion that the great operational concept of its creator, as it was transformed into deed, was not endangered by the deployment that had been chosen, but had already been clouded in the mind of the person who had been called on to execute it.

---

[16] In fact, in Moltke's 1906 *Generalstabsreise West*, Moltke let the right wing advance through Belgium proceed! The exercise demonstrated nevertheless that the Germans had to divert forces from the right wing to Metz. Moltke's 1906 exercise is in fact very similar to Schlieffen's 1st 1904 *Generalstabsreise West*. That is, *both* Schlieffen and Moltke came to the conclusion that if the French made their main effort in Lorraine, then the decisive battle would be fought in Lorraine. See Zuber, *op. cit.*, pp. 191–200, 224–8.
[17] By 17 August 1914 at the latest, Moltke knew that while the French had committed strong forces to an offensive in Lorraine, their main body was north of Metz. Foerster's argument concerning these two war games, in which the French did commit their main body to Lorraine, is therefore pointless. See Zuber, *op. cit.*, p. 268.
[18] If it could be shown that the war could have been won without the invasion of Belgium – or indeed if this invasion could have been limited to Belgium south of the Meuse – then the General Staff was in serious trouble. Hence Foerster's emphasis on the essential nature of the attack through Belgium.

19

1920/1929: Groener Explains the Schlieffen Plan[1]

Almost simultaneously with Kuhl, Groener presented the Schlieffen plan to the public.

Groener's first essay is a long discourse on German foreign policy and society before 1914 as seen by the nationalist Right. Only the parts concerning the war plan are translated here.

'The Liquidation of the World War'[2]

[43] Indeed a man lived in Germany who well recognized the looming danger. He occupied the modest position of the Chief of the General Staff and worked tirelessly on the question of victory. But he was not a king or a statesman. He had his limited responsibility, which it was not customary to exceed. Count Schlieffen suffered the same fate as Bismarck. He was dismissed too soon, but left behind a rich legacy, even as Bismarck had done: [44] his operational concept, in which his political concept was hidden. Unfortunately, the statesmen never found it.

If Germany was determined not to allow its freedom of development to be limited and would not shy away from war, as difficult as it might be, for the security and future of the Reich, then it was demanded of the statesman to choose a course that would foster the battle in the west according to the operational concept, with the highest possible degree of protection for the rear in the east. When the political constellation was favorable, the statesman must recognize it in time and lead policy in an appropriate manner, in order to thoroughly prepare for the use of military means. No one will deny that the operational thought of Count Schlieffen was well-suited to the period of Russian weakness during the East Asian war and immediately thereafter, just as was that of Prince Bismarck, although in another manner than previously. The difference was that Prince Bismarck sought and attained protection in the rear through a policy of understanding with Russia, while in a later period chance temporarily provided protection in the rear in the form of a weakening of Russian power.

---

[1] Zuber, *Inventing the Schlieffen Plan*, pp. 36–8.
[2] Wilhelm Groener 'Die Liquidation des Weltkrieges', in: *Preußischer Jahrbücher* Band 179 Januar bis März 1920, pp. 36–61, 172–84, 337–58, Band 180, April bis Juni 1920, pp. 21–31, 161–78, 305–14.

The course of events did not lead to unity of objectives. Many Germans hoped to attain great success from an accommodation with Britain rather than by breaking the encirclement with force. [Groener said that Germany's objectives – increased influence in the East, colonies and a fleet – were incompatible with the modest gains that could be made by a peaceful policy of accommodation.]

[46] 2. Count Schlieffen and the operational concept

As Field Marshall Count Schlieffen closed his eyes on 4 January 1913, he left as his legacy the secret of victory in a two-front war. To the hour of his death his restless spirit worked on the problem, the solution of which he had spent his entire adult life. Seven years before, he had left his place of work on the Königsplatz – the General Staff – in the secure possession of the secret of victory. Seven more years have passed since that January 4th, and we, who believed we were in possession of the secret of victory, stand by the grave of German power and splendor . . . .

The greatest army in world history moved over the Rhine in August 1914, ready for combat and confident of victory. It returned over the river a year ago, undefeated but broken and worn, to die in lunatic disintegration . . . .

However, on this the day of Schlieffen's death, a reasonable person should immerse himself in his spirit and recognize that we have sinned against this spirit, which was given and bequeathed to the German people, in order to once again gain and possess what our fathers had achieved on the fields of battle in 1870/71.

[48] The operational concept that contained the secret of victory is simple and clear:

The quickest, most complete decision against our strongest and most dangerous enemy in the west. A colossal strategic Cannae! Left wing held back and firmly anchored on the Moselle position Metz–Diedenhofen with the flank bent to the rear. Right flank in a powerful *bataillon carrée*, direction of march through Brüssels on Abbéville–Amiens, from the sea to the Moselle, left wheel march – in the same manner as Frederick the Great – to the tune of the *Pariser Einzugsmarsch* [the march music written to enter Paris in 1871]. Then on further over the lower Seine, strong enough, not only to close off Paris to the west, but also to continue the operation against the French flank and rear, be it on Orleans or Le Mans. If the *bataillon carrée* meets up along the way with the British, who have landed on the coast of Flanders or France, the wheel temporarily stops, the British are beaten and rendered harmless, and the march is continued. In order to be sure to have the force necessary for all the missions on the right flank, all the men at home that could be found, young and old, all the muskets and canons, were to be sent there.

In the meantime the French could attack in Alsace and Lorraine. They could even cross the upper Rhine and threaten southern Germany: so much the better for us. For they were removing themselves from the battlefield where the decision of the entire war would fall.

"Only make the right wing strong" admonished Count Schlieffen as the shadow of death was hovering before his eyes . . . .

The results of the Battle of the Marne in September 1914 prove that this red thread was lost . . . .

[Groener then critiques the military operations of the remainder of the war.]

The Testament of Count Schlieffen[3]

[A 224-page critique of the German army in the first months of the war, according to Groener's interpretation of Schlieffen's principles. Groener's intent is to show how Schlieffen would have won the war. Groener's critique is quite detailed. Only the sections pertaining directly to pre-war planning are translated here.]

[6] It may be true that Count Schlieffen never recommended a preventive war to the Chancellor. Out of principle, he steered clear of mixing in politics. The question should be presented in another fashion. Did the Chancellor ever come to Count Schlieffen to ask the responsible authority if under the conditions obtaining in 1904/05 it was not indicated that Germany should break the encirclement with force? The Chancellor would not accept the uncertainties of a war. He sought to go around the dangers, which piled up year after year, with more malleable policies. He pursued World Power, without having adequately secured Germany's continental position. Count Schlieffen was of the opinion that the decision concerning Germany's power position was not going to be determined on the sea or in faraway lands, but solely on our eastern and western borders, and that all efforts should be made to create the best possible preconditions for a victory of German arms on land. In the first years after his retirement the preconditions were not unduly unfavorable. Russia had been severely weakened. In Berlin there lived the man, who though retired, still retained remarkable mental alertness, and who guarded the secret of victory. With the eyes of a seer he looked into the future and perceived the World War approaching in all its enormous extent. Not only that, he foresaw all of the mistakes that would be made and wrote his fingers raw, counseling and warning. With a burning soul and youthful boldness he revealed to the entire world the secret of victory [7] in his writings in the years from 1906 to 1912. They are like burning beacons, lighting the way . . . .

Seldom has there been such an bequest of wisdom and boldness as that of Count Schlieffen . . . .

[15] These same ideas that Count Schlieffen discussed publicly in 1909 are to be found years before in his military test problems, studies and war games, but particularly in his last *Denkschrift* written shortly before his retirement from the position of Chief of the General Staff in 1905. The Reichsarchiv called this *Denkschrift* Schlieffen's military legacy to his successor, the younger Moltke. In the operations plan for 1905 Schlieffen completely applied his strategic ideas in the most perfect manner. Today it sounds very simple when we read: "We must continually seek, by attacking their left flank, to push the French to the east against their Moselle fortresses, the Jura and Switzerland. The French army must be destroyed. The essential point for the conduct of the operation is to form a strong right flank, to win the battles with it and by means of continual pursuit with the same strong wing time after time force him to withdraw." In Lorraine "we must seek to fix the largest number of French forces as possible with the fewest German forces". Even if the French, against all probability, would cross over the upper

---

[3] Groener, *Das Testament des Grafen Schlieffens* (2nd edition, Berlin, 1929).

Rhine, the plan was to be changed as little as possible: "If the Germans continue their operation, they can be sure that the French will immediately turn around, and not to the north, but to the south of Metz in the direction from which the threat comes. It is therefore imperative that the Germans are as strong as possible on the right wing, for the decisive battle can be expected here." For the younger Moltke, Schlieffen's plan was obviously too bold. In opposition to his advice, from 1909 on, the force ratio between the German right and left wings was changed. While it was 7:1 in the last Schlieffen plan, later it was shifted to 3:1. It is plain that such a shift in forces was a fundamental offense, contrary to the "highest law of decisive combat" and against the ideas of Count Schlieffen. [17] Through the concentration of forces in Alsace-Lorraine the danger arose that the troops opposite the French fortress front would run their heads directly against it, which is what actually happened.

[17] In the 1905 *Denkschrift* Count Schlieffen left no doubt that a French counter-offensive against the German phalanx advancing through Belgium could only be an advantage for the Germans – it would represent a French *Liebesdienst*.

[79] So 1909 arrived, the decisive year for Moltke's future. In this year he decided to weaken Schlieffen's envelopment concept and to change the deployment in the west. He proceeded on the not incorrect assumption – as also happened during the war – that recently the French had decided not to remain on the defensive any longer, but to attack with strong forces into Alsace-Lorraine in order to re-conquer it. In this case, Moltke expected that the decision would come in Lorraine and considered it "pointless" to continue the great wheel through Belgium. On the contrary, he wanted to march all available forces to the south for the [80] decisive battle. Like a *fata morgana* a new Sedan between Metz and the Vosges appeared before his eyes. In changing the operations plan Moltke disregarded the fact that Schlieffen's great envelopment, though originally intended for a French defensive, was best suited for a French offensive into Alsace-Lorraine. That was precisely the greatness of the Schlieffen plan, that the German leadership would not be faced with uncertainty or become dependent on French operations, but could use the plan in any situation. The more consistent, the better! Count Schlieffen could justifiably view his plan not only as another operations study, but as the culmination of his life's work. It would have been well for his epigones, before they set to work moving the load-bearing columns of the structure, to have consulted the Master. But such pilgrimages to one's predecessor were not customary: they easily led to inconveniences and ill feeling. It was only human that the opinion of the old man who is finished and done with is considered dispensable. In the years after 1909 Moltke seemed to be at the height of his powers and he clearly moved away from the intellectual legacy of Count Schlieffen. When the war demanded that Moltke give proof of his capacity as a commander, old Schlieffen was dead. His last warning, which he presented in a *Denkschrift* a few days before his death, went unnoticed. Had he been able to maintain his position a few years longer, perhaps his plan would not have been changed, even though he would not have lived to see the war.

[196] If we want to obtain complete clarity concerning the operations in 1914, we must hold the mirror of Schlieffen's ideas before the army, the more so since critics maintain that the Schlieffen plan was a fantasy because there were never

adequate forces available to execute it. Count Schlieffen was a sober thinker. Illusions were as foreign to him as sentimentality. His sarcasm protected him against it. He thought matters through to the final conclusion. He was not deterred by traditional glory when it was a question of finding the secret of victory. He was conscious that "from old experience" "offensive warfare requires and uses up strong forces, and that these forces continually become weaker while those of the defender become stronger, and that this is particularly true in a country that bristles with fortresses".[4] (Reichsarchiv) We cannot be strong enough at the spot where we seek the decision. That is the *Leitmotiv* of his December 1905 *Denkschrift*. Behind the fighting front on the right wing we must follow with a second, third, fourth line or echelon, or whatever one prefers to call it. All men capable of bearing arms are to be called up and set in motion. Schlieffen had no doubt that the forces raised in the mobilization plans of 1905 were too weak for his plan. He therefore already used more forces during the initial deployment, when he retired at the end of that year, in order to encourage their establishment in case of war. Even that was not enough for him. He demanded the immediate mobilization of the Landsturm and its employment in the combat zone. Unmobilized Landwehr troops still at home were also to be moved to the field. Security and labor-service functions in the homeland were to be given to non-deployable and untrained personnel. The ersatz units, filled with trained personnel, were not to be allowed to populate the home garrisons. They were to be formed into combat-capable units. "We cannot wait to raise these new formations until the need is painfully evident, when the operation has been brought to a halt, but rather immediately after the mobilization of the other units." "This is the absolute minimum that our duty demands we accomplish." Count Schlieffen saw in his recommendations nothing more than what necessity and duty demanded. His testament laid down not only a victorious operations plan, but it was also concerned with creating the army that was necessary to execute it. The *Denkschrift* was a program [197] for expanding the army and for the mobilization. His ideas did not fit in with previous practice nor with routine operations, both of which played a role in the mobilization plan. The voice of the strategist faded away, unheard. General von Moltke, inexperienced and not trained in such questions, did not take up the program, although he retained the operations plan until 1909. Therein was a contradiction. General von Moltke could hardly have thought himself capable of obtaining victory with weaker forces than Schlieffen, the creator of the plan. That the expansion of the army did not commence immediately is not surprising, considering the attitude of the personalities involved. From 1906 to 1909 there was no inclination to demand large sums from the Reichstag to expand the army. Russian strength was at its nadir, German policy was pacific; no one expected a war due to the Risk Theory of the High Seas Fleet either. The army was good enough. Not even the Bosnian Crisis of 1909 awakened military defense from its slumber. Suddenly the Morocco Crisis sounded. The danger of war stood outside the door. Terror seized the General Staff. The political

---

[4] Groener neglected to include the preceding line: "These preparations can be made any way that you like: it will soon become clear that we are too weak to continue the operation in this direction."

leadership hoped to preserve peace. It did not seem necessary to dig deep into the public purse. The War Minister chose the middle path. It was decided to do something for the good old army, which had fallen behind in the competition with the navy. What could already have been done in 1906 on the basis of Schlieffen's *Denkschrift* was in part made good by the Army Bills of 1912 and 1913. If these measures had been taken five years earlier, it would have meant a half-million more men for the field army, while in actuality they did not even produce 150,000 men by the outbreak of the war. In the last hour before the war General von Moltke finally pressed for the complete implementation of universal conscription. It was too late. The good-hearted, distinguished man had no success as the organizer of the army either.

[201] Perhaps his [Schlieffen's] counsel was not even correctly understood. The few people who at that time saw the 1905 *Denkschrift* disregarded it or didn't think it worth the effort to dig for its riches through immersion into the ideas of the immortal Schlieffen . . . .

The giant fortress of Paris was to be besieged by ersatz troops . . . . There was doubt if the weapons and equipment [of the ersatz units, Landwehr and Landsturm] were adequate . . . . In any case this second field army would not be provided with the artillery and cavalry that is desirable for combat operations. In 1914, when the recommendation was strongly made to send ersatz battalions, recruit depots and Landsturm battalions to Belgium to establish peace and order there, it was rejected with a laugh. This was against conventional practice.

[202] In order to relieve General von Moltke of the charge of not having adequately increased the size of the army, it has been said that during his own tenure Count Schlieffen did nothing either to create the ersatz corps or for the employment of the Landsturm in enemy territory. Had the war broken out in 1905, Schlieffen himself would not have had the forces that he considered necessary. To this it may be replied that he did not write the *Denkschrift* of 1905 for himself, but for his successor. If there had been a war in 1905, he would have known what to do.

In 1905 Count Schlieffen intended to use the entire German field army in the west. Russia's weakness at the time allowed him to leave the land east of the Vistula without protection. If necessary, the deployment of an *Ostarmee* in the strength of 3 active corps, 4 reserve divisions, 7 Landwehr Brigades and 2 cavalry divisions had been prepared. As has been mentioned, in his programmatic *Denkschrift* Schlieffen assumed that more forces were available than was actually the case. Since for our observations it is not a question of the actual strength of the German forces in 1905 but rather of the forces that Count Schlieffen thought were necessary to conduct his plan, we must compare the numbers in his plan with the actual forces in 1914.

First we must compare total strengths. In doing so, the garrisons of the border fortifications will not be considered. As was usual, the Guard Reserve Corps will be considered as the equivalent of an active army corps. The Landwehr corps raised in Silesia in 1914 has been counted in the Landwehr and ersatz numbers. According to the Schlieffen plan the total strength of the army was:

26½ active corps
14   reserve corps

11 cavalry divisions
26½ Landwehr brigades.

The total strength in 1914 was:
26   active corps
13½ reserve corps
11   cavalry divisions
28½ Landwehr brigades.

[203] The difference is not significant. The actual army was only a half an active corps and a half a reserve corps smaller than that in the Schlieffen plan. A larger difference appears in the reinforcement for the field army that Schlieffen wanted to receive from ersatz, Landwehr and Landsturm troops. In the east Schlieffen provided 3 active corps, 2 reserve corps and 2 cavalry divisions for the eventuality that the situation would not permit exposing the land to the east of the Vistula. In 1914 the 8th Army in East Prussia initially was a reserve division, a cavalry division and four Landwehr brigades weaker, but was reinforced in August with the Landwehr division from Schleswig-Holstein . . . . The execution of the Schlieffen plan in 1914 was not influenced by the allocation of forces to a greater degree than that considered acceptable by Schlieffen in 1905. That is was possible or permissible in 1914 to "sacrifice" the land east of the Vistula is very questionable. In the nine years since Schlieffen had written his *Denkschrift* the Russian army had not only recovered from the East Asian war and the first Revolution, it had accelerated its mobilization and found itself in the hands of the Grand Duke's pan-Slavic party . . . . Therefore the political and military circumstances in 1914 required the creation of a German *Ostarmee*, though a weak one.

When the troops required for the east are subtracted, we have the following numbers for the west:

1905: 23½ active corps
        12   reserve corps
         9   cavalry divisions
        19½ Landwehr brigades. [204]
1914: 23   active corps
        12   reserve corps
        10   cavalry divisions
        21½ Landwehr brigades.

(After the withdrawal of 4 Landwehr brigades for the north, 17½ Landwehr brigades deployed to the west . . . .)

. . . . The *Westheer* in 1914, aside from half an active corps and two Landwehr brigades, was no smaller than that of 1905.[5]

---

[5] This is a fraud. The 1905 *Denkschrift* was for a one-front war, not a two-front war, included 8 ersatz corps that Groener has left out completely, and required a total of 48 corps. In fact, the *Westheer* in 1914 was 12 corps short of the force required by the 'Schlieffen plan'.

Shortly before the war it was decided to plan for the establishment of part of the ersatz troops as ersatz divisions and ersatz brigades. Schlieffen had required a minimum of 8 ersatz corps. In 1914 6½ ersatz divisions and 2 ersatz brigades for the Landwehr corps were created. In spite of the small numbers of ersatz divisions, they would initially have been adequate had they been employed at the correct place, on the right rather than the left wing. Even though their weapons and equipment were insufficient for their intended operational employment, they could have been equipped in an improvised manner. In addition to captured equipment, Belgium offered considerable resources.

[235] For our study we have used the strength of the 1905 Schlieffen plan without subtracting an army for the east, in order to emphasize the concept that Schlieffen left to his successor with the minimum amount of change. If we subtract one cavalry and nine infantry divisions for the east according to the organization for combat of 1914, the question arises where these forces could most easily have been spared from the *Westheer*. The cavalry division is not important: it can be withdrawn from the middle or from Lorraine. As for the rest, in Count Schlieffen's time the contingency for a deployment in the east was covered by subtracting divisions equally along the right wing, so that after their subtraction the force ratio among the individual army groups would be changed as little as possible. In both cases the number of divisions in Lorraine remained the same. However, Schlieffen did intend, as has been often mentioned, to transfer two corps from Lorraine to the right wing as soon as possible, where they could compensate for the loss of the east corps . . . .

The loss of the eastern corps (I, XVII, XX Corps, I Reserve Corps and 3rd Reserve Division) did not significantly hinder the execution of the operation in the west. We demonstrated that to the French themselves in 1914. In spite of the sweeping changes in the German deployment in 1909 it would [236] not have been particularly difficult for a leader congenial with old Schlieffen to have conducted the operation as of 20 August in the spirit of the Schlieffen plan and crowned it with a glorious victory. The French leadership could not have prevented him.

20

1929: Ludendorff Critiques the Schlieffen Plan[1]

During the era of the Great War Erich Ludendorff was arguably the single most important officer in the German army. From 1908 to 1912 he was the head of the deployment section under the younger Moltke. He was the conqueror of Liège and the de facto *victor of Tannenberg in 1914, as well as the real head of the German army from mid-1916 to October 1918. The last article in this book gives Ludendorff's opinion of the Schlieffen plan.*[2]

General von Kuhl has written a large two-volume work, *The World War 1914/18*.

It does full justice to the incomparable heroic deeds of our army and brings clarity to most of our operations. Whether he does so for the political affairs remains to be seen . . . .

I disagree concerning some things, for example the deployment plans of Count Schlieffen in 1905 and the deployment of the German army in 1914, which was conducted according to the instructions of General von Moltke. I must state my opinion for the benefit of the military education of coming generations. I would explicitly like to make reference to page 74 of my book *Kriegführung und Politik* (War Leadership and Politics) which I wrote in 1921. I said there that the decision-making officers in the Great General Staff, next to General von Moltke, were the *Oberquartiermeister*, that the section chiefs were not decision-makers, and that I did not see any reason to conduct the deployment other than in the manner that General von Moltke did, on the advice of General von Stein.

I assume that the fundamental concepts of the deployment plan of Count Schlieffen are well known. It stated that the *Schwerpunkt* of the advancing German army would be placed on the right wing north of the Meuse at Liège–Namur, and that the advance itself would consist of a huge left wheel from the line Aachen–Diedenhofen, while holding fast to the pivot at Diedenhofen. Meanwhile a very weak force in Lorraine would protect the left flank of this huge movement against an enemy attack between Metz and Strasbourg. Such an attack could reach the German lines of communication at Saarbrücken three to four days before the wheeling German right, after the lengthy march through all of Belgium, could reach the French communications in France. A success against the German left

---

[1] Erich Ludendorff, 'Der Aufmarsch 1914' in: *Ludendorff's Volkswarte* Folge 31 vom 24. Dezember 1929.
[2] Zuber, *Inventing the Schlieffen Plan*, pp. 35–6.

flank in Lorraine could cut the German army off from their lines of communication and the homeland and push it against the Dutch–Belgian border, while in case the French army were enveloped, it had the depth of the hinterland in its rear. Further, "holding on to Diedenhofen" was questionable as long as there was not adequate strength for the maneuvering wing to reach far into France, or at least to Paris. If the forces for this were not adequate, holding onto Diedenhofen gave the deployment plan a dangerous rigidity.

General von Kuhl sees the deployment plan of Count Schlieffen as an infallible recipe for victory, as do probably all military critics. I do not at all fail to recognize its greatness and genius, but I doubt that the conditions of 1914 were the same as those on which Schlieffen based his 1905 plan.

Specifically, on page 10 General von Kuhl writes: "The forces on which Count Schlieffen based his plan were in fact not entirely available. He employed as many forces as he thought necessary for the operation, and thereby established a program for the necessary expansion of the army."

I have always considered it unusually dangerous that in his studies Count Schlieffen counted on forces that did not exist. This would not have mattered, if these studies had remained studies. That must change the moment that studies based on non-existent units are transformed into a deployment plan, which naturally cannot be written using non-existent units. General von Kuhl is incorrect when he says that Count Schlieffen "established a program for a necessary expansion of the army". Unfortunately, Count Schlieffen never did enough for the expansion of the army: in any case he did not somehow overcome existing difficulties. The expansion of the army could also not be based on a particular plan, but could only be realized purely and solely by the implementation of universal conscription. In this regard General von Moltke, who succeeded him on 1 January 1906, did infinitely more than General Count von Schlieffen. Unfortunately, after I became section chief on 1 April 1908, I was not able to convince him to commit himself and his office fully to the implementation of universal conscription. In spite of my most strenuous efforts the horrible fact must be recorded that at the beginning of the war 5½ million German men who were capable of bearing arms had not received military training. It would have been possible to establish a considerably larger number of units than either those on which Count Schlieffen based his studies or those he even considered creating. Then the OHL would have needed simply to assemble the army, without having to worry about the left flank, which could have been adequately protected. Unfortunately, that didn't happen.

In his 1905 study Count Schlieffen used 40 corps (including reserve corps), 8 ersatz corps and 11 cavalry divisions. Of that, 35 corps were to deploy on the line north [east?] of Liège–Metz, 5 corps and 3 cavalry divisions between Metz and Strasbourg, and at the beginning of the advance the 8 ersatz corps were to follow behind the right wing.

Count Schlieffen therefore used 80 infantry divisions, 16 ersatz divisions and 11 cavalry divisions.

In 1905 the Germany army consisted of only 72 infantry divisions and 11 cavalry divisions. It was 24 infantry and ersatz divisions short of the ideal number!

In 1905, according to the instructions of Count Schlieffen, the German army deployed with:

Debate: Ludendorff Critiques the Schlieffen Plan

10 infantry divisions in East Prussia
62 infantry divisions in the west with
    54 divisions between Aachen and Metz and
    8 divisions in Lorraine
of the cavalry divisions
    1 was in the east
    7 in front of the army
    3 on the left wing

There were no ersatz divisions.

These were massively different numbers than the 1905 study, which assumed a one-front war in the west.

Critics generally refrain from mentioning or acknowledging this significant difference between the number of units on which Count Schlieffen's study is based and the number of units that were actually available, and that given the actual force structure Count Schlieffen's plan would have to be changed. About a quarter of the forces used in the plan did not exist.

When General von Moltke became the Chief of the General Staff on 1 January 1906, he may well have adopted a brilliant plan from his predecessor, but not the troop strength that was necessary to execute it. General von Moltke's strategic vision has often been underestimated. When, after 1908, I assisted him at strategic war games, I frequently observed it with pleasure. He did not lack the vision to lead the army, but rather the firmness of character and nerves.

Because the lacking troop strength could not be made available, but the march through Belgium on the way to Paris alone seemed to guarantee a victorious conclusion to the war, the basic idea of Count Schlieffen's plan had to be retained, but the number of the available troops were to be multiplied through mobility, so that the plan could actually be conducted without making it likely that a crisis for the entire strategic situation would occur due to the weakness of the left wing. Even in the west it was a question of a part of the troops operating according to the given situation and then employing them within Count Schlieffen's concept. How that was to be accomplished was demonstrated in the campaign in the east. With the addition of only limited reinforcements, the same troops fought the Battle of Tannenberg, then the Battle of the Masurian Lakes in September, the campaign in south Poland from Krakow to the Vistula in October. Following the completion of the withdrawal to the Polish–Silesian border they conducted the campaign in northern Poland from Hohensalza and Thorn in November. Each time a different group of enemy forces was defeated or operationally fixed in place.

The deployment chosen by General von Moltke could have allowed the same operational maneuver and a multiplication of German forces and thereby the execution of the brilliant plan of Count Schlieffen.[3]

---

[3] Here Ludendorff obviously means a Schlieffen plan along the lines of the November–December 1905 war game and not the 'Schlieffen plan' *Denkschrift*. In the same manner, Ludendorff is now discussing the actual 1905 deployment and not the 'Schlieffen plan'.

In 1914 General von Moltke had available, in addition to the 11 cavalry divisions, not 72 divisions, but 79 infantry divisions and 6½ ersatz divisions: 13½ divisions more than General Count Schlieffen.

General von Moltke divided them so that 9 divisions were sent to East Prussia, one division fewer than Count Schlieffen had provided.

The German right wing deployed between Aachen and Metz with 54 divisions, the same number provided by Count Schlieffen, with a strong, mobile group of 16 divisions in the 6th and 7th Armies in Lorraine and the upper Alsace.

General von Moltke thus employed the newly created divisions [in Alsace-Lorraine].

[Ludendorff included a "Map for the 1914 Deployment" which showed the German right wing meeting the French left *inside Belgium*, while 12 divisions of the German left defended against an attack by 18–29 French divisions in Lorraine, and nothing more, that is, no great wheel through France.]

In addition, the 6½ ersatz divisions were retained as a reserve. The allocation of cavalry divisions remained the same.

According to the available information – I do not know if this was available in 1905 – General von Moltke expected an early attack by the French 7th Corps into the upper Alsace and a strong early attack by the French right wing into Lorraine. This seriously threatened our left wing before the right wing would be engaged. Therefore the opportunity was present here to win early, significant successes, after which, because there would no longer be a threat to the German left wing east of Metz to worry about, those troops could be employed in a timely manner to support the part of the army that had begun the wheeling movement. The enveloping movement through Belgium would have proceeded so far that by this time the French, whose offensive in Lorraine had failed, must have become concerned. If the French did not attack in Lorraine, the corps deployed here could have easily been moved through Diedenhofen to the wheeling front and the right wing shifted immediately further to the north or north-west.

If only 8 divisions had actually been deployed in Lorraine, as Count Schlieffen had wanted, on 20 August these 8 divisions would have been opposed by 24 French divisions, and to be precise, immediately on the lines of communication of the German army.

Given this ratio of forces, it cannot be said with certainty how the battle would have turned out. A French success was possible. Knowing the personalities involved as I do, I doubt if the nerves of the German leadership would have been adequate to overcome the terrific tension that this situation would have produced. In my opinion to create such a situation without compelling reasons, which did not exist, would have meant taking an unnecessary risk and playing a desperate strategic game.

General von Moltke therefore deployed four divisions in the upper Alsace, which defeated the invading French 7th Corps, although not as decisively as they could have. But this was not his fault.

He then moved these four divisions to a second operation in Lorraine and committed the ersatz divisions there as well, so that 22 German infantry divisions and 3 cavalry divisions were massed here. The possibility of a great early German success beckoned here. But the 6th Army under Crown Prince Rupprecht of Bavaria understood how to obtain it as little as did OHL. The enemy was nevertheless beaten. The threat to the left flank was thereby eliminated. In fact, on about 25 August at least part of the forces should have been moved from Lorraine either by rail as far as possible towards the German right wing or pushed through Metz–Diedenhofen in such a manner that they could be inserted in the wheeling front, so that this front would reach all the way to Paris. The decisive day on the Battle of the Marne was 9 September, and by that time troops could have been moved considerable distances.

Instead, the instructions from OHL resulted in the 6th Army becoming committed in the direction of Toul–Epinal and therefore not available for the Battle of the Marne. This had not the slightest thing to do with the deployment itself. The deployment had even less to do with the fact that later reinforcements for the east were taken from the right wing, although I did not think that they were necessary so long as the situation in the west was still uncertain.

In the meantime OHL had in the course of the operation lost sight of the concept of Count Schlieffen's plan, that is, that the strong right wing would reach to the immediate vicinity of Paris. They finally followed Schlieffen's plan only at its weakest point, that is, OHL held the wheeling front firmly attached to the pivot Diedenhofen (Verdun) and therefore did not come to the idea of moving the 6th Army through Diedenhofen, thereby allowing the right wing to be extended to Paris.

Naturally, conducting operations with numerically inferior forces presents great dangers. It is much easier to assemble strong bodies of troops and just march them forward, driving the enemy in front of them. If the forces available are not strong enough for this, there is no other alternative but maneuver. This was the situation facing General von Moltke in 1914 in the west. The fundamental concept was not any different than that in the east, only much simpler.

Given the situation on both sides in the west, I believe that the deployment plan of General von Moltke in 1914 was better than the instructions of Count Schlieffen, according to which at the beginning of the deployment the right wing was made stronger and the left wing weaker. I have stated my reasons. The ersatz divisions, which lacked cohesion, would have been employed more effectively by immediately marching them behind the right wing. I can also think of another method to employ the cavalry divisions. But for me that is not the problem here.

I want to warn against placing hopes on plans or programs. Correct basic concepts and effective education of the intellect of the leaders are necessary for success. The rest is determined by his will, strength of character and readiness to assume responsibility.

The Schlieffen Plan Debate in *War in History*

T. Zuber, 'The Schlieffen Plan Reconsidered' in: *War in History*, 1999; 3: pp. 262–305.

T. Holmes, 'A Reluctant March on Paris', in: *War in History*, 2001; 2: pp. 208–32.

T. Zuber, 'Terence Holmes Reinvents the Schlieffen Plan' in: *War in History*, 2001; 4, pp. 468–76.

T. Holmes, 'The Real Thing' in: *War in History*, 2002; 1: pp. 111–20.

T. Zuber, 'Terence Holmes Reinvents the Schlieffen Plan – Again' in: *War in History*, 2003; 1: pp. 92–101.

R. Foley, 'The Origins of the Schlieffen Plan' in: *War in History*, 2003; 2: pp. 222–32.

T. Zuber, 'The Schlieffen Plan was an Orphan' in: *War in History*, 2004; 2: pp. 220–5.

T. Holmes, 'Asking Schlieffen: A Further Reply to Terence Zuber' in: *War in History* 2003; 4: pp. 464–79.

T. Zuber, 'Any Plan Was the Schlieffen Plan' in: *War in History* (in press).

Further Reading in English

Albertini, Luigi, *The Origins of the War of 1914* (3 vols., Oxford, 1952–7).
Berghahn, V. R., *Germany and the Approach of War* (2nd edn., London, 1933).
Bucholz, Arden, *Moltke, Schlieffen and Prussian War Planning* (New York, 1991).
Craig, Gordon, *The Politics of the Prussian Army* (2nd rev. edn., Oxford, 1964).
Depuy, T. N., *A Genius for War: The German Army and General Staff 1807–1945* (Englewood Hills NJ, 1977).
Foley, Robert (trans.), *Alfred von Schlieffen's Military Writings* (London and Portland OR 2002).
Goerlitz, Walter, *The German General Staff* (New York, 1963).
Herwig, Holgar, *The First World War: Germany and Austria-Hungary 1914–1918* (London, 1997).
Kennedy, Paul, 'The Operational Plans of the Great Powers 1880–1914: Analysis of Recent Literature' in: *Militärgeschichtliche Mitteilungen* 19 (1976), 189–207.
Kennedy, Paul (ed.), *The War Plans of the Great Powers 1880–1914* (London, 1979).
Kitchen, Martin, *A Military History of Germany* (Bloomington IN and London, 1975).
Langdon, John W., *July 1914: The Long Debate 1918–1990* (New York and Oxford, 1991).
Liddell-Hart, Sir B. H., *The Real War 1914–18* (1930).
May, Ernest R., *Knowing One's Enemies: Intelligence Assessment Before the Two World Wars* (Princeton, 1984).
Miller, Steven, *Military Strategy and the Origins of the First World War* (Princeton, 1995).
Millet, Allen and Murray, Williamson (eds.), *Military Effectiveness. Volume I: The First World War* (Winchester MA, 1988).
Mombauer, Annika, *Helmuth von Moltke and the Origins of the First World War* (Cambridge, 2001).
Paret, Peter (ed.), *Makers of Modern Strategy from Machiavelli to the Nuclear Age* (Princeton, 1986).
Ritter, Gerhard, *The Schlieffen Plan: Critique of a Myth* (London, 1958).
Ritter, Gerhard, *The Sword and the Scepter: The Problem of Militarism in Germany* (2 vols., Miami, 1969).
Showalter, Dennis, *Tannenberg: Clash of Empires* (Hamden CT, 1991).
Snyder, Jack, *The Ideology of the Offensive: Military Decision-Making and the Disasters of 1914* (Ithica NY and London, 1984).
Stevenson, David, *The Outbreak of the First World War: 1914 in Perspective* (London and New York, 1997).
Strachan, Hew, *The First World War. Volume I: To Arms* (Oxford and New York, 2001).
Taylor, A. J. P. *War by Timetable: How the First World War Began* (London, 1969).
Tunstall, Graydon A., *Planning for War Against Russia and Serbia: Austro-Hungarian and German Military Strategies 1871–1914* (Highland Lakes NJ, 1993).
Wallach, Jehuda, *The Dogma of the Battle of Annihilation* (Westport CT, 1986).

Index

Aachen 75, 155, 175, 207–20, 267, 280, 300
Abbéville 282, 290
Africa 36
Aillevilliers 26, 28
Aisne 22, 192, 195, 196, 197, 280
Albrecht, Archduke 126, 127
Algeria 10
Alle 145, 149, 170, 172
Allenstein 82, 108, 140, 145, 171
Alma 165
Alsace 22–7, 75, 109, 120, 123, 155, 174, 181, 193, 207–20, 249, 255, 272, 274, 280, 285, 290, 300
Alsace-Lorraine 56, 67, 83, 152, 232, 266–7, 283–7, 292
Altbreisach 99
Alzette 184
Amagne 33
Amance 235, 236
America 262
Amiens 282, 290
Angerapp 65, 96, 145, 147
Angerburg 144, 170, 171
Antwerp 157, 179, 180, 181, 192, 193, 200, 202, 251, 280, 281
Apremont 26
Ardennes 194
Arlon 225, 230
Arys 105
Attigny 43
Aufmarsch I 92, 95, 96, 98
Aufmarsch II 92, 95–7, 246
Aufmarschanweisung (5th Army) 228–30
Aufmarschanweisung (6th Army) 223–7
Aufmarschplan 50, 54, 55–6, 65, 77, 89, 122, 126, 253, 279
Austria 76, 116, 123, 129, 143, 214, 249
Auxerre 282
Avricourt 9, 43, 238

Baccarat 225, 232, 238, 253
Baden 226, 227, 274, 285

Baghdad 96
Ballon de Severance, Fort 188
Bar le Duc 18, 22, 23, 26, 43, 44, 48
Baritey 18
Barten 149
Bastnach 219
Bayonne 42
Beck, Freiherr von 64, 123, 126, 127, 128
Belfort 11, 19, 23, 25, 26, 30–2, 37, 38, 43, 93, 120, 157, 164, 175, 187–9, 194, 196, 197, 209, 215, 226, 240, 249, 250, 279
Belgium 12, 13, 23, 34, 35, 43, 72–3, 74, 76, 77, 94, 104, 114, 120, 140, 155, 157, 160, 161, 175, 178, 179, 189, 194, 198, 203, 212, 214, 262, 267, 272, 277, 283, 285, 294, 300
Bellingen 237
Bensdorf 87
Berlin 55, 157, 291
Besançon 10, 19, 26, 32, 37
Beseler 104
Bethmann-Hollweg, Theobold von 264
Bettemberg 230
Beuthen 126, 128
Bialystock 135, 252
Bingen 210
Bismarck, Prince Otto von 71, 248–9, 289
Bitche 161
Blâmont 225, 236
Blesmes 11
Borchersdorf 137
Bordeaux 42
Boulogne 18, 36, 43
Bourg 37
Boyen, Fort 143, 144, 168
Breslau 153
Breusch 285
Brieg 128
Brienne le Château 18
Bromberg 65, 135, 136
Bronsart von Schellendorff, Walter 62–3, 78, 79, 117, 120

Brühl 208, 210
Brumath 161
Brun, General 27
Brussels 183, 193
Buchy 238
Budki 173, 174
Budry 237
Bülow, Major Carl von 91, 101, 127, 128, 129, 270, 275

Calais 36, 43, 168, 175, 195
Cambon, Paul 278
Challerange 12
Châlons 11, 26, 27, 37, 43
Châlons sur Marne 10, 28, 30
Chamberlain, Austen 101
Champenoise 28
Charleroi 183
Charleville 33, 38, 48
Charmes 32
Château Salins 163, 238
Château Thierry 37
Chatel sur Mer 26
Chatillon sur Seine 32
Chaumont 18, 32, 48, 100
Chenevières 236
Cherbourg 42
Chiny 230
Cholm 151
Chorzele 173
Cirey 163, 236
Clausewitz, Karl Marie von 168
Coblenz 175, 178, 199, 208, 210, 212, 268
Col du Bonhomme 43
Cologne 155, 175, 178, 180
Commercy 23, 33, 43
Contchen 56
Coulommiers 37
Cracow 127
Crefeld 280
Cuperly 37

Damblain 18
Darkehmen 65, 105, 107
Deime 133, 143, 170, 172
Deines, Colonel von 126
Delbrück, Hans 272–8
Delme 238
Demer 178, 182
Denkschrift (1871–1914) 245–57

Denkschrift (1877) 249
Denkschrift (1879/80) 249–50
Denkschrift (1884) 251
Denkschrift (1885) 8–10
Denkschrift (1886) 250
Denkschrift (1887) 10–11
Denkschrift (1888) 12–13, 250
Denkschrift (1889) 14
Denkschrift (1890) 15, 252
Denkschrift (1891/92) 15–16, 252
Denkschrift (1893–95) 17–19, 67, 70, 71, 252–3
Denkschrift (1896–98) 19–21, 74, 77, 89, 93
Denkschrift (1899/1900) 21–3, 253
Denkschrift (1905) 23–5, 253–5, 291–6
Denkschrift (1907) 25–31
Denkschrift (1909–11) 31–4
Denkschrift (1912) 34–8, 255
Denkschrift (1914) 38–48, 255–7
Denmark 214
Deutsch Eylau 134, 138, 140
Diedenhofen [Thionville] 56, 75, 82–9, 92, 103, 104, 110, 114, 120, 184, 199, 209, 215, 217, 225, 228, 229, 230, 265, 290, 297, 298, 300, 301
Diekirch 219
Diest 178
Dietrichsdorf 148
Dieulouard 43, 236
Dijon 38
Dirschau 133, 136
Dôle 32, 38
Dommes, Lieutenant Colonel or Oberstleutnant, von 247
Donchery 94
Donon 155, 233, 234, 237
Doulcon 32
Dounoux 26
Drewenz 134
Dubno 126, 151
Dudy 173
Duisburg 207–20, 210
Dun 10, 32, 33
Dunkirk 36, 168, 189, 192, 195, 197, 280
Durbuy 184
Düsseldorf 207–20
Dyle 178, 182, 200

East Prussia 61, 65, 76, 79, 82, 108, 117, 126, 149, 254, 263, 300

Index

Echternach 109
Eifel 155, 207–20, 210, 212
Eising 134
Elbing 152
Epernay 18, 28
Epinal 9, 10, 18, 23, 26, 31, 34, 35, 74, 94, 103, 118, 155, 157, 178, 187, 188, 232, 240, 247, 249, 252, 253, 267
Esch 218, 219
Eupen 109
Euskirchen 212

Falkenberg 56, 237
Falkenhausen, Generalmajor Freiherr von 133
Falkenstein, 86
Fall I 102, 106, 108, 109, 112–14
Fall II 102, 105, 106, 108, 109, 111–12, 114
Fashoda 21
Filipow 108, 146
Fitzendorf 148
Flanders 290
Florenville 230
Foch, Marshal 266, 270
Foerster, Lieutenant-colonel Wolfgang 50, 51, 273, 276
Forest of Haye 32
France 87, 118, 123, 151, 188, 194, 198, 207–20, 250
  Plan VII (1885/86) 7–8, 10
  Plan VIII (1887/88) 10–11, 13
  Plan IX (1888/89) 11–13
  Plan X (1889/90) 13–14
  Plan X M (1890) 14–15
  Plan XI (1891/92) 15–16
  Plan XII (1893/94) 17–18
  Plan XIII (1895/6) 18–19
  Plan XIV (1898/99) 19–21, 31, 99–100
  Plan XV (1903) 21–3, 23–31
  Plan XV*bis* (1907) 23–31
  Plan XVI (1909) 31–8
  Plan XVII (1914) 39–48
  war game 1906 (Hargon) 26–7
Frankfurt 251
Franz Joseph, Emperor 127
Frederick the Great 154, 263, 275, 276, 278, 290
Fresnes-Thiaucourt 75
Friedland 170, 171

Friedrichshof 149
Frisching 170
Frouard 9, 232
Frouard, Fort 57, 94

Galicia 55, 108, 123, 126, 127, 140, 263, 273
Gallieni, Governor of Paris 269
Gayl, Colonel Freiherr von 133
Geistkirch 238
Generalstabsreise (1908–1910) 34
Generalstabsreise West (1904) 4, 155–65
Generalstabsreise West (Moltke, 1906) 288
Generalstabsreise West (Moltke, 1908) 4, 207–20
Generalstabsreisen Ost (1894) 4, 133–9
Generalstabsreisen Ost (1901) 108, 140–2
Generalstabsreisen Ost (1902) 4, 143–50
Generalstabsreisen Ost (1903) 4, 151–4
Gerardmer 234
Germersheim 238
Gilgenberg 138
Givet 184, 209
Gneisenau, 275
Goßler, Generalleutnant von 80–1
Goeben, General von 146
Goltz, Colmar Freiherr von der 83, 88, 120
Gondrecourt 44
Grandpré 33, 43
Graudenz 65, 145
Gravelotte 154
Gray 24
Great Britain 72–3, 76, 91–2, 207–20, 213
Greiner, Hellmuth 7
Große Schobensee 173
Grodno 135
Groener, Wilhelm 245
Gross Puppen 144
Gross Tännchen 56
Gumbinnen 107, 126, 252

Hagenau 161
Haldane, General 36
Han an der Nied 87
Hargon, General 26, 27
Hasselt 178
Hausen, Generalmajor Freiherr von 134
Heilsberg 171

Index

Hentsch, Lieutenant-colonel 270–1, 275
Hindenburg 273
Hirson 48, 189, 194, 202
Hohendorf 136
Hohenloehe, Prince von 63
Hohes Venn 155, 181, 210
Holland 34, 35, 161, 178, 179, 189, 200, 203, 214
Holstein, 91
Hötzendorff, Conrad von 254
Hülsen, Count 127
Hungary 52
Hüningen 175
Huy 192, 216

Insterburg 65, 82, 107, 126, 170
Is sur Tille 24
Istein 175
Italy 250
Ivangorod 65, 126

Jarotschin 126
Jeandelaincourt 235, 236
Jeaseler, Graf 87
Joffre, General Joseph 33, 266
Johannisburg 108, 144, 168, 173
Joinville 100
Jura 189, 198, 291

Kaiser Wilhelm II, Fort 92, 105, 226
Kalisch 64
Kaltenborn-Stachau, War Minister Generalleutnant von 62, 78, 117, 119
Kamoniken 149
Kappel 99
Kenzingen 99
Kholm 153
Kibarty 108
Kielzy 64
Kiev 255
Kluck, Generaloberst von 270, 275
Königgrätz 138, 142, 165
Königsberg 82, 108, 133, 136, 143, 153, 170, 171
Königsberg, Fort 141
Köpke, Generalmajor 69, 70
Kovno 173
Kowno 135, 252
Krakow 299
Krasnick 126

Kriegsspiel (1905) 167–85
Kryksztany 147
Kuhl, General Hermann von 265, 275, 276, 277, 297, 298
Kurland 135
Kuropatkin, General 172

La Fère 22, 24, 28, 38, 189, 192, 194, 195, 197, 199, 280, 282
La Nouvion 43
Labiau 145
Lacroix, General 29–30, 31
Laggerben 148
Landremont 236
Langres 10, 11, 24, 32, 266
Laon 22, 27, 28, 189, 197, 280
Lautenburg 96, 105, 108, 136, 138
Le Cateau 43
Le Havre 43
Le Mans 290
Leipzig 154
Lemberg 273
Lérouville, Fort 30
Leuthen 160, 185
Leyr 236
Liart 28, 33, 38, 48
Liège 104, 155, 157, 178, 179, 181, 192, 193, 196, 200, 203–4, 209, 212, 215, 253, 256, 298
Lille 36, 175, 189, 194, 197, 202, 280
Limburg 267
Lithuania 168, 277
Lodz 64
Loison 157
Lomza 52, 114, 252
London 36
Longwy 74, 194
Lörchingen 56
Lorraine 22, 24, 32, 34, 35, 104, 188, 207–20, 225, 226, 232, 254, 266, 267, 274, 280, 282, 286, 290, 291, 297–8, 300
Lötzen, Fort 133, 145, 168
Louvain 182
Löwentinsee 168
Lozdzieje 147
Lublin 126, 128, 151, 153
Lublinitz 127
Ludendorff, Erich 256, 266, 274, 278, 284, 297
Lunéville 75, 225, 234, 236, 252, 253

Lure 19, 28, 32, 37, 43
Lutzelstein 219
Lutzk 151
Luxembourg 12, 13, 34, 43, 74, 103, 109, 110, 114, 120, 140, 155, 157, 189, 195, 207–20, 225, 228, 268, 283, 285
Lyck 108, 252
Lyon 37

Maastricht 179, 196
MacMahon, Marie Edmé 180
Madoce 32
Madon 43, 157
Maggrabowa 108
Mahrung 134
Mailly 42
Mainz 175, 251
Maizieres 238
Malmedy 104
Mamer 225, 230
Manchuria 174, 185, 217
Manonviller, Fort 226, 235, 236, 274
Marchand 11, 13, 14, 17, 20
Marche 184
Marien 134
Marienburg 133, 135, 141, 152
Marienwerder 134, 135, 141
Markirch 99
Marne 100, 194, 195, 198, 266, 267, 268, 269, 270, 271, 275, 277, 278, 282, 290, 301
Marsal 238
Massaunen 148
Masurian Lakes 82, 96, 114, 144, 147–8, 168, 173, 174, 299
Maubeuge 34, 36, 37, 48, 175, 184, 189, 197, 202, 209, 215, 280
Maunoury 269
Mayen 208
Mecheln 178, 180
Memel river 145
Metz 56, 75, 82–9, 92, 103, 105, 107, 110, 114, 120, 121, 155, 160–2, 164, 174, 178, 183, 192, 193, 198–200, 207–20, 225–38, 249, 251, 265, 267, 280–92, 298, 300, 301
Metzinger, General 27
Meurthe 43, 57, 189, 226, 232, 234, 237, 252, 253, 274, 286
Meuse 27, 28, 30–5, 38, 57, 74, 75, 94, 99, 103, 110, 118, 120, 151, 152, 155, 157, 161, 174, 178–83, 189, 192–6, 200, 202, 216, 280
Mézières 10, 12, 27, 33, 43, 157, 189, 192, 194, 196, 228, 229, 280, 281
Michel, General 32
Mikusch-Buchberg, Generalleutnant von 133
Mirecourt 18
Mlawa 134, 147, 171
Molsheim 162, 164
Moltke, Helmuth von 51–2, 64, 66, 68, 72, 82, 123, 128, 154, 175, 180, 188, 189, 192, 202–4, 213–19, 247, 250–6, 265, 267, 273–7, 283–7, 293, 294, 297–300, 301
Moncheux 237
Mongwy 230
Mons 266
Mont Toulon 236
Montanari 255
Montbéliard 19, 38, 43
Montfaucon 33
Montjoie 181, 212
Montmedy 27, 74, 155, 157, 194, 230
Montmirail 270
Mörchingen 87
Moscow 168
Moselle 9, 23–8, 32, 43, 56, 70, 74, 86, 94, 106, 114, 118, 151, 152, 155, 157, 160, 161, 163, 164, 174, 175, 178, 179, 180, 183, 188, 192, 193, 196–9, 212, 217–18, 226, 232, 246, 252, 253, 255, 267, 269, 274, 282, 286, 290–1
Mouzon 33, 228, 229
Mühlhausen 38, 266
Mukden 217
Müller-Löbnitz 276
Mutterhausen 218
Myslowitz 128
Myszyniec 149

Nackel 135
Nahe 155, 207–20
Namur 104, 155, 157, 180, 182, 183, 192, 193, 196, 200, 209, 218, 268, 280, 281
Nancy 19, 22, 23, 30, 57, 58, 69, 75, 94, 98, 103, 110, 118, 188, 189, 193, 198, 234, 235, 236, 240, 252, 253, 267, 282, 286

Nantes 42
Napoleon Buonaparte 154, 185, 275
Narew 52, 66, 105, 108, 114, 126, 144, 153, 173
Neidenburg 65, 96, 145, 147
Netze 152, 200
Neubreisach 114, 226
Neuerburg 109
Neufchâteau 10, 28, 35, 48, 208, 229
Nied 56, 57, 193, 233, 234, 282
Niedenburg 66
Niedersee 168
Niemen 52, 55, 105, 108, 144, 147, 252
Nikolaiken 144
Nizza 250
Nogat 153
Nomény 237
Novion Porcien 28

Oberstein 210
Offenburg 99
Oise 189, 194, 195, 196, 197, 269, 282
Omet 172
Omuleh 148
operations plan (1909) 240–1
operations plans (1890–95) 51–66
Operationsstudie (1900) 104
Orléans 32, 290
Orlowen 105
Ortelsburg 65, 114, 127, 143, 144, 147, 252
Orzyc 148, 171, 173
Ostaufmarsch 58–66, 114
Osterode 108
Ostrolenka 66, 173
Ottenheim 99
Ourcq 270
Ourthe 181, 183, 184

Paris 8, 20, 32, 35, 37, 42, 74, 157, 168, 194–200, 207–20, 268, 269, 277, 282, 290, 294
Peitschendorf 149
Pfalzburg 234, 251
Pillkallen 105
Pitkleisen 252
Podolia 52, 55, 64, 252
Poix 43
Poland 51, 144, 168, 277, 299
Pont à Mousson 75, 225, 232, 234, 235, 237
Pont St Vincent, Fort 9, 57, 94, 118
Posen, Fort 55, 82, 152, 153
Prague 165
Pregel 140, 170, 171, 172
Preussisch Holland 138
Prüm 106, 181
Przasnyßcz 173
Przerosl 146
Pußczanskie 173
Pultusk 114

Radom 64
Raon l'Etape 237
Rastenburg 170, 171
Reims 11, 13, 19, 20, 22, 27, 33, 37, 38, 48, 160, 189, 194, 195, 197, 209, 280
Rethel 22, 23, 27, 38, 192, 194
Revigny 18, 27, 43
Rhein 149
Rhine 99, 113, 120, 155, 160, 161, 164, 175, 182, 199, 207–20, 234, 235, 249, 251, 274, 280, 285, 290, 292
Rhone 25
Roberts, Lord Frederick 179
Roer 181
Rohr, Captain von 10
Rosenberg 108
Rosheim 56
Rothe, Colonel 118
Rothfließ 149
Rowno 126, 151
Rozan 66, 173
Rudczanny 105, 114, 145, 149
Rumania 129
Rupprecht, Bavarian Crown Prince 301
Russia 52, 64, 76, 79, 80–1, 87, 89, 97, 101, 117, 118, 123, 129, 135–6, 140, 143–4, 151–2, 213, 249, 250, 262, 277, 290

Saales 43
Saalfeld 138
Saar 54, 114, 155, 193, 225, 233, 234, 238, 251, 282
Saarbrücken 94, 106, 114, 160, 253, 297
Saarburg 54, 87, 94, 99, 105, 107, 120, 163, 174, 175, 178, 207–20, 235
Saargemund 218
Saarlouis 114

Index

Saboy 250
St Dié 38, 234, 237, 253
St Dizier 23, 38, 43
St Hilaire 11
St Hubert 218
St Mihiel 32, 225, 228, 229
St Nicolas du Port 236
St Privat 217
St Quentin 28, 38, 48, 146, 268
St Vith 75, 207–20
Ste Génevive 235
Ste Menehould 10, 26, 27, 33, 43, 189
Salisbury, Lord 87, 101
Sallbach, Gereralleutnant 58
Sambre 157, 197
San 65, 127
Schelde 200
Schimonken 144, 149
Schirmeck 163
Schirwindt 108
Schlettstadt 99
Schlieffen, Alfred von 8, 9, 246, 247, 265–7, 272–91, 298–9
Schlieffen plan 187–204
Schlieffen plan (Dieckmann) 51, 52–121
Schlucht pass 43
Schmerfeld, 51
Schmolleningken 105
Sedan 26, 33, 43, 142, 154, 273
Seine 194, 195, 269
Semois 184
Sensburg 149, 171
Sereje 147
Sick, Generalmajor von 133
Sierck 87, 104
Signy l'Abbye 43
Silesia 65, 126, 128, 152, 252
Sint Truiden 218
Sixt von Armin, Major 117
Skrwa 173
Soissons 28, 37, 38, 48, 270
Sokal 126
Soldau 65, 126, 133, 136, 138, 145, 147, 153, 171
Solferino 142
Sommesous 18, 28
Sorcy 24, 26
Sorquitten 149
Spirdingsee 168
Stallupönen 105
Stein, General von 274

Stenay 20, 33, 94, 228, 229
Strasbourg 56, 65, 83, 92, 105, 108, 134, 138, 147, 160, 161, 162, 163, 164, 174, 175, 212, 215, 232, 235, 238, 249, 251, 253, 280, 283, 284, 285
Strasbourg, Fort 226
Suippes 33, 43
Switzerland 189, 198, 199, 214, 291
Szittkehmen 108

Tannenberg 273, 299
Tapui 143
Tarnowitz 128
Thaon 26
Thiaucourt 213
Thorn 65, 82, 96, 105, 108, 127, 134, 136, 145, 147, 152
Tienen 218
Tilsit 145
Tirpitz, Alfred von 276
Toul 10, 19, 22, 26, 30–5, 43, 75, 94, 95, 98, 99, 110, 155, 157, 178, 187–9, 192, 197, 232, 240, 247, 252, 267
Townsend, General 36
Trier 199, 207–20, 210, 212, 253
Troyes 20, 38, 282
Turkey 76

Ulzette River 163
Urft 181

Verdun 9, 10, 12, 23, 27, 30–5, 43, 57, 70, 71, 74, 75, 93, 95, 98, 103, 104, 110, 155, 157, 160, 175, 179, 188, 189, 192, 193, 194, 196, 197, 199, 209, 212, 215, 216, 228, 229, 269, 277, 279, 280, 281, 283, 301
Verdy-Program 53
Vervin 48
Vesdres 181
Vesoul 10, 18, 20, 38, 48
Vienna 64, 255
Vistula 51, 62, 64, 82, 95, 126, 133–5, 138, 143, 151, 152, 153, 168, 250
Vitry 11
Vitry la Ville 28
Vitry le François 18, 27, 28, 37, 43
Void 43
Volhnya 52, 252, 277
Vosges 12, 13, 19, 24, 32, 34, 38, 43, 54,

92, 114, 155, 175, 189, 210, 217, 226, 233, 237, 251, 256, 269, 288
Vouziers 43

Waldersee, Count Alfred 64, 66, 68, 71, 123, 250, 251, 252
Wallersberg 163
Warsaw 64, 66, 123, 126, 127, 145, 151, 153
Warthe 152
Wasselnheim 56, 87, 251
Waterloo 165
Wehlau 144
Wellington, Arthur Wellesley, Duke of 275
Wenninger, Karl Ritter von 240
Wesel 155, 192

West Prussia 55, 61, 65, 149
Westaufmarsch (1899) 98
Westaufmarsch (1903) 151
Westaufmarsch (1905/6) 279
Westaufmarsch (1914) 284–8
Westaufmarsch 246
Wilhelm II, Kaiser 63, 66–7, 73, 76, 80–1, 84, 86–9, 254, 263
Willenberg 65, 173
Wloclawek 151
Wolseley, Field Marshal Garnet 275
Wyschtynez 108

Zawichost 126
Zielun 136
Zuccari, Chief of General Italian Staff 255

Warfare in History

Already published

The Battle of Hastings: Sources and Interpretations
edited and introduced by Stephen Morillo

Infantry Warfare in the Early Fourteenth Century
Discipline, Tactics, and Technology
Kelly DeVries

The Art of Warfare in Western Europe during
the Middle Ages from the Eighth Century to 1340 (second edition)
J.F. Verbruggen

Knights and Peasants:
The Hundred Years War in the French Countryside
Nicholas Wright

Society at War:
The Experience of England and France during the Hundred Years War
edited by Christopher Allmand

The Circle of War in the Middle Ages:
Essays on Medieval Military and Naval History
edited by Donald J. Kagay and L.J. Andrew Villalon

The Anglo-Scots Wars, 1513–1550: A Military History
Gervase Phillips

The Norwegian Invasion of England in 1066
Kelly DeVries

The Wars of Edward III: Sources and Interpretations
edited and introduced by Clifford J. Rogers

The Battle of Agincourt: Sources and Interpretations
Anne Curry

War Cruel and Sharp
English Strategy under Edward III, 1327–1360
Clifford J. Rogers

The Normans and their Adversaries at War
Essays in Memory of C. Warren Hollister
edited by Richard P. Abels and Bernard S. Bachrach

The Battle of the Golden Spurs (Courtrai, 11 July 1302)
A Contribution to the History of Flanders' War of Liberation
J.F. Verbruggen

War at Sea in the Middle Ages and Renaissance
edited by John B. Hattendorf and Richard W. Unger

Swein Forkbeard's Invasions and the Danish Conquest of England, 991–1017
Ian Howard

Religion and the Conduct of War, c.300–c.1215
David S. Bachrach

Warfare in Medieval Brabant, 1356–1406
Sergio Boffa

Renaissance Military Memoirs
War, History and Identity, 1450–1600
Yuval Harari

The Place of War in English History, 1066–1214
J.O. Prestwich
edited with an introduction by Michael Prestwich

War and The Soldier in the Fourteenth Century
Adrian R. Bell